T0283224

Praise for *The Future of Foreign Policy is Feminist*

'I have known Kristina for several years – as a co-conspirator, critic and ally. Over the years, we have celebrated feminist civil society's wins, had thought-provoking conversations, and brainstormed the ways that all of us in our various manifestations – activists, civil society actors, feminist academics and allies – can create systemic change. I've also challenged and debated her and seen her grow as a person and as a feminist and leader. Now, I am honored and pleased to be writing this comment on her book – the first of many yet to come, no doubt. I believe that this book will make you question the status quo of security and foreign policy and rethink it in a more humane, effective and inclusive way. It illustrates the connections and intricacies of the most pressing issues of our time – the climate crisis, pandemics, growing inequalities and inequities at every societal level – and emphasizes what feminist civil society knew for a long time: there's no peace without feminism and no policy decision should be made without those it affects – nothing about us without us.

Kristina is a remarkably bold thinker in foreign policy. She's persistent, hard-working, well-reflected, empathetic, determined, and doesn't take no for an answer. Crucially, she is aware of the shoulders she stands on and the work of those that came before her. She knows that it's not individuals but social movements that change history and make herstory. Kristina and the Centre for Feminist Foreign Policy, now an internationally renowned organization she built from scratch, challenge the status quo of foreign policy – a status quo that works for the few and marginalizes those it affects most – while offering sustainable intersectional feminist solutions for a better future: a future built by and for all. In short, Kristina knows that the future of foreign policy is feminist!'

Madeleine Rees
Secretary-General of the Women's International
League for Peace and Freedom

'The future of foreign policy is feminist. When I announced Sweden's feminist foreign policy as foreign minister in 2014, making Sweden the first country in the world to adopt and pursue a feminist foreign policy, I didn't imagine that, by now, many countries, including Mexico and Canada, would follow suit. Today, we stand on the shoulders of all the trailblazing activists who have paved the way for a new sustainable and human-security focused vision of foreign policy: feminist foreign policy. Frankly, we cannot speak about foreign policy without speaking about feminist foreign policy.

I am grateful that civil society persistently continues to push and expand the feminist foreign policy agenda further. Kristina's book and the work of the Centre for Feminist Foreign Policy does exactly that – it describes a bold vision for a sustainable future that centres human security. Kristina challenges the status quo of foreign policy and security and explores the tensions and opportunities that lie at the nexus between diplomacy and activism. She portrays leading thinkers in foreign policy and inspires readers to demand a foreign policy serving those affected by it. In this book, she illustrates what a feminist foreign policy entails, explains why it is the most effective way to address the challenges of our time, and emphasizes the imperative for all countries to adopt a feminist foreign policy.'

Margot Wallström
Former Foreign Minister of Sweden

'Kristina Lunz shows the possibility of a more just and secure world – and thus a way out of the current crisis.'

Emilia Roig, founder and Executive Director
of the Center for Intersectional Justice

'Kristina Lunz puts her finger on the wound and makes an eloquent and astute case: A feminist foreign policy is urgent and necessary.'

Kübra Gümüsay, author of *Speaking and Being*

'There is only one sustainable and safe future: one without indiscriminate weapons, violence and the destruction of our ecosystem. Kristina Lunz shows how this is possible.'

Beatrice Finh, former Executive Director of
International Campaign to Abolish Nuclear Weapons,
2017 Nobel Peace Prize Laureate

'*The Future of Foreign Policy is Feminist* is a timely and thought-provoking exploration of the vital role that feminism plays in shaping the international landscape. Drawing on her expertise, Lunz highlights the urgent need for feminist approaches in foreign policy to address the root causes of conflict and build sustainable peace.'

Oleksandra Matviichuk, head of the Centre for
Civil Liberties, 2022 Nobel Peace Prize Laureate

'Kristina Lunz's *The Future of Foreign Policy is Feminist* tackles the pressing questions that feminism brings to power and global politics in a comprehensive and conscientious way. With her nuanced and persuasive arguments, Lunz inspires us to reimagine what foreign policy can be and to work towards a more equitable and beautiful world.'

Minna Salami, author of *Can Feminism be African?* and
Sensuous Knowledge: A Black Feminist Approach for Everyone

'Kristina Lunz is an innovative, forward thinking, creative and resilient leader – something the world needs now more than ever. This book, and her vision throughout it, demonstrates every one of these qualities. It brings to life a new way of seeing and believing in the world we live in.'

Jennifer Cassidy, diplomatic scholar at the University of Oxford

'Through an impressive combination of rigorous research, keen analysis and personal reflection, Kristina Lunz has produced a persuasive critique of the dominant paradigm of international relations. More importantly, she offers a compelling alternative vision "fit for purpose" for the twenty-first century, based on feminist principles and values including respect for all life, justice, empathy and humility. Only if we are guided by these principles and values are we likely to manage successfully the profound challenges of our times – violent conflict, the climate crisis, the denial of basic human rights, pandemic disease and deep economic disparities. Lunz shows us that we can be robust in our military support for Ukraine while pursuing longer term strategies focused on building a better and safer world. Men, above all, should read this book.'

Stephen Heintz, President & CEO, Rockefeller Brothers Fund

The Future of Foreign Policy is Feminist

The door has been pushed open. I hope many will walk through it.
For all those whose expertise is dismissed
because they dare to imagine
a new – feminist! – society,
moving away from the patriarchal status quo,
towards justice.
They are the only hope we have.

THE FUTURE OF FOREIGN POLICY IS FEMINIST

KRISTINA LUNZ

Translated by Nicola Barfoot

polity

Originally published in German as *Die Zukunft der Außenpolitik ist feministisch*
© Ullstein Buchverlage GmbH, Berlin. Published in 2022 by Econ Verlag

This English edition © Polity Press, 2023

All illustrations © Katie Turnbull

Excerpt from 'The Transformation of Silence into Language and Action' in *Sister Outsider* by Audre Lorde included by permission. Copyright © 1984, 2007 by Audre Lorde

Excerpts from *The Mother of All Things* by Rebecca Solnit, Haymarket Books, 2017, used by permission of the publisher

Excerpt from *My Seditious Heart*, page 204, by Arundhati Roy, 2019, included by permission of Roam Agency

Excerpt from *Invisible Women* by Caroline Criado-Perez. Copyright © 2019 Caroline Criado-Perez. Used by permission of Abrams Press, an imprint of ABRAMS, New York. All rights reserved

Excerpt from *Invisible Women* by Caroline Criado-Perez published by Chatto & Windus. Copyright © Caroline Criado Perez, 2019. Reprinted by permission of The Random House Group Limited

Polity Press
65 Bridge Street
Cambridge CB2 1UR, UK

Polity Press
111 River Street
Hoboken, NJ 07030, USA

All rights reserved. Except for the quotation of short passages for the purpose of criticism and review, no part of this publication may be reproduced, stored in a retrieval system or transmitted, in any form or by any means, electronic, mechanical, photocopying, recording or otherwise, without the prior permission of the publisher.

ISBN-13: 978-1-5095-5783-7 – hardback

A catalogue record for this book is available from the British Library.

Library of Congress Catalog Number: 2023931484

Typeset in on 12 on 15.5pt Adobe Garamond
by Cheshire Typesetting Ltd, Cuddington, Cheshire
Printed and bound in Great Britain by CPI Group (UK) Ltd, Croydon

The publisher has used its best endeavours to ensure that the URLs for external websites referred to in this book are correct and active at the time of going to press. However, the publisher has no responsibility for the websites and can make no guarantee that a site will remain live or that the content is or will remain appropriate.

Every effort has been made to trace all copyright holders, but if any have been overlooked the publisher will be pleased to include any necessary credits in any subsequent reprint or edition.

For further information on Polity, visit our website:
politybooks.com

CONTENTS

Contents

Contents

Contents

Contents

ACKNOWLEDGEMENTS

There are many wonderful people without whom this book would not exist. First and foremost the trailblazers, the pioneering thinkers and visionary women on whose shoulders I stand.

The book would definitely not exist without the two women who helped me hands-on to bring it into the world: my editors Silvie Horch (from Econ – the whole Econ/Ullstein team is amazing!) and Heike Wolter. I've learned so much from both of you – thank you! And the English version would not exist without the wonderful team behind my English publisher Polity Press, first and foremost Elise Heslinga and Nicola Barfoot.

My Berlin team at the Centre for Feminist Foreign Policy contributed a lot of the research and facts and figures mentioned in the book. That's not all, though; they also offered enthusiastic support throughout the writing process. Thank you to Nina Bernarding, Damjan Denkovski, Anna Provan, Sheena Anderson, Annika Droege and Annika Kreitlow.

The book could not have come about without the experts who shared their knowledge with me, time and time again. Thank you for your generous support and patience, Louise Arimatsu, Heidi Meinzolt, Leonie Bremer, Juri Schnöller, Emilia Roig, Alice Grindhammer, Aron Haschemi, Tiaji Sio, Laura Hatzler, Jutta von Falkenhausen, Thomas Grischko, Gotelind Alber, Janika Lohse, Lea Börgerding, Kaan Sahin, Nicola Popovic, Elvira Rosert, Aleksandra Dier, Annette Ludwig and Madeleine Rees. For the German paperback edition I also received fantastic support from Sarah Farhatiar, Nahid Shahalimi, Gilda Sahebi, Katharina Rietzler, and government employees of the states that already have a feminist foreign policy. I'm very grateful.

Thank you Nes Kapacu for the fabulous cover – and special thanks for your patience!

And a huge thank you for your love, your emotional support, and

Acknowledgements

your help in deciding on the title and cover design of the original German edition: Beggy, Nina, Kaan, Alice, Waldemar, Bianca, Yara, Jeannette, Lisa, Sophia, Jutta and Mama. Love you.

ABBREVIATIONS

ACLED   Armed Conflict Location & Event Data Project
ACLJ   American Center for Law and Justice
ACLU   American Civil Liberties Union
ADF   Alliance Defending Freedom
Afd   Alternative for Germany
AFD   Agence Française de Développement – French Development Agency
ATT   Arms Trade Treaty
BIPoC   Black, indigenous & people of colour
CAT   Convention Against Torture and Other Cruel, Inhuman or Degrading Treatment or Punishment
CCW   Convention on Certain Conventional Weapons
CDU   Christlich Demokratische Union Deutschlands – Christian Democratic Union of Germany
CEDAW   Convention on the Elimination of All Forms of Discrimination Against Women
CEPI   Coalition for Epidemic Preparedness
CFFP   Centre for Feminist Foreign Policy
CPED   International Convention for the Protection of All Persons from Enforced Disappearance
CRC   Convention on the Rights of the Child
CRPD   Convention on the Rights of Persons with Disabilities
CSW   UN Commission on the Status of Women
DGAP   Deutsche Gesellschaft für Auswärtige Politik – German Council on Foreign Relations
DoC   Diplomats of Color
ECLJ   The European Center for Law and Justice
FARC   Fuerzas Armadas Revolucionarias de Colombia – Revolutionary Armed Forces of Colombia
FDP   Freie Demokratische Partei – Free Democratic Party
Gavi   Global Alliance for Vaccines and Immunization

GBD	Global Burden of Disease study
ICAN	International Campaign to Abolish Nuclear Weapons
ICERD	International Convention on the Elimination of All Forms of Racial Discrimination
ICESCR	International Covenant on Economic, Social and Cultural Rights
ICRW	International Center for Research on Women
IMA	Interministerielle Arbeitsgruppe im Auswärtigen Amt – Interministerial Working Group in the Federal Foreign Office
IMF	International Monetary Fund
IPCC	Intergovernmental Panel on Climate Change
IUCN	International Union for Conservation of Nature
JCPoA	Joint Comprehensive Plan of Action
KADEM	Women and Democracy Association (Turkey)
LGBTQ+	lesbian, gay, bi, trans, queer and other orientations and identities
LSHTM	London School of Hygiene and Tropical Medicine
MAPA	most affected people and areas
MEP	Member of European Parliament
NAP	national action plan
NATO	North Atlantic Treaty Organization
NDG	nationally determined contribution
NTD	neglected tropical disease
OECD	Organization for Economic Co-operation and Development
OHCHR	Office of the United Nations High Commissioner for Human Rights
OSCE	Organization for Security and Co-operation in Europe
P5	Permanent 5 – permanent members of the UN Security Council
SAP	structural adjustment programme
SGBV	sexual and gender-based violence

Abbreviations

SIPRI	Stockholm International Peace Research Institute
SPD	Sozialdemokratische Partei Deutschlands –Social Democratic Party of Germany
SRHR	sexual and reproductive health and rights
TPNW	Treaty on the Prohibition of Nuclear Weapons
UDHR	Universal Declaration of Human Rights
UNDP	United Nations Development Programme
UNFCCC	United Nations Framework Convention on Climate Change
UNHRC	United Nations Human Rights Council
UN OCHA	United Nations Office for the Coordination of Humanitarian Affairs
UNSCR	United Nations Security Council Resolution
WCAPS	Women of Color Advancing Peace, Security and Conflict Transformation
WHO	World Health Organization
WIDF	Women's International Democratic Federation
WILPF	Women's International League for Peace and Freedom
WPS	Women, Peace and Security – UN Resolution 1325 and its related resolutions
WTO	World Trade Organization

PREFACE TO THE 2023 EDITION

'Totally out of place and yet highly topical':* this was the comment in a TV item on my book shortly after it was published early in 2022. To be precise, the date of publication was 24 February 2022, the very day on which Vladimir Putin began his war of aggression against Ukraine. The numerous newspaper, radio and TV interviews scheduled for the book's publication ended up focusing almost exclusively on the war and paying little attention to the vision of a feminist foreign policy. On 27 February 2022, the German chancellor, Olaf Scholz, announced a 'turning point' (*Zeitenwende*)in foreign policy and a €100 billion special fund for the armed forces. This seemed to define the general direction of future foreign policy activities: more militarization and a greater emphasis on military security. In an emergency such as the murderous war in Ukraine, when one particular response predominates and appears to be the only right thing to do (in this case, more weapons and a stronger army), then other ideas for the future and possible solutions are quickly rejected and the people associated with them attacked and vilified. This is exactly what happened to me, and others had similar experiences. One of these was Beatrice Finh, who had been awarded the Nobel Peace Prize in 2017 on behalf of her organization, the International Campaign to Abolish Nuclear Weapons (ICAN), for their work towards the Treaty on the Prohibition of Nuclear Weapons. On 27 February 2022, online news portals announced that Putin had put his nuclear forces on high alert. Overnight, organizations that had campaigned to end nuclear deterrence for decades were dismissed as pointless. For me, however, these events made it clearer than ever that the work of organizations such as ICAN is exactly what we need – and we need much more of it, not less.

There is no doubt that people who are acutely affected by brutal and deadly violence need help – help that meets their demands and

* MDR Artour, 3 March 2022, www.mdr.de/tv/programm/sendung-733162.html.

enables them to defend themselves as effectively as possible. At the same time, however, it is both true and empirically evident that more weapons and militarization today will lead to more violence, wars and conflicts in the future. The hypermilitarized state of our world is not a law of nature but the result of decades – centuries! – of old political decisions. In 2021 (in the middle of the pandemic, when money was too tight to distribute vaccines equitably worldwide or to provide sufficient hospital beds and medical personnel), more than $US2 trillion was spent globally on defence and militarization – the highest value ever recorded.* In contrast, only about $6.45 billion was made available in June 2022 for the UN's peacekeeping operations for the year. That's less than 0.4 per cent of the military spending. Albert Einstein supposedly said that problems can't be solved with the same thinking that caused them. But this is exactly what our society attempts to do – again and again.

Feminists in foreign and security policy are very good at distinguishing between short-term, medium-term and long-term goals. In a hypermilitarized world, supplying arms to help people in imminent danger is the right thing to do in the short term. At the same time, more sustainable solutions are needed in the medium and long term. These include special funds for civil crisis prevention, (nuclear) disarmament, the strengthening of international law and human rights, and support for human rights defenders and (feminist) civil society worldwide.

This edition of the book incorporates answers to the many questions I have been asked since the outbreak of war. It contains numerous updates to the previous German version and new (sub)chapters. In chapter 13, which is completely new, I both take a closer look at Putin's war in Ukraine and the feminist revolution in Iran and write about the relevance and practice of feminist foreign policy in times of war and conflict. The earlier edition, with a copy deadline of early December

---

* www.sipri.org/media/press-release/2022/world-military-expenditure-passes-2-trillion-first -time.

2021, was also unable to deal fully with another important development that was taking place in Germany. In late November 2021, the new government announced in its coalition agreement that Germany would henceforth pursue a feminist foreign policy. Since then, Foreign Minister Annalena Baerbock – the first female foreign minister in the 151-year history of the Federal Foreign Office – has consistently drawn attention to the rights of women and minorities and has emphasized human security as a crucial expansion of the narrow focus on military security. Since the announcement of Germany's feminist foreign policy, Baerbock has repeatedly led the German Foreign Office in new and unaccustomed directions. One example is the appointment of the former head of Greenpeace, Jennifer Morgan, as state secretary and special envoy for international climate action. Another is the successful proposal (with Iceland) of a UN Human Rights Council resolution to investigate the violence of the Iranian regime against protesters. I scrutinize Germany's feminist foreign policy in the revised chapter 7.

We must not forget that humankind was facing a multitude of simultaneous crises even before the Russian war of aggression: the long-standing climate catastrophe, the pandemic, and the steady rise in armed conflicts involving states. In the last ten years, the number of such conflicts has nearly doubled, from thirty in 2010 to fifty-six in 2020. In the same period, the number of people killed in conflicts and wars has doubled, as has the number of refugees. In 2010, there were 41 million displaced persons worldwide; in 2020 this figure had risen to 82.4 million.* Russia's war is exacerbating all these trends. When, if not now, will we as a society finally realize that 'business as usual' is not an option and that traditional political approaches do not lead to a fair, peaceful or sustainable world? We have to finally stop applying 'solutions' that will become tomorrow's problems.

Kristina Lunz
Berlin, January 2023

---

* www.sipri.org/research/peace-and-development/environment-peace.

1 PROLOGUE: THE PERSONAL IS POLITICAL

What I most regretted were my silences. . . .
And there are so many silences to be broken.
Audre Lorde, 'The transformation of silence into language and action',
in *Sister Outsider* (Feasterville Trevose, PA: Crossing Press, 2007)

It helps to be naive. Sometimes it's even a blessing. If I'd realized, in 2014, what happens when a woman takes a public stand and calls out injustices, I probably wouldn't have started a campaign against sexism and the degradation of women in Germany's top-selling tabloid, *Bild*. But I was naive. I had no idea of the extreme hatred and violence that confronts women in the public arena – especially when they criticize the status quo.

Not knowing all this, in October 2014 I launched the petition 'Zeigt allen Respekt – Schluss mit Sexismus in BILD!' (Show respect for everyone – no more sexism in *Bild*!). The campaign was born of the tremendous anger I felt towards the newspaper. 'Anger at injustice and inequality is in many ways exactly like fuel',[1] writes Rebecca Traister in *Good and Mad: The Revolutionary Power of Women's Anger*. Here she shows how the anger of women – from the suffragettes to the legendary Black* civil rights activist Rosa Parks, #MeToo or the Women's March – unleashes a transformative force. This has also been the experience of my friend and mentor Dr Scilla Elworthy. Born in

---

* While opinions differ about the capitalization of 'Black' and 'White', I have chosen to capitalize both these words throughout as a matter of racial sensitivity. For a more detailed explanation, see Ann Thúy Nguyễn and Maya Pendleton, 'Recognizing race in language: why
we capitalize "Black" and "White"', Centre for the Study of Social Policy, 23 March 2020,
https://cssp.org/2020/03/recognizing-race-in-language-why-we-capitalize-black-and-
white/.

Scotland in 1943, founder of numerous organizations and three times a Nobel Peace Prize nominee, she gave me this insight: anger is like gasoline. If you spray it around thoughtlessly it can spark a fire and cause massive destruction. But if you use it carefully, it can serve as fuel for your inner motor.

My feminist awakening . . .

So there it was, the anger. I was in my mid-twenties and studying for my first master's degree at University College London. That in itself was surprising, given that my parents hadn't been to university. In Germany, parents' income and level of education are the main determinants of their children's career path. While 79 per cent of the children of university graduates go to university, only 27 per cent of the children of non-graduates do so. Only 11 per cent of the children of non-graduates do a master's degree, as opposed to 43 per cent of the children of graduates. The class we're born into determines our life to a significant extent. Individual social capital – the social group we belong to, the people we know – is a door-opener.[2]

In London I was overwhelmed by pretty much everything: the size of the city, the language, and the elite environment. I was intimidated and had a constant feeling of inadequacy. My fellow students had done their undergraduate degrees at Cambridge, Oxford, or other international universities; I came from an ordinary university in Germany. I buried myself in books; I had a lot of catching up to do. My main reading material was feminist literature: I'd barely had any contact with this before, but for many of my fellow students it was standard fare.

My struggles were partly to do with my origins. I grew up in a village of eighty inhabitants in a picturesque corner of Bavaria as the youngest of three children – my twin brother is five minutes older than me. It was a sheltered childhood, in a very loving and warmhearted family. In my teens, however, I began to feel increasingly uncomfortable in my surroundings. Everything about the community was very traditional. All the positions of power – the priest, the pub owner, the heads of the sports clubs, the mayor, the doctor, the driving instructor – were (and still are) occupied by men, and these men were treated with great respect. At the same time, some of them failed to show respect for me and other young women. At village festivals or sports days, they stood much too close to us at the bar, made sexualized allusions, and overstepped boundaries. When I wanted to gain my driving licence, it was an open secret that young women shouldn't take their lessons with the head of the driving school, who was widely known to have wandering hands. But in my time no one did anything about it – it was the norm.

Respect was a core tenet of my upbringing: it was extremely important to my parents to teach me and my siblings to treat our fellow humans respectfully. Dismissive terms such as 'idiot' were not used in our home. Even if there were differences of opinion, there was never any shouting or disparaging language. Appreciation, reliability and helpfulness were the virtues we were measured against. My father, during his lifetime, worked long hours but was always there for the family and other villagers if they needed help in the evening or weekend – whether it was tying a necktie or laying cables (he was a trained electrician). The word 'kindness' is probably the best description for the feeling our parents gave us. And it was this that I found hard to reconcile with the highly unpleasant feeling that many men inspired in me as a child and teenager. On the one hand, a great deal of respect was paid to these men in positions of leadership; on the other hand, it seemed that some of them exploited this status and behaved in a manner that was anything but kind – particularly towards us young girls and women. Yet my father's example showed me, even as a child, that there was another way.

In London, thanks to feminist literature and an international, cosmopolitan environment, a new world opened up to me. All at once, there were concepts and explanations for the many unpleasant situations and injustices that I'd sensed for years but had never been able to frame or even articulate. The time in London was my feminist awakening. I learned, for example, that whenever a group of people is collectively objectified – by sexualization, for example – these individuals are dehumanized. This objectification makes it easier to inflict violence on them. In early 2021, a study by UN Women in the UK showed that 97 per cent of women aged eighteen to twenty-four had experienced sexualized violence in the form of harassment in public spaces.[3] Girls in Brazil are between nine and ten years old, on average, when they first experience sexual harassment.[4] Almost none of the perpetrators are ever held accountable. In Germany it is estimated that fewer than 1 per cent (!) of all rapists (not just those whose victims report them) are brought to justice.[5] Also in Germany, one man attempts to kill his female partner or ex-partner every day. Every second to third day, one of them succeeds. It is a scandal that femicide is not a specific criminal offence, punished with the utmost severity, in German courts.

In short, I was far more aware of the malign influence of the patriarchy by the time I returned home at the end of my first term in London. Paying for petrol, I saw the *Bild* newspaper lying in front of me at the checkout. The front page showed photos of the cleavage of famous women and an invitation to vote for the 'best bosom on German TV'. I was disgusted by the degrading treatment of these celebrities – and of women in general. As one of Germany's top-selling newspapers, *Bild* contributes to the preposterously high rate of male violence against women. At the time, I had no idea what activism was, or how to change things. But I wasn't prepared to tolerate this discrimination and sexualization of women, however widely it was accepted in our society.

When I talked to friends and acquaintances about my anger, many of them thought I shouldn't make such a fuss. After all, it was normal. But who defines what is normal and accepted? I remembered my feeling of powerlessness as a young girl, when I'd see *Bild* lying on my grandmother's kitchen table in front of my assembled family, male members included. The front page showed news stories – mainly about men – and the '*Bild* girl', the German version of the page 3 girl, the sexualized representation of a female body. I felt ashamed, sullied and humiliated. Would I be ogled later in life, like them? Would my body be commented on and sexualized? Would I be seen as an object, while the men around me were valued as subjects, playing active and dominant roles in politics, business, society and culture?

I sat down at my desk and wrote an open letter to Kai Diekmann, the editor-in-chief of *Bild* at the time. This became the start of a petition and a campaign. I wrote: 'It's time all people were treated with the same respect in *Bild* and *Bild.de*: women are not society's sex objects!' Nearly 60,000 people signed. It was a much needed step to counter the silencing of women, which the patriarchy – smothering every truth that does not serve it – has practised for millennia.

This is also shown by the many examples of sexualized violence against women that have been discussed in public – as well as all the anonymous or unreported cases. It is shown by experiences such as those of Chanel Miller (raped by Brock Allen Turner on the campus of Stanford University in 2015), Nafissatou Diallo (who accused Dominique Strauss-Kahn, then head of the IMF, of sexual assault in 2011), Christine Blasey Ford (who accused Supreme Court judge Brett Kavanaugh of sexual assault in 2018) and Nika Irani (who accused the rapper Samra of raping her in June 2021). And it goes on – for example, with the many women harmed by the film producer Harvey Weinstein and by Donald Trump, and the countless survivors of Bill Cosby's violence. Every time women stand up to their male tormentors, they and their credibility are called into question; it is not uncommon for them to be threatened with rape (again) and murder. And yet we wonder why 90 per cent of rape victims do not report the crime. This is part of the strategy of patriarchal societies: hold your tongue or you're in for even more violence.

Tabloids such as *Bild* and rappers with lyrics like 'Ich fick sie fast tot, sie liegt im Wachkoma' (I fuck her nearly to death, she's a vegetable now)[6] show how widespread misogyny is. Men are the doers; women become sex objects. This toxic masculinity, visible in media, politics and culture, is tolerated by society and is also played out in private and professional settings. So it comes as no surprise to learn that the former editor-in-chief of *Bild*, Julian Reichelt, abused his power over young female employees. The scandal was first revealed by the news magazine *Der Spiegel* in March 2021, in an article entitled 'Vögeln, fördern, feuern' (Shag, promote, fire), but did not lead to Reichelt's dismissal from *Bild* until the *New York Times** ran the story in mid-October 2021. Why would someone responsible for the devaluation of women in a mass medium treat them any differently in real life? And the more powerful the man, the greater the impact: Donald Trump, accused of sexual abuse by at least twenty-six women, began his term of office with presidential decrees that radically restricted women's rights.[7] Of course it is not just these individual misogynists who are the problem – it is entire systems, patriarchal systems, which protect and tolerate these men, allowing them to act.

Back then, in my naivety, I didn't know what feminists, female activists, and women taking a stand in public had to put up with on a near daily basis. I wouldn't learn until later that 88 per cent of the internet users who had witnessed digital violence said that the hate was aimed at women;[8] that 58 per cent of the girls and young women questioned in a 2020 study by Plan International had been harassed online;[9] or that, in a survey of 70 million reader comments in 2016, *The Guardian* had found that eight of the ten journalists subjected to the most threats were women, and that the two men among the top ten were Black. The person who attracted the most hatred and attacks was the feminist writer Jessica Valenti.[10] White men are not exposed to this violence.

If I'd known all this, who knows whether I would have dared to raise my voice. As it was, a wave of digital violence rolled over me when Kai Diekmann mocked me and my petition on his Twitter account, inviting me to procure him more '*Bild* girls'. My inboxes and social media accounts filled up with messages from men who hoped I would

---

* In Germany it was mainly research by Juliane Löffler and the Ippen investigative team that confirmed and concretized the suspicions.

be raped or threatened to rape me themselves and inflict violence on my family. I felt paralysed; I broke down and cried a lot. At first I was convinced that my future role would be limited to silent observation of the oppressive patriarchal system. I couldn't understand that my request for a respectful representation of women had been met with graphic descriptions of the sexual abuse men wanted to inflict on me. It was only the solidarity of other women activists that gave me the courage to carry on. And the knowledge that using (online) violence to silence me as a woman was exactly what those men wanted. I refused to give them that satisfaction. I wasn't just angry and hurt, I was determined.

. . . and where it led

Solidarity with other women and women activists meant that I refused to be silenced, in spite of this violence. In 2000, scientists from the University of California in Los Angeles found that the conventional 'fight or flight' narrative – the notion that people under stress either attack or flee – was incomplete. Their study[11] showed that women were more inclined to 'tend and befriend': to care for each other, show solidarity, and offer each other support and advice. This gives protection, reduces stress and consolidates networks. To this day, the first place I turn when I need support is my network of wonderful women. And whenever one of us needs the same thing, I do my very best to offer her this protection and a place of emotional refuge. Talking and listening, sharing experiences (especially of violence) and supporting each other: this is the strength of friendships among women. '[T]he women's movement was born of women talking to each other',[12] wrote the great feminist Gloria Steinem. And this is also what enables the feminist movement to grow stronger. 'We are volcanoes', the US author Ursula K. Le Guin once said. 'When we women offer our experience as our truth, as human truth, all the maps change. There are new mountains.'[13]

Just as landscapes are gradually altered by pressure from climate and tides, the '*Bild* girl' was eventually abolished under Julian Reichelt in 2018. The tabloid's explanation was: 'In recent months we've had the feeling that many women see these pictures as offensive and degrading, both in our editorial team and among our female readers.'[14] Various media outlets saw a connection with my campaign.

The campaign against *Bild* was the beginning of my feminist activism. Many other campaigns followed. After the sexualized attacks on hundreds of women on New Year's Eve 2015–16 in Cologne, I joined a feminist collective of twenty-one women. Under the slogan 'Against sexualized violence and racism. Always. Anywhere. #ausnahmslos' ('NoExcuses'), we formulated fourteen demands for politicians, society and the media. We wrote: 'It is harmful for all of us if feminism is exploited by extremists to incite against certain ethnicities, as is currently being done in the discussion surrounding the incidents in Cologne. It is wrong to highlight sexualized violence only when the perpetrators are allegedly the perceived "others".' When we issued the press release at the beginning of January, our appeal was published on the online front pages of most of the major media outlets. A few weeks later we received the Clara Zetkin Prize for political intervention, awarded by the German Left Party (Die Linke) and named after a famous early twentieth-century communist, pacifist and feminist. Ours was the first intersectional feminist campaign to attract so much attention. On that day, we made feminist history.

In the months that followed, the campaign #NeinheißtNein (No Means No) gained momentum. I advised UN Women Germany and helped to devise their campaign to change German criminal law. We wanted to introduce a new criterion for the definition of 'rape', which would finally make lack of consent for the sex act the decisive factor. Instead of the victims (in most cases women) having to defend themselves physically against their (usually stronger) attacker, the word 'no' would suffice. At the start of the campaign I wrote, in an article for *Zeit Online*: 'There is no rational argument against this, except for the desperate attempt to preserve a system in which the rights of men count more than those of women.' When the German Bundestag (federal parliament) voted unanimously to tighten the law on sexual offences in July 2016, there was great jubilation in feminist civil society. Some organizations, such as the Deutscher Juristinnenbund (German Women Lawyers Association), the Deutscher Frauenrat (National Council of German Women's Associations) or bff – Frauen gegen Gewalt e.V. (bff – Women Against Violence e.V.), had been fighting for years to achieve this important milestone for the feminist movement.

While campaigning on feminist issues in Germany, I was living in Oxford. I first went there to study diplomacy, on a full scholarship from the university, then worked briefly for the Blavatnik School of Government, an institute for research and teaching on international politics and the government sector.

My studies offered a complete contrast to my political activism. At university I listened to lectures about fragile states, development policy and diplomacy, all from a fairly traditional perspective, and learned about 'great' diplomats such as Niccolò Machiavelli (1469–1527). This historian and philosopher, one of the first influential diplomats, saw male qualities as the prerequisite for developing and guiding relations between states. And he was just one example of the lack of diversity in the diplomatic realm – it almost seemed as if the world hadn't changed at all in the last five hundred years.

In my course I was frequently amazed at the absence of any perspectives from people outside the 'old, White, male' category. My questioning was reinforced by campaigns such as #RhodesMustFall, aimed at the decolonization of the curriculum. Inspired by students in South Africa, this movement reverberated as far as Oxford, where I became a supporter.

Certain formative political events took place in 2016 and 2017. In autumn 2016 I spent a few months working for the feminist organization Sisma Mujer in Bogotá, Colombia. Sisma played a major role in ensuring that the peace treaty between the guerrilla group FARC and the Colombian government, aimed at ending one of the longest-running civil wars in Latin America, was framed in historically inclusive terms. Unfortunately, the agreement was narrowly rejected by the population in a referendum one day after my arrival (though the government and the FARC agreed on an amended version some weeks later). During my time in Bogotá we regularly took to the streets with thousands of people to demonstrate for peace and tried to stand up to anti-democratic and antifeminist attacks on the peace process.

In 2016 I was also very much preoccupied by Brexit and Donald Trump's election victory. On the day of his inauguration in January 2017 I landed in New York City, where I would be working for the United Nations Development Programme (UNDP) for the next few months. I booked a flight that would allow me – a few hours after my arrival in the middle of the night – to catch one of the many buses going to Washington, DC, for the historic Women's March. The day gave me hope; it electrified me. On that day, Women's Marches were taking place on every continent, and millions of people were chanting feminist demands. It was a tremendous, historic example of the resistance that will change our society.

In spring 2017 I moved to Yangon, Myanmar, to continue my work for UNDP. It was the year of the genocide committed by the Myanmar military against the Rohingya Muslim minority in the western state of Rakhine. So I was working for the United Nations, an organization officially committed to ensuring that genocide – ignored by the international community – would never happen again. And I was in a country where genocide *was* happening again, and the UN was repeatedly accused of not doing enough to protect the population. A feeling of powerlessness dogged me in my work, and I felt a loss of confidence in international provisions for the protection of human rights, in particular the rights of minorities. Sexualized violence and rape as a weapon of war were widespread. This same military carried out a putsch in February 2021 and declared a two-year state of emergency. In the months that followed, thousands of people were killed in protests against the military coup. Feminists have played a prominent role in the resistance against the military; Nandar, whom I know personally, is one of them. Nandar, one of the best-known feminists in Myanmar, was among the first to stand up to the military. As she and other feminists know, the military is one of the worst manifestations of the patriarchal state – especially when it turns against its own population.

My years of expertise as a feminist activist, coupled with my experience in the field of international politics in the UK, Colombia, the USA and Myanmar, inspired an increasingly strong desire to bring feminist critique into the field of diplomacy and international politics. It was more important to me to change attitudes in these areas than to continue to pursue a career in an established organization. I still remember one of the triggers for this: the UNDP Christmas party in December 2017 in Yangon. It was summer, and we were standing barefoot in the garden of the UN building. Outside, Myanmar was in turmoil, with hundreds of thousands of people murdered or forced to flee. A representative of senior management thanked us, the staff, for the 'sacrifices' we were making to help the people in this economically poor country. I felt a strong sense of discomfort. Sure, many people at UNDP were undoubtedly working very hard to support the country's development. But I don't think that 'making sacrifices' is an appropriate term for this – not for the privileged Western staff. As employees or consultants with UN contracts, we were earning very well, paying above average prices to live in the nicest apartments and houses, eating out in the city's best restaurants and buying the finest products. We were contributing to the distortion of rents and the emergence of a two-tier society: the mainly White aid workers on one side and the mainly poor local population on the other. These are typical patterns which are still very much present in 'development cooperation' today.

These North–South relations, which I experienced for myself at the Christmas party in Myanmar, and the resulting financial and political dependency are often referred to as 'neocolonialism'. Imperial colonialism ended in most countries with the wave of decolonization in the 1950s and 1960s (or as early as the nineteenth century in Latin America), yet dependence, exploitation and repression continue to exist, and it is always the former colonies who suffer. This takes many forms, such as loans and debt programmes with international financial institutions, the shipping of waste to poorer countries, the exploitation of raw materials, the lack of say in major international committees such as the UN Security Council, or nuclear weapons testing on the territory of former colonies. All these things consolidate the power imbalance between North and South and therefore White domination.

My desire to integrate feminist critique into international politics became a reality in 2017, when I decided to found the Centre for Feminist Foreign Policy (CFFP) with Marissa Conway. Marissa was an American living in London, whom I'd met digitally through a mutual friend while I was working in New York. I'd already published work on feminist foreign policy, and Marissa had launched a Twitter account and a website entitled *A Feminist Foreign Policy* just a few months earlier. In 2018 CFFP was also established in Germany, where I direct it in tandem with my second co-founder, Nina Bernarding (since 2022 CFFP has existed exclusively in Germany).*

The founding of CFFP has turned my life upside down. Never before have I done anything that has been so overwhelming and so fulfilling at the same time. Founding an organization or business, taking responsibility for employees, formulating strategies that will enable the organization to survive and thrive, and simultaneously dealing with hostility and hurdles because we're challenging the status quo – all these things are exhausting. Yet at the same time, it's the greatest gift I could ever have been given. I would never want to give up the freedom of thought and action that I've gained from developing and leading CFFP.

At the end of 2022, in our fourth full year of operation, the Centre for Feminist Foreign Policy gGmbH in Berlin consisted of sixteen employees. We're enormously proud of this, given that female founders and feminist work receive little or no funding, and civil society groups as a whole are systematically underfunded and undervalued. New grassroots political organizations and charities founded by

---

* A profile of Nina Bernarding can be found at the end of chapter 4.

women with little capital, challenging the status quo, are virtually non-existent; the patriarchy doesn't fund those who want to overthrow it.

The men in the village where I grew up who abused their power and overstepped boundaries are ultimately no different from the Putins, Bolsonaros, Trumps and Erdoğans of this world. They have different degrees of impact, but their attitude of entitlement is the same. This is because they know that their behaviour will have no consequences in our patriarchal society and will probably go unpunished. I'm not prepared to accept their influence, their destructiveness; I'm not prepared to be discouraged. There will always be naysayers who find countless reasons why something shouldn't be attempted. Whatever campaign or initiative I've started, whatever I've done in my life – in the beginning, the small number of people who encouraged me were vastly outnumbered by those who explained, in great detail, why my plans were stupid, naive, and doomed to failure. And yet we need more people who are curious, more people who question what we see as the 'norm' (nuclear weapons in foreign policy, for example) and why we see it that way. People who then consider whether there are better options and act accordingly. People who are able to think long term and formulate visions for the future. People who are not afraid to be seen as ridiculous and to make waves. This is my personal aspiration, both in my day-to-day work as co-CEO of the Centre for Feminist Foreign Policy and in this book. I hope it will provoke readers, bring joy and inspire criticism. Constructive and sympathetic criticism allows us to develop ideas and advance whole subject areas. We need people who can turn their vision into reality – people prepared to take a leap into the unknown. After all, society only changes when people call it into question.

I therefore hope that this will be only the first book on feminist foreign policy, and not the last. I liked what Kamala Harris said when it became clear in November 2020 that she would be the first woman – and the first woman of colour – to become vice president of the USA: 'I may be the first, but won't be the last.' For me, her statement means that the door has been pushed open and that the first steps, however imperfect, have been taken. But at least the door is now open for others to follow – all those who were previously excluded, along with their ideas, with all the force of the patriarchy's interpretive sovereignty and dominance. Of course this book can't be compared to a vice presidency. Nonetheless, Kamala Harris's words meant a great deal to me as I wrote the German edition of this first book on feminist foreign policy, and I'm grateful for them. I'm also grateful for the intellectual work already done in this area, which underpins my work.

I'm not perfect, and the same goes for this book. There's a limit to how much a single person can read, research, reflect and write. And yet the field of foreign and security policy, with its history, its international agreements, its different actors, and its thematic and regional areas of expertise, is so extraordinarily wide-ranging that it would take several standard works on feminist foreign policy, each thousands of pages long, to rethink every single sub-area. I'm therefore hoping that this book will be constructively criticized, and that we will begin to write those standard works on feminist foreign policy together. If the book could be read with an attitude of 'Yes, and . . .' rather than 'Yes, but . . .', we would be taking a huge step forwards. Vilifying women and denying their professionalism is as old as the patriarchy; baseless accusations, insinuations and defamatory statements – which I've already experienced during the writing process and even more after the book was first published in German – have no place in the debate about a new approach to foreign policy. Every such attack costs us, as women operating in the public sphere, vital emotional resources which could be better used elsewhere.

I'm writing this book about diplomacy and foreign policy even though my CV is rather different from that of most actors in this field. In fact that's exactly why I'm writing this book. For all those people who, at the age of twenty, had no idea what a diplomat actually did. For all those people who have a certain interest in foreign policy but are repelled by the ideas and the basic assumptions behind foreign policy actions. For many years, I myself did not see foreign policy as a subject area that might be relevant for me or one where I might have a place: too elitist, too far removed from the reality of my life and my origins, pervaded by ideas and beliefs that utterly horrified me. For example, the idea that the deadliest weapons invented by humanity – weapons of mass destruction such as nuclear bombs – contribute to international security. This idea is so abhorrent to me that I almost completely ignored foreign policy topics for years. If you've ever felt the same way, this book is for you.

For more than two hundred years, the feminist movement has been extraordinarily successful in bringing about radical and lasting social change. Just over one hundred years ago, feminists began to radically rethink international politics. I want this book to be a contribution to the feminist movement within international relations. Because the greatest challenges of our time – be it wars and conflicts, attacks on women's and human rights, (nuclear) arms proliferation, the climate crisis or pandemics – can only ever be resolved internationally, not nationally. And, without a feminist approach, all attempted solutions would exacerbate existing injustices and power imbalances. The future of foreign policy, then, can only be feminist.

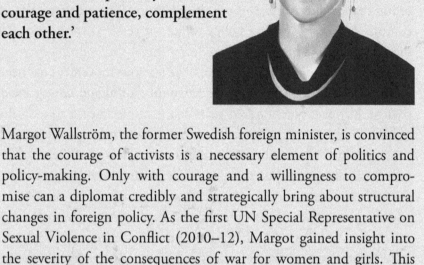

Margot Wallström:
'Activism and diplomacy, that is,
courage and patience, complement
each other.'

Margot Wallström, the former Swedish foreign minister, is convinced that the courage of activists is a necessary element of politics and policy-making. Only with courage and a willingness to compromise can a diplomat credibly and strategically bring about structural changes in foreign policy. As the first UN Special Representative on Sexual Violence in Conflict (2010–12), Margot gained insight into the severity of the consequences of war for women and girls. This experience was deeply depressing. At the same time, meeting the survivors and witnessing their determination to bring about social change gave her hope.

As Sweden's foreign minister, Margot decided to create an innovative form of foreign policy which focused for the first time on women's rights and equality: feminist foreign policy. Sweden demonstrated this commitment when it took a seat in the UN Security Council from 2017 to 2018. In every session, in the context of every resolution, and in every briefing, Sweden asked: 'Where are the women?' Under Margot's feminist leadership, her country helped to create a political culture in which women were finally taken into consideration.

A particularly memorable moment for Margot occurred during a visit of the entire Security Council to the African country of Mali, when Malian women explicitly thanked the Swedish delegation for this work. Without Sweden's persistence, a Security Council resolution on the conflict in Mali would not have included a passage on women's participation. And, without this, the women would not have been able to meet the president of their country. This would make it harder to exclude women from future meetings, and it signalled the beginning of a change in thinking about the role of women. Margot says that it is moments like these – and seeing other governments and civil society organizations such as CFFP continuing to pursue feminist work – that fill her with the greatest pride.

A book that has impressed Margot is *Say Nothing*, a true story about the conflict in Northern Ireland by Patrick Radden Keefe.

2 WHY FOREIGN POLICY MUST BECOME FEMINIST

Foreign and security policy is complex. So is feminism. Turning the former upside down to reconcile it with the latter is even more complex. In this chapter I introduce some terms and concepts that will be helpful later on, when we get down to business. These include patriarchy, feminist peace, the nation state, human and feminist security, and intersectionality.

But before our heads start spinning, I'll try to begin on a very basic level: international politics and diplomacy are about entities (such as states or organizations) working out how to get on with each other. The question is: what's the best way to do this?

The beginnings of feminist foreign policy

'The sea was rough. Not only icebergs, but also military hazards lay in wait for the Dutch ship SS *Noordam* on its route across the North Atlantic', writes the historian Wolfgang U. Eckart.[1] It was spring 1915, early in the First World War, and the German Empire had recently begun to wage submarine warfare against the Allied Powers. The passengers on this perilous journey included diplomats, businessmen, private travellers, and also forty-seven feminists and women peace activists from the USA. They were on their way to The Hague, to meet nearly 1,200 like-minded women from both neutral and belligerent countries. The dominant mood in Europe at the time was one of euphoric enthusiasm for war. But there were also women who refused to join in the general jubilation, and from 28 April to 1 May 1915 they met for the First International Congress of Women in The Hague. Three visionary women's rights activists had jointly convened the congress: Anita Augspurg and her partner (in life and work) Lida Gustava Heymann, both from Germany, and the Dutch doctor Aletta Jacobs.

Feminist foreign policy and my work at CFFP would not be possible without these historical foundations: the feminists who came before us. We stand on the shoulders of giants. The congress of 1915 and the subsequent congress in Zurich in 1919 led to the founding of the Women's International League for Peace and Freedom (WILPF). The courage, resilience and persistence of the feminists at The Hague have inspired and encouraged me to fight for justice at the intersection of activism and diplomacy, as they did. Without them, this book would not exist.

What these women showed, even then, was that activism and diplomacy go together brilliantly. And yet they are usually perceived almost as opposites. According to this view, activists are noisy troublemakers, determined to assert their ideals regardless of the consequences. Diplomacy, on the other hand, involves finding compromises that all parties can live with, despite different ideas and interests. Of course I don't agree with this oppositional view – in fact, this whole book contradicts it.

It is particularly vital that we as women call into question the underlying traditions and patterns of thought and make it clear that these are not laws, and that we *can* change things. This goes for both private and political life, as well as for the international arena. For example, who decided which states had a right of veto in the UN Security Council? How could it ever have been seen as fair that, even today, no African, Middle Eastern or Latin American state has a permanent seat? Who decided which offences were 'crimes against humanity', and who agreed that threatening to use weapons of mass destruction was legitimate diplomatic behaviour?

Feminist movements have shown, again and again, that they are not inhibited by a fear of being unable to bring change. On the contrary, feminist movements are the deciding factor – often the only factor – that brings change with regard to women's rights and therefore human rights.[2] According to a study by Mala Htun and Laurel Weldon, based on four decades of data from seventy countries, the mobilization of feminist civil society is the decisive factor when measures and laws are adopted to curb and punish violence against women. The study demonstrates that a strong women's movement is much more important for such changes than national prosperity, left-wing parties, or the presence of women in government.[3] Another study shows that law reform relating to women's rights is less likely if feminist civil society does not intervene.[4]

Feminist coalitions have brought about a fundamental shift in the way people think about equity between the sexes and the importance they ascribe to it. From the creation of the UN Commission on the Status of Women (CSW) in 1946 to the introduction of the Women, Peace and Security agenda in the UN Security Council in 2000 and the negotiations that led to the UN Sustainable Development Goals (one of which is gender equality) in 2015, the pressure on governments to include gender equity and women's rights in international agreements and norms has always come from feminist civil society.[5]

Feminism for everybody

Time and time again, people ask me whether feminism is the right term for what I'm doing. After all, they say, CFFP and I are not just campaigning for women's rights – so maybe a new term needs to be invented. My answer is, no, definitely not. For me, feminism is a collective term for theories and movements that demand and drive political organization and activism. It is a tool for analysis, and it challenges existing power hierarchies. It articulates utopias and visions for a fair and equal society in which everyone is free of oppression, marginalization and exclusion. This means an end to injustices and power hierarchies, including sexism, racism, colonialism and classism. Unfortunately, these kinds of discrimination have also manifested themselves within the feminist movement – one distressing example was the exclusion of women of colour from the battle for women's suffrage. CFFP and I are therefore concerned with the everyday experiences of marginalized people with diverse backgrounds, experiences and identities. So, yes, it's true that the feminist movement has its origins in the fight for women's rights – hence the name. And a commitment to the rights of women is still a major focus of the movement, since women are the largest politically marginalized group in our society. Yet today's feminism has evolved and now includes all forms of oppression and marginalization – as the oppression of women is directly linked to the oppression of other marginalized groups. The mechanisms and the underlying ideology are almost the same. This is why intersectionality is a core element of feminism as I understand and practise it.

The concept of intersectionality was developed at the end of the 1980s by the law professor Kimberlé Crenshaw (though crucial ideas had already been formulated by Black activists and teachers in the 1970s). In the course of her work, Crenshaw had come across a legal dispute from 1976: Emma DeGraffenreid, along with several other Black women, had sued General Motors for discrimination. Their complaint was that the company did not employ Black women. The court found no discrimination, however: since General Motors employed both Black men and White women, it could not be accused of either racial or sex-based discrimination. The injustice perceived by DeGraffenreid and her co-plaintiffs was a blind spot in the justice system – and Crenshaw decided to change this. Her concept describes how different forms of discrimination intersect and overlap, giving rise to new forms and qualities of discrimination. Crenshaw's original aim was mainly to draw attention to the whiteness in mainstream feminism: the voices of non-White and, in particular, Black women have often been ignored and pushed aside because Black men's experiences of racism and White women's experiences of sexism have been seen as the norm.[6] Intersectional feminism analyses and challenges power structures and demands the just distribution of power, resources and opportunities in our society. This is only possible if patriarchy is abolished.

People also ask me: if we're championing intersectional feminism, why not just opt for humanism? Shouldn't human rights be for everyone? Yes, of course. But since this has not been the case for thousands of years, and the rights of a small group have always been prioritized over those of the numerical majority, we need a term that highlights these thousands of years of oppression and exploitation. Humanism doesn't do this, and it can't do this as long as women, people of colour, people with disabilities and those with queer gender identities – along with many others – do not enjoy the same rights and protections as the White male minority. Anyone who demands that we refer to emancipatory movements such as feminism or antiracism as 'humanism' is failing to see this oppression. Such demands show a lack of understanding and knowledge – for example, of the fact that Enlightenment humanists themselves were often misogynist and racist. Such demands also remind me of slogans such as 'All Lives Matter' in response to 'Black Lives Matter', or '#NotAllMen' in response to '#MeToo'. We could talk about humanism instead of feminism if we had a society in which the lives of people of colour and Black people were valued just as much as those of White people, in which young women were not almost all subjected to sexual harassment, and in which one woman in three did not experience more explicit forms of male violence. However, as long as the members of a powerful, privileged minority deny or relativize problems because they themselves are not affected by them, we are still far removed from such a society.

In *Why We Matter: Das Ende der Unterdrückung* (Why we matter: the end of oppression), the political scientist Emilia Roig writes that slogans such as 'All Lives Matter' or calls for 'humanism' instead of feminism are not only counterproductive 'but also oppressive, because they deny the experience of separation and division. The voices in the struggle for social justice are silenced and delegitimized by such messages.' Roig argues that emancipatory movements are seeking not to cause division but to repair the damage done by separation, division and classification.[7]

Though this new form of feminism goes much further than earlier concepts, it is still not the same thing as humanism. Cinzia Arruzza, Tithi Bhattacharya and Nancy Fraser, the authors of *Feminism for the 99 Percent*, write: 'The time for fence-sitting is past, and feminists must take a stand: Will we continue to pursue "equal opportunity domination" while the planet burns? Or will we reimagine gender justice in an anticapitalist form – one that leads beyond the present crisis to a new society?'[8] For me as a feminist working in diplomacy and foreign policy, there is no doubt that this is also our goal. Feminist foreign policy is an intersectional project.

Marginalization and vulnerability

Vulnerability, as used in the social sciences and psychology, is not just a lack but a social condition characterized by insecurity and defencelessness.[9] Vulnerable people and population groups are exposed to shocks and stress factors and have difficulty coping with them. It is precisely these groups that are often simultaneously marginalized – that is, pushed to the edges of society's consciousness.

Yet many reports and studies, especially those by international organizations such as the United Nations, go no further than labelling these groups, stating that poor and marginalized people in our societies are especially vulnerable. This reductive approach annoys me. Like 'violence against women' and other such terms, it says nothing about how this direct or structural marginalization comes about. It may be true that poor and marginalized groups are structurally vulnerable in many societies. But this statement obscures what is probably the most important question: what is the cause of their vulnerability? Or, as in the case of 'violence against women', who perpetrates this violence? It is not a natural law that has caused our societies to develop in this way, condemning the majority of people to experience structural violence, i.e. marginalization. Our societies were deliberately designed to privilege only one small subgroup of humanity. In the words of the Filipino climate activist Mitzi Jonelle Tan, 'The system is not broken – it was built to be unjust.'[10]

Less patriarchy, more security

In *The Creation of Patriarchy*, the historian Gerda Lerner writes that the establishment of patriarchy was not a single event but a gradual process over a period of nearly 2,500 years, from around 3100 to 600 BC. The word *patriarchy* means 'the rule of the father' or 'the law of the father'. It describes a social order in which the male head of the family has legal and economic power over the female and male family members who depend on him.[11]* *Patrilineality* means that the male line determines naming and social position; *patrilocality* that the wife joins the household of the husband's family after marriage (as is still the norm in Asia, Africa and the Middle East in particular). For millennia, this has ensured that male networks are strengthened, while women's social networks are destroyed when they marry and move away – this is why the construction of networks among women is an inherently feminist act. In short, patriarchy is an ancient social order in which men have a privileged position both in the family and in the state.

Here the categories 'man' and 'woman' are not understood in a biological sense (i.e. as sexes); instead they are seen as social constructs (i.e. genders) and as a product of our socialization. For the American philosopher Judith Butler, the division into two genders is the result of an act of cultural production. In the words of the pioneering feminist thinker Simone de Beauvoir, 'On ne naît pas femme, on le devient.'[12] We are not born as women, we become women. The interplay between language, knowledge and power means that the relatively small differences between the sexes define our social relationships. Butler speaks of the 'performativity' of gender in the tradition of de Beauvoir: our gender is not determined solely by biological parameters; ultimately, it is created in our speech and actions. Butler also calls this 'doing gender'. So I'm not read as a woman primarily because of my biolog-

---

* In India, for example, women own only 13 per cent of the land, while studies have shown that women who own land have more negotiating power in the home and are less often affected by male domestic violence.

ical sex but because I mostly behave in 'typically feminine' ways – as defined by our patriarchal society.[13] All those who don't fit the stereotype of the masculine are devalued, oppressed and disadvantaged. This affects women, members of the LGBTQ+ community,* and people who are vulnerable or don't participate in the performance of the male role.

It should be noted that patriarchy itself is hierarchically structured. Men of different classes, races† or ethnicities, sexual orientations, religious affiliations, etc., occupy different places in this hierarchy. White European men from the upper classes have a higher position than non-White working-class men. Heterosexual men enjoy more social privileges than homosexual men. Intersectionality allows us to see and understand these nuances. But by and large, from a historical perspective, the one thing all these men in our patriarchal societies have in common is that they dominate the women around them – both in the family and in the state.

Patriarchy is based on misogyny on the one hand and androcentrism on the other. The latter is a point of view that sees men as the centre, yardstick and norm. According to the philosopher Kate Manne, author of *Down Girl: The Logic of Misogyny*, misogyny should not be understood primarily as men's hatred of women. What it's really about is controlling and punishing all women who challenge male dominance. Research shows that women who are more resolute and assertive are more likely to be sexually harassed and attacked[14] – the same violence I got a dose of when I launched the campaign against *Bild*. Or 'No Means No'. Or the vilification that we get for our work on feminist foreign policy at CFFP – since we too are challenging

---

* LGBTQ+ stands for lesbian, gay, bisexual, trans and queer; the + sign covers other identities.

† In using this term I refer to the political scientist Dr Emilia Roig. Although races do not exist in a biological sense, they do exist as socio-political constructs, with clear impacts on the personal experiences of different people. This is why Roig argues that the term 'race' should not be deleted from Article 3 of the German Basic Law. See Roig, *Why We Matter: Das Ende der Unterdrückung*. Berlin: Aufbau, 2021.

hegemonic masculinity. Every woman who calls into question the patriarchal status quo experiences this violence. In contrast, women who help to cement the status quo are rewarded by the system.

To understand this book, it is vital to be aware of the triad of misogyny, androcentrism and patriarchy. This combination, with its links to Eurocentrism, imperialism and racism, explains the exclusion of women from the history of diplomacy and international relations, and it explains why the practice of international policy and politics is objectively unjust for the majority of society.

As a consequence, our form of society is intolerable for anyone with a sense of justice. It is unjust that, during the Covid pandemic from March 2020 to March 2021, the wealth of the planet's more than 2,000 billionaires grew by $US4 trillion, or 54 per cent (note that nine of the top ten billionaires are men),[15] while global poverty is estimated to have undergone an unprecedented rise in 2020 (with women particularly affected).[16] It is not acceptable that women worldwide are expected to carry out unpaid care work and have most of the responsibility for childcare, the care of sick relatives, and housework.[17] It is scandalous that there are only six countries in the world where women have the same employment rights as men[18] and that men are disproportionately represented as decision-makers in business and politics. On a global scale, it is not acceptable that large parts of the Earth will be uninhabitable by the end of this century. The more patriarchal a society, the more likely it is to exploit the environment. The oppression of women goes hand in hand with that of 'Mother Nature'. It is neither normal nor acceptable that we women are, too often, still not permitted to make decisions about our own bodies. As a result, secret or unsafe abortions are (according to the World Health Organization) the third most common cause of maternal mortality* worldwide.[19] That's patriarchy. Although the harm done by the patriarchal order is clearly visible, its defenders

---

* Women who die because of an unsafe abortion are classified by the WHO as 'maternal deaths'.

are becoming ever louder and more numerous, as I show later in the book.

And yet we as a society should all be working to make patriarchy a thing of the past. The benefits of feminism for women are self-evident – the great writer and civil rights activist Maya Angelou is reported to have said that she was obviously a feminist, since it would be stupid not to be on her own side. But men should support feminism too. Feminism has never been targeted at men themselves but always at a system. Feminism needs men as fellow fighters, and men need feminism even more. Because they too suffer from patriarchal structures and demands – their suicide rate, for example, is much higher than that of women worldwide. The patriarchy convinces them that they're not allowed to be vulnerable, let alone ask for help, and the consequences can be deadly.

But the consequences of patriarchy go even further than this. The patriarchal social order determines war or peace. Working with other scholars, the US political scientist Valerie Hudson,* a member of CFFP's advisory council, used data records from 176 countries to investigate the effect of gender hierarchies on governance and security. In their 2021 book *The First Political Order: How Sex Shapes Governance and National Security Worldwide*, Hudson and her colleagues show that control over women and their bodies creates hierarchies and normalizes violence all over the world. The empirical analyses carried out by the researchers vividly demonstrate that the oppression of woment is directly connected to the well-being of nations. The more a society disregards and oppresses women, the greater the negative consequences: poorer governance, worse conflicts, less stability,

---

* A portrait of Valerie Hudson can be found at the end of chapter 3.

† Hudson and her team use the following variables to measure the oppression of women: the prevalence of male violence against women and the social sanctions for this violence; the prevalence of patrilocal marriage; the prevalence of marriage between cousins; the preference for sons and abnormalities in the sex ratio; the legal age of marriage for girls; general injustice in laws regulating family matters (e.g. laws of succession), which privilege men; the prevalence of polygamy; and property rights for women in law and practice.

lower economic output, less food security, poorer health, worse demographic problems, less environmental protection and social progress. If, for example, women's bodies and sexuality are the property of the heads of their families and are seen as crucial for the preservation of the family honour, then (extramarital) sex can lead to reprisals against the woman and the murder of the accused man, potentially triggering a clan conflict. And when contempt for women leads to disproportionate rates of abortion of female foetuses or the neglect of girls – it is estimated that there are 130 million girls missing worldwide – this means that far too many men remain single. Frustrated men are often dangerous. Lena Edlund from Columbia University and her co-authors discovered that the rate of violent crime and property crime in China increased by 3.7 per cent for every 1 per cent rise in the ratio of men to women. There is also more violence against women in the parts of India with particularly high numbers of excess men. The uprising in Kashmir no doubt has political roots, but (as pointed out in an article in *The Economist*) it is also not helpful that this state has one of the most distorted sex ratios in India.[20] Another article in the same issue of the magazine suggests it is probably no coincidence that all twenty of the world's most fragile states, as listed in the index of the Fund for Peace, practise polygamy. Globally, only 2 per cent of people live in polygamous households, but in Mali, Burkina Faso and South Sudan the proportion is more than a third, and in north-eastern Nigeria, where the jihadis of Boko Haram control large parts of the country, 44 per cent of women aged fifteen to forty-nine live in polygamous households.[21] If the richest 10 per cent of men have four wives each, then the poorest 30 per cent, for whom marriage with a bride price is much harder to achieve, will have none. This can lead to violence. Polygyny – i.e. the form of polygamy in which a man has several wives – has distinctly negative consequences for women and their rights, as well as for war and peace.[22]

The oppression of women is maintained through violence and the threat of violence; disarmament and an end to the arms trade are therefore fundamental feminist concerns. In every country of the world, female perpetrators of violent crime are outnumbered roughly ten to one by male offenders. The US psychologist David P. Barash puts it very clearly: 'The overwhelming maleness of violence is so pervasive in every human society that it is typically not even recognized as such; it is the ocean in which we swim.'[23] Violent, patriarchal social orders create insecurity not only within states but internationally. The way women are treated is directly linked to war and conflicts worldwide. The empirical findings of Hudson and her team make it clear that the patriarchy must be disrupted and dismantled in order to create and maintain peace, stability, security and resilience.

Yes, states do go to war because of oil and scarce resources. But they are more likely to do so if norms of violence based on gender inequality have become established in their societies. Societies that accept domestic violence and sexual assaults (as supposedly 'personal' or 'private' matters) are more likely to go to war; so are societies where 'rape culture' – the widespread acceptance of gender-based violence – is part of the national DNA. Without feminism, there can be no lasting peace.

Feminist security beyond the nation state

When feminists talk about peace, they mean 'feminist peace'. This is the basis of feminist foreign policy, which sees peace and security as more than just the absence of violent conflicts, international or otherwise. Instead of upholding the prevailing militarized conception of state security, feminist foreign policy focuses on the idea of feminist security (an extension of human security) and is committed to justice and equity.

The United Nations defines human security as 'the right of people to live in freedom and dignity, free from poverty and despair. All individuals, in particular vulnerable people, are entitled to freedom from fear and freedom from want, with an equal opportunity to enjoy all their rights and fully develop their human potential.'[24] But feminists go a step further. The concept of human security does highlight the things that make people genuinely secure, such as the observance of human rights, the protection of livelihoods and ecosystems, food security, healthcare and economic security. It does not, however, differentiate between groups of people and individuals who have different security needs and experiences because of structures of oppression such as sexism, racism and classism. 'Human security' is based on a universalizing understanding of 'human' and is therefore unable to adequately analyse power dynamics within society. This inadequate analysis then hinders the development of a comprehensive solution, capable of dismantling the above-mentioned systems of oppression. 'Feminist security', on the other hand, illuminates these power dynamics from an intersectional perspective.[25]

When I think of feminist security, I am thinking explicitly of the countries of the 'Global South' and the 'Global North'. These concepts, developed in the late twentieth century, have made the discourse on development policy more progressive and more equitable. People used to speak (and unfortunately often still do) of 'developing' and 'industrialized' countries, or 'First World' and 'Third World' countries. These terms have colonialist roots and are discriminatory. They present a hierarchy, and they suggest that 'development' should and does go only in one direction – that of the industrial nations – and that other countries need to catch up. To avoid these connotations, the terms now used in development cooperation are 'Global North' and 'Global South'. These are to be understood in a geopolitical rather than a strictly geographical sense, and they are not solely designed to replace discriminatory language. They refer to colonialism and neo-imperialism, which have led to the prevailing power relations between ex-colonies (the Global South) and ex-colonizers (the Global North). These terms highlight the ongoing inequalities in lived realities, living standards and access to resources – and thus the different needs that must be addressed to achieve feminist security.[26]

Feminist foreign policy criticizes putative security measures that promote or normalize militarism, and it makes demilitarization a core theme. Peacetime does not automatically mean that women and other political minorities can live in peace and freedom. So peace cannot be understood solely as the absence of war (negative peace); instead, structural violence – including poverty, hunger, social injustice and inequality – must be abolished and a positive peace achieved. In this process, feminist foreign policy insists on inclusivity and transparent decision-making, from local to global level, in all questions of peace and security.

At this point it is important to note that the nation state, from a feminist perspective, is a fundamentally patriarchal and imperialist institution. The concept emerged with the Peace of Westphalia (1648) at the end of the Thirty Years' War and was given the finishing touches in the French Revolution. It contains the idealistic notion of a homogeneous ethnic community (the 'people' or 'nation') which coincides with the territorial-legal government (the 'state').[27] This leads to claims of absoluteness towards other states and intolerance of minorities. Nation states are therefore not really compatible with the concept of feminist foreign policy.

The political scientist Toni Haastrup* emphasizes that there were two main reasons for the emergence of the nation state: control and expansion. Slavery and exclusion have played a major role in the history of the nation state, as has control – of everyone, not just women. Nation states are closely interwoven with colonialism and have repeatedly extended their territory at the expense of others. The concept of the nation both props up nationalism and patriarchy and presses women into a sex- and gender-stereotyped role as wives and producers of offspring, functions that are essential for the nation's survival. This also explains the extremely close links between nationalism, fascism and antifeminism. Of course, as is often the case in life, things are not completely clear-cut. The former German foreign minister Sigmar Gabriel points out that it is (democratic) nation states that have created and defended constitutions based on the ideas of enlightenment, emancipation and democracy, and that, for many nations of the Earth,

* A portrait of Toni Haastrup can be found at the end of this chapter.

the nation state is therefore synonymous with freedom from external domination. Furthermore, he argues, there is no institution outside the nation state that protects people's constitutional rights. 'Without the nation state, which marks its own borders and accepts those of its neighbouring states, and which upholds both democratic freedoms and its monopoly on the use of force, there could have been no Helsinki Accords, no European Union, and no German reunification.'[28] This very positive narrative of the nation state dominates the social discourse, which is why I feel it's important to present a contrasting view, such as that expressed in my opening lines about the nation state. I believe it's important to acknowledge and highlight different positions – this is why I'm writing this book. But the historical understanding of foreign and security policy is one-dimensional, and this is a problem.

Conclusion: why (feminist) foreign policy concerns us all

All the concepts presented here are essential for the foundation of a feminist foreign policy and have far-reaching consequences for such a policy. It should have become clear that feminist foreign policy and its activists are not fighting simply to secure a place at the table. What we want is to destroy the old table and build a new one. This is our motivation for founding the Centre for Feminist Foreign Policy, the first organization worldwide specifically dedicated to this cause. We are committed to a global security policy that focuses on people, not states, and gives a voice to previously marginalized groups, in line with the principles of intersectional feminism.

Feminist foreign policy applies to all areas of diplomacy and of foreign and security policy. It offers a new perspective, since it is clear that we cannot go on with 'business as usual'. Besides the above-mentioned concepts, it is based on human rights and shaped by civil society; it is transparent, anti-militarist, and focused on climate justice and cooperation rather than domination over others.

Foreign and security policy often seems very far removed from our everyday experience. It isn't, though. For millions of people, war and conflict are part of everyday life. And even in ostensibly peaceful societies, the effects of decisions made internationally in foreign policy arenas extend into everyday life. International, legally binding agreements on climate protection and climate justice influence the decisions of our own national governments, which we then have to live with. Decisions about development cooperation change the market – for example, for clothing, foodstuffs or energy. If international arms proliferation is proceeding at such a pace that a child born today is more likely to experience a nuclear war than not,[29] then it is clear that decisions in the fields of diplomacy and foreign and security policy have concrete and in some cases deeply personal effects on our lives. This is why we have to get involved in these fields – and why they have to become feminist.

My aim in this book is to present the fascinating history of feminist foreign policy, as well as its theory and practice. The more theoretical sections will include discussions of specific areas of application and personal anecdotes. To make it clear that this is not simply about getting more women into consulates and embassies and into senior foreign policy positions, I will finish by outlining a vision for the future. Each chapter ends with a portrait of one of the thirteen pioneering thinkers I interviewed for this book, women whose research and actions have helped to make the book possible.

Toni Haastrup:
'Home was never a place for me.'

This is how the Nigerian-born, US-trained academic Toni Haastrup, currently living in the UK, describes the origins of her fascination with international relations. Toni has taken on the task of radically questioning the traditional conception of international relations and, instead, considering the subject from a postcolonial perspective. Postcolonialism denies the premise that the state must be the starting point for thinking about international relations and focuses its analysis on nexuses of power.

International relations are always about power, in particular relative power: 'State A has power if State A has more power than State B.' This raises the question of what grounds there are for criticizing the growing power of nations such as China, which are traditionally not part of the Global North. Is it really their abusive human rights practices? Or is it the mere fact that power gains by for example China mean power losses for the historical colonial powers?

Toni stresses that feminism is not always compatible with the idea of the nation state. There were two main reasons for the emergence of the nation state: control and expansion. The history of the nation state shows that this construct has reinforced the tendency to exclude people. Slaves, women, and all those who were 'different' had to be controlled – for example, by limiting the right to vote. Furthermore, the nation state gave rulers legitimation for expanding their territory by colonial conquests. In Toni's view, these principles – colonialism, militarism and oppression – are precisely what feminism is fighting against.

If we believe in the transformative power of feminist foreign policy, such a policy can only ever be an ideal that we strive for as feminists. This is because a genuinely feminist foreign policy would not stop at the mere inclusion of women in the existing system; it would revolutionize our socio-political systems and create new social structures. This means, according to Toni (a great advocate of feminist foreign policy, it should be noted), that feminist foreign policy can never actually exist: once it has achieved its transformative purpose, the idea of the nation state will be obsolete, thus rendering feminist foreign policy itself obsolete.

Toni's favourite authors include Toni Morrison and John Irving.

3 DIPLOMACY: IT'S A MAN'S WORLD

For the women who persist: keep on being bloody difficult.
Caroline Criado-Perez, *Invisible Women*
(London: Chatto & Windus, 2019)

It was early January 2020. For the past year I'd been working four days a week as an advisor in the German Foreign Office; my evenings, nights and weekends were reserved for CFFP. My mission was to build up a women's network between Latin America, the Caribbean and Germany under the auspices of the then minister for foreign affairs, Heiko Maas (SPD). The network was named 'Unidas', and I made sure it was resolutely feminist. During this period I was a regular visitor to the headquarters of the Foreign Office in Berlin, and I was present at the celebrations for its 150th anniversary. And on that occasion I heard something I couldn't believe I was hearing. I was standing with hundreds of other staff members in the atrium, the impressive, light-flooded visitor entrance to the Foreign Office. There were drinks and snacks; Niels Annen (SPD), a minister of state at the time, gave a speech. And then, towards the end, he uttered these words:

And, last but not least, I know this is still a tricky topic, we should think about how to create a 'house culture' that is appropriate for our century. Team spirit rather than blind acceptance of authority, knowledge sharing rather than knowledge hoarding, and – I'm allowed to say this as a man – feminism rather than patriarchy. These are the conclusions to be drawn from a responsible approach to our history.

There it was: feminism rather than patriarchy. Explicitly called for by a minister of state in that same Foreign Office which, in its

150-year history, had largely been a natural habitat of the patriarchy. Anyone who has witnessed the speechwriting process for the leadership of the Foreign Office knows how many people have to have their say and give their blessing: different departments, the minister's team and the speechwriters. I was moved; I felt like an old woman smiling to herself and murmuring: 'Never thought I'd see the day!'*

A rocky road

Women as diplomats? Certainly not! That was the near unanimous response of the ambassadors surveyed for the British Foreign Office by Charles Howard Smith, an assistant undersecretary at the UK Foreign Office, in 1933. The question was whether women should be admitted to His Majesty's Diplomatic Service. As Helen McCarthy states in *Women of the World: The Rise of the Female Diplomat*, Smith was determined to find all the ammunition he could to demolish the proposal. He put in considerable effort. After all, he needed to find good reasons why the UK should deny women something that was permitted and practised in both the USA and the Soviet Union at that time. So Smith sent letters to all the British ambassadors asking whether they believed women would do just as good a job as men. With very few exceptions, the answers were consistently negative: the respondents advised and even warned against admitting women to the diplomatic service. Some of the ambassadors went to great pains to put their aversion to female diplomats on record. The gentlemen from the embassies in Brazil, France and the USA all wrote eight-page justifications. Sir Claud Russell, the British ambassador in Portugal, took fifteen whole pages to express his contempt for women, culminating in terms such as 'unthinkable' and even 'criminal'. Women would not only destroy

---

* Just two years after Niels Annen uttered these words, and six months after I wrote these lines, the new 'traffic light' coalition of the SPD, FDP and Greens included feminist foreign policy in its coalition agreement. This shows how quickly things can change – for the worse but also for the better.

the efficacy of British diplomacy, they would drag the reputation of His Majesty's government through the mud. Admitting women would simply be too expensive and troublesome, because new accommodation would have to be built and new dress codes established. Russell also suspected that other 'less civilized' nations would not be able to cope with women in these positions. Furthermore, women would not be able to put up with the rougher side of diplomacy, such as dealing with drunken sailors, and, on top of all that, female diplomats would never find husbands willing to travel around with them. Smith was successful: the British diplomatic service remained closed to women until 1946 (compared to 1949 in the two German states). Even then, the 'marriage bar' was maintained, and women had to give up their diplomatic career when they married. It was only in 1973 – not long ago, really – that this rule was dropped, allowing women to be both diplomats and wives.

The views of Smith, Russell et al. had a long history. Niccolò Machiavelli had a clear opinion on women and their role. He insisted that women were unsuited to diplomacy simply because of their sex. They lacked the 'uniquely masculine' attributes required to succeed in diplomatic circles, he claimed.[1] Many others supported his position. Women were therefore excluded from the diplomatic service in most countries for many years. 'Women are prone to qualities of zeal, sympathy and intuition which, unless kept under the firmest control, are dangerous qualities in international affairs,'[2] argued the diplomat Sir Harold Nicholson (1886–1968), husband of the writer Vita Sackville-West (1892–1962). And he wasn't alone in this opinion. The patriarchal, misogynist attitude of leading diplomats and foreign policy figures explains why women were excluded from the field of diplomacy for so long – and still are.

Kings and princes, sultans and emirs, prime ministers and presidents with their ambassadors and representatives – since the beginning of human history, men have always been the main protagonists of geopolitics.[3] It took a long time for women to gain a hearing and become successful in this field. Diplomacy and foreign policy are highly conservative, elitist areas in our society, and elites – especially political ones – have always been male-dominated. Women served as the secretaries of their diplomat husbands or engaged in charitable work; they were seen solely as appendages and had difficulty pursuing a career of their own because they had to move so often.[4]

It was not until the twentieth century that women gradually gained access to the world of diplomacy. Bulgaria, for example, had its first female diplomat in 1920, Chile in 1927, Japan in 1958. This was the century in which, little by little, the feminist movement successfully fought for suffrage, property rights, and unrestricted access to education and the labour market. Helen McCarthy points out that it is not easy to establish exactly how and when women gained access to diplomatic careers worldwide; much more research is required. She also notes that it is impossible to identify with complete certainty the first fully accredited female diplomat in the world. There are two contenders for this title: Rosika Schwimmer, who took part in an international conference in Bern in 1919 as Hungary's 'plenipotentiary', and Nadeja Stancioff, a Bulgarian envoy in Washington.[5]

Female diplomacy in Germany

The German Foreign Office has its very own history of excluding women. As part of the celebrations for International Women's Day on 8 March 2020, the minister of foreign affairs at the time, Heiko Maas, presented an unprecedented report: *Gender Equality in German Foreign Policy and in the Federal Foreign Office*. Among other things, the report deals self-critically with equality in the Foreign Office: 'As recently as the 1980s, if a woman shone on the diplomatic stage, it was often not by representing Germany abroad as an ambassador or by conducting political discussions. Rather, the only role available to women was mostly that of a diplomat's wife: organising receptions, entertaining guests and volunteering for social causes.'[6] Although women had gradually been admitted to positions in the Foreign Office as early (!) as 1914, these were limited to support roles such as typists, office clerks, registrars, secretaries or interpreters.

A small breakthrough came in 1950. The economist Helen Schoettle-Bourbon (1919–1997) became the first woman in West Germany to complete the first phase of training (alongside eighteen men) for the senior foreign service – i.e. the pathway to a diplomatic career. A tradesman's daughter from Cologne, Schoettle had studied economics and social science, and her previous jobs had included work for the British military government. When she married in 1951, this had a negative impact on her career: 'Several months after her marriage she was due to be posted to a diplomatic mission abroad. This did not happen due to reservations on the part of the head of mission, who feared possible problems with protocol relating to social interaction and the position of the husband accompanying a female diplomat.'[7] She ended her career with postings to Mumbai and Montreal as consul general.[8] In the thirty years following Schoettle's debut, from 1950 to 1980, an average of only two women per year were admitted to the senior foreign service.

East Germany, though more emancipated than West Germany, was not really much more advanced when it came to female participation in international relations. The first female diplomat in the East German Ministry for Foreign Affairs was Änne Kundermann (1907–2000).[9] A woman from a working-class family, she took charge of the diplomatic mission of the GDR in Bulgaria and became ambassador in Sofia in April 1950.[10] In the years that followed she was also posted as ambassador to Poland and Albania. East German diplomacy nonetheless remained very male-dominated.

Even in the 1990s, after the reunification of Germany, women still made up, on average, only 20 per cent of new recruits in the higher foreign service. At present around 45 per cent of the annual intake of trainees for the diplomatic service are women. But because women have been disadvantaged for so long, and because there are still structural reasons, even today, that make it difficult to perform such a role, only around 27 per cent of ambassadors, the highest position in the diplomatic service, are women.*

It was not until 1969 that West Germany had its first woman ambassador, Ellinor von Puttkamer (1910–1999). The top-selling tabloid, *Bild*, could hardly contain its amazement; its headline 'Eine Frau wird deutscher Botschafter!' (A woman becomes German ambassador!) incongruously uses the masculine form of 'ambassador', underlining how strange and unexpected this development was. Ellinor von Puttkamer, born into an old aristocratic family, for nine years led the Foreign Office department responsible for dealing with the UN and other international organizations, then headed the permanent representation of West Germany at the Council of Europe from 1969 to 1973. In October 2020 the press briefing room at the Foreign Office was renamed the 'Ellinor von Puttkamer Room' – the first time a room in this ministry had been named after a woman.[11] Two years earlier, female diplomats had established the organization 'frauen@ diplo' to build networks between female staff members and ensure better articulation and recognition of their needs. CFFP has been in regular contact with this group since it was founded. Change always works best on a foundation of solidarity, with pressure exerted from both inside and out.

Many of those in positions of responsibility in the Foreign Office cynically justify their current inaction by pointing out the decades-long exclusion of women from the diplomatic service. At events at the Foreign Office, I've repeatedly been told that, if you wait long enough, things will work out on their own. This is clearly just a lazy excuse, and it says more about how little desire there is for action than about how many competent women are available. The Canadian example shows this. Where there's a political will, there's a way. In 2013, under Prime Minister Stephen Harper, only 29 per cent of top diplomatic

---

* The proportion of women in senior positions abroad was 27.1 per cent in August 2022. This also includes senior roles in multilateral delegations (such as Germany's delegation at the United Nations) and consulates general. Two years earlier, this figure was only 20 per cent, so things seem to be moving in the right direction.

posts (ambassadors, high commissioners and consuls general)* were held by women, while 71 per cent were held by men. By 2017, 44 per cent of the top diplomats were women and 56 per cent men.[12] And this was purely because Justin Trudeau, who became prime minister in 2015, did not just pay lip service to the fair representation of women (since 2018, there has been near parity; currently, 48 per cent of these top Canadian diplomatic positions are held by women, according to information from staff at Canada's foreign office). And, anyway: shouldn't the argument be that, *because* women have been deliberately disadvantaged and excluded for centuries, it's time to make amends? Historical oppression must not be accepted as a justification for continuing exclusion.

While Germany is still a long way from Trudeau's ethos, there have already been some changes in the Foreign Office, under the new Foreign Minister Baerbock, with regard to the fair distribution of power for women but also for other disadvantaged groups (for example, there is now a separate unit on 'gender equality and diversity'). This is shown, among other things, by the figures already mentioned. Still, I remember an invitation issued on the intranet during my time as advisor at the Foreign Office (before Annalena Baerbock took office and a feminist foreign policy was announced): an event was being held for male staff who had concerns and questions about the promotion of women. This was because male diplomats kept complaining – at internal meetings or to the HR department – that nowadays only women had a chance of making a career. Enough was enough, they felt. A high-ranking diplomat once said, to my face, 'Wouldn't you like to become a diplomat? Your chances are good; men have no hope of a career here any more.' Evidently, men have a hard time imagining that true merit-based selection (as opposed to the historical privileging of

---

* Ambassadors represent their country's government in the host country. Consuls general and their staff primarily uphold the interests of citizens of the home country, for example by issuing passports and giving support in emergencies. High commissioners hold top positions in international organizations, focusing on such things as refugee issues, human rights or the protection of minorities.

men) is statistically likely to lead to parity. According to this interpretation, the main reason why women are diplomats is that they are given preferential treatment. If some people think the attempt to achieve greater fairness feels like oppression, then this says a great deal about the many privileges they enjoy and do not wish to lose.

Although women now have almost equal access to a diplomatic career in many countries, diplomatic circles and foreign policy are still dominated by men. This becomes apparent if we look at the distribution of the highest diplomatic positions worldwide. A study published in 2017 (with figures from 2015) shows that, at the time, only 15 per cent of the ambassadors of the fifty richest nations were female.* The analysis also reveals that women are much less likely to be posted to major military powers or countries in crisis. And yet it is postings to trouble spots that advance a diplomat's career. In international politics, women continue to be associated with 'soft' topics such as development cooperation, culture and peace. These traditions mean that it is mainly men who are able to prove themselves in the countries and policy areas perceived as more complex and more important. This then enables them to rise through the ranks and make the most central and weighty diplomatic decisions.[13]

Shecurity: an indicator of fairness

While the distribution of ambassadorial posts has become fairer since 2017, our society is still far too many years away from real fairness when it comes to politically influential positions.[14] A team led by Hannah Neumann, a member of the European Parliament, shows this unsatisfactory reality with *The Shecurity Index 2022*. This is based on an analysis of 106 data sets in six areas of analysis (politics, diplomacy, military, police, international missions, and

---

* See the infobox on 'Shecurity' on the next page for current figures. Another index, the *AGDA Women in Diplomacy Index 2021*, which examines the world's forty largest economies, concludes that only 20.7 per cent of ambassador posts were occupied by women in 2021.

arms manufacturers) taken from all EU and G20 member states, the EU itself, and all states that have formulated a national action plan to implement the Women, Peace and Security agenda. The findings: the higher and more prestigious the position, the lower the representation of women; in some areas of leadership women's representation is even decreasing. In politics, for example, women make up only 27.4 per cent of parliamentarians across all regions, so it will take another thirty-five years to reach global parity in national parliaments. For defence ministers, the time frame to reach gender parity is estimated at thirty-eight years. In diplomacy, only 23.1 per cent of ambassadors were women in 2021 (a decrease from 2020, when 25.5 per cent of ambassadors were women), resulting in an estimated thirty-eight years, on average, until parity. In national armies, women occupied only 12.6 per cent of roles in 2021 – so it would take another 154 years to achieve parity in this area. *The Shecurity Index 2021* also scrutinized foreign and security policy think-tanks and found that men were strongly overrepresented in European and US think-tanks, occupying 75 to 77 per cent of the leading positions.

Fair representation – not just for women

It is not only women who are trying to break through patriarchal structures and tear down concrete walls in international politics and diplomacy. Other politically underrepresented people have also fought for years for respect, recognition and equal status. For example, the group Rainbow was set up in the German Foreign Office in the 1990s to fight for LGBTQ+ rights. One of their first campaigns was for equal treatment of same-sex partners on overseas postings. This wasn't always a given: without same-sex marriage, even after the introduction of civil partnerships in 2001, there were major legal difficulties for diplomats wanting to be accompanied by their same-sex partners. And, even today, many states do not grant same-sex spouses of diplomats the same diplomatic immunities and privileges as opposite-sex spouses. This can mean that same-sex spouses, unlike those of the opposite sex, are not granted residence in the host country. A classic solution in such countries is for same-sex partners to be officially registered as domestic staff. This becomes untenable if homosexuality is criminalized in the host country: if there is no protection from prosecution, then both the home state and the couple have to consider carefully what risks the posting would entail for the same-sex spouses – and for the work of the embassy.

In Russia, for example, there is no recognition for same-sex partners. China grants a residence permit and minimal rights, but only if the sending state gives an assurance that the same-sex spouses will not appear as a couple at official events of the host country. The same-sex partners are thus officially confined to the closet. And yet a guarantee of diplomatic immunity from criminal prosecution is essential, especially in countries where homosexuality is criminalized. How is a diplomat supposed to represent or assert the interests of her own state when a sword of Damocles hangs over everything she does in the host country – the danger that her wife might have to go to prison because of their relationship? This highlights the challenges ahead for a feminist foreign policy approach aimed at guaranteeing the same career prospects to all diplomatic staff, regardless of sexual orientation. In the summer of 2022 another network was formed by the staff of the German Foreign Office: 'Inklusiv'. The initiative aims to represent the around 300* staff with severe disabilities and to contribute to making the Foreign Office more inclusive.

Another network within the German Foreign Office is Diplomats of Color (DoC), founded in 2019. It is now part of 'Diversitry',† a network established in May 2021 to promote diversity across the whole German federal administration. Diversitry explains: 'According

---

* The German Foreign Office has around 13,000 staff.
† This is a BIPoC network: the acronym stands for Black, indigenous, & people of colour.

to a study by the Federal Institute for Population Research, only around 12 per cent of those employed in the federal administration come from a "migration background", compared to 26 per cent in the population as a whole. Those 12 per cent are more often employed in short-term contracts or in lower-skilled positions.'[15] Diplomats of Color also campaigns for a critical examination of the colonial past of the Foreign Office. According to its founding president, Tiaji Sio, the discourse on structural racism has now made its way to Germany, following various racially motivated killings in Germany in the 2000s and 2010s and the murder of George Floyd in the USA in 2020. She continues: 'I want the German government to recognize that diversity and equal opportunities are beneficial for all of us, and to make up for what has been neglected up till now, despite the urgent need for action.'[16] Yet, in spite of sizeable 'post-migrant' communities within German society, there is not a single ambassador of non-European ancestry representing Germany abroad.

But it is not just German diplomacy that has a racism problem. Institutions of international politics such as the United Nations have also repeatedly been accused of racism, a lack of diversity and neo-colonial attitudes. One indication is the passports held by UN staff: European countries such as the UK, France, Italy and Spain are dis-proportionately represented among UN employees, which means that these states have more influence. The best-paid jobs in the UN headquarters in New York and Geneva go to employees from Western countries. In some UN agencies, such as the United Nations Office for the Coordination of Humanitarian Affairs, virtually all executive roles are occupied by White people, and White privilege and the resulting White gaze have particularly powerful effects on development coop-eration.[17] An internal survey in spring 2021 found that, of the nearly 3,000 UN employees of African descent surveyed, over 50 per cent had experienced racism in their work. A former UN official is quoted as saying: 'The United Nations is a Western-built institution. Western countries dominate the international policy apparatus just as much as the human resources side.'[18]

At a commemorative meeting at the UN General Assembly on the International Day for the Elimination of Racial Discrimination on 21 March 2021, the US ambassador to the United Nations, Linda Thomas-Greenfield, a Black woman herself, spoke very plainly: 'And because Black Lives Matter, we need to dismantle White supremacy at every turn.'[19] White supremacy goes hand in hand with the devaluation of non-White lives. This White supremacy and the devaluation of countries of the Global South is part of the DNA of the United Nations. It explains, among other things, (neo)colonial structures such as the composition of the permanent members of the UN Security Council (USA, Russia, China, France, UK) and the structural racism within the organization. 'The creation of the United Nations was based on a new global consensus around equality and human dignity. And a wave of decolonization swept the world,' said UN Secretary-General António Guterres in the annual Nelson Mandela Lecture in July 2020.* 'But let's not fool ourselves. The legacy of colonialism still reverberates.'[20]

The United Nations was founded by fifty countries in 1945. At the time, many of the founding states (including France, the UK, Italy, Belgium and Portugal) were still colonial powers, and too many people were still suffering under colonial rule, especially in Africa and Southeast Asia. For centuries, almost the entire world was under the control of European states. White supremacy had justified genocides, exploitation, slavery and plunder all over the globe. Globally, there are only four states that never suffered any form of European colonization: Japan, Korea, Thailand and Liberia. The impact of colonization can therefore be felt all over the world, to this day, and it is still highly relevant for the understanding and practice of international politics. So, yes, the work of the United Nations during the period of decolonization means that it is associated – probably more than any other international organization – with the fight for equal rights and

---

* In the annual Nelson Mandela Lecture, organized by the Nelson Mandela Foundation, prominent speakers talk about important social challenges.

racial justice. And, yes, it also deserves praise for supporting the US civil rights movement and the fight against apartheid in South Africa. However, there is still a structural problem with racism and neocolonial power relations within the UN.

These neocolonial tendencies are not only to be found at the United Nations, of course. They also pervade the whole system of international diplomacy, and especially the area known as 'development cooperation'. The International Monetary Fund (IMF), the World Bank and the World Trade Organization (WTO) are regularly criticized for neocolonial practices and structures. The points of criticism include structural adjustment programmes,* unfair trade agreements, and the suppression, in poorer countries (ex-colonies), of policies that once allowed rich countries (ex-colonizers) to become wealthy. For example, states such as the USA achieved economic prosperity partly by means of protectionism – i.e. by imposing duties on foreign products – and only later subscribed to the ideals of 'free trade'. Yet they demand that countries of the Global South open their borders to free trade, without allowing them the same opportunity to generate wealth by means of protectionism.[21]

Organizations at the heart of international diplomacy cannot contribute to fair foreign and international policy based on feminist security when their own structures are so marked by oppression. Patriarchal structures (the UN, for example, has never had a woman as its secretary-general) and White supremacy still make their presence felt. This cannot and should not be the case. Not in organizations committed to human rights, human dignity and justice.

---

* Structural adjustment programmes (SAPs) were large-scale loans granted to countries of the Global South on favourable conditions by the International Monetary Fund and the World Bank. The condition was that the receiving country would implement a jointly conceived development programme, focusing mainly on the elimination of perceived structural weaknesses (public budget, foreign trade, infrastructure, etc.). According to critics, SAPs exacerbate social injustice, since their aims include the privatization of state services.

Making women visible

In day-to-day life, I'm constantly reminded of this dominance of the experiences, needs, ideas and achievements of White men. Minor, everyday events emphatically demonstrate their connection to global power shifts. One example is a discovery I made in spring 2019. As part of my work as an advisor to the Foreign Office, I had accompanied the then foreign minister Maas and his delegation to Salvador da Bahia in Brazil, Bogotá in Colombia and Mexico City. The purpose of the trip was to introduce the feminist network Unidas, linking Latin America, the Caribbean and Germany. When the work was done I seized the opportunity to stay a few more days in Mexico City. I love travelling alone, letting my intuition guide me through towns and cities. One day in early May I was strolling through the Mexican capital and happened to discover, in the Museo de la Ciudad de México, an exhibition on Aurora Reyes (1908–1985). Reyes was Mexico's first female muralist, a friend of Frida Kahlo, and an impressive feminist.

I'd never had a particular affinity with art. It didn't play a major role in my life when I was growing up. That had to do with my origins, but it also had a lot to do with the artistic canon. I just wasn't interested in how all those White men whose works filled the museums saw the world. The White male gaze had no relevance for me. But all that changed when I became aware of the work of (feminist) women artists. Their portraits, sculptures, performances and other works fascinate me, because I can identify with them. They can be role models for me. That was why I was so delighted to encounter Aurora Reyes and her works in the exhibition in Mexico City. At the same time, it reminded me once again how little we know about the women who came before us, and how many pioneering women have been left out of our history books. The Mexican woman who guided me through the exhibition commented: 'We live in such a macho society that very few people know of Aurora Reyes – the work of women artists is barely acknowledged. Everyone knows Diego Rivera (who was also a muralist). Reyes was Mexico's first female *muralista*, yet we're not taught about her story.' We can only build on people's experiences, perspectives and accomplishments if we know about them, if they and their history are visible. Women occupy a mere 0.5 per cent of about 3,500 years of recorded history.[22] We need more than one perspective to grasp the complexity of our world.

Making women visible is important not only in relation to history but also for our future. This process must be supported by political decision-making. Only then will boys cease to be born into a world in which they grow up believing they are superior – a world where they see it as their natural right to dominate the public arena, acquiring fame, honour, and the top positions in politics, business, culture and society. Because, wherever they look, they see themselves represented: in newspapers, on television, in (text)books, or in the portrait galleries in government ministries. Wherever power and repute are to be found, men are overrepresented. Boys grow up believing that this is their rightful place. While girls, far too often, are still taught to be quiet and take up as little space as possible. This has a formative effect. In 2017, an American study showed that boys and girls already believed at the age of six that 'brilliance' was a masculine quality.[23] All over the world, contrary to scientific findings, men believe that they are more intelligent than women. Confidence and competence often do not coincide, and, if a person is highly confident of his own abilities, others may confuse this with actual competence. This fact is the basis for the *Harvard Business Review* article 'Why do so many incompetent men become leaders?'.[24] And the same phenomenon is manifest in many areas of everyday life. In her book *Untenrum frei* (Freedom 'down there'), Margarete Stokowski writes: 'The boys around me speak of themselves as philosophers as if it were self-evident, as if they'd been baptized by Plato himself.'[25]

Oppression and violence – women's lives past and present

It is important to understand how much discrimination occurs routinely in our society. When women or other political minorities successfully fight for visibility and agency, this is often presented as though a woman or person of colour were finally good enough to keep up with the men, who have been in their positions for so much longer. This narrative is as false as it is dangerous. When Kamala Harris became vice president of the USA in January 2021, it was high time: high time for the first woman, the first Black woman, and the first person of South Asian descent to take this role. But, at the same time, we have to remember: as a Black person in the USA, she would still have been enslaved until 1865; as a woman, she would not have been allowed to vote until 1920; and, as a Black woman, she would have been actively hindered from using her right to vote, especially in the southern states, until 1965.[26] She would have had to attend racially segregated schools until 1954, and she would not have been allowed to have her own credit card until 1974. All those years, White men were presidents of the USA and therefore shared the responsibility for this systematic and inhuman oppression of women and Black people. Back in 1837, the abolitionist Sarah Grimké summed up these injustices with the following words: 'I ask no favours for my sex. . . . All I ask of our brethren is, that they will take their feet from off our necks, and permit us to stand upright.'[27]

In the German Empire the oppression of women continued into the twentieth century. Often women were not even allowed to go out walking or eat at a restaurant alone; any woman who did so risked being mocked as an old maid, condemned as a lesbian, or treated as a prostitute. Worse still, the regressive family law at the time meant that, if such 'suspicions' arose, relatives could have the woman committed to a psychiatric ward and subjected to forced treatment. 'Any woman suspected of prostitution could be arrested and forcibly examined. And anyone who was out alone was under suspicion.'[28] Despite these adverse conditions, outstanding women and feminists took up the fight against various forms of injustice and discrimination. Some organized themselves in feminist women's associations, which were influential in the early twentieth century. Yet the Prussian law on associations prohibited these groups from expressing their political views.

This was hardly surprising. Men wanted to maintain the oppression of women, using the social and institutional structures they had established. Fighters such as Anita Augspurg and Lida G. Heymann were undeterred. These are two of the most famous feminists in German history, and they played a pioneering role in introducing feminist ideas to foreign and international policy.

There are reasons for the realities described above: patriarchy and misogyny. Women are controlled, and those who challenge male dominance are punished. One of the (far too) many examples is the feminist Olympe de Gouges. In 1791, during the French Revolution, she demanded equality for men and women in her revolutionary 'Declaration of the Rights of Woman and the Female Citizen'. The first article reads: 'Woman is born free and remains equal to man in rights.' Two years later, this courageous and ground-breaking thinker was beheaded by the Jacobin government. The judges justified her execution with the words: 'She wished to be a statesman, and it seems that the law punished this conspirator for forgetting the virtues proper to her sex.'[29] Equally threatening was the brute male force – such as violent arrests and force feeding in prisons – inflicted on British women's rights activists in the early twentieth century because of their campaign for female suffrage.[30] The argument was that they had no business in the public arena and were neglecting their children and households. Kathrine Switzer, born in Germany in 1947 as the daughter of a US army major, was the first woman to officially run the Boston Marathon in 1967. The organizers tried to forcibly remove her from the course: real women were supposedly too delicate to run marathons. A further example consists of the insults, humiliations and innuendo aimed at female politicians in West Germany before reunification. A 2021 documentary, *Die Unbeugsamen* (The unyielding ones), shows the sexism inflicted on female members of parliament such as Herta Däubler-Gmelin (SPD), Rita Süssmuth (CDU) and Petra Kelly (Greens). Male MPs were unrelenting in their efforts to convince them that parliament was not a natural environment for women.

Men's feeling that they have a natural right to occupy positions of power is painfully evident in the most routine behaviours. In February 2021, the front-page story of the news magazine *Der Spiegel* was 'Feindbild Frau – Die dunkle Welt enthemmter Männer: und was gegen den Hass hilft' (Women as the enemy – the dark world of men who have lost their inhibitions: and what can be done to combat the hate). The story confirmed the shocking conditions facing female politicians even in today's German parliament: '69 per cent of the female MPs who responded to the survey [sixty-four out of the 222 who were sent the questionnaire] have experienced misogyny, 36 per cent have been attacked'; and when asked whether they had experienced misogyny within parliament from colleagues or staff, 72 per cent of the sixty-four MPs said they had.[31] In the article, female politicians such as Ute Vogt (SPD) reported that the hate messages were no longer all anonymous. Vogt had received messages, with the sender's name and address, calling her a 'filthy refugees' whore' and a 'repulsive piece of shit.' Lisa Paus (Greens) told of phone calls where she was insulted as a 'slut', 'bitch' or 'cunt'. MP Yasmin Fahimi (SPD) had had bullets posted to her, and Aydan Özoğuz (SPD) had required protection from the BKA (Federal Criminal Police Office) on several occasions and was no longer able to leave the door in her constituency office open. Here racism and misogyny are combined in a particularly dangerous mix.

An especially tragic example is Marielle Franco, a young lesbian Afro-Brazilian from the favelas. In 2016 she achieved something that had previously seemed impossible: this young woman from the working class was elected to the city council of Rio de Janeiro. She campaigned for the rights of women, especially Black women, for the LGBTQ+ community, and against police brutality and corruption. She had been in office for less than a year when she and her driver were shot and killed on their way back from a political event. This barbaric murder was not just about silencing Marielle herself. It was aimed at all women, Black women in particular, who dare to seize political power. Patriarchy and racism go hand in hand.

Conclusion: diverse and efficient

Taking into consideration the lived realities of different people leads to a better politics, meeting a wider spectrum of needs. In *Invisible Women*, Caroline Criado-Perez uses multiple studies to show that the presence of women in politically powerful positions is beneficial for women.[32] This also applies to other politically underrepresented groups. In the end, the quality of policies depends on the diversity of the people behind them. Not because diversity makes political processes more efficient, but because it allows different lived realities and perspectives to feed into political decision-making. Women and other politically marginalized groups have the right to seize power and to be represented at all levels of decision-making in accordance with their group size – simply because they're entitled to this, and because a disproportionate emphasis on a particular social group always points to unjust processes. This also applies to diplomacy and foreign policy. If we want to tackle and solve the greatest global challenges successfully, we can't afford to keep limiting our options for interpretation and decision-making.

Yet oppressive patriarchal structures will not be smashed just by achieving fair representation. We also need to question and rethink conventions, paradigms and dogmas. So strengthening women and other politically marginalized groups and getting them into important positions is only the beginning. Feminist content has to follow.

Valerie Hudson:
'What a long, strange trip it's
been.'

This is how the political scientist, author and lecturer Valerie Hudson describes how she became a feminist and found the focus for her research: the connection between the security of states and the oppression of women. The journey began during Valerie's studies, where she encountered a complete absence of women in science, politics and history. This invisibility of women, coupled with experiences such as her work in the Special Forces, clearly showed her that we see the world through men's eyes and through the definitions men have created. In doing so, we overlook women's expertise and experience, and we ignore the fact that the stability of a nation state is linked to the degree of gender equality in that country. There was a shortage of data, however: until then, nobody had comprehensively analysed women's situation and their safety worldwide. Valerie therefore launched the WomanStats Project, a database that now includes information about the safety of women in 176 countries. One of Valerie's findings is that the most significant factor affecting a state's willingness to use violence domestically and abroad is the level of gender equality within the country. This is a more statistically significant factor for predicting state security than gross domestic product or form of government. Yet it is difficult to gather quantitative data, since most states simply don't record statistics on women's lives. For example, there are around thirty countries that do not keep any records on rape.

In her latest book, *The First Political Order: How Sex Shapes Governance and National Security Worldwide*, Valerie shows how these gender inequalities have come about. The extensive research and data collection required for this were funded by a $1.3 million grant from the US Department of Defense. Valerie argues that the 'first political order' on which every society is based is determined by the relationship between the sexes. In many societies this relationship is seen as a hierarchy and is manifested in the oppression of women by means of control and exploitation. These mechanisms, she argues, are then transferred to all other individuals and groups who are regarded as 'different' because of, e.g., their skin colour or religion.

Valerie's favourite book is *Parity of the Sexes* by Sylviane Agacinski.

4 OLD WHITE MEN IN THEORY

*Representation of the world and the world itself are the work of men.
Men describe it from their own point of view, and they confuse this with
the absolute truth.*

Simone de Beauvoir, *The Second Sex*

My personal sense of unease

It was 2014, and I'd made it – or so I thought. I'd moved to Oxford to study diplomacy. It sounds elite, and it was. That's what diplomacy is like. Some of my fellow students were already diplomats, or are now; they came from elite universities such as Yale and now work for the United Nations, national governments, big tech companies or consultancies, or in human rights advocacy. Our lecturers were the best in their field. It couldn't get any better than this, I thought.

But doubts soon crept in. Why were nearly all our lecturers men? And why, in courses such as 'Security Issues in Fragile States', were the oppression of women and patriarchal social orders never mentioned as important criteria for understanding state fragility? For decades, feminists have been pointing out how personal difficulties experienced by women are linked to political problems.[1] The slogan 'the personal is political' comes from an article with this title by the US feminist Carol Hanisch, published in 1970 in the anthology *Notes from the Second Year: Women's Liberation*. Violence experienced in private is linked to state violence; injustice experienced 'personally' on a mass scale has a political and structural dimension. The research by Valerie Hudson and her team, discussed in previous chapters, makes this clear.[2]

There was no mention of this in my degree course. Most of the required reading was dominated by White, Western male theorists.

Some textbooks on the history of diplomacy, such as *Diplomatic Theory from Machiavelli to Kissinger*, referred exclusively to the ideas of men. None of this felt right, and the focus on these theories diminished my interest in studying diplomacy. I wasn't the only one to feel this way, either.

My frustration became productive when I met Jennifer Cassidy.* At the time, she was still working on her doctorate in the department where I was studying, having completed the same master's programme as I had a few years earlier. Like me, she was struck by this gap in the course and began to research women in diplomacy. When she searched online for 'women' and 'diplomacy', however, almost all the information that appeared was about ambassadors' wives.† Jennifer wasn't prepared to accept this state of affairs, and in 2017 she published the edited volume *Gender and Diplomacy*. In the introduction, she and Sara Althari describe androcentrism in the (international) political arena and criticize its consequences for women. Today Jennifer is not just a highly valued friend, fellow fighter and member of the CFFP advisory council, she's also one of the most sought-after political commentators in the UK and Ireland, with over 170,000 followers on Twitter.

I still remember how electrifying my exchanges with Jennifer were. During a dinner at my college, St Cross, in 2014, she told me that the Swedish foreign minister, Margot Wallström,‡ had just announced that Sweden was adopting a 'feminist foreign policy' – the first country in the world to do so. Given that most women and feminists had been excluded from all areas of public life for thousands of years, this was an extraordinary step. I was thrilled – and full of enthusiasm for Margot Wallström, who is now on the advisory

---

* A portrait of Jennifer Cassidy can be found at the end of chapter 8.
† The historian Katharina Rietzler, an expert in the history of women's international thought, points out that an ambassador's wife held an important role as, in the context of the gender conventions of early modern and modern diplomacy, circa pre-1945, this was one major route for a woman to participate in international politics.
‡ A portrait of Margot Wallström can be found at the end of chapter 1.

council of my organization, CFFP. She's still someone I look up to enormously.

The imperial brotherhood, or: androcentrism is everywhere

This devaluation or even negation of women can have dangerous effects, as highlighted by the feminist author Caroline Criado-Perez in her 2019 bestseller *Invisible Women*. She shows what happens when our society is constructed around the needs, ideas and norms of men.

Since men are the standard, towns are planned and built to be safe and accessible for them. Urban infrastructure is not designed to suit women's lifestyles and therefore disadvantages them. For example, men more often drive, while women tend to walk or use public transport. Funding for infrastructure, however, is more likely to be used to improve roads than to provide wider, interconnected pedestrian paths. This means that women and children face a higher risk of serious injury in a traffic accident.

In medicine, the male body has been the norm since the ancient Greeks. Male and female bodies were regarded as essentially the same except for their reproductive functions and size. Even today, the female body is often seen as a deviation from the male standard. Most medical research uses male subjects, working on the false assumption that the results can simply be transferred to women's bodies. This is despite the fact that there are sex-specific differences in the tissue and organ system of the human body, and illnesses differ in severity depending on sex. For example, women have a higher risk of suffering from right-sided colon cancer, which often develops more aggressively. However, the method often used to detect this disease, a stool blood test, is less reliable for women than for men. The androcentric norm also makes it harder to identify heart attacks in women. As a result, women have a 50 per cent greater chance of their heart attack going undetected or being misdiagnosed.[3] Androcentrism operates on many levels and can have fatal consequences.[4]

So the problem is not simply that history has been written by (predominantly White)* men. It is also that the human past as recorded and interpreted is incomplete, because it includes next to no women. As noted earlier, only 0.5 percent of recorded 3,500 years of human history is about women. That equates to 17.5 years – or as *New York Times* journalist Maya Salam wrote, the acknowledged written history of women isn't even old enough to vote.[5]

This applies just as much – or even more – to the major paradigms of the supposedly male domains of diplomacy and foreign policy. An important theoretical component is 'realism', the most influential school of thought within International Relations (liberalism and constructivism are similarly influential, at least in theory). Realism, not to be confused with *Realpolitik* as a guiding principle for political action, is focused on the state, state power and interests, national security, and the threat or use of force. Realism sees the coexistence of states without a supranational government as anarchy. In order to be influential and powerful in this situation, states attempt to dominate and oppress others – preferably by military strength and armed force. Individuals and their needs play no part in this concept, or if they do it is only in terms of the desire to gain control over others – 'man over man'. The precursors of realism include the ancient Greek military commander and thinker Thucydides (ca. 460 to 395 BC), the previously mentioned Italian poet, diplomat and philosopher Niccolò Machiavelli, the philosopher and political theorist Thomas Hobbes (1568–1679) and the US political scientist Hans J. Morgenthau (1904–1980). The term 'realism' is based on the belief of these men (and their advocates) that their thoughts and actions were a neutral, objective reflection of reality. Yet nothing could be less neutral, objective or real than the limited perspective of an exclusive – predominantly male – minority.

---

* Of course men of colour have also engaged in historical writing – one important example is Ibn Khaldun – but the issue was more about whose knowledge and writing was considered important. I deal with this topic later in this chapter. And while humans in all cultures have engaged in historical writing, it can be assumed that, because of patriarchal exclusion and oppression, these humans were mostly male.

Unfortunately, the assumptions and ideas of men have also shaped movements that are generally regarded as progressive, such as the Enlightenment. In *Emile, or On Education*, Jean-Jacques Rousseau, viewed as one of the great figures of the Enlightenment, explains that women lack the rationality required for participation in public life, being slaves to their sexual passions. He concludes that they should be excluded from public life and confined to the private, domestic sphere. Thomas Hobbes also thought that women's role should be restricted to the home, in keeping with their duties of nurture and care. And Machiavelli, in his major work *Discourses on Livy*, spends a whole chapter describing how women seduce (states)men into mixing private and public affairs. (The narrative of women seducing men and causing their downfall has defined the DNA of Christian societies ever since Eve's 'transgression' in the Garden of Eden.) According to Machiavelli, (states)men are to be judged on their actions in the public interest of the state, while women are to be judged on their private actions. The political scientist Barbara Finke sums it up as follows: 'At the centre of the classical realist school is the concept of the (masculine) public interest in the tradition of Machiavelli, which must not be mixed with (feminine) private matters.'[6]

Is it any wonder that the study of Machiavelli and his successors didn't inspire me to care about the content of my course? Machiavelli's *The Prince* (1513) is regarded as one of the first works – if not *the* first work – of modern political philosophy. In this text and his theoretical *Discourses on Livy*, he purges moral and religious ideals from political action. In his view, preserving power and securing domination are the core aims of governance; in politics, moral action is condemned to failure. He gives tips, for example, on how to establish and maintain a dictatorship. His whole analysis is based on a pessimistic view of humans as ruthless egotists. 'Of men, this can generally be said: they are generally ungrateful, over talkative, imitators, dissimulators, cowardly in the face of danger, and greedy for money.'[7] Machiavelli's advice is to use whatever means are necessary to extend and preserve one's power, including ruthlessness and force.

Today Machiavelli's book is regarded – wrongly, I believe – as one of the most important works of modern political philosophy. It is generally understood to be based not on moral ideals but on political 'reality'. In fact this is the reality only of a rather small subgroup of society, but one with the power to interpret its own reality as universal. The political scientist Herfried Münkler, well known for his research on Machiavelli, writes that Machiavelli is often assumed to have replaced an ideal of politics with political reality.[8] Münkler himself interprets Machiavelli differently: not as an amoralist but as the founder of an ethics of political responsibility – the same interpretation as that presented by the sociologist and economist Max Weber in his lecture 'Politics as a Vocation' (1919).

But how exactly is patriarchy connected with realism as a political paradigm? Since realism centres on the state, state security and military strength, and since these are exclusively associated with men, realism cements patriarchal structures and the dominance of men over women. Dominating others and using force to assert men's interests and gender hierarchies: this is the core of patriarchy. In 1981 the political scientist Zillah R. Eisenstein wrote that '[u]ntil feminists are aware of the state's involvement in protecting patriarchy as a system of power, much in the same way as it protects capitalism and racism as systems, feminists will be unable to see why a reform politics, though necessary, is insufficient. A feminist theory of the state is necessary to understand why this is so.' Realism, however, is not based on any such feminist theory.[9]

(Classical) political realism cannot be explained without the work of Hans J. Morgenthau, who drew on the writings of Hobbes and Machiavelli. In his principal work *Politics among Nations* (1948), the German-American political scientist and advisor to the US Department of State explains how he sees the international system of nations: as a state of anarchy, with constant power struggles and conflicts of interest. Viewed in this light, international politics is an eternal battle for domination. Morgenthau's book was a success, probably partly because of its timing: it came out just as the USA was recalibrating its foreign policy after the Second World War, with the founding of NATO and the new policy of containment towards the USSR.[10]

In *The Inevitability of Tragedy: Henry Kissinger and His World*, Barry Gewen quotes Kissinger, the former US secretary of state and national security advisor, as saying that anyone who teaches International Relations must begin with Morgenthau's ideas. As Gewen sees it, anyone using the term 'national interest' as an analytical tool is following in Morgenthau's tradition.[11] 'Few scholars can be said to have invented an entire discipline, but Morgenthau comes close.'[12] Morgenthau held that politics was based on objective laws, which were in turn based on unchanging human nature. This made it possible to establish a rational, objective theory. Moral deliberations, he argued, were incompatible with successful political action and obstructed the goal of expanding power. Anyone acting morally in international politics was bound to fail, since everyone else was behaving immorally.

The most famous contemporary of Morgenthau to subscribe to realism was probably Henry Kissinger, who played an influential role in US foreign policy for decades. Despite his Nobel Peace Prize, Kissinger is highly controversial. Some see him as one of the greatest figures of twentieth-century foreign policy. Others – such as the journalist Christopher Hitchens in his book *The Trial of Henry Kissinger* – regard him as a war criminal who should be brought to justice for his role in calamitous strategic and military decisions. These include bomb attacks in Cambodia during the Vietnam War (1973), the failure to react to Indonesia's invasion of East Timor (1975) and the sabotaging of Allende's socialist government in Chile (1973).* Gewen writes that Kissinger was such a fervent proponent of *Realpolitik* that he even advocated suppressing the attempts of other countries to establish democracy – if these efforts were contrary to the interests of the USA. Hence the frequent comparisons with Machiavelli.[13]

---

* The aim of the USA in Chile in 1970 was to prevent the election of the socialist Salvador Allende. This was not successful, but political and economic interventions later contributed to the coup against President Allende in September 1973, enabling the dictator Augusto Pinochet to come to power.

Kissinger's often-cited *Realpolitik* stands for 'the attempt to bend reality until it fitted into the corset of cast-iron precepts',[14] according to the historian and American studies scholar Bernd Greiner. Greiner has written a critical biography of Kissinger, whose principles he refers to as 'force, power and hegemony'. He quotes a statement by Kissinger: 'How is one to carry out diplomacy without the threat of force? Without this threat, there is no basis for negotiations.'[15] According to this view, diplomats must 'master the craft of coercion'.[16] Greiner believes that Kissinger's status as an original thinker has been overestimated; he sees him, instead, as an effective 'advertiser and impresario of himself'.[17]

Yet Kissinger clearly impressed a lot of people, including Morgenthau. For decades the two men carried on an intellectual exchange. 'It is probably no exaggeration to say that there was no thinker Kissinger respected more than Morgenthau. And Morgenthau considered Kissinger one of the best secretaries of state in American history,' writes Gewen.[18] 'Morgenthau was a Realist down to his bones.'[19] The influence of classical realism on Kissinger's foreign policy is obvious. Ideas do not simply remain ideas; they have the power to guide our behaviour. Or the foreign policy of a state.

An analysis by the political scientist Robert D. Dean shows the devastating consequences certain ideas and principles can have in political reality. His book *Imperial Brotherhood: Gender and the Making of Cold War Foreign Policy* deals with Kissinger's role as national security advisor and US secretary of state in the Vietnam War and the Cold War. Dean describes the prevailing masculinized culture of the adherents of political realism, a culture that dominated US foreign policy (and that of other countries) in the second half of the twentieth century. Secretary of Defense Robert McNamara, Kissinger and their entourage were all part of an elite defined by a supposedly masculine toughness, the breeding ground for some disastrous decision-making. Dean argues that the mindset of those in authority in Washington was largely to blame for the extremes of destruction, death and suffering caused by the Vietnam War. This tallies with the description by McNamara, whose views are considered realist. In his memoirs, the former secretary of defense retrospectively categorizes many of his actions as errors: 'We of the Kennedy and Johnson administrations who participated in the decisions on Vietnam acted according to what we thought were the principles and traditions of this nation. We made our decisions in light of those values. Yet we were wrong, terribly wrong.'[20]

Dean refers to the underlying culture as an 'imperial brotherhood' – an imperialist, dominant understanding of masculinity, obsessed with strength. It was the result of socialization during education and training and elite men's clubs; the effects of the McCarthy era and homophobic denunciations also played a part. '[T]he actions and attitudes of foreign policy decision makers were grounded in prescriptive lessons learned in a series of exclusive male-only institutions – boarding schools, Ivy League fraternities and secret societies, elite military service, metropolitan men's clubs – where imperial traditions of "service" and "sacrifice" were invented and bequeathed to those that followed,'[21] writes Dean. Even if the failures and brutality of the decision-makers at the time were their individual responsibility, they were nonetheless acting in the context of prevailing socio-political structures – a culture that equated diplomacy with appeasement, weakness and homosexuality, thus reinforcing a toxic understanding of masculinity. 'The politics of manhood crucially shaped the tragedy of Vietnam,'[22] argues Dean.

Are humans essentially selfish?

Different disciplines share the rationalist premises of realism and its pessimistic view of humanity. In economic theory, for example, reflections and models are based on the concept of *homo economicus*. This is rational, selfish man (an echo of Machiavelli's ideas), always intent on the maximization of profit. But such a negative view of humanity does not account for phenomena in our society such as care work, charitable giving, and voluntary or humanitarian work. In her bestseller *Unsere Welt neu denken* (Rethinking our world), the German political economist Maja Göpel explains how all the structures of our society were created on the basis of the *homo economicus* concept and therefore encourage selfish behaviour – a self-fulfilling prophecy. In a world of depleted planetary resources, inexorable population growth and increasing inequality, Göpel argues, it is disastrous to continue to base our social and economic systems on this negative view of humanity, focusing on the needs of a *homo economicus* who seeks only to maximize his own benefit.

The Dutch author Rutger Bregman goes a step further. In his book *Humankind: A Hopeful History*, he investigates whether people are actually bad, as assumed by many in the Western tradition of thought, or are in fact fundamentally good. He wonders whether men such as Hobbes, Machiavelli and their modern counterpart, the US psychologist Philip George Zimbardo, were wrong after all. Zimbardo was responsible in 1971 for the famous Stanford Prison Experiment, which supposedly proved that people become evil and abuse their power because of situational and social factors. Bregman cites numerous examples in support of his contrary hypothesis – that people are basically good. There are, for instance, many controversies around Zimbardo's prison experiment, and there is much to contradict his diagnosis of the natural malevolence of the participants. One of Bregman's main points, however, is the relevance of the stories we tell ourselves as a society. They influence the way we see ourselves, what we believe in, how we live and how we act. Bregman quotes the media scholar George Gerbner, who sums up the effect of social narratives as follows: 'Who tells the stories of a culture really governs human behaviour.'[23] And of course these stories can also be positive.

It is truly astounding that the proponents of such a negative view of humanity are seen as realists, when their perception of the world is clearly at odds with reality. Scholars such as the Berkeley professor Dacher Keltner have investigated how realistic Machiavelli's analyses – and his understanding of how power is acquired and maintained – really are. In *The Power Paradox*, Keltner argues that people acquire power not through coercion and oppression (as posited by Machiavelli) but through socially intelligent and empathetic behaviour.

Against this background, theories such as those of Morgenthau and other advocates of realism should be seen not as reality but as self-fulfilling prophecies – prophecies that uphold patriarchal power, which is particularly oppressive for women and political minorities. If representatives of states largely assume the worst about other states and their representatives, this will influence their foreign policy behaviour. Conflict and aggression can then become their preferred strategies for the retention of power. Such problematic assumptions justify dogma such as 'international security and peace can only be achieved by nuclear deterrence.' Weapons are then presented as guarantors of peace and security, even though their purpose is to extinguish hundreds of thousands of human lives at the touch of a button. This perverts the idea of lasting peace. Ultimately, this kind of politics is based on fear and fragility – in egos and in ideas.

The strongest critics of this pessimistic view of humanity are people with a different reality, people whose lives are not shaped by the privilege of possessing power. At first glance this seems absurd, since these are the people most likely to be oppressed by the conduct of the powerful. It seems they would have every reason to develop a pessimistic view of humanity. Yet the opposite is true. Feminists, for example, have long since criticized this view of humanity.* It is typically masculine and equates power with force. The Black feminist author Minna Salami writes that men, over the course of history, have always used their power of definition to define power in a manner that benefited them. As a consequence, the traditional patriarchal understanding of power has three common features: first, the linking of power with the state and its institutions (government, the military, parliament, constituencies), which are all male-dominated; second, a definition that

---

* Of course feminists tend to take a negative view of masculinity, based as it is on misogynist and androcentric socialization. However, their fundamental understanding is that this can be changed – this is one of the very motors of feminist activism.

is synonymous with dominance, authority, violence, oppression and coercion; third, power as a measurable concept.[24] Historically, many philosophers – mainly White European men – have understood power as 'power over'. '[I]t is no surprise that the same three characteristics can be traced at least to renaissance philosopher Niccolò Machiavelli's treatise on the topic, *The Prince*,' Salami concludes. Later power was conceptualized positively as 'power to', for example by Hannah Arendt and the American political scientist Hanna Pitkin; here the aspect of oppression is omitted. The etymology of 'power', from the Latin verb *potere*, to be able, suggests that power is something that enables.[25]

A destructive view of humanity and understanding of power is problematic for the utopia of a just society, as the Dutch author Joke J. Hermsen argues in her book about Rosa Luxemburg and Hannah Arendt, *A Good and Dignified Life*. 'Rosa Luxemburg goes further than Arendt in denouncing capitalist society more radically, arguing that it is based on the fundamental misapprehension that a just world can be created on the basis of competition, contest, and exploitation of others.'[26] And this is precisely the point: a society that takes such values as its foundation and perpetuates them in its narrative can never be just. As long as international politics relies on exploitation, dominance and destruction, it will never contribute to lasting peace. Theories and assumptions form the basis for real political measures and decisions. This is why it is so important to call them into question. Patriarchal, violent theories inevitably lead to disastrous policies.

In the 1980s this thinking gradually changed in International Relations. After the Second World War the focus had initially been on national security, military debates and the nuclear arms race. Now, however, efforts to develop international cooperation and norms slowly emerged. One sign of this is Hedley Bull's 1977 book *The Anarchical Society*, in which he defines values such as peace and the reduction of violence as the main goals of an international community. Yet the dominance of the militarized discourse and the prioritizing of national over human security was – and is – undeniable. The world was split into two halves, the capitalist West under the leadership of the USA (the NATO states) and the communist East (the states of the Warsaw Pact). The Cold War ruled the world. The number of nuclear weapons available worldwide peaked in 1986[27] at nearly 65,000; the figure now is around 13,000,[28] though today's weapons are far more destructive. The arms race between the two opposing systems was just one aspect of the rivalry between them, but it was a powerful element in the ideological propaganda of the superpowers and their allies. There was never a direct military confrontation between the USA and the Soviet Union and their military blocs, but there were proxy wars, e.g. in Korea, Vietnam and Afghanistan. And there were precarious situations that almost led to a 'hot' war: the Berlin Blockade in 1948–9, the Cuban Missile Crisis of 1962, and the conflict over the deployment of medium-range missiles between 1979 and 1982–3.

With the end of the Cold War in 1989, new approaches, methods of analysis and priorities attracted more interest in the field of International Relations. This also applied to feminist perspectives on international politics.[29] Where previously the political theory of realism had dominated, the liberal internationalist school of thought now challenged this focus on power and the state. 'At least since the overcoming of the East–West conflict in 1989, liberalism has played a leading role in International Relations as a research paradigm,' write Daniel F. Schulz and Jan Tilly in their contribution to the *Casebook Internationale Politik*.[30] In contrast to realism, they explain, liberalism does not consider the (supposedly anarchic) international system to be the primary determinant of state behaviour. Instead, this is thought to be affected by internal factors such as government type, constitutional order, domestic politics, human rights and civil society. These factors are seen as essential for an understanding of the behaviour of states – and not just their desire for greater power.

From the end of the 1980s, academic feminists began to address theories of International Relations. Pioneering thinkers such as J. Ann Tickner, Chandra Mohanty, Cynthia Enloe, Gayatri Chakravorty Spivak, Christine Sylvester, V. Spike Peterson, Rebecca Grant, Kathleen Newland, Anne Sisson Runyan, Carol Cohn and Sandra

Whitworth critically examined the predominant ideas of realism. Feminist approaches in political science derived their energy from feminist movements. Socialist and anti-imperialist women's groups in particular (especially East–South alliances) insisted from a very early stage on linking the topic of women's rights to colonialism, imperialism and arms proliferation and thus seeing it as part of foreign policy, or at least international relations. Academics such as Kristen R. Ghodsee[31] (whose works include *Why Women Have Better Sex under Socialism*) remind us that feminist movements in the Global South and in socialist states such as the USSR were crucial for the development of international politics from the 1950s onwards. Ghodsee points out that the Soviet Union and its allies also dominated the debate on women's issues in the UN in the early 1970s. The same goes for various congresses organized and sponsored by the Women's International Democratic Federation (WIDF). The WIDF had been founded by left-wing women in Paris in 1945 as the umbrella for a number of women's organizations. Women from forty countries took part in the inaugural meeting.

These global feminist movements became more radical in their demands and more critical of the system. Feminists from (ex-)colonies and socialist systems combined the question of women's rights with that of class and with demands for an end to racism. There were bonds of solidarity between feminist movements in socialist states and in (former) colonies, and the former supported the latter in their strivings for independence. Lily Monze, a great pioneer in the fight for women's rights in Zambia, said: 'Cooperation with the women from socialist countries helped us a lot. For example with scholarships for study or with reciprocal visits, and sometimes they paid for us to take part in these conferences.'[32]

In 1975 there was no denying it any more: the issue of women's rights had developed international momentum. On the initiative of the WIDF, the UN declared 1975 International Women's Year. This marked the start of a whole 'Women's Decade': three major international congresses on the question of women's rights were held (in Mexico City in 1975, in Copenhagen in 1980, and in Nairobi in 1985), and the whole decade had a progressive feminist agenda. According to Ghodsee, this was mainly thanks to women from the Eastern bloc and the Global South.[33]

Academic feminism within the field of International Relations also emerged – and benefited – from the feminist movements of the 1960s and 1970s. One of its concerns was to refute the idea that international politics was practised mainly between states. Feminists argued that international politics was also played out between international organizations (such as the UN, NATO, the OECD and many others), social movements such as antiracist or pacifist movements, civil society, and other non-state actors such as transnational companies, international financial organizations, and human rights organizations.[34]

Feminist thinkers place particular emphasis on the significance of (feminist and women's) civil society. Civil society (i.e. politically and socially active citizens), and especially the feminist movement, is the most effective agent of social change leading to a fairer society. From the 1990s, a broader understanding emerged in International Relations about who the relevant actors were – civil society and NGOs gradually became accepted as objects of mainstream research. A principle expressed in 1959 by the West German politician and government minister Käte Strobel (1907–1996) eventually became widely accepted: 'Politics is far too serious to be left to men.'[35]*

International Relations: the revolution begins

The special issue of *Millennium* published in 1988, 'Women and International Relations', has been recognized as the beginning of academic feminist engagement with international theory.[36] In this issue J. Ann Tickner† – a pioneering feminist theorist of International

---

* The next chapter, especially the paragraphs on the Paris Peace Conference, will provide strong examples for this.
† A portrait of J. Ann Tickner can be found at the end of chapter 10.

Relations – deconstructs the political realism of Hans J. Morgenthau. In her article 'Hans Morgenthau's principles of political realism: a feminist reformulation', she writes: 'International politics is a man's world, a world of power and conflict in which warfare is a privileged activity.'[37]

This text laid the foundation for a feminist revolution in the discipline of International Relations. Tickner regards Morgenthau's principles as a highly simplified description of international politics, based on a one-sided view of humanity which privileges masculinity and disparages the feminine. Morgenthau himself, she argues, stands for the male, patriarchal perspective. The way he interprets 'power' or defines 'security' is based mainly on the experiences of White, European men.

Tickner astutely dissects Morgenthau's theoretical constructs and builds an alternative, feminist political theory. She argues that some of Morgenthau's central concepts need to be redefined. Objectivity must become dynamic objectivity, so as offer us a view that is truer to reality and has less potential for dominance. National interest is multidimensional and context-dependent and goes far beyond power-related interests. Solving global problems requires cooperation rather than zero-sum approaches. Instead of power that is associated with domination and control,* we need power that is understood as collective empowerment. Morality cannot simply be separated from political action. All political actions have moral significance. Traditional 'realists' prioritize the morality of order over the moral values of justice and the fulfilment of basic needs. Feminists attempt to find shared moral ideas. This offers a basis for de-escalating international conflicts and creating an international community. In our Western political culture, autonomy is presented as purely masculine. This denies

---

* The equating of power with dominance and control is a narrative that feminist intellectuals have repeatedly criticized and deconstructed over the decades. See, for example, Minna Salami, *Sensuous Knowledge: A Black Feminist Approach for Everyone*, or, for the history of women's exclusion from traditional spheres of power, Mary Beard, *Women & Power: A Manifesto* (London: Profile Books, 2018).

pluralist conceptions of human nature and excludes the concerns of women, which are not associated with the narrow, autonomous political sphere.

When I interviewed J. Ann Tickner for this book, she stressed that she did not believe Morgenthau's 'political realism' was completely wrong – especially in view of the global pandemic. Nonetheless, she felt it was important to point out that his representation of reality was far from the full picture. Political realism and *Realpolitik*, she argues, are scarcely relevant for the lived reality of most of the population. People become ill, they need a functioning healthcare system, they worry about their families and fellow humans – these are our everyday needs. Very few people are interested in obliterating another nation at the touch of a button, as the *Realpolitik*-inspired foreign policy of the Cold War era suggests. These are, quite simply, unacceptable ideas created by men and the patriarchy and maintained by a small, powerful elite, which keep us all in a state of uncertainty and insecurity.

Samantha Power,* director of the US Agency for International Development (USAID), would probably confirm this. In her professional life she has often been confronted with the consequences of the realist paradigm. Power, who was senior director for multilateral affairs and human rights and later US ambassador to the UN (both under the Obama administration), describes the dominance of this worldview and understanding of security in her autobiography, which bears the telling title *The Education of an Idealist*. Writing about her time in the US National Security Council, she says that government officials do not explicitly identify with labels such as 'realist' or 'liberal internationalist', which are common in academia. Nonetheless, the predominant view is based on *Realpolitik*, in which 'values' are seen as secondary. 'Many US officials considered prioritizing human rights to be in tension with, if not antithetical to, our traditional security concerns.'[38]

---

* A portrait of Samantha Power can be found at the end of chapter 12.

When reality overtakes you

In phases in which traditional political themes take a back seat to global challenges, it becomes particularly clear how important the theory and practice of human (and feminist) security are. During the Covid-19 pandemic, we heard nearly daily reports of over-burdened health systems all over the world. Too often we simply accept (and I am no exception) that this is an unavoidable phenomenon. We must not forget that such situations are not natural but are the result of conscious political decisions about resource distribution. Such decisions are not laws of nature. Our capitalist system and the different resources allocated to particular areas of life and government spending are based on political decisions. How is it possible that, in Germany in 2020, defence received more funding (8.98 per cent of the federal budget) than health (8.11 per cent)?[39] And even this figure is only due to frantic efforts to combat the pandemic, leading to supplementary budgets in the health sector. The International Campaign to Abolish Nuclear Weapons (ICAN), winner of the Nobel Peace Prize, has looked at what the nuclear states France, the UK and the USA spend on the maintenance, improvement and development of their nuclear arsenals compared with their spending on healthcare. The results are (sadly) unsurprising and were particularly striking during the pandemic: if the money spent on nuclear weapons had been invested in the health sector, it could have saved thousands of lives.[40]

Historically, both in theory and in practice, it is overwhelmingly White men who have (re)produced knowledge, led debates, conducted politics and shaped diplomacy. Such contributions as women have made are too often forgotten or dismissed – an equally serious problem. A few decades of the feminist movement do not make up for 4,000 to 6,000 years of patriarchy, in which women and other politically underrepresented groups have been excluded and marginalized. But since the 1980s at least, the perspectives of men in International Relations have increasingly been called into question. Thank goodness for that!

The political scientist Elvira Rosert writes: '(Neo-)realism is now less present, and cooperation is not neglected. There are major new strands of research such as research on norms, which focuses on normativity, progress and rule-based action in international politics – rather than on the state of conflict.'[41] If we really want to create a fairer and more peaceful world – a goal that has always motivated political theorists – then this is the path we need to take.

Epistemicide – the destruction of knowledge

Let's take a step backwards. The obvious question is: how could this have happened? How did the ideas, thoughts and theories of a minority – White men from Italy, France, Britain,* Germany and the USA – come to dominate the world of knowledge and university courses out of all proportion to their numbers? And how were they able to claim objectivity, neutrality, and interpretive authority for their work?† The Puerto Rican sociologist Ramón Grosfoguel, wondering how men from these five countries were able to impose their knowledge as universally valid and superior to traditional forms of knowledge, talks about 'epistemic‡ privilege'. The other side of the coin is epistemic inferiority, and the coin itself is epistemic racism and sexism.[42]

In her bestseller *Why We Matter: Das Ende der Unterdrückung* (Why we matter: the end of oppression), the political scientist Emilia Roig explores these questions with impressive rigour. The main reason she identifies is the erasure of knowledge systems in the course of Western colonization, a process that the Portuguese sociologist Boaventura de

---

* As well as Britain's settler colonies: Canada, Australia, New Zealand and South Africa.
† This section is very much inspired by Emilia Roig's book *Why We Matter: Das Ende der Unterdrückung*.
‡ 'Episteme' comes from ancient Greek and refers to knowledge, science or understanding.

Sousa Santos has called 'epistemicide'. Discussing the meaning of epistemicide, Roig writes that 'today's universities and schools only reflect
a very small part of the world's extensive and diverse knowledge. They
exclude many of the diverse systems of knowledge, including those of
indigenous peoples and excluded, minoritized ethnic groups, as well
as the knowledge of people excluded on the grounds of gender, class or
sexuality.'[43] Knowledge from the Global South, less influenced by the
Enlightenment and based more on traditional knowledge and experience, is considered inferior; the same goes for women's knowledge.
Though I wasn't aware of these concepts at the time, it was precisely
this one-dimensionality that caused me such unease when I was studying diplomacy in Oxford. This is why programmes such as women's
studies are so essential. Roig refers to Ramón Grosfoguel, who argues
that the one-dimensional nature of knowledge today – which he calls
intellectual colonization – goes back to the four epistemicides of the
long sixteenth century.[44] The first was the expulsion of the Jewish and
Muslim populations during the conquest of al-Andalus. The second
was when the Spaniards began to colonize indigenous peoples, first in
America, then in Asia. The third is the transatlantic slave trade, during
which millions of people from the African continent were dehumanized, enslaved and murdered. The fourth is the 'witch hunts', in which
tens of thousands of Indo-European women were burnt at the stake
'because their practices of knowledge could not be controlled by men',
writes Roig.[45]

Women were affected by all these epistemicides; around three-
quarters of the victims of the witch hunts were female. The murder
of these women was a deliberate, strategic attempt to erase knowledge, spirituality, intuition and (especially) practices that were specific
to women. This centuries-long massacre of women – which began
in the fifteenth century and ended in 1782, when the last woman
defamed as a witch was executed in Switzerland – also ushered in the
Enlightenment era. 'The movement that tried to kill the witches is
also, unwittingly of course, that which paved the way, later on, for
the lives and thought of Montesquieu, Voltaire and Kant,' writes his-

torian Guy Bechtel.[46] The perception that the Age of Enlightenment was overwhelmingly positive and progressive can once again be attributed to the interpretive authority of a small male elite.* This is all the more disastrous if we look at the way famous Enlightenment thinkers perceived the world and humankind. Immanuel Kant, for example, was an anti-Semite who formulated a hierarchic race theory and considered White people to be superior – not unlike Voltaire, who also doubted that Black people were human.[47] Seen in this light, the Enlightenment is not just an 'incomplete project of modernity', as Jürgen Habermas once said. It is, to quote the philosopher and cultural studies scholar Iris Därmann, a 'halved matter' ('eine halbierte Angelegenheit'), which included neither non-males nor slaves in the colonies.[48]

The postcolonial perspective

In academia, the methods and concepts of postcolonial criticism offer an indispensable tool for understanding international politics and foreign policy and avoiding Eurocentrism. That is, the idea that the Global North, Europe in particular, is unique and superior and is therefore the centre of modernity and of all international politics.[49] This is just as false as the idea that Columbus discovered America.

Early in the summer of 2020, not long after the murder of the Black US citizen George Floyd by a White policeman, the political scientists Kelebogile Zvobgo and Meredith Loken wrote an article in *Foreign Policy* entitled 'Why race matters in International Relations'.[50] Here they argue that considering race is not just a necessary perspective

---

* Although it is generally presented in a mainly positive light, for example in the school curriculum, there have always been theorists who have taken a critical approach to the Enlightenment and the associated concept of progress. Examples in the twentieth century include Hannah Arendt ('Aufklärung und Judenfrage' [Enlightenment and the Jewish question], 1932), Theodor W. Adorno and Max Horkheimer (*Dialektik der Aufklärung* [*Dialectic of Enlightenment*], 1944) and – clearly postcolonial in focus – Edward Said (*Orientalism*, 1978).

in the discipline of International Relations but also vital for an understanding of international politics. Since European states brought
nearly all the countries in the world under their colonial rule at some
point in history, these past and ongoing relationships have to be taken
into account when we analyse international relations and judge foreign policy actions today. The authors also analyse the containment
policy of the USA during the Cold War – i.e. the attempt to prevent the expansion of communism and Stalinism. Anti-communism
and racism, they argue, were inextricably linked in attitudes towards
Africa, Asia, Central America, the Caribbean and South America.
Racist prejudices also play a significant role in the 'War on Terror',
declared after 9/11, and in efforts to prevent extremism and terrorism.

Racism and the accompanying imperialism, slavery and colonization can be traced back to the Peace of Westphalia in 1648, at the end
of the Thirty Years' War. This gave rise to the principles of statehood
and sovereignty which are still accepted today. As a result of these
nationally oriented definitions, the world was divided into 'civilized'
and 'uncivilized' parts; this then served to justify invasion, plunder
and genocide.[51] These beliefs were reaffirmed at the Berlin Conference
of 1884–5 (also known as the 'Congo Conference'), to which Otto
von Bismarck invited representatives of the major European powers,
the USA, Russia and the Ottoman Empire. The delegates decided how
Africa was to be divided into colonies, drawing borders with a ruler.
This partition was then brutally implemented. The plan was to 'civi-
lize' Africa, raising the continent to the same level as Europe in social,
cultural (including linguistic and religious) and economic terms.

Ideas and actions that seem unimaginable today nonetheless have
an ongoing legacy. Even today, important events in international politics can be understood in all their complexity only if we consider
them from a postcolonial and decolonial perspective. For example, the
financial crisis of 2007–8 and the ensuing European sovereign debt
crisis showed how colonial ideas of the inferiority of other countries
could be invoked even within Europe. At the time, the EU decided
on a very strict austerity policy towards Greece. Again and again, the

image of the 'lazy Greek' was used to legitimize and enforce the policy of austerity. Such justifications are not new. In the colonial period, the European rulers justified their exploitation and oppression in the colonies with the argument that the population was inferior, lazy and uncivilized. The measures towards Greece were also reminiscent of the 'structural adjustment programmes' (SAPs) and the subsequent poverty reduction strategy papers. SAPs are economic measures, such as budgetary discipline, subsidy cuts and deregulation, imposed in countries of the Global South. From the 1980s, they were the precondition for loans or debt waivers from financial institutions such as the International Monetary Fund (IMF) and the World Bank. Not long after the introduction of the SAPs, they were the target of outspoken feminist criticism from the likes of Ester Boserup, Maria Mies and Chandra Mohanty.* These women argued that the SAPs had a particularly severe impact on marginalized population groups, and that the relationship of dependency between the Global South and the Global North made them neocolonial in nature.

SAPs have a strong emphasis on the reduction of the public sector and privatization. For my final thesis at University College London in 2013, I studied the case of Ghana to see how this affected women and their rights. During my research visit to Accra, I learned about the catastrophic effects of this policy. If the public sector is reduced and jobs in administration are cut, this more often affects women, since they are more likely to work in this area. And if more and more public services are scrapped – e.g. in the education and health sectors – this also has a greater impact on women. All over the world, women are still expected to carry out the majority of housework and care work, so when public services are cut it is usually women who have to provide these services in the family. In short, neocolonial dependencies and international policies that fail to consider gender help to cement injustices such as racism and sexism. It is structures such as these that decolonial feminist foreign policy seeks to dismantle.

---

* A portrait of Chandra Mohanty can be found at the end of chapter 5.

The 'international development cooperation' sector (formerly known as 'development aid') is particularly vulnerable to accusations of neocolonialism. In May 2021 the organization Peace Direct, founded by my mentor Scilla Elworthy (and now directed by Dylan Mathews) published the report *Time to Decolonise Aid*[52] in partnership with Adeso (African Development Solutions), the Alliance for Peacebuilding, and WCAPS (Women of Color Advancing Peace, Security and Conflict Transformation), founded by Bonnie Jenkins.* In this report, the authors and the experts consulted explain how deeply structural racism is embedded in development cooperation and peacebuilding. Many bilateral partnerships – between individual countries, between organizations of the Global North and the Global South, or between donor organizations such as the UN and recipient countries in the Global South – are based on former colonial relationships. And some things have only changed marginally: there are parallel employment systems in which staff from the Global North are paid substantially better than those from the Global South. The structure and research design of many programmes are based on Western values and standards, with no adjustments made for local needs or circumstances. The perspectives of intersectionally marginalized groups – such as members of the LGBTQ+ community or people with physical disabilities – are often not taken into consideration.

This structural racism is also apparent in the language used. One example is the concept of 'capacity building'. It implies that there cannot be abilities and knowledge without experts from the Global North, and it perpetuates the myth of 'uncivilized' societies. No less problematic is the mentality of many international development workers from the Global North, who clearly see themselves as 'White saviours'† – a mindset that also has its origins in colonialism.

---

* A portrait of Bonnie Jenkins can be found at the end of chapter 11.
† The term 'White saviour complex' is used to describe the phenomenon in which (mainly White) people from the Global North go to the Global South to 'help' in different projects. However, the aim of these projects is often not to provide useful support but to boost the self-presentation and self-aggrandizement of the White 'helpers'. Many of the projects do

When I myself was working in the United Nations Development Programme (UNDP) in Yangon, Myanmar, I had moments of great unease on a near daily basis without really being able to articulate what was troubling me. I was conscious of how wrong it was that I – just two years out of university – was given more responsibility and more interesting tasks than many of the local staff. This was despite the fact that they often had decades of professional experience and, of course, knew the political, social and economic situation of their country much better than I did. All I'd done in preparation was to read a few books about Myanmar, one of which was a guidebook. It was absurd: although I had no geographical expertise and only a limited knowledge of the topic, I was expected to write strategies for 'Women, Peace and Security', while more experienced Burmese women did the groundwork for me. This is neocolonialism: the belief that superficial conceptual and functionalist abilities, developed in European conditions, are more important than situated knowledge.

The *Decolonise Aid* report demands that all these problems be recognized and eliminated. It demands a fundamental questioning of prevailing power dynamics and a completely new culture of self-reflection and honesty in which criticism can be expressed openly. Funding systems must be reformed to support creative new projects and less established applicants. There must also be investment in the use of local, indigenous knowledge.[53]

Although race and racism are central for an understanding of international politics, this has been a severely under-researched area for far too long. Between 1945 and 1993, in the five most relevant academic journals, only one article with the word 'race' in its title was published.[54] Yet whether we are talking about colonial politics, imperialism, or the way decision-making power within international organizations is concentrated in the West, or about nuclear weapons tests in former colonies, structural adjustment programmes, refugee

---

not integrate local voices but function more as a tourist industry for (young) people from the Global North.

81

policies, global vaccine distribution, or the War on Terror, one thing is certain: international politics can only be understood if we take race into consideration.

Conclusion: old White men – a narrow outlook

'The narrative through which we view knowledge is both the seed and the fruit of the culture it produces. To produce nourishing fruit, we need to plant sublime seeds,' writes Minna Salami in *Sensuous Knowledge: A Black Feminist Approach for Everyone.*[55] It is vital to understand both where the origins of political theory and diplomatic practice lie and how women and other political minorities are fighting against them – so as to establish a feminist form of knowledge, thinking and action and place this at the heart of diplomacy. Only then can we comprehend the staggering consequences of patriarchy and toxic masculinity, from nuclear deterrence, neocolonial politics, and attacks on the human rights of women or the LGBTQ+ community to the destruction of our planet. And only then can we choose a different and better course of action.

Nina Bernarding:
'Gendering is a way of structuring power.'

'If you come from such a privileged background as I do, you have a responsibility to advocate for and support those that are not so fortunate.'

Before deciding to join forces with me to co-found CFFP, Nina worked with traditional actors in the field of peacebuilding and international security. Over time, however, she became frustrated with the lack of focus on building societies that work for everyone – and not only for those that shout the loudest or have the best military equipment. In building CFFP, she saw the opportunity to work for structural change that lays the foundation for a more equal and just society.

Nina's main areas of work are disarmament and arms (export) control. She focuses on highlighting the fact that the international arms trade benefits mainly those already in power and helps sustain patriarchal and exclusionary structures. She also works on raising awareness of the influence of arms manufacturers on foreign and security policies – while feminist civil society is burdened with the proof of demonstrating the links between arms (exports) and gender inequality.

Nina also works to highlight and counter the international antifeminist attacks, both in Europe and beyond, which actively work to undermine and restrict the rights of women and LGBTQ+ communities, in particular in the areas of sexuality education and reproductive rights.

What Nina wants for the future is this: that we understand the need for a feminist foreign policy as an imperative rather than a question. This impetus will generate energy, which can be invested in implementing – rather than just advocating for – a feminist foreign policy.

Nina's favourite books are *Freedom is a Constant Struggle* by Angela Davis and *The Eighth Life* by Nino Haratischwili.

5 THE BEGINNINGS OF FEMINIST FOREIGN POLICY

I first met the former Swedish foreign minister Margot Wallström in 2018. She was visiting Berlin for a meeting with the German minister of foreign affairs, Heiko Maas, and took the opportunity to invite a small group of civil society representatives to lunch. This was just after I had founded CFFP in Germany. Meeting her in person and giving her a copy of our print magazine, *Disrupted*, meant a lot to me. Since that evening in Oxford when Jennifer Cassidy had told me that Wallström had established a feminist foreign policy in Sweden, I'd been paying close attention to her work. Three years later, in spring 2021, I was delighted when Wallström accepted our invitation to join CFFP's advisory council.

Whenever there's talk of feminist foreign policy and its history, eyes turn to Sweden and Margot Wallström's visionary work. In 2014, Sweden became the first country to proclaim a feminist foreign policy – a huge step forward not just for feminism but also for an effective global peace and security policy. Sweden's declaration was an inspiration both for other states and for civil society. CFFP probably wouldn't exist if it hadn't been for Margot Wallström and her courage. Yet it is equally true to say that Wallström could never have announced a feminist foreign policy if it hadn't been for the decades of previous work by feminists in international politics.

The pioneering Black feminist campaigner Audre Lorde wrote:

By ignoring the past, we are encouraged to repeat its mistakes. The 'generation gap' is an important social tool for any repressive society. If the younger members of the community view the older members as contemptible or suspect or excess, they will never be able to join hands and examine the living memories of the community, nor ask the all-important question, 'Why?'. This gives rise to a historical amnesia that keeps us working to invent the wheel. . . .[1]

Her message is that we should acknowledge and appreciate the feminist ancestors on whose shoulders we stand. As their inheritors, we have the duty and responsibility to carry on the fight, never ceasing and never resting, because there can be no pause in the battle for human rights and justice. In this feminist struggle, women stand shoulder to shoulder, each generation forming a base for the next, enabling the movement and its influence to grow. Without the strong shoulders of these countless former fighters, there would be no CFFP, this book would never have been written, and no state would ever have announced a feminist foreign policy.

1915: it all began in The Hague

Feminist foreign policy was not dreamt up in a government department. It was developed by activists, who analysed the causes of conflicts and violence and wanted to use the lessons learned to prevent wars. The American women who made the dangerous journey across the Atlantic to the international women's congress in The Hague in 1915 (see chapter 2) are perfect examples.

The law professor Freya Baetens refers to the 1915 International Congress of Women as the 'forgotten peace conference'. It was the last of three peace conferences in The Hague, all of them influential for the course of the twentieth century. The first took place in 1899 on the initiative of the Russian Tsar Nicholas II. The conference had two objectives: to curb the arms race between the major European powers and to resolve international conflicts peacefully. Representatives of twenty-six countries were present (men only; women were not admitted). Despite its failure on these two points, the conference was regarded as a success. In the first Hague Convention, the participants agreed on basic principles that now form part of international humanitarian law. These are essentially about giving the greatest possible protection

86

to people, infrastructure and the environment during military conflicts. The appetite for war showed no signs of abating, however, with the Second Boer War in South Africa (1899–1902) and the Russo-Japanese War (1904–5). A second peace conference was therefore held from June to October 1907, this time with representatives from forty-three countries.[2] Seven years later, the First World War broke out.

During this pre-war period concern was also growing among feminists in the German Empire, and many women's associations discussed disarmament. But war fever was rampant, and anyone talking of disarmament was quickly branded unpatriotic or even traitorous.[3] Two women were undeterred, however. Seeing that the arms race was in danger of leading to war, Anita Augspurg and Lida G. Heymann took up the fight for disarmament. The two women, partners in life as well as fellow campaigners, would go on to lead the German women's peace movement during the First World War.[4]

Augspurg and Heymann were part of the 'radical' wing of the bourgeois women's movement[5] and were later among the first people to demand Hitler's expulsion from Germany following his attempted putsch in 1923. They achieved a great deal for the rights of women: they co-founded the German Association for Women's Suffrage, edited their own feminist pacifist journal, *Die Frau im Staat* (Woman in the state), and established the women's association Frauenwohl (Women's welfare), which campaigned for equality in all areas. In 1897 Augspurg became the first woman in Germany to earn a doctorate in law. Like Rosa Luxemburg, she had to go to Zurich to study, as women were not admitted to German universities at the time.

Heymann and Augspurg were alarmed when the Reichstag adopted the first Naval Law in 1898, authorizing the rapid expansion of the German navy. Shortly afterwards, a 'patriotic naval association' was founded, campaigning for a military build-up and a politics of power. It soon had a million members. Wanting to counter this trend, just before the first peace conference in The Hague in 1899 Heymann and Augspurg organized a week of women's protests demanding an end to the arms race. Compared to international participation in the protests, the response in Germany was feeble, with demonstrations held in only six German cities. Heymann and Augspurg were aware how far their country lagged behind international developments. Meetings with international feminists from the women's suffrage movement helped to introduce more progressive thinking into the German Empire.[6]

In August 1914, the First World War began. Heymann and Augspurg were horrified at the enthusiasm shown by many intellectuals, parts of the media and the German population. 'There was an elation, a delirium, the like of which had never been experienced by those alive at the time. The German people, otherwise riven by dissent, suddenly felt united, like a mighty colossus. . . . Anyone who had dared to stand up against this unity would have been stampeded, crushed, lynched.'[7] Augspurg and Heymann, however, were convinced that the war was 'the greatest crime' and the 'culmination of male greed and destructiveness'.[8] The two women refused to give up their anti-war campaign. Soon after the start of the war, they helped to bring together feminists from enemy countries: in February 1915, women activists met in Amsterdam to plan the first international women's congress.[9] Lida G. Heymann was subsequently summoned to the Bavarian war ministry, where she was ordered not to carry out any further action against the war. But the preparatory work done by Heymann, Augspurg, the Dutch doctor Aletta Jacobs and English suffragists bore fruit: the third peace conference in The Hague – which was also the first international women's peace congress – took place from 28 April to 1 May 1915. The Netherlands had been chosen as the location because of its neutrality. The conference can be seen as the founding moment of feminist foreign policy.[10]

Over a thousand women from twelve countries took part. And it could have been many more if the feminists' efforts to participate had not been thwarted on a massive scale. Only twenty-eight women were able to come from Germany, for example, because the authorities – for various reasons – refused to grant passports to many of those wanting to attend. English women had played a major role in the preparations, and 180 women from England had registered to participate. Only five reached their destination, however, because Winston Churchill, first lord of the admiralty at the time, prevented any of the delegates from crossing the Channel. The ship with the forty US delegates was also briefly detained by the British navy in Dover but was released to avoid any diplomatic upsets with the USA.[11] Such attempts to sabotage women's work are typical of the patriarchy. It always acts like this when its critics become too strong, using any means it can find to stop them. The patriarchy realizes how powerful feminists can be. Most of the participants were suffragists, united in organizations such as the International Woman Suffrage Alliance (IWSA).[12] They knew one another from earlier congresses, where they had met to strategize the fight for women's suffrage.[13] But the women gathered at The Hague wanted to talk about something else, about no less a topic than war and peace. It is impossible to overstate the revolutionary nature of this gathering: a group regarded as politically powerless, a group that lacked even the right to vote, was meeting not only to discuss the current war but to develop concrete proposals for an end to the conflict, disarmament, and a new international legal system to prevent future wars.

Yet there were also differences of opinion and problematic behaviour among the women. The French women's rights movement boycotted the congress because they were unwilling to participate alongside German women. And some women – we'll get to specific cases later – were outspokenly opposed to women's suffrage and peace.[14] Women from the colonies were not even invited, and the few women of colour who attended were not treated as equals by the majority. This wasn't the first time that White feminists had displayed racist behaviour and treated Black women as inferior.

The organizers asked the American campaigner Jane Addams (1860–1935), one of the most highly respected social reformers of her time, to lead the congress – partly because the USA was not yet involved in the war. This reflected the women's desire for a non-partisan event. Addams was one of the co-founders of the American Civil Liberties Union (ACLU), which has campaigned for human rights since 1920, and of the National Association for the Advancement of Colored People (NAACP), one of the oldest and most influential Black civil rights organizations in the USA. She was also a noted feminist activist and was elected president of the newly founded International Committee of Women for a Permanent Peace, renamed the Women's International League for Peace and Freedom (WILPF) in 1919. Addams presided over the congress with two other American women: Emily Greene Balch (1867–1961), professor of economics and sociology at Wellesley College,[15] and Alice Hamilton (1869–1970), who was to become the first female (assistant) professor at Harvard Medical School.[16] Balch became secretary and treasurer of WILPF and succeeded Addams as honorary president. Both women later received the Nobel Peace Prize.

Augspurg, Heymann, Addams, Balch, Hamilton and many of their fellow campaigners fought against militarism and for peace and social justice throughout their lives. At CFFP, we're fighting the same fight. Without these visionaries, our work would not be possible.

The women's resolution

At the end of the congress, the feminists agreed on a twenty-point resolution. One of their main demands was that the current war be ended immediately and – a revolutionary idea – that war be made illegal in international law.

The women called for immediate mediation by neutral states, the activation of an international organization as an authority, and the establishment of an international court of arbitration.[17] They agreed on basic principles for a peace and planned to meet immediately after the end of the war to influence the peace negotiations. Many of their demands, proclaimed over a hundred years ago, are still relevant today. As Anna Dünnebier and Ursula Scheu note, similar ideas had been discussed at the previous Hague conferences, but no resolutions had been reached. One of the women's demands – that national territory should never be transferred to another state without the consent of its citizens – was partly targeted at Germany's objective of annexing Belgium and part of France. They also demanded nationalization of the arms industry, state control of the arms trade, and universal disarmament, arguing that arms profiteering was incompatible with lasting peace and non-violence. Another key demand was the abolition of secret diplomacy and the introduction of democratic scrutiny by equitably elected women and men.[18]

At the time, far too little attention was paid to these demands. The feminists presented their proposals in person to several male heads of state but were largely ignored. It was only in subsequent decades that their resolutions were (partially) implemented. This shows how radical their vision was and how far ahead of their time they were. One example is their demand that war be considered illegal and a violation of international law. This did not become a reality until after the Second World War, when the Charter of the newly established United Nations set out to ban international aggression and wars of conquest. The Charter stipulated – thirty years after the feminists had made this demand – that member states should refrain from the threat or use of force in their international relations.

Another radical aspect was the call for democratically elected parliaments at a time when most countries were not democracies. Equally revolutionary – in 1915, when women had the vote in only five countries worldwide – was the demand for female suffrage.[19] The feminists were also visionary in their views on the importance of children's education. At a time without compulsory schooling, when children in the poorer social strata were mainly exploited as cheap labour in factories or on farms, the feminists placed great emphasis on the rights of children. They advocated the provision of high-quality education, which would teach children the ideals and the value of constructive peace.[20] The women's demands for a general assembly of nations and a court to resolve economic conflicts laid the foundations for the subsequent creation of the UN General Assembly and the World Trade Organization. The latter was founded in 1995, eighty years after the women at The Hague had made their resolutions. And their demands that conflicts be peacefully resolved by arbitration and mediation and that social, moral and economic pressure be exerted on states that use force formed the basis for the mechanisms of implementation and enforcement used by the League of Nations and later the United Nations. The only one of their core demands that has not yet become part of international law is the demand for universal disarmament and an end to the private arms industry.[21] Even today this is dismissed as naive.

In addition, the feminists discussed mass rape as a war strategy and war crime. Right at the beginning of the congress, Lida G. Heymann was loudly applauded when she addressed one of the greatest taboos of all wars: 'We've had enough of hearing that women are protected by war. No, we are raped by war!'[22] It was not until the 1990s, with the International Criminal Tribunals for Rwanda and the former Yugoslavia, that international law finally caught up with the women's congress of 1915: mass rape was recognized as a weapon of war deployed against women and as a deliberate strategy to humiliate entire nations. In 2002, almost a century after the feminists in The Hague had made this demand, the Rome Statute of the International Criminal Court declared rape a crime against humanity and a war crime in international law.

It is remarkable not only *what* the feminists achieved but also *how* they did it under the given conditions: while the national propaganda machines were busy branding other countries as enemies, they came together and made collective demands which are still relevant today. This shows the key characteristics of feminist civil society: solidarity, a vision far ahead of its time, and cooperation that pays no heed to borders.

Delegations with a mission

The feminists decided to send delegations led by Aletta Jacobs and Jane Addams to a number of heads of government and heads of state to present and discuss their proposals. They met with prime ministers and other high-ranking politicians in many countries: the Netherlands, the United Kingdom, Germany, Austria, Hungary, Switzerland, Italy, the Holy See, Belgium, Denmark, Norway, Sweden, Russia and the United States. In Germany they were received by Gottlieb von Jagow, secretary of state at the Foreign Office; in Norway they had an audience with the king; and in Rome they spoke to Pope Benedict XV.[23] Yet, wherever they went, their efforts to bring peace and mediation met with little sympathy. The general mood was one of patriotic belligerence.[24] Pacifists were 'submerged by the flood-tide of militarism', as Jane Addams put it.[25]

There were also other ways to disseminate these demands. Emily Greene Balch used contacts from her studies at Bryn Mawr College. This women's college, founded in 1885, was the first US university to confer degrees on female graduates; it even allowed women to complete PhDs. Because Balch had been a student of Woodrow Wilson, who was now the US president, she was able to meet him several times and hand him the resolutions of the congress. She urged the president to initiate a mediation process, to be led by the neutral states Sweden, the Netherlands and the USA. In the long term, the idea was that the process would lead to an international organization for conflict resolution and the prevention of future wars. Wilson saw the women's demands as politically astute and forward-looking.[26] He is quoted to have said to Jane Addams, who also spoke to him personally: 'I consider them by far the best formulation which up to the moment has been put out by anybody.'[27] He adopted most of their proposals (especially that of founding an international institution, as well as the call for all territorial transfers to be backed by popular consent, the end of secret treaties, and the idea of international mediation of disputes),[28] revised them, and presented the new version to the US Congress in January 1918. His 'Fourteen Points' propose a peace with neither victorious nor vanquished parties – but make no mention of the feminists' work.[29] Even today, students learning about the League of Nations – founded in 1919 to arbitrate conflicts, promote disarmament, and establish a system of collective security – are told that

Wilson was its main architect. In 1919 Wilson actually received the Nobel Peace Prize for helping to end the First World War and establish the League of Nations. The history of patriarchy is also the erasure of women's achievements – especially those of feminists.

Although the feminist delegations and their talks with politicians did not lead to the direct implementation of their demands, they did generate international interest. This international publicity was also influential, Balch argued. In retrospect, however, I think her assessment is much too modest. The feminists not only spoke out and gained public attention but also changed the international discourse and reconceptualized foreign policy. They laid the groundwork for subsequent feminist thinking and activism in international politics and policy-making.

1919: a continent rearranged

The feminists had of course called for women to be represented at the post-war peace conference. Unfortunately, their efforts were unsuccessful. The war ended with the armistice of 11 November 1918, negotiations began at the Paris Peace Conference in January 1919, and the Treaty of Versailles was signed on 28 June 1919. Representatives of twenty-seven states were involved in the conference, with the victorious powers (the USA, France, the UK and Italy) presiding. Pacifists were not invited, nor were the defeated countries Germany and Austria-Hungary.[30] All the delegates were men,* and the negotiations took place behind closed doors, preventing women and pacifists from contributing their ideas and objections.

At the end of the 1915 congress in The Hague, the feminists had agreed to reassemble after the war at the time and location of the official peace talks. But the feminists from The Hague were not the

---

* The only Allied woman officially appointed a member of a national peace delegation was the Chinese feminist Soumay Tcheng. For more background, see Mona L. Siegel, *Peace on Our Terms*.

only women to organize and lobby for inclusion in the Paris Peace Conference and for a new liberal international order, including women's suffrage. As a direct consequence of the exclusion of women from the Versailles negotiations, the French suffragist Marguerite de Witt-Schlumberger, vice president of the International Woman Suffrage Alliance (IWSA), organized the Inter-Allied Women's Conference in Paris. Commencing on 10 February 1919 (and ending in April), the conference brought together several dozen prominent suffragists, including Millicent Garrett Fawcett, who led the British delegation and was the president of the British National Union of Women's Suffrage Societies at the time.[31] The women were not only denied a seat at the negotiating table, but, despite extensive lobbying by feminists and repeated meetings with Wilson in Paris, their demands were not officially included in the negotiations.* The women delegates of the Inter-Allied Women's Conference requested an official women's commission 'staffed by competent female leaders and tasked with advising the peacemakers on all matters relating to women and children',[32] but the Supreme Council, the central body of the Paris Conference, rejected the proposal. The statesmen argued that the political status of women and women's suffrage were of no relevance to the peace conference. Siegel concludes: 'Wilson . . . was happy enough to appear as women's champion (for which he received a lot of gratitude from the women), but he did not want to waste any valuable political capital on their behalf.'[33]

The absence of women from the talks in Paris in 1919 was definitely not for want of trying. One week after the armistice, in November 1918, Marguerite de Witt-Schlumberger had asked President Wilson to take female delegates to the peace talks. But there was resistance, and not only from men. One opponent of the proposal was Alice Hay Wadsworth, a leading campaigner against women's suffrage. She and

---

* The American historian Mona L. Siegel, author of the book *Peace on Our Terms: The Global Battle for Women's Rights after the First World War*, comprehensively describes the efforts by different women's and feminists' groups to influence the peace negotiations in Paris.

her husband, US Senator James W. Wadsworth, were fiercely opposed to women's suffrage, arguing that government should be left to men. For a while Alice Hay Wadsworth headed the National Association Opposed to Woman Suffrage, an organization founded and run by women. It appealed mainly to wealthy families who wished to preserve the status quo, as well as to plantation owners in the southern states who feared that more rights for women would also mean more rights for political minorities, in this case African Americans. It is misguided to believe that women are incapable of antifeminism and even misogyny in their efforts to uphold patriarchy – and racism.

Wadsworth did not want to see women in general excluded from the negotiations, just pacifists – as she called the feminists around Jane Addams and Emily Greene Balch. Wadsworth feared that these women would demand more merciful terms for the defeated countries. And so President Wilson set out for Paris without any women in his delegation. Ultimately, women and feminists were excluded from the peace talks in Paris for a reason that seems almost comical: the negotiators were worried that these women would advocate peace and would be susceptible to Germany's demands for a more lenient punishment.[34] How ironic – not inviting feminists to a peace conference because they might push for too much peace! Siegel summarizes the statesmen's successful attempts to exclude women from the conference as follows: 'From their initial refusal to seat women as peace delegates, to their rejection of a Women's Commission, to their final decision not to appoint women to existing commissions, the male peacemakers had done their utmost to minimize women's influence in the negotiations.'[35] The Inter-Allied women were ultimately invited to address two commissions, the Labour Commission (where they articulated their basic demands, including identical work conditions and labour laws for both sexes – except in the case of maternity – and equal pay for equal work) and the League of Nations Commission (where they continued to demand women's equal political participation and suffrage). President Wilson informed them that all League of Nations positions would be equally open to men and women. The biggest achievement of the Inter-Allied Women's Conference, according to Siegel, was that, with their relentless demands for a seat at the negotiating table, 'Schlumberger and her Allied collaborators advanced the idea that women's cooperation was vital to building a just and democratic world order and to securing a lasting peace.'[36]

It was only after the end of the Inter-Allied Women's Conference that the women who had met in The Hague in 1915 gathered for their follow-up conference. However, as the German and Austrian delegates were barred from entering France as citizens of enemy states, the original plan had to be changed and a neutral location found. In May 1919 around 150 women from fifteen countries gathered for the Women's Peace Congress in Zurich. Lida Heymann began her speech with the following words: 'Five years of war and armistice have turned the world into a madhouse! We women can build a new world, a world founded not on lies and hatred, but on justice, love and understanding.'[37] A key difference between the Inter-Allied Women's Conference and the WILPF Congress was that the latter changed location to enable women from the defeated powers (Germany and Austria-Hungary) to participate. The aim was to reintegrate them into the international women's movement in an effort to challenge wartime animosities.[38]

The feminists were a significant group on the international stage, who discussed the Treaty of Versailles and condemned many of its terms. One idea that they did welcome was the League of Nations. They hoped that this might help to achieve their transnational vision of overcoming nation states and national thinking. But even here they criticized some of the proposed rules – for example, that not all states who wanted to join would be admitted. The women interpreted the planned League of Nations as an alliance of the victors against the vanquished. Unless the existing paradigms were overturned, they argued, the power of one group of states over another would be reinforced, further cementing the old order that had led to world war. The delegates brought their Women's Charter to Paris, calling for its content – the vision of a society based on equality and justice – to be included in the Treaty of Versailles.[39] And they passed the following unanimous resolution: 'This International Congress of Women expresses its deep regret that the terms of peace proposed at Versailles should so seriously violate the principles upon which alone a just and lasting peace can be secured, and which the democracies of the world had come to expect.'[40] Siegel describes the feminists' deep frustration with the Versailles Treaty and their conviction that men could no longer be trusted to manage global affairs. 'Deeply disappointed in the peace forged at Versailles, they refused to bow to pressure to confine their activism to "women's issues" and leave diplomacy to the men,' Siegel concludes. She adds: 'In 1919, together with participants in the Inter-Allied Women's Conference in Paris, delegates to the International Women's Congress in Zurich unabashedly challenged men's hold over peacemaking and asserted that global stability hinged, to no small degree, on women's ability to help shape the terms of collective security both within and between nation-states.'[41]

One idea, already proposed in 1915, illustrates the possible role of a peace project designed with the participation of women. This is the principle that territories should not be handed over to other nations without the consent of the affected populations. This feminist demand was discussed during the negotiations for the Treaty of Versailles but was rejected. As a result, the Nazis were able to use the terms of the Treaty of Versailles for their propaganda. Again and again, they emphasized the humiliation suffered by Germany, which had lost substantial parts of its territory to the victorious Allies. This made the people in areas such as Alsace-Lorraine, West Prussia and Upper Silesia susceptible to the Nazis' nationalist propaganda. A new narrative was invented: that the outcome of the war and the harsh terms of the peace were the fault not of the Empire (which had lost the war) but of the democratic forces within Germany. This was the perfect breeding ground for the seeds of authoritarianism.[42]

Two women were of particular importance for the feminist movement – and even greater importance for the racial justice movement – during the months of the Paris Peace Conference. These were Mary Church Terrell and Ida Gibbs Hunt, two American women of colour. Terrell and Gibbs Hunt were two of the very few non-White women lobbying the statesmen of the peace negotiations. In fact, Terrell was the only non-White member of the American WILPF delegation to the Zurich congress and 'the only woman at this congress . . . who has a drop of colored blood in her veins',[43] as she observed during her speech in Zurich. Both made history. Gibbs Hunt's major contribution was her role in organizing (with W. E. B. Du Bois) the Pan-African Congress,* which opened on 19 February 1919 in Paris, alongside the peace conference. She was also an 'intellectual heavyweight'[44] on questions of anti-imperialism. Terrell was instrumental in putting racial justice prominently on the agenda at the Zurich conference. After the statesmen at the peace conference refused to include racial justice as a principle in the future League of Nations, Terrell put forward a resolution on the subject in Zurich. This was accepted unanimously by the women delegates. Siegel concludes that, for both women, the greatest shortcoming of the peace settlement was its failure to address the question of racial equality: 'The peacemakers' refusal to include a "racial equality clause" in the Covenant of the League of Nations underscored a broader unwillingness to confront, let alone address, inequities stemming from the long history of slavery and imperialism that would continue to imperil global peace and stability for decades to come.'[45] Racist oppression continued and was not addressed by the Paris conference. In fact, the Mandate System of the League of Nations Covenant simply placed former German colonies in Africa under French, British, Belgian or White South African tutelage. The demands of the Pan-African Congress were not met at all: White rule continued throughout the European colonies in Africa. According to Siegel, the Paris peace negotiations did 'little to nothing for people of African descent, but it did help draw together American civil rights activists and European, Caribbean, and African colonial

---

* The goals of Du Bois for the Pan-African Congress were 'to collect documentation on the experiences of African American troops in the Great War, to represent people of African descent at the peace conference, and to convene a separate Pan-African Congress to unite the "dark races" of the world around a common agenda' (Siegel, p. 70).

nationalists for the longer fight that lay ahead. Women – including Mary Church Terrell and Ida Gibbs Hunt – would play a central role in building this new, trans-Atlantic movement for racial justice.'[46]

The other women presented here also had a lasting influence on the constitution of a feminist foreign policy: at the end of the 1915 congress, Jane Addams had been nominated president of the newly created International Committee of Women for Permanent Peace. At the 1919 peace congress in Zurich, at Anita Augspurg's suggestion, this was renamed the Women's International League for Peace and Freedom (WILPF).[47] Jane Addams was elected president, Emily Greene Balch became treasurer and secretary, and Lida G. Heymann was elected to the committee. Heymann served as vice president of WILPF from 1919 to 1924 and remained honorary vice president of the organization until her death in 1943. Anita Augspurg was on the committee of the German branch of WILPF until 1933, when she was forced into exile and the Nazis banned the organization. The German branch was not re-formed until the 1950s, during the protests against the rearmament of Germany. It subsequently played an important role in the international organization and work of WILPF, which has its headquarters in Geneva.

A central element of WILPF's work has always been the demand for an end to racism, ethnocentrism, religious hatred, and all other sources of oppression. Years later, Ida Gibbs Hunt also joined WILPF. In fact, the majority of the women of colour who were active in Paris in 1919 subsequently joined WILPF, turning it into the international women's organization most committed to racial justice and most willing to confront questions of colonialism in the interwar decades.[48] Yet its biggest concern has always been to end violence against women on both an individual and a global political level. Right from the start, the feminists of WILPF have understood that patriarchy, bolstered by violence against women, is the main cause of militarization and war.[49]

Women and peace talks

There can be no peace without women. Yet women are still massively underrepresented in peace negotiations worldwide. Given the proven positive effects of female participation in state conflict management, this is disastrous. Studies have shown that a peace treaty is 64 per cent less likely to fail if civil society groups (including women's organizations) have played a significant role. And the likelihood that a peace treaty will last at least fifteen years is 35 per cent higher if women have been involved.[50] When women take part in peace processes, this is incredibly effective in reducing conflicts and promoting long-term stability. This is partly because of the topics they bring to the negotiations, as shown by the peace processes in Northern Ireland and Colombia. Between 1992 and 2019, however, women made up only 13 per cent of negotiators, 6 per cent of mediators, and 6 per cent of the signatories in major peace processes around the world.[51] In around 20 per cent of the peace processes there were no women involved as mediators or signatories, and in nearly 30 per cent of cases the participants provided no gender-specific data. So up to 50 per cent of peace processes may have had no female participation whatsoever. It is therefore absolutely vital to boost the role of women in critical peace talks. The former US ambassador to Austria, Swanee Hunt, has done much to bring about change with her Women Waging Peace network. This has not only conducted studies to highlight the crucial role of women in peace processes; it has also helped to create a network of highly qualified women who are potential mediators and who can also identify other suitable women.[52] In recent years, many regional 'women mediator networks' have been established worldwide. Today there are around a dozen such regional, subregional and national networks bringing together women in peace mediation. Examples are the FemWise Mediation Network, founded by the African Union, the Scandinavian network Nordic Women Mediators, and Women Mediators Across the Commonwealth. These networks differ in their structures and mandates. All, however, have been created in reaction to the ongoing exclusion of women from peace processes, and all aim to strengthen the position of women in mediation.[53]

Yet these networks are controversial, even within the feminist community, because they saddle women with so much responsibility for bringing about change. The networks may be able to help change structures, but much more is needed. As I have already written, it is not enough simply to bring women or other political minorities to the table; we need to smash the table and build a new one. Content and agendas must be revised. We need to rethink how peace talks are organized, what topics are discussed, and who is allowed to participate (in terms not only of gender but also of status – should civil society be represented as well as governments?).

What would our history books tell us today if, back in 1915, the leaders had listened to the feminists and included women in the peace negotiations? Could the Second World War, with its millions of deaths, have been prevented? What positive developments would have happened much earlier? How much closer might we be to a just and peaceful international community?

From 1920: the re-emergence of hope

WILPF intensified its work towards disarmament in the period between the wars, but the Second World War was a massive setback. The organization was banned in the fascist countries, and women were persecuted for their membership in WILPF, their commitment to pacifism, their women's rights work, and their fight against human rights violations. Some died in concentration camps.

When the war was over, the United Nations was born. WILPF was one of the first NGOs with official observer status.* It was also one of the first organizations to publicly express shock at the nuclear bombing of Hiroshima and Nagasaki by the USA in August 1945. Its cam-

---

* This status makes it possible to take part in certain meetings and events, but without the right to vote or propose resolutions.

paign against the nuclear arms race became one of the main activities of the organization, which had always defined universal disarmament as one of its core objectives. In the 1950s, as more and more formerly colonized nations regained their independence, WILPF showed solidarity with these countries, especially with the women who were at the forefront of the independence movements.

From the mid-1970s there were numerous international gatherings of the women's rights movement, and various initiatives were launched. In 1975 the first UN World Conference on Women was held in Mexico City, then the decade beginning in 1976 was declared the United Nations Decade for Women. In 1979 the UN General Assembly adopted the Convention on the Elimination of All Forms of Discrimination Against Women (CEDAW). The second UN World Conference on Women took place in Copenhagen in 1980, the third in Nairobi in 1985, and the fourth and probably most famous in Beijing in 1995. The final document, the Beijing Platform for Action, states that the rights of women and their equal participation are human rights. It names twelve areas in which national governments should introduce strategic steps towards equality: poverty, education, health, violence against women, armed conflicts, the economy, power and decision-making, institutional mechanisms for promoting equality, human rights, media, the environment, and girls.[54]

Feminist civil society was also behind a small revolution that took place in the UN Security Council in autumn 2000: the unanimous adoption of Resolution 1325 on Women, Peace and Security (followed by nine related resolutions in subsequent years). This was the first resolution concerned with the significance of women in conflicts and conflict resolution and with the experiences of women in wars – and it is such an important resolution that I have dedicated a whole chapter to it.

Feminist international law

International law is not some newfangled invention. Its origins lie in the Middle East, long before the birth of Christ,* and important developments also took place during the European Renaissance. However, the concept and impact of international law made significant advances in the twentieth century. The process began with the conferences in The Hague and accelerated in response to the Second World War. Key milestones were the founding of the United Nations and its Charter (1945),† the establishment of the International Court of Justice, the adoption of the Universal Declaration of Human Rights, and important international agreements – above all the nine core treaties that make up the human rights system.

When feminist intellectuals and academics began to shake up the field of International Relations in the late 1980s and early 1990s, towards the end of the Cold War, similar changes were occurring in other scientific disciplines, including international law. In 1991 Hilary Charlesworth, Christine Chinkin and Shelley Wright published an article entitled 'Feminist approaches to international law',[55] laying the foundations for a feminist approach to this discipline.

Charlesworth and her colleagues criticize the androcentrism and Eurocentrism of international law and its imperviousness (at the time) to feminist analysis. They show how necessary such an analysis is. 'A feminist account of international law suggests that we inhabit a world in which men of all nations have used the statist system to establish economic and nationalist priorities to serve male elites, while basic human, social and economic needs are not met.' It is no different in international institutions, they argue. This is still true today. The

---

* We know of international treaties from the Mesopotamian city-states of Lagash and Umma, for example, as well as from ancient Egypt or between sovereign Greek city-states.
† The Charter of the United Nations is its founding agreement. Its universal aims and principles, accepted by all 193 member states, form the constitution of the international community. The statutes of the International Court of Justice are an important component of the Charter.

international legal order reflects the priorities and views of privileged White men and ensures their continuing dominance. Men are over-represented in the main subjects of classic international law – i.e. states and international organizations – and the exclusion of women at senior level is clearly visible. Furthermore, international law still has a strong Eurocentric bias; it is a legal system created to protect the interests of powerful states over those that were not so imperialistic and, even more crucially, to mediate conflicts between the imperial nation states that had colonized much of the globe. It is a two-tier system between the so-called civilized nations and those outside that standard.[56]

International law consists mainly of political agreements and trea-ties negotiated on the international stage. Political power and domi-nance play a key role in determining what is agreed on and in what detail. A veto by a permanent member of the UN Security Council can virtually paralyse the development of laws.

This means that our current international legal system, despite its claims to neutrality, is not neutral at all – either in its development or in its implementation. On the contrary, it has been developed and agreed on largely by and for men. This is apparent in attitudes to women's rights. Even though violence against women was already rec-ognized as a human rights violation by CEDAW* in 1979, it was only in the Vienna Declaration† of 1993 that women's rights were

---

* The UN Convention on the Elimination of All Forms of Discrimination Against Women (CEDAW) is the most important human rights instrument for the rights of women. It was adopted by the UN General Assembly on 18 December 1979 and came into force in 1981. Since it was adopted, 189 states have ratified the convention. This gives its provisions the same status as national laws in those countries.

† The Vienna Declaration and Action Programme (VDPA) is the final document of the UN World Conference on Human Rights in 1993. It was the basis for a resolution of the UN General Assembly in December 1993, leading to the appointment of a UN high commis-sioner for human rights. The declaration was also important for the legitimation of human rights, since the 171 countries assembled all recognized their human rights obligations. The Universal Declaration of Human Rights of 1948 had been adopted only by around fifty-seven countries, since many of today's states did not exist at the time, and many coun-tries that are independent today were still under colonial rule.

recognized as human rights in a wider sense. And it was not until the late 1990s that sexual and gender-based violence (SGBV), which mainly affects women, was recognized as an offence in international criminal law. This happened when war crimes tribunals for the former Yugoslavia and Rwanda classed SGBV as a war crime, a crime against humanity, and even genocide.* However, as noted by Nicola Popovic, an expert on gendered peace and security issues, 'the weakest point is implementation, and unequal access to the resources that are needed to actually bring charges in such cases. Women are disadvantaged structurally and in virtually every other respect, and it's also extremely difficult to prove SGBV and bring charges.'[57]

The impact of the law extends into our social relations. As long as the legal frameworks with their patriarchal norms do not change, equality will remain a utopia. Instead of calling this inequality into question, the current legal system has legitimated the unequal status of women and other political minorities all over the world.

The historical division into public/male and domestic/female spheres of action is another reason for the persistently patriarchal struc-ture of international law. Charlesworth, Chinkin and Wright argue that all laws, including international human rights norms, are based on the assumption that there really is a distinction between the public and the 'domestic' or private sphere – as if human society and human life could be divided into two distinct spheres. This split, they con-tinue, is an ideological construct, which excludes women from public and political power and claims this is a rational principle. It also allows the perpetuation of repressive systems of control over women. While men claim that they are fulfilling their duty of protection by restrict-

---

* This is of legal significance because it means that, under CEDAW, both the CEDAW Committee and (in case of doubt) human rights courts can require states to react more appropriately to violence against women. Since the 1990s, in extreme cases (of systematic and pervasive use of this violence), international courts no longer have to deal with the states but can use international criminal law to pursue and bring to justice individual per-petrators. Jurisprudence has progressed to the point that SGBV is no longer an accepted by-product of conflicts but an offence of serious violence – comparable to torture.

ing women to the private/domestic sphere, in actual fact this excludes women from the protection that human rights guarantees afford to actors in the public sphere.

These human rights and guarantees play a significant part in international law. The human rights system differs from 'classic' international law in that the main point of reference is protection of the rights of individuals and not of states. The state is responsible for observing, protecting and fulfilling the obligations that arise from the ratification of human rights instruments. Human rights call into question the centrality of the state in international law (though states retain their core role, since they still have to sign and implement international human rights treaties). This is an achievement: human rights legislation has raised the profile of humans and human security in the historically state-centred field of international law. It has also ensured that states can be held accountable if, for example, they do not sufficiently protect women from violence. Regional enforcement mechanisms enable accountability if courts have been set up. There is a limit, however. Accountability within the framework of the different treaty bodies is limited: states can be urged to take measures to remedy violations, but this cannot be enforced by the international community.

In recent decades there has been progress: a normative development towards more rights for women, LGBTQ+ people, indigenous people and other politically underrepresented groups. Yet these human rights agreements are often poorly implemented (or not implemented at all). States often refuse to allow inspections, or ignore calls to implement human rights from international commissions and even courts. International law and therefore also human rights treaties need the consent of states (ratification) in order to be valid within their jurisdiction. And even ratifying states can declare 'reservations' against particular clauses of international agreements; this means that these points are not unconditionally valid in their country. Incidentally, more reservations have been declared against CEDAW than any other convention. This shows how controversial women's basic rights are – even today.

So we may be on the right track, but there still needs to be more transformative change in international law. In academia, feminist research continues to have niche status in this discipline. In the 2000s, only 2.3 per cent of journal articles in this field took a feminist approach, and between 2010 and 2016 this figure was even lower.[58]

UN human rights conventions

A brief digression on the sources of international law and the obligations it imposes.

The following nine UN conventions constitute the international human rights framework:[59]

- the International Convention on the Elimination of All Forms of Racial Discrimination (ICERD)
- the International Covenant on Civil and Political Rights (ICCPR)
- the International Covenant on Economic, Social and Cultural Rights (ICESCR)
- the Convention on the Elimination of All Forms of Discrimination Against Women (CEDAW)
- the Convention Against Torture and Other Cruel, Inhuman or Degrading Treatment or Punishment (CAT)
- the Convention on the Rights of the Child (CRC)
- the International Convention on the Protection of the Rights of All Migrant Workers and Members of Their Families (ICMW)*
- the Convention on the Rights of Persons with Disabilities (CRPD)
- the International Convention for the Protection of All Persons from Enforced Disappearance (CPED).

---

* Most European countries have neither signed nor ratified this convention.

In international law, states must not only sign an agreement but also formally ratify it. Only then does it become legally binding and require the ratifying state to respect, protect and fulfil the rights enshrined in it, in accordance with Article 13 of the 1986 Vienna Convention on the Law of Treaties.

Alongside these obligations, which require explicit consent, countries are bound to customary international law, which applies to all states regardless of their consent and ratification. This includes, for example, the Universal Declaration of Human Rights (UDHR). The resolutions of the UN Security Council are also binding for member states, according to Chapter VII of the UN Charter.* However, the clauses in most resolutions on Women, Peace and Security (WPS) use non-binding language, which makes them harder to enforce. A declaration issued by the UN General Assembly is not legally binding, but it can become customary law – or form the basis for a legally binding Security Council resolution.†

Christine Chinkin – one of the pioneers of feminist international law – spoke at an event on the subject at CFFP. She emphasized that, though there has been progress in this area, it has not been enough to challenge the underlying structures.[60] Scarcely any attention is paid to important elements such as the interpretation of treaties, rules on jurisdiction, assumptions and rules on sovereignty, rules on state

---

* In actual fact the topic is somewhat more complex. There are some law scholars who claim that only resolutions based on Chapter VII are binding. Others would claim that every decision of the Security Council is legally binding for the member states, regardless of whether the text explicitly refers to Chapter VII or not. To establish whether a particular clause of a Security Council resolution is legally binding on the member states, including the specific addressee of the resolution (i.e. whether it is a 'decision' of the Security Council), the key question is whether the Security Council has chosen to use words indicating an intention to create a legally binding obligation (as a rule – though not necessarily exclusively – this occurs in resolutions based on Chapter VII).

† Although most resolutions of the UN Security Council (UNSC) are in theory legally binding on member states, there is no enforcement mechanism. This effectively reduces them to toothless tigers (or 'soft law').

responsibility, and the fundamental structures of international law. Chinkin noted that there have been discernible changes in specialized areas of international law, such as the international human rights system, international criminal law, or international environmental law. There have, for example, been advances in the criminalization of sexualized violence and in the human rights of women. Yet this has been done without looking at and tackling the underlying system. SGBV and especially conflict-related sexualized violence are an expression of gender hierarchies and gender inequities, which international (criminal) law cannot address because gender hierarchies and inequities are not criminal offences per se.[61]

So women's rights are certainly something that feminism has achieved in international law. But of course this isn't nearly enough. Power must be examined and recalibrated in all areas. Although international law is traditionally law by and for states, the role of civil society has grown over the years. Civil society movements have been the catalyst for several international treaties. For example, the feminist Jody Williams received the Nobel Peace Prize for her work to ban landmines, resulting in the Anti-Personnel Mine Ban Convention (the Ottawa Treaty). The International Campaign to Abolish Nuclear Weapons won the Nobel Peace Prize for its contribution to the Treaty on the Prohibition of Nuclear Weapons. And the Convention on the Rights of Persons with Disabilities was also triggered by civil society actors. In each case, members of civil society perceived a problem, formed coalitions and movements, wrote a draft treaty, and gradually gained the support of states, until the regulation became enshrined in international law.

Intersectional feminism, which aims to advance decolonization and eliminate Eurocentrism from international law, focuses on regional as well as international human rights agreements. An example of such an agreement is the 2003 Maputo Protocol (full title: Protocol to the African Charter on Human and Peoples' Rights on the Rights of Women in Africa). This was the result of work by African women and is more progressive than CEDAW.

Another speaker at the CFFP event on feminist international law was Akila Radhakrishnan, president of the Global Justice Center in New York. Akila offered this advice: 'You have to take validation in all of the places where you are creating friction. Because where we are making things uncomfortable for people is where we know we are pushing all the right buttons.'[62] She related this to her experiences around sexual and reproductive health in armed conflicts and the way this is dealt with in international humanitarian law. Her work in this area has met with considerable resistance and triggered serious controversy. One of the aims of the Global Justice Center is to compel states to pay for medical care and abortions in cases of rape as an obligation under international humanitarian law. Many reject such initiatives. This is what happens when structures are created by people who are unlikely to experience certain things and therefore do not feel threatened by them.* These experiences are ignored, and the attempts to change outdated structures are resisted.[63]

In view of ongoing transnational challenges such as the Covid-19 pandemic, the global assault on women's and LGBTQ+ rights, and the climate emergency, the world desperately needs a responsive, intersectional feminist international legal system. This must acknowledge the lived experience of vulnerable and disadvantaged social groups such as women and take their reality as the starting point for legislation. Yet so far not one of the states with a feminist foreign policy has taken a serious interest in feminist analyses of international law. Major international feminist agreements (such as CEDAW, WPS or the Beijing Action Platform) generally form the basis for national feminist foreign policies, but I see no real willingness to rethink international law from a feminist perspective. International justice can only be achieved within a just legal framework.

---

* Even women who have never experienced sexualized violence fear it throughout their lives – unlike men.

Conclusion: the shoulders of giants

Feminist advances in the post-war period would be unthinkable without the courageous women who came before us: activists such as Augspurg, Heymann, Terrell, Gibbs Hunt, Addams and Balch. The extent of their commitment becomes clear when we realize the price they paid for their fight against patriarchy.

Let's start with the American feminists. When the USA entered the war in April 1917, the political and social climate changed. Suddenly the pacifist positions the feminists had advocated were seen as unpatriotic and un-American. Jane Addams and Emily Greene Balch were subsequently declared opponents of the state; Balch's name appeared on official lists of 'subversives', and in 1918 she was dismissed from her post as professor at Wellesley College.

When the US military intelligence agency handed the Senate a list of sixty-two 'dangerous, destructive and anarchist individuals' in January 1919, the names of Emily Greene Balch and Jane Addams were on it. A report by the US Secret Service in 1920 about 'revolutionary radicalism' explicitly mentioned the two women, describing them as agents of Imperial Germany and the Soviet Union – because they had opposed the USA's entry into the war in 1917.[64]

Things were no better in Europe. In 1917 Lida G. Heymann was expelled from Bavaria because of 'pacifist machinations', but she managed to go underground in Munich until the end of the war. In 1923, WILPF was classified as subversive.[65] Like Heymann, Anita Augspurg had to endure repeated expulsions, bans and house searches. In spring 1933, the two women were unable to return to their apartment in Munich after a winter trip to the Mediterranean. 'Since 1923 their names had been on the Nazis' list of persons to be liquidated. All that remained of their possessions was the content of four travel bags.' In her memoirs, Heymann recalled that the most painful loss was the archive of the women's movement and their extensive library.[66] The Nazis destroyed all their papers, records and correspondence.[67]

Even international accolades did not necessarily bring domestic approval. In 1931 Jane Addams became the first American woman to win the Nobel Peace Prize, 'for [her] assiduous effort to revive the ideal of peace and to rekindle the spirit of peace in [her] own nation and in the whole of mankind.'[68] In 1946 Emily Greene Balch became the second American woman to receive the prize, for her courage, her clear-sightedness, and her commitment to people regardless of race, religion, class, sex and nationality.[69] Yet Balch's exclusion continued, and neither President Harry S. Truman nor any other member of the US government congratulated her.[70]

It must have been extraordinarily difficult for these women to face exclusion and opposition at the highest political level because of their commitment to a just society. Yet this is still everyday reality for human rights advocates all over the world.

I myself know what it's like to have others try to silence me with hate speech, fantasies of violence, and even threats. This is infuriating and frustrating, and it never seems to stop. Yet I lead a privileged life in twenty-first-century Germany. All my experiences pale in comparison to what feminist campaigners had to endure in the past – and still have to endure in many other countries.

I find it extraordinary how little we as a society appreciate the great women of history and remember them and their work. In his biographical text on Emily Greene Balch, Christian Ritz mentions that WILPF organized a commemoration of the fiftieth anniversary of Balch's Nobel Peace Prize at Wellesley College in November 1996.[71] It turned out, however, that hardly a single student or lecturer had heard of this Nobel laureate who had taught at the college a hundred years earlier. We all learn so much about men and their heroic deeds, and so little about women, especially feminists. This deprives feminists of the opportunity to build on the thoughts, words and achievements of their predecessors – and forces them to keep reinventing the wheel, as Audre Lorde put it. In her preface to the book that tells the story of Augspurg and Heymann, *Die Rebellion ist eine Frau* (Rebellion is a woman), the veteran German feminist Alice Schwarzer recalls:

When we young feminists took to the streets in the early seventies with the same old demands, we thought they were new. We thought we were the first, and we started – once again – from scratch. Instead of climbing on the shoulders of our predecessors so we could finally get a clearer view. Unfortunately, the first German women's movement had been more or less completely forgotten by then.[72]

Around 1900, activists such as those mentioned here confronted society with radical demands. In the late 1980s, academics such as J. Ann Tickner, Chandra Mohanty and Cynthia Enloe* began to dissect the theories of 'old White men' in political science, building on early leaders in international thought such as the Black feminist scholar Anna Julia Cooper (1858–1964).[73] And, at some point, politicians introduced these ideas to parliaments and ministries. These processes eventually led to Sweden's announcement of a feminist foreign policy, later followed by countries including Canada, France, Mexico, Luxembourg, Spain, Chile, Scotland and Germany.

This isn't the whole story, of course; in reality, many more processes, events and experiences have contributed to the present situation. A multitude of stories from far and near, past and present, help to explain why there are now eleven countries worldwide with an officially feminist foreign policy.

I hope these untold stories will eventually be written and shared. But words alone are not enough; we have to act! It is our duty to build on what has already been fought for and won. To carry on where others stopped – or were forced to stop. This is the most important form of recognition.

---

* A portrait of Cynthia Enloe can be found at the end of chapter 7.

Chandra Mohanty:
'My loyalty was never to an institution'

Professor and author Chandra Mohanty calls herself a 'scholar activist'. She uses this term to criticize the fact that knowledge is developed and applied mainly in academic and institutional contexts and is too often understood in isolation from the lives and struggles of its subjects. Activism, Chandra believes, creates a different kind of knowledge, which foregrounds the struggles, power relations and real everyday lives of individuals. Activism activates certain critical forms of thinking and knowledge about justice.

For Chandra, feminism (especially anticolonialist and antiracist feminism) is essential, as it puts gender and sexuality at the centre of our understanding of states, societies and social relations. Feminism also draws attention to the impact of political decisions on the most marginalized groups. In some states, for example, certain groups are subjected to mass incarceration and systematically disenfranchised. This marginalizes these groups and deprives them of their social existence.

Chandra emphasizes the need for a transnational feminism which connects the local with the global, across national borders. Borders are the product of colonialism and imperialism. Chandra has often been told that decolonization has already taken place: countries have freed themselves from colonial rule and are now self-determined. But she argues that this understanding of colonialism is too simplistic: it is still deeply embedded in the underlying structures of our society, in our minds, and in the history that we teach and learn. For Chandra, a central concern of feminist foreign policy is to connect the history of colonialism and capitalism with the marginalization of people on the basis of their sex or skin colour. Justice, she says, should always be considered from the point of view of the most marginalized groups.

Formative influences for Chandra's activist scholarship include her childhood in India and her own experience of a colonialist education system in Nigeria, as well as the community of feminist activists that she helped to develop when she was in her twenties.

Chandra's favourite authors include Toni Morrison, Arundhati Roy, Angela Davis, Silvia Federici, Louise Erdrich, Leslie Feinberg and Cherríe Moraga.

6 FEMINIST ACTIVISM: UN RESOLUTION 1325

Who is heard and who is not defines the status quo.
Rebecca Solnit, *The Mother of All Questions*
(London: Granta, 2017)

In the UN Security Council

One sunny day in March 2017, I attended my first ever UN Security Council meeting. At the time I was working with UNDP, and I actually had more than enough work to keep me at my desk. But when colleagues and I heard who was going to be speaking to the Security Council that day, I knew I had to be there. That's how I came to witness an excellent speech by an impressive woman, the famous human rights lawyer Amal Clooney. Speaking alongside Nadia Murad, a survivor of the Islamic State (IS) genocide against the Yazidi in Iraq (who would later receive the Nobel Peace Prize), Clooney accused the members of the Security Council of not doing enough to punish the crimes of IS terrorists in Iraq.

Obviously these two women wouldn't have been given this opportunity to speak if it hadn't been for the respect they enjoy worldwide. Twenty years earlier, their presence here (especially that of Nadia Murad) would have been most unlikely: the experiences and needs of women and other political minorities have played next to no part in the nearly eighty-year history of the UN and its Security Council. Historically, the Security Council has always been a boys' club – like foreign and security policy in general.

According to Article 24 of the UN Charter, the Security Council is the body responsible for preserving world peace and international security. It has fifteen members: alongside the five permanent members with right of veto (the P5), ten other states are elected to the Council for two-year periods by the UN General Assembly.

The ideologies of the P5 could hardly be more different – (il)liberal democracy and capitalism rub shoulders with authoritarianism. This means there is little unity among them, and the right of veto is used more and more often. Russia, for example, often vetoes resolutions proposed by the USA, and vice versa. This paralyses the Security Council and impedes collective action. Vetoes have blocked measures to alleviate humanitarian disasters and have hampered the resolution of conflicts in Bosnia-Herzegovina, Palestine, Syria and Yemen. The ineffectiveness of the Security Council weakens its international credibility and encourages member states to disregard its decisions – or those that manage to pass without a veto. For example, the UN arms embargo against Libya, which has been in place for ten years, is regularly ignored; a report by UN experts in spring 2021 described it as completely ineffective.[1]*

Another great weakness is that the composition of the Security Council reflects the geopolitical power relations of 1945, when the victors of the Second World War were made permanent members. Among the P5 there is no representative of Latin America, Africa or South Asia; this creates a legitimacy deficit. The right of veto allows the P5 – even though they constitute only 3 per cent of UN member states – to make decisions that affect all countries. Though many attempts at reform have been initiated, none has yet been successful. For over a decade, a transnational group within the UN has been trying to develop a proposal for reform.[2]

The Security Council has various tools to enforce its decisions and can vote to make these decisions binding resolutions. Its tools include sanctions, humanitarian interventions (Responsibility to Protect, R2P) and the deployment of UN peacekeeping troops ('Blue Helmets'). Yet, if the Security Council really wanted to work towards sustaina-

---

* For example, Germany supplies arms to Jordan, which circumvents the embargo to supply arms to Libya; see note 1.

ble worldwide peace, the best thing it could do would be to actually meet an obligation enshrined in Article 26 of the UN Charter:[3] arms control.

> *Article 26*
> *In order to promote the establishment and maintenance of international peace and security with the least diversion for armaments of the world's human and economic resources, the Security Council shall be responsible for formulating . . . plans to be submitted to the Members of the United Nations for the establishment of a system for the regulation of armaments.*[4]

This article is completely incompatible with a reality in which the P5 are the only five states authorized to possess nuclear weapons, according to the Convention on the Non-Proliferation of Nuclear Weapons of 1970 (in actual fact four other states – Israel, North Korea, Pakistan and India – also have such weapons). The obligation to control armaments also clashes with a reality in which all five permanent members of the Security Council are among the biggest arms exporters in the world and earn billions from this trade.[5]

It is highly problematic that arms control or disarmament is often played off against the right to self-defence, which is also enshrined in the UN Charter (Article 51). This is a serious misunderstanding. The right to self-defence is used to justify supplying weapons to states all over the world. The Security Council's mandate to regulate armaments, as formulated in Article 26, is ignored. Disarmament is interpreted as allowing states the weapons they need to ensure internal order and security. As if security could only be guaranteed by weapons! In this patriarchal understanding, state security, enforced by arms, continues to be prioritized over human security. This is something that feminist analyses of foreign policy and international security architecture have consistently criticized. The security of people – and not the protection of state territory – must be at the centre of political decision-making.

For feminists such as Madeleine Rees* and Ray Acheson of WILPF, the UN Charter 'is not sufficiently designed for its stated end' – i.e. to create and maintain peace and security. Instead it helps to preserve the 'militaristic structures and thinking that led to the need for its creation in the first place.' They go on to argue that the Charter 'failed to set out the institutional structures and philosophical or intellectual approach to prevent war and weaponization.'[6] Militarized structures – created by the production, export and proliferation of arms, all authorized by the UN Charter – foster conflicts and wars, which in turn require weapons and militarized structures. This vicious circle can only be broken if we finally concentrate on human and feminist security.

In her book *The Education of an Idealist*, Samantha Power, the former US ambassador to the UN, writes about the need to actively campaign for human rights within the UN, despite these difficulties and limitations. Bringing about change in institutions and systems is always a laborious, frustrating process, she says. But no progress can be achieved without people who are willing to fight tirelessly for their values and ideals, despite all resistance. Samantha Power was inspired by the work of the Polish Jewish lawyer and peace scholar Raphael Lemkin. In 1947, despite resistance and setbacks, Lemkin drafted the Convention on the Prevention and Punishment of the Crime of Genocide. This was adopted unanimously and almost without changes a year later. Instead of completely giving up on the Security Council, we must critically examine its values and goals. Only then can it be equipped to meet the challenges of the twenty-first century.

This is exactly what feminists have been trying to do for decades: make the Security Council fit for the future. With the adoption of Resolution 1325 (UNSCR 1325) in 2000, and the subsequent agenda for Women, Peace and Security (WPS), they have partially succeeded.

If reforms are not being initiated from within, then pressure from

---

* A portrait of Madeleine Rees can be found at the end of chapter 13.

civil society can bring about the necessary change. My team and I are trying to do both things at once: to bring change from the outside with campaigns and advocacy, but also to exert influence from within – e.g. by providing advisory services to political institutions such as the German Foreign Office. We believe in combining clear but constructive criticism with support for existing structures.

The idea of a feminist security council

In 2018 WILPF produced a remarkable publication: *Towards a Feminist Security Council*. The authors argue that it is not enough merely to respond to active conflicts with sanctions, interventions or other repressive measures. Instead the Security Council must make a sincere effort to perform the mandate enshrined in the UN Charter: to ensure international peace and security. It must, they argue, create lasting and genuinely democratic peace and a society in which all people are safe. This could best be achieved with the local expertise of women and feminists in the areas in question. The authors therefore demand that the Security Council expand its collaboration with feminist civil society. For example, the Security Council should invite more women and feminist civil society actors to deliver briefings and should take on board their analyses, expert opinions and recommendations. On 2 December 2016, Victoria Wollie, national coordinator in Liberia for the West Africa Network for Peacebuilding, became the first civil society briefer to address the Security Council on a geographic agenda item. It says a lot about the historical disregard for civil society expertise that it took the Council so long to listen to a local geographical assessment for Liberia.[7] Since 1992, however, it has been holding what are referred to as 'Arria formula' meetings.* These informal meetings can be held on the initiative of one or more members of the Security Council to gather information and expert knowledge – usually from civil society – on a particular topic.[8]

---

* These informal meetings were initiated by the Venezuelan ambassador, Diego Arria.

WILPF calls on the Security Council to support local, national and regional peacemaking efforts and to require mediating teams and peace talks to include at least 30 per cent women. Another demand is that gender conflict analyses* be carried out in the missions of the Security Council, along with local needs assessments, and that relevant resources be made available for experts. WILPF also argues that reports and analyses by experts on gender and women's rights should feed into any Security Council debate on crisis areas. Gender inequity is one of the main causes of conflicts, as shown in research by Valerie Hudson and her colleagues (see chapter 2). If these dynamics are disregarded, the analyses and measures chosen cannot contribute to lasting peace. The WILPF paper also demands the implementation of Article 26 of the UN Charter and more work towards universal disarmament. This includes reports and analyses on how the arms trade affects the lives of women.

United Nations Security Council Resolution 1325

In normal times, when there's no pandemic on, thousands of feminists and activists flock to the UN headquarters in New York every March, the month of International Women's Day. Their destination is the most important women's conference of the year, the Commission on the Status of Women (CSW). In countless main and side events, organized by the UN, governments and civil society, feminist concerns are discussed: climate justice, peace talks, mediation, international trade, and much more. All of these could be part of a feminist security council.

A model already exists. Every year, UNSCR 1325 (passed in 2000) and the related agenda for Women, Peace and Security (WPS) are prominent topics in the events. 1325 is one of the best-known

---

* This involves adding the category of gender to typical elements of a conflict analysis, such as key actors, main causes of conflict, conflict dynamics or opportunities for peace. This allows a better understanding of power hierarchies.

resolutions of the highest decision-making body of the UN. The influence of the resolution extends into countless governments, as well as into 'classic' military organizations such as NATO. During my time with UNDP in New York, at one of the many events around CSW 2017, I met a woman who made a lasting impression on me. This was Sanam Naraghi Anderlini,* who had played a central role in the creation of 1325. If someone had told me then that this inspiring and impressive expert would later be a regular collaborator with CFFP and a member of our advisory council, I would never have believed it.

In a panel discussion, Sanam argued that it was a misunderstanding of the WPS agenda to try to get more women into the military, as many countries were doing. Instead we should be dismantling destructive, militaristic structures, so that neither sons nor daughters have to join the military and fight in violent conflicts. The point was to prevent conflicts, not to make them more equal.

When the Security Council unanimously adopted Resolution 1325 on 31 October 2000, this was unprecedented. It was the first time that this important international body, the arbiter of war and peace, had acknowledged the concerns, experiences and needs of women, and the significance of gender-related issues. Until then, women and their rights and perspectives had been regarded as irrelevant for peace and security.

In her chapter in the *Oxford Handbook on Women, Peace and Security*, and in our personal conversations, Sanam Naraghi Anderlini vividly describes the origins of Resolution 1325. These clearly lie in feminist civil society. Although it was ultimately members of the Security Council who had to vote on the resolution, they were not involved in its creation.

Sanam remembers how the ball got rolling in May 1998. This was in London, at an international conference convened by the

---

* A portrait of Sanam Naraghi Anderlini can be found at the end of this chapter.

organization International Alert. It was the first global conference on the experiences of women in conflicts and peacebuilding. Around fifty women from conflict regions all over the world took part – from Guatemala, South Africa and Rwanda to Afghanistan and Israel. The discussion covered all the issues that personally affected these women and influenced their lives: human rights and human security; the effects of armed conflicts on women; collective strategies for peace and security; democracy and peacebuilding; and much more. The demands articulated here had their seeds in the Fourth World Conference of Women in Beijing three years earlier, in 1995. As a result of lobbying by feminists from Northern Ireland, Israel, Palestine, Guatemala, Rwanda, Bosnia and elsewhere, the final document of this conference, the Beijing Action Platform, had announced a focus on 'women and armed conflicts'.

Sanam talks about how extraordinary it was to find that all these women, despite their different origins and national specificities, had one experience in common: that they as women suffered disproportionately from the conflicts in their home countries. This became the motivation for Resolution 1325 and for the Women, Peace and Security agenda: these experiences had to be heard and given due consideration at the heart of international politics – the UN Security Council.

Women, Peace and Security

The WPS agenda consists of the following ten resolutions: 1325, which laid the foundation, and the related resolutions 1820, 1888, 1889, 1960, 2106, 2122, 2242, 2467 and 2493. The agenda is based on four pillars: (1) the **participation** of women in peace-building; (2) conflict **prevention** by the inclusion of gender-specific perspectives; (3) the **protection** of women and girls in armed conflicts; and (4) gender-specific help, reconstruction and reintegration (**relief and recovery**). These are referred to as the three Ps and R&R.

Resolution (year of adoption)	Content
1325 (2000)	For the first time, the Security Council thematizes the disproportionate effects of armed conflicts on women and recognizes that women's contributions to conflict prevention, peacemaking and conflict resolution are neither sufficiently appreciated nor adequately integrated. This resolution emphasizes how important full and equal participation by women is for peace and security.
1820 (2008)	Sexualized violence is recognized as a weapon and tactic of war. This means that rape and other forms of sexualized violence can meet the criteria for war crimes, crimes against humanity or genocide. The resolution calls both for training to prevent sexualized violence and for more women in peacekeeping missions.
1888 (2009)	Sexualized violence and its consequences are central here. This violence can exacerbate armed conflicts and jeopardize international peace and security. The resolution calls for teams of experts to be deployed after incidences of sexualized violence.
1889 (2009)	This resolution is concerned with all phases of the peace process, especially the participation of women in the peacebuilding stage after conflicts.
1960 (2010)	This resolution reiterates the call for an end to sexualized violence in conflicts and establishes a 'naming and shaming' mechanism. It sends a clear message that sexualized violence will be rigorously punished – for example, by naming parties suspected of these crimes in the annual reports of the UN Secretary-General, by referrals to UN sanctions committees

and the International Criminal Court, and by international condemnation and reparations.

2106 (2013) This resolution highlights existing commitments. This is the first of the resolutions to acknowledge that sexualized violence also affects men and boys.

2122 (2013) This resolution systematically addresses the deficit in women's participation and recognizes the need to remedy the underlying causes of armed conflicts and security risks for women. It links disarmament with gender equity, mentioning the Arms Trade Treaty twice.

2242 (2015) This resolution connects efforts to counter violent extremism and terrorism with the WPS agenda and calls for these problems to be analysed in terms of gender. It also emphasizes the importance of collaboration with civil society.

2467 (2019) This resolution acknowledges that sexualized violence in conflicts is part of a continuum of violence against women and girls. It emphasizes the need to give survivors a key role in managing this issue and to involve marginalized groups in prevention. And it underlines the responsibility of individual states to tackle the causes of structural gender inequality and sexualized violence. However, the topics of reproductive and sexual health were removed from the draft resolution because the USA was threatening a veto.

2493 (2019) The resolution emphasizes the ongoing validity and necessity of existing commitments and demands more information on progress and setbacks in the implementation of the WPS agenda.

A few months after the London conference, the feminists began their campaign. One strategy was to send postcards to the UN Secretary-General: in 2000, feminists from all over the world wrote to Kofi Annan. Among other things, they demanded the inclusion of women as decision-makers in peace talks, better protection and representation for refugee women, and an end to impunity for crimes against women.

In the 1990s there had been high hopes of strengthening human rights. But it was also a decade of wars: in Bosnia, Somalia, Rwanda, the Congo and Liberia. Women were raped in these wars; sexualized violence was a widespread tactic and weapon of war. The two international criminal tribunals set up by the UN in the 1990s for the former Yugoslavia and Rwanda, in combination with the International Criminal Court established in 1998, made it possible to use international law to punish sexualized and gender-based violence – as crimes against humanity, war crimes and genocide. Despite this, not a single Bosnian woman (nor any other female voice) was involved in the peace talks that ended the conflict in Bosnia, held in November 1995.

Wolfgang Ischinger, the former German ambassador to the USA and former chairman of the Munich Security Conference, describes these talks in detail in his book *Welt in Gefahr: Deutschland und Europa in unsicheren Zeiten* (World in danger: Germany and Europe in uncertain times). The conference took place far from the battlefields of Bosnia, at a US Air Force base in Dayton, Ohio, and lasted twenty-one days. Ischinger led the German delegation. It was, he writes, 'the first time in years that the Serbian president Slobodan Milošević, the Croatian president Franjo Tuđman, and the Bosnian president Alija Izetbegović had been in the same room.'[9] The talks were supported by the Contact Group, consisting of diplomats from the USA, France, the UK, Russia and Germany, which had undertaken to manage the crisis in the Balkans eighteen months earlier. The EU was also represented. On 21 November 1995 all the negotiating parties agreed to a peace treaty in Dayton, and on 14 December 1995 the agreement was signed in Paris. In his chapter on Dayton,

Ischinger admits various failings. But the biggest mistake, he believes, was leaving Bosnia and Herzegovina to their own devices, politically, in the period after the agreement.[10] From a feminist perspective, we have to add that one of the major errors was the attempt to build peace without including half the population and their experiences during the war, and without acknowledging their need for a new order after the conflict. The UN estimates that between 20,000 and 50,000 girls and women were raped in the war in Bosnia. Toxic patriarchal structures – such as a rigid hierarchy, maintained by the use of (sexualized) violence against women and other political minorities – lead to conflicts and wars. If these structures are not dismantled, lasting peace is not possible.

All these international developments symbolized the end of the Cold War. This also meant a partial end to the paralysis of the Security Council, since the division of the world into opposing blocs had ended. In the context of developments in international women's rights, such as the Beijing Action Platform and the condemnation of crimes relating to sexual violence, activism for Resolution 1325 grew louder and more effective. The activists began to form partnerships with government delegations at the UN and with civil society organizations. They also founded the Ad Hoc Working Group on Women, Peace and Security. This is still a very important organization in New York, with which we have worked closely on several occasions.

The objective of the 1325 activists was to change the paradigms behind discussions on war and peace, to overturn fundamental assumptions, and to demand equal rights for women. The aim was to ensure that no one would ever have to experience the horror of war again. The women took part in numerous events in regions affected by conflict, carried out interviews and kept gathering knowledge. They wanted to show that there can be no peace when the needs and personal experiences of half of humanity are ignored. This seems obvious and straightforward in theory but is challenging in practice because of patriarchal structures and the overrepresentation of men and male perspectives in peace processes. The involvement of women in peace processes had to be facilitated, not actively suppressed as it had been so far. This, however, required a binding resolution. Feminist civil society wrote the first draft of Resolution 1325; Sanam, WILPF and a remarkable coalition of feminist NGOs played leading roles. The core concern was to prevent conflicts from happening in the first place. So the aim was not to make wars safer for women and other political minorities but to bring about the end of warfare.

In October 2000, Namibia presented the resolution to the Security Council during its presidency as a non-permanent member. During the negotiations between Council members, important aspects were lost, such as the accountability of states and the call for disarmament. Nonetheless, there was great jubilation among feminist actors when the resolution was unanimously adopted on 31 October 2000. For the first time in history, members of the UN Security Council had acknowledged that peace could only be created and maintained if women participated in all respects.

Lobbying and activism paved the way for 1325, the most famous feminist resolution of the UN Security Council. This proves that diplomacy and activism are an excellent combination. Without feminist activism in diplomacy, there can and will be no lasting peace.

In the end, this feminist success was a compromise. If you succeed in gaining recognition and agency within the system, and then try to change things from within, the sluggish nature of the system will severely limit your options. It's always much easier to criticize from the outside. Once you're inside, you have to be far more strategic.

This is something I experience in my everyday work. Of course I usually try to demand the utopian maximum – this is the motivation for all my work. At the same time, I also need to be sensitive to what is actually possible (and when and how it might be possible). Political influence is complex and involves give and take. For example, when I was working as an external advisor at the German Foreign Office in 2019, other civil society actors accused me of being too close to the government. This is the fate of those who come from 'outside' to change something on the 'inside'. Those who are still working solely on the outside think you're too close to the government. And those working next to you on the inside still see you as an outsider.

The reason I'm emphasizing feminist civil society here is that the movements and grassroots work behind many successes are often forgotten and ignored. Resolution 1325 was the achievement of feminist civil society. The Women, Peace and Security agenda exists because feminists and women from conflict areas, often in the Global South, shared their experiences and articulated their demands. The agenda is one in a long line of achievements that we do not owe to governments. Women's suffrage, the end of racial segregation, same-sex marriage and many other things would never have been possible without civil society and its actors. These achievements are widely appreciated today, but the people involved were often subjected to severe violence at the time. Around 1900, suffragettes on hunger strikes were force-fed in the UK. In 1969, during the Stonewall riots in Christopher Street in New York, lesbians, gay men and trans people suffered serious police violence. Anyone who says 'But that was all decades ago!' needs to be reminded that the violent police response to antiracism protests in the USA or the suppression of feminist protests – e.g. in Iran or Turkey – are far from ancient history. These and many other examples show that civil society activists still have a crucial role to play.

The example of Colombia

Colombia's peace process is regarded as a textbook example of how the United Nations and its Security Council can support local peace actors instead of taking control. In 2016, after several years of negotiations, the process led to official peace between the Colombian government and the left-wing guerrilla movement FARC. On 2 October 2016 a referendum was held to secure the people's consent for the agreement. At the time I was about to start work for the feminist organization Sisma Mujer in the centre of the Colombian capital, Bogotá. I landed in the city on the eve of the referendum.

On the morning of the referendum it was raining in Bogotá. There was also heavy rainfall on Colombia's Caribbean coast, where the president and key negotiator of the proposed peace deal on the government side, Juan Manuel Santos, had many supporters. In some cases the weather made it difficult to access the polling stations. When my Colombian flatmate set out into the rain to cast his vote in the north of the city, I went with him. People streamed into the polling station from all directions, and a long queue formed. I thought the turnout seemed high, but later in the day I learned how wrong I'd been: in actual fact only 37.4 per cent of the electorate had voted.

That afternoon I joined a guided tour of the city centre, beginning at the Museo del Oro. The fact that our group could move about freely was not something to be taken for granted. Ten years earlier, the guide told us, the security situation would have made this impossible. Proud of the positive developments in her city, she viewed a 'yes' as the only possible answer to the referendum. She saw the vote as a real opportunity to bring lasting positive change to the country. After the polling stations closed at 4 p.m., the first provisional results were expected at 5.

After the tour I took a taxi along the steep slopes in the east of the city to the Parque de los Hippies in order to await the result with my flatmate's friends. The taxi driver told me he was confident of the outcome; he too wanted to see peace in his country. But just at that moment we turned the radio on. Ninety per cent of the votes had been counted, and they were saying that 'no' had won by a small margin. The taxi driver had tears in his eyes, and when I got to the park many people were embracing and weeping. Not far from the park, those who had invested no hope in the peace treaty and had voted against it were celebrating. A large screen showed the result: the 'no' campaign, led by the former Colombian president Álvaro Uribe, had won by a 0.4 per cent margin, just 54,000 votes. 2016 was already the year of the Brexit vote; it was to become the year of Trump's victory. And now it was the year of the failed Colombian peace referendum. Yet the country's civil war, begun in the mid-1960s, had cost the lives of more than 220,000 people. More than 6 million people had been displaced.

'Nearly all current conflicts have their origins in the inequality, poverty and injustice which were created by the colonization process,' says Nicola Popovic, one of Germany's leading experts on gender, peace and security. She's the director of Gender Associations International Consulting, based in Berlin, which specializes in these issues. The civil war in Colombia clearly had its origins in colonization – in the marginalization of the indigenous people, the influence of the Catholic Church, and the extreme socio-economic inequality. The war was also partly caused by a global imbalance: the illegal but lucrative cultivation of coca to produce cocaine for the Global North. Further factors were a security sector in desperate need of reform and an army that regularly violated human rights. Nicola Popovic adds: 'As Europeans, we mustn't shirk responsibility for these present-day conflicts by only considering the postcolonial dynamics, and thus shifting the blame outside Europe to the Global South.'[11]

Although there had already been many unsuccessful attempts to make peace, the 2016 referendum was the first time in Colombian history that the people had been able to vote on a peace treaty. The treaty, the Acuerdo Final Para La Terminación Del Conflicto, is nearly 300 pages long and is divided into six areas, partly inspired by UNSCR 1325: land reform, political participation of citizens, end of the conflict and political integration of the guerrillas, resolution of the drug problem, compensation for the victims, and implementation of the peace treaty. The peace talks in Havana, Cuba, had lasted nearly four years. The treaty presented to the people for their approval was one of the most inclusive in world history. Part of my work at Sisma Mujer was to analyse how often and in what context the terms *género* (gender), LGBTQ+ and *mujer* (woman) appeared in the text.

Support for the peace treaty was strongest among people who had experienced terrible violence. In Bojayá, in the Chocó Department, where the FARC guerrillas had killed nearly 120 people in a massacre in May 2002, 96 per cent voted 'yes'. But analyses indicated that one of the most critical factors for voting behaviour was 'Uribism': loyalty to the former president Uribe, who had taken a hard line against the FARC during his time in office. Uribe's supporters and his Centro Democrático party largely rejected the treaty. In doing so, they turned the vote into a referendum on the government of his successor, Santos. The Uribe camp rejected the concessions made to the FARC, which allowed it to transition into a political movement. They were also opposed to the inclusivity of the treaty, as manifested in the LGBTQ+ rights that it contains. It was during my stay in Bogotá and my work in the context of the Colombian peace process that I first realized how powerful the opponents of human rights, women's rights and LGBTQ+ rights are.

The 'no' result in the referendum on the peace treaty was therefore also a 'no' to a more equal society. A peace process regarded as exemplary by feminist civil society worldwide was anathema to the conservatives and populists in Colombia. Under the guise of protecting the family and family values, they had vilified the treaty as *ideología de género*, gender ideology.* And yet it was an extraordinary achievement for Colombian victims' associations and women's rights organizations, who had played a key role in the treaty's development.

Although the agreement in its original form was rejected on 2 October 2016, it was still the first peace treaty worldwide to give such prominence to the gender perspective and the rights of women and the LGBTQ+ community. It did so in response to UNSCR 1325, which acknowledges the different experiences of men and women in conflict and calls for the active involvement of women in peace processes. The resolution provides a legal foundation for gender-sensitive peacemaking and peacekeeping. In Colombia, for example, a subcommission on gender was created to insert a gender perspective into the peace treaty – the first time this had happened in a peace process. The subcommission incorporated representatives of both the FARC and the government. Eighteen women's and LGBTQ+ organizations were

---

* In chapter 8 I discuss in detail the origins of the antifeminist construct of 'gender ideology'.

involved in the formulation of the peace treaty, and ten experts were consulted on the topic of 'sexualized violence'. This alone is a historic achievement, if we consider how few of the negotiators and mediators in official peace processes are women.[12] Research has shown that more inclusive peace treaties and processes lead to longer-lasting peace.[13] So the 'no' vote felt like a slap in the face to victims' associations and women's rights organizations.[14]

When the revised agreement was finally signed by the government and the FARC on 24 November 2016 (this time without a referendum), this was a historic event, despite the antifeminist attacks, because it acknowledged the perspectives of women and other political minorities. More than 100 provisions referred to gender relations. One example was the section on the redistribution of land, which – in Colombia as in the rest of the world – is mainly in the hands of men. Another example was the stipulation that there must be zero tolerance for sexualized and gender-based violence. The peace agreement also led to one of the most successful arms amnesties in history: nearly 9,000 weapons were handed in.[15] And the revised version that was eventually signed is still inclusive, though much less so than the original version. For example, the terms 'LGBTQ+' and 'gender' were largely deleted, with the latter replaced by 'women'. This is a typical approach for those who oppose an equal society and cling to a binary, patriarchal social order which pushes men and women into traditional roles.

Although other governments and organizations strongly supported the process, it was Colombian feminist civil society that ensured the progressiveness of the peace treaty. This was brought home to me one evening in mid-December 2016, when my boss at Sisma Mujer (a woman known throughout Colombia as a feminist and human rights defender) invited me to attend a meeting in a boutique hotel in Bogotá. I was surprised to see armed security guards at the door of the conference room. I hadn't been fully aware of the danger facing human rights defenders in Colombia. The room was full of leading human rights and women's rights activists, including professors, lawyers, directors of NGOs and representatives of the FARC. You might assume they were arch-enemies, but they'd come together to discuss the practical implementation of the peace treaty and its concessions to women and other socially oppressed groups (such as LGBTQ+ people, Afro-Colombians, and the indigenous population). 'Even if we don't agree on everything, we need to pull together,' said one of the feminists sitting at my table on that December evening. Although they were on different sides, they were united by their desire for a more equal society.[16]

A few days later, at 11 p.m. on 23 December, I got a message from my boss. She wasn't writing to wish me a merry Christmas. In an SMS sent to all the staff, she informed us of the new emergency measures taken by the Colombian government to protect human rights defenders. In 2016, the year that officially brought peace to Colombia, more human rights defenders had been murdered than in any of the last six years. Eighty people paid the ultimate price for their commitment. And, in the first half of the following year, 31 per cent more human rights defenders would be murdered than in the first half of 2016.[17] The trend continued in the years that followed. 2020 was Colombia's deadliest year ever for human rights defenders and activists working for peace or environmental protection, with 199 murders.[18] A country where human rights defenders are being killed is not a country at peace.

The Colombian peace process can still be seen as exemplary. It's true that the original version was not accepted, and it's true that many activists were threatened and even murdered after it was signed – but despite all this it's an example of how peace processes can become more inclusive and more humane.

The example of NATO

Governments are not the only entities engaging intensively with WPS. The same goes for the EU and for many international organizations and alliances, such as the Organization for Security and Co-operation in Europe (OSCE), the Organization for Economic Co-operation and Development (OECD) and NATO. In some cases they have their own action plans and strategies, tailored to their specific tasks and structures. I find this especially interesting in the case of NATO. After all, it was founded in 1949 as a Cold War military alliance, a classic defence alliance to guarantee 'collective security' for the West and its allies. In recent decades, NATO has undergone a transformation. The defence alliance has become an institution of security management, which sees itself 'to an increasing degree as a military-political organization serving to provide comprehensive security'.[19]

As part of the strategic 'NATO 2030' process, I was invited to take part in a panel discussion in October 2020. I was excited – this was a chance to voice my criticism of NATO in the presence of Secretary General Jens Stoltenberg. This was important to me because Stoltenberg describes himself as a feminist and has repeatedly acknowledged the significance of WPS. The other speakers included Melanne Verveer, the former US ambassador-at-large for global women's issues and current executive director of the Georgetown Institute for Women, Peace and Security, and Radmila Šekerinska Jankovska, the defence minister of North Macedonia at the time.[20] The topic was the future of WPS at NATO. The briefing document I received from NATO in preparation for the panel discussion was self-critical: 'While we may not have understood it at our founding in 1949, a gender lens is vital in order to reflect the whole of the population that the Alliance serves and the communities in which we engage. Only by applying a people-centric and gender approach will NATO be able to respond to new and non-conventional security trends.'

This new approach from NATO has a lot to do with vocal feminists at NATO such as Clare Hutchinson and Irene Fellin. From January 2018 to November 2021 Clare was the Secretary General's Special Representative for Women, Peace and Security, a position created in 2012. Irene Fellin, also an outspoken women's rights advocate, is her successor. In an interview with CFFP, Clare said that she considered armed forces to be essential – though she acknowledged that many other feminist intellectuals and activists working on foreign and security policy see this very differently.[21] The question of the compatibility between patriarchal military structures and feminist foreign policy is highly controversial, even within the feminist community.

It is also thanks to the personal efforts of Clare and Irene that NATO is well positioned with regard to WPS. Yet they are far from the only ones who have contributed to this slow but steady progress within NATO. In *NATO, Gender and the Military: Women Organising from Within*, the authors describe how women and men have been working within NATO for decades to bring about a change in culture. Their aim has been to make this supremely patriarchal organization – which tends to equate protection with masculinity – more feminist and more progressive and to discard old ideals of hegemonic masculinity. NATO has been working on WPS since 2007, and there have been initiatives exploring gender dynamics since 1961, such as the Committee on Women in NATO Forces and its successor, the NATO Committee on Gender Perspectives.[22]

The influence of feminist civil society on UN resolutions

But how exactly is the influence of feminist civil society reflected in the resolutions? And what effect does it have when powerful governments pursue their own goals in this process? I want to illustrate this with Resolution 2467, which was closely interwoven with my work. I have strongly criticized this resolution, for reasons that will become clear below.

In the second to last week of April 2019 I was putting in long hours at the German Foreign Office. I'd been working there for about three months as an external advisor, building up the feminist network Unidas with my diplomat colleagues. Now the time had come for the official launch of the network in Latin America. The plan was to launch Unidas at the Goethe Institute in Salvador da Bahia, Brazil; we'd arranged for feminists from different parts of the continent to fly in for the occasion. The next day we were to travel on to Bogotá and then to Mexico City, where more events with South American feminists would take place. In order to get everything ready, I was leaving for Salvador two days before the foreign minister, along with the diplomat who shared an office with me and colleagues from the Deutsche Gesellschaft für Internationale Zusammenarbeit (GIZ, German Agency for International Cooperation). The planning had been very time-consuming, and in the days before our flight I'd generally not been leaving the Foreign Office until shortly before midnight.

In those same two days before our departure, when I was burning the midnight oil in the Foreign Office, I was also kept very busy criticizing the work of the ministry and the minister in the UN Security Council. There was much to criticize, and I did so both on social media and in interviews, along with my co-director Nina Bernarding.[23] Criticism and support are not mutually exclusive.

This was what had happened. When Germany became a non-permanent member of the UN Security Council for two years, beginning in 2019, the German Foreign Office put Women, Peace and Security right at the top of its agenda, particularly the fight against sexualized violence in conflicts. A good idea in theory. But it's the practical implementation that counts. Other WPS resolutions had already dealt with sexualized violence in conflicts (see information box). The plan was to present a related resolution, the ninth in the WPS agenda, during Germany's presidency of the Council in April 2019. To persuade other states, Foreign Minister Heiko Maas secured the high-profile support of the actress Angelina Jolie and the Nobel Peace Prize laureate Denis Mukwege – the Congolese gynaecologist who treats women raped in war. Resolution 2467 was intended to be a great step forward. But for months feminist civil society had been alarmed by the composition of the UN Security Council, which included states with authoritarian leaders such as Trump and Putin. The nearer the date came, the more urgent and worried were the phone calls from civil society colleagues in New York City, the headquarters of the UN. They warned us that the USA was unwilling to accept important points on sexual and reproductive health – such as access to abortions for women raped in conflicts – and was threatening a veto. Nina and I, in collaboration with other feminists, wrote numerous emails and made countless phone calls between New York and Berlin. We urged the Foreign Office not to back down. But it was all in vain. Under pressure from the USA, the German negotiators removed these vital clauses from the text. The United States under Trump was on a mission to take away women's autonomy over their own bodies – and this campaign extended to the United Nations. I spoke about this in an interview at the time: 'Trump's government is once again showing, clearly and shamelessly, the misogynist face of its right-wing ideology. In its repugnant determination to deny women's autonomy over their own bodies, it has blackmailed the UN Security Council by threatening to block a resolution designed to take a more targeted approach to some of the worst crimes of humanity. This is absolute insanity.'[24] The foreign minister, Maas, described the resolution as ground-breaking. I was less euphoric. In the same interview, I pointed out:

The resolution does advance the WPS agenda in crucial ways. However, Germany and the entire UN Security Council have given in to pressure from the USA to delete every mention of reproductive and sexual health from the draft resolution – otherwise the USA would have used its right of veto to block the resolution. This is particularly painful given that the UN Security Council had agreed on language about reproductive and sexual health in previous resolutions on sexualized violence.[25]

Legally – i.e. in terms of international law – nothing had changed, but politically this was a bitter blow. Just a few weeks earlier, in March 2019, a broad coalition of German organizations, including CFFP, had written a press release aimed at the German government. Here we'd warned about just such attacks on democratic values, and especially on sexual and reproductive health and rights. We'd made the following demand: if there is a danger that anti-democratic forces in Russia, China and the USA, all permanent members with veto powers, will try to water down a resolution, then Germany should not put this resolution to the vote. We were very clear.[26] And yet our voices were not heard.

The lawyer Madeleine Rees, secretary-general of WILPF, also laments the fact that the threat of a US veto succeeded, and that states such as Germany accepted a weakened WPS agenda – at the expense of those the resolution was meant to protect. But she emphasizes that the USA was heavily criticized by many countries for its opposition to reproductive rights. Thus there were more states advocating than opposing the recognition of fundamental rights to self-determination. Rees views this normative shift in discourse as significant progress.[27]

Germany's national action plan

To ensure worldwide implementation of the WPS agenda, governments have written national action plans (NAPs) setting out how the individual points will be put into practice in their national policies. Just over 100 countries (as of November 2022) now have an NAP.[28] A striking aspect of these plans is that countries of the Global North see WPS mainly in terms of foreign policy; they also describe how they can meet WPS requirements in relation to countries of the Global South and regions of conflict. Countries of the Global South, on the other hand, outline how they can implement the requirements in their own countries. This has an unsavoury, neocolonial aftertaste, as if countries such as Germany had no need to make their own policies more feminist.

As part of the NAP process in Germany, the civil society actors working on WPS (a coalition of CFFP and other groups known as Bündnis 1325) meet with the Interministerial Working Group (IMA) twice a year to discuss the progress of 1325. The meetings take place in the Foreign Office. The IMA includes representatives of the Foreign Office and experts from several other federal ministries: Justice; Family Affairs, Senior Citizens, Women and Youth; Defence; Economic Cooperation and Development; and Interior and Community. Here

CFFP has repeatedly pointed out the incompatibility between domestic and foreign policy and the lack of coherence in these areas. For example, the Foreign Office deserves credit for its increasingly strong defence of sexual and reproductive rights around the world. It seems to have recognized that there can be no advances in democracy as long as half the members of society cannot even decide what happens with their own bodies. And yet abortion is still not legal in Germany. According to paragraph 218 of the German Criminal Code, it is exempt from punishment only under certain conditions: the woman must attend a counselling session and observe certain time limits. It's scandalous that Germany is still clinging to an obsolete law. Denying women autonomy over their own bodies is the perverse culmination of patriarchal oppression.

The input of feminist civil society is crucial here; its expertise and commitment have transformative power.

But knowledge and passion alone are not enough. Activists also need financial support to carry out essential research and educational work. Too often, these social movements – especially in the Global South – receive virtually no funding, since funds usually go to short-term 'empowerment' projects, not to the movement itself. But empowerment-based approaches – which suggest that women simply have to become 'better', and which demand nothing more radical than women's integration into socio-political systems – are not sufficient to bring about systemic change and create new power structures. If systems are to be changed, there needs to be investment in the movements themselves.[29] Nobody else is as effective as social movements. That's why I believe ministries such as the Foreign Office should trust our expertise when we intervene and tell them what needs to change.

Before the Foreign Office began its work on the new NAP for the WPS agenda in 2020, my organization, as part of Bündnis 1325, put several demands to the ministry. We began by pointing out that a commitment to lasting peace can never be reconciled with Germany's position as the world's fourth biggest arms exporter. The substantial expansion of humanitarian aid – Germany is now the second biggest aid donor in the world – doesn't make up for this.[30] Isn't it bizarre? First, German weapons contribute massively to worldwide destruction, and afterwards we send humanitarian aid – e.g. funding to support democratic development projects.

The main motivation of Resolution 1325 is to prevent conflicts, and militarization is one of the core causes of conflict. Our list of demands consisted of thirty-six points. These included institutionalized changes (e.g. the appointment of a special envoy for 1325) and 'focal points' (i.e. contact persons) for this topic in all German diplomatic missions – this demand was actually turned into reality with Germany's announcement of a feminist foreign policy in November 2021. We also urged the German government to resolutely oppose those international actors who deny sexual and reproductive rights and bodily autonomy, and who attack people because of their sexual orientation. The government, we demanded, must acknowledge the connection between German arms exports and violent conflicts (and sexualized violence) and work towards a complete ban on arms exports in the medium term. Human rights defenders at home and abroad must be protected and financially supported, and the Paris Climate Agreement must be fully implemented.[31]

At the end of February 2021 the German government adopted its third NAP for the WPS agenda. Compared to the previous two German NAPs, this latest one is a substantial improvement. Clearly the government has taken its cue from other progressive states. It has also taken into account some of the demands from the policy briefing of Bündnis 1325 (*The Women, Peace and Security Agenda: Implementation Matters*),[32] which my co-director Nina was instrumental in preparing.

There are some positive points that deserve acknowledgement. Politically and conceptually, the explicit mention of an intersectional perspective is a major step forward for the German government, as is the explicit mention of the LGBTQ+ community as a concerned party. We're also pleased that the government emphasizes the increased risks facing women and minorities because of the international decline in democracy and attacks on women's and LGBTQ+

human rights – and that it acknowledges its special responsibility for protecting and extending these rights. This includes rights to reproductive health and sexual self-determination.[33] This is also the first time the German government has acknowledged that an intersectional and human-rights-based approach is needed to prevent conflicts and promote peace. And, lastly, the third NAP establishes a mechanism to assess the impact of the measures taken – something civil society has been demanding for many years.

But there is still room for improvement – hence our ongoing criticism of the current NAP and our suggestions for the next one. Firstly, the next NAP must concentrate on disarmament and the control of arms exports, especially in the area of conflict prevention. Secondly, civil society must be better integrated into the creation and evaluation of the NAP. And, thirdly, there has to be more political will to strengthen the WPS agenda in international organizations and forums.

In the third NAP, the German government once again refrains from any explicit commitment to peace. It doesn't so much as mention the conflict-fuelling effect of arms exports or indicate that it has any intention of stopping this trade. It doesn't acknowledge that a policy of disarmament is integral to crisis and conflict prevention, and it makes virtually no commitment to disarmament or controls on arms exports. The NAP should have included commitments to ending arms exports in the long term, to ratifying the Treaty on the Prohibition of Nuclear Weapons (in 2022 Germany at least became an observer to the treaty, only the second NATO country to take this step), and to actively supporting an international convention banning autonomous weapon systems ('killer robots').

Another shortcoming of the third NAP is that it contains no domestic measures for crisis prevention. Victoria Scheyer, co-chair of the German branch of WILPF, writes: 'In Germany, insecurities and threats are not caused by heavily armed military vehicles and soldiers, but by deep-seated misanthropic ideologies. These are institutionalized in extreme right-wing parties, groups and movements, whose agendas usually include misogyny, hostility to migrants, anti-Semitism and racism, and who pursue nationalist and anti-democratic goals.'[34] The connection between gender and violent extremism and terrorism is set out in WPS Resolution 2242, adopted in 2015. The third NAP would have been an opportunity to explore this in detail.

Demanding the maximum and negotiating compromise

Feminist criticism and feminist activism have made their way into the UN Security Council via the WPS agenda and have had a substantial impact within the last two decades. Yet feminist achievements within one of the most powerful institutions of international politics have frequently been co-opted for other agendas, leading to some rather unfeminist compromises. Professor Dianne Otto, a human rights expert who teaches at the University of Melbourne, has critically examined the achievements of the WPS agenda in light of these problems.[35] According to Otto, the success of the resolutions has gone hand in hand with the loss of important feminist principles. In the UN Charter, 'peace' is mentioned forty-five times, but usually in connection with security rather than development or human rights. Otto therefore finds it unsurprising that the WPS agenda presents a military understanding of security instead of prioritizing feminist peace. This same feminist understanding of peace – not the absence of military conflicts, but the realization of feminist security – was the foundation for the twenty resolutions formulated by the feminists in The Hague in 1915. The acceptance of the WPS agenda in the Security Council, says Otto, has led to a shift in the focus of feminist peace activism: from seeking to make armed conflict illegal (*ius ad bellum*) to trying to humanize the laws of warfare (*ius in bello*). Instead of ending war once and for all, the aim is now to make war safer for women. This smacks of political horse-trading. Looking at the women of The Hague, Otto argues that WPS has betrayed the hopes of its feminist forebears. Instead of transforming dominant ideas and practices on international peace and security, the original demands of the feminists have been twisted so as to actually expand the justifications for military intervention. For example, armed force can now be authorized as a response to sexualized violence.

Sara E. Davies and Jacqui True[36] are less severe in their analysis and advocate a pragmatic approach. They suggest that we need to consider which feminist aims really can be fully achieved within patriarchal structures; aims that allow compromises are most likely to be achievable. If no solution can be reached within patriarchal structures, or if compromises are not possible, then the agenda must be pursued outside these structures. Davies and True argue that the pragmatic approach taken so far has led to some achievements, such as the deployment of women's protection advisors and gender protection advisors (experts who consider gender hierarchies and the needs of women in conflict situations) on peace missions and the establishment of the Informal Expert Group on WPS, a coalition of states within the UN Security Council who want to advance the WPS agenda. They also mention the inclusion of feminist civil society in peace missions, which allows feminist demands to be heard.

Conclusion: she who fights with monsters

Ultimately the question is this: should radical feminist demands, which could bring about real transformative change and even lead to completely new systems, be softened by compromises to the point where they are accepted within institutions but lose their transformative power? Or should such compromises never be made, even though this might mean that feminist demands never make it as far as the decision-makers in the halls of power?

For activists this is a crucial and difficult question that cannot be answered with a simple 'yes' or 'no' but depends on the situation. As Friedrich Nietzsche said: 'He who fights with monsters should be careful lest he thereby become a monster. And if thou gaze long into an abyss, the abyss will also gaze into thee.'[37]

I walk this tightrope every day in my work. Since the beginning of my public commitment to feminism, I've had to work hard to strike the right balance, often under heavy criticism. In 2016, when I was part of a loose coalition of feminist civil society groups and activists working towards reform in Germany of the law on sexualized violence, we demanded that the expression 'no means no' be included in the law. Until then, criminal proceedings for a sexualized attack, assault or rape were possible only if the perpetrator had used or threatened violence and if the victim had physically resisted. Some of the feminists I talked to refused to be part of the campaign because they wanted the law to say 'yes means yes' instead. I didn't take this lightly; I even engaged in written debates with law professors to get my head around the different positions and work out what we could achieve. And I came to the conclusion that 'no means no' was the best we could hope for. A much more experienced activist once told me: 'Don't let the perfect be the enemy of the good.' So I stuck with 'no means no'. That doesn't mean I was right, of course. It was simply my assessment of the situation: pragmatism over idealism.

When it comes to German foreign policy, however, I've never been prepared simply to accept what was supposedly achievable at a given moment. This goes for both my time as an advisor in the Foreign Office and CFFP's interactions with Foreign Office representatives. Usually the ministry would promise 'more women in foreign policy' as soon as we expressed our feminist demands. But, in our eyes, this simply wasn't (and isn't) enough. Feminism is so much more than 'more women'. If I'm asked: 'How much utopia is possible, given the limited options?', it's not easy for me to give a definite answer. But there's one thing I'm sure of: if a society produces such injustices as ours does, our demands should be as utopian as possible, and we should be calling for a just world as loudly as we possibly can. If we begin with the most utopian demands we can formulate, then we may eventually achieve a result we can build on.

Sanam Naraghi Anderlini:
'Who fights for human rights?
Women do.'

'If the country you're growing up in implodes, you understand that there are turning points at which history can either take a negative turn or be transformed.'

Sanam Anderlini has taken on the task of helping to shape these moments of transformation and has been involved in numerous peace processes. She was born into the Iranian elite, moved to the UK during the Iranian Revolution of 1979, and now divides her time between the USA, where she works as the founder and director of the International Civil Society Action Network, and London.

Sanam derives her motivation from the life stories of women who have had similar experiences to hers and responded in similar ways. Despite great personal losses suffered in war, they have, in the moment after the conflict, chosen humanity and empathy and have opted to make peace instead of seeking revenge.[38] Sanam is often asked whether women are more peaceful than men. Her response is that empathy depends not on one's biological sex but on one's experience of life: the oppressed must understand the oppressors and the powerful and anticipate their actions if they are to survive unscathed. She is thinking in particular of peace workers, because they seek the humanity in others, even the oppressors, and try to understand this humanity in order to find a path of transformation and shared peace.

For Sanam, feminism is inextricably linked with anti-militarism. She distinguishes between a feminism that aims to integrate women into existing structures and one that fundamentally questions these structures. And she observes a generational divide in the West. The 'Hillary Clinton generation', fighting for equal opportunities in a patriarchal, militaristic system, often lost sight of the anti-militarist element of feminism and the goal of challenging the status quo. The younger women, in contrast, refuse to accept any destructive, patriarchal structures within their feminism.

For Sanam, this is about the struggle for transformative equality. Her aim is not to give everyone an equal chance of killing or being killed as a soldier but to ensure that nobody has to experience the horrors of war.

One of Sanam's favourite authors is Isabel Allende, and one of her favourite books is *Daughter of Persia*, written by her aunt, Sattareh Farman Farmaian.

7 THE STATUS QUO OF FEMINIST FOREIGN POLICY

Those who do not move, do not notice their chains.

Rosa Luxemburg, *The Accumulation of Capital*
(London: Routledge, 2003)

In October 2014, after the parliamentary elections in Sweden, something unusual happened. The newly appointed foreign minister, Margot Wallström, announced a feminist foreign policy for Sweden – the first country in the world to take this path. Many observers couldn't believe their ears. Surely Sweden couldn't be serious, at a time like this, when Russia was behaving more and more aggressively towards Sweden and the Baltic states[1] and had violated international law by annexing Crimea just a few months earlier? Wasn't it a bit utopian? Feminist demands were instantly put in the 'naive' corner, alongside pacifism. Anyone familiar with Wallström's biography would probably have been less surprised, though. After her stint as vice president of the European Commission, she had been the UN special envoy for sexualized violence in conflicts from 2010 to 2012. And she herself had experienced sexualized violence from an ex-partner.[2]

Wallström, who joined the Swedish Social Democratic Party in her mid-twenties, has been a resolute activist and feminist for decades. She supported the Treaty on the Prohibition of Nuclear Weapons (TPNW) (instigated by civil society) in 2017 and has campaigned – so far unsuccessfully – to have it ratified by Sweden. (Germany hasn't ratified it either.) This caused much displeasure among friendly nations belonging to NATO, an alliance firmly committed to nuclear (and conventional) deterrence. But Wallström is ahead of her time; she's the kind of woman who forges her own path and doesn't care about conventions. A portrait by the *New York Times* quotes her as follows:

'I have very little time. I don't have time to walk around cocktail parties. I don't think that is the work of a diplomat.'[3] So it is particularly tragic that Sweden, a role model to many other states that have since adopted a feminist foreign policy, no longer has such a policy itself. The new government formed in October 2022 is a right-wing three-party coalition with the additional support of the far-right Swedish Democrats in parliament. Very shortly after the public announcement of the new cabinet, the foreign minister, Tobias Billstrom, abandoned the country's pioneering feminist foreign policy.[4]

Nonetheless, there are now eleven countries in the world which have officially announced or are developing a feminist foreign policy:* Canada, France, Mexico, Luxembourg, Spain, Germany, the Netherlands, Chile, Liberia, Scotland† and Colombia. There are also parliamentary groups calling for a feminist foreign policy in the USA[5] and the EU.[6] In some countries, e.g. India, civil society actors are campaigning vigorously on this issue.[7] As I write this book, I hear reports from reliable sources that Argentina is on the point of announcing a feminist foreign policy. And Denmark, Norway and Switzerland emphasize gender equality in their foreign policies.

In November 2020, the majority of MPs in the European Parliament voted for a feminist foreign policy (though it has to be said that the parliament has no legislative authority, and the foreign minister of the EU, officially the 'High Representative of the Union for Foreign Affairs and Security Policy', has no great clout). The vote was based on a report by Green MPs Hannah Neumann and Ernest Urtasun. Earlier that year they'd asked CFFP to write the first comprehensive report on the subject. In this document, *A Feminist Foreign Policy for the European Union*, my co-founder Nina and I presented our vision.[8]

---

* Or feminist development policy or feminist diplomacy – in the following I will talk about feminist foreign policy and go into more specific details in the sections on different countries.
† Scotland is, of course, not an independent state but a nation within the United Kingdom; nonetheless, its government formulates its own policies in various areas.

CFFP's work on feminist foreign policy is based on the understanding that we can't just carry on with 'business as usual'. Traditional foreign policy isn't capable of developing equitable and effective solutions to the most urgent global crises of our time – e.g. the climate crisis, attacks on human rights, or (nuclear) arms proliferation – because it perpetuates existing injustices. In order to create lasting peace and a world where no one is left behind, we need new approaches, new perspectives and a recalibration of power dynamics – in short, a feminist foreign policy. The core principles are a comprehensive and inclusive understanding of gender, intersectionality, antiracism, and coherence between domestic and foreign policy. Feminist foreign policy is based on human rights and is developed with input from civil society. It is transparent, anti-militaristic, and focused on climate justice and cooperation, not domination over others. Its aim is to overturn patriarchal structures within foreign and security policy.

At CFFP we define feminist foreign policy as a political framework necessary for the well-being of marginalized people. It rejects the emphasis on military force, violence and dominance and formulates an alternative, intersectional understanding of security from the perspective of the weakest members of global society. It aims to improve the experiences and agency of women and marginalized groups. It unmasks destructive forces such as patriarchy, colonization, heteronormativity, capitalism, racism, imperialism and militarism, and it shows more equitable alternatives.

Let's take a look at the different ways this approach is implemented in the countries that already practise feminist foreign policy.

Sweden

Although Sweden launched its feminist foreign policy in 2014, it wasn't until 2018 that the government published a handbook explaining the policy. A year after the publication of this handbook, I ran into a senior representative of the Swedish government at a meeting and asked about her experience of the implementation of feminist foreign policy. She mentioned various successes but also had the honesty to say: 'We started to drive the car before we'd finished putting it together.' Even though the details hadn't been fully thought through in 2014, Sweden set off on its journey. That's OK, though. It's even necessary – to encourage others and to bring change. If we always waited until all the issues had been sorted, we'd never get started. Wallström's announcement enabled feminist civil society to hold the Swedish government accountable and demand genuinely feminist behaviour.

The handbook explains the aims of Sweden's former feminist foreign policy. At its core were the three Rs: promotion of the human rights of all women and girls, fair representation of women and girls in all decision-making positions, and the allocation of sufficient resources to facilitate gender equality. There was also a fourth R, for reality: the whole process was based on empirical facts.[9] Valerie Hudson and her team of researchers were able to show empirically that there can be no peace or non-violence as long as patriarchal structures remain in place.[10] This, not Morgenthau and Kissinger's version, is the true reality.

Before the 2022 elections, Sweden had divided its foreign policy into three areas: first, traditional foreign and security policy; second, development cooperation and humanitarian aid; and, third, trade policy. The area of foreign and security policy comprised peace and security, human rights, democracy and the rule of law, and disarmament. Development cooperation and humanitarian aid covered the climate, the environment, and gender equity. Feminist trade policy included sustainable economic activity. The strategies spanned several years, and the specific goals were defined in action plans. The last action plan, for 2019–22, focused on securing all human rights for women and girls; stopping physical, psychological and sexualized violence against them; and ensuring their participation in the prevention and resolution of conflicts. Further goals were to encourage the involvement of women and girls in all areas of society; to empower them economically; and to protect their sexual and reproductive health and rights.[11]

Sweden's feminist foreign policy was not created in a vacuum, of course; it was based on important international agreements. These included the Universal Declaration of Human Rights, the Convention on the Elimination of Discrimination Against Women (CEDAW), the action plans of the Beijing Platform for Action (1995) and the International Conference on Population and Development in Cairo (1994). Also important were the Women, Peace and Security agenda (including UNSCR 1325), the UN's Sustainable Development Goals (Agenda 2030) and the EU's commitment to equality in its external relations.

The Swedish government appointed an 'ambassador for gender equality and coordinator of feminist foreign policy', who, assisted by a small team (just two people), supported the implementation of feminist analyses and measures throughout the Swedish Foreign Service. There were also 'focal points' (i.e. designated contacts) for feminist foreign policy in all departments within the Swedish Ministry for Foreign Affairs and in all diplomatic missions. They served as local points of contact, leaders and coordinators, but every member of staff was responsible for considering the gender perspective in his or her own work. To support this, the Ministry for Foreign Affairs developed several tools, including the above-mentioned handbook, an action plan (updated annually), a website on this topic (which was immediately taken offline after the new foreign minister announced that Sweden was dropping its feminist foreign policy), and e-learning on the intranet. The Government Offices (the ministries and other agencies supporting the work of the government) were also assisted by a department for gender equality, which helped to build capacity and ensured that all ministries considered the gender perspective in their work.

Margot Wallström showed the transformative and progressive aspirations of feminist foreign policy in spring 2015, when she publicly criticized the women's rights and human rights situation in Saudi Arabia, in particular the flogging of the blogger Raif Badawi. In response, Wallström's invitation to speak to the Arab League was withdrawn. Sweden then cancelled an arms trade agreement with Saudi Arabia, whereupon Saudi Arabia recalled its ambassador from Stockholm, and Swedish businesspeople lost their visas for the kingdom.[12] At the time, many 'experts' opined that, with these actions, Wallström and Sweden had lost all authority in matters of foreign policy. It was felt that the country could no longer be taken seriously in foreign policy decisions and that its bid for re-election as a non-permanent member of the Security Council in 2017–18 was dead in the water.[13] What actually happened, however, was just the opposite: Sweden *was* elected to the Security Council, and during its two-year tenure it persistently put women's rights and conflict prevention on the agenda. At the end of this period, the country could look back on a number of successes. It had (according to the Swedish Ministry of Foreign Affairs) consistently sought to advance the WPS agenda by ensuring that it was taken into account in all discussions and decisions. During its presidency of the Council in July 2018, it had made history by inviting equal numbers of male and female experts to give briefings. It had initiated debates on the climate crisis and security to ensure that the connection between them was taken seriously.[14] And in 2017 it had introduced a Security Council resolution to make sexualized and gender-based violence grounds for economic sanctions.[15] In 2015, Wallström had launched the Swedish Women's Mediation Network to increase the participation of women in peace processes.[16] The country had also helped to contribute to the inclusion of gender equality aspects in Colombia's 2016 peace deal and supported new legislation on gender equality in over twenty countries.[17] And for several years it was the leading OECD donor country for aid targeting gender equality.

At the same time, there was criticism. Actors in Swedish civil society lamented their country's failure both to mention disarmament or non-proliferation of arms as a factor in conflict prevention and to acknowledge how the proliferation of small arms and light weapons is linked to male violence towards women.[18] Actors in Swedish feminist civil society mainly criticized the country's continuing arms exports, which were incompatible with the official agenda of a feminist foreign policy. Sweden continues to supply weapons to conflict areas and to regions where women are denied their most basic human rights. The states that received military equipment from Sweden in 2018 include Saudi Arabia, the United Arab Emirates, Jordan, Kuwait, Bahrain and Qatar – all countries involved in the armed conflict in Yemen. This has become one of the world's worst humanitarian crises, with devastating consequences for women and girls. Sweden's weapons exports continue to reinforce the patriarchal and militarized structures that feminist foreign policy is working to remove.[19]

Sweden's feminist foreign policy didn't just come out of nowhere. Sweden had, at the time, a self-declared feminist government and a widely shared feminist outlook. The Swedes are a few decades ahead of the Germans. In Germany, for example, tax law treats married couples as a single unit, thus discriminating against unmarried people while encouraging married women to stay at home; this has remained unchanged despite years of campaigning. In Sweden, spouses have been taxed separately since 1971. Sweden also became the first country to introduce paid parental leave for both mothers and fathers, back in 1974.[20] Combating male violence against women is officially a national priority in Sweden; Germany, in contrast, still has no national strategy to combat male violence against women or any coordinating body for tackling the problem. Since 2007, Sweden has had a minister for equality.

Despite the criticism, the launch of a feminist foreign policy in Sweden – a world first – paved the way for countries such as Canada, France and others to announce similar policies. Sweden was an inspiration for many states. Wallström and Sweden were truly visionary in proclaiming a feminist foreign policy. They proved that women's rights are relevant for war and peace; that cooperation is more important than domination; that human security outweighs military security; and that it's time to end the patriarchy's stranglehold on international politics. The scrapping of its feminist foreign policy is tragic, because – as I argue in an article co-authored with other leading international feminist foreign policy advocates – Sweden's decision to call its foreign policy feminist gave hope and inspiration to feminist activists around the world. Women human rights defenders knew they had an ally on the global stage. This solidarity is particularly vital as attacks on feminist activists and LGBTQ+ people increase globally.[21]

Canada

In June 2017, Canada adopted a Feminist International Assistance Policy (FIAP),[22] designed to fight poverty by promoting gender equality. The policy calls on Canada to adopt a feminist, intersectional and human rights-based approach to its international assistance. One of its aims was to ensure that 95 per cent of its bilateral international development assistance either targeted or integrated gender equality and the empowerment of girls and women by 2021–2.* Canada's FIAP covers six action areas: gender equality and the empowerment of girls and women (core action area); human dignity (health and nutrition, including sexual and reproductive health and rights; education; humanitarian action); growth that works for everyone; environment and climate action; inclusive governance; and peace and security. Canada has also introduced a number of additional measures to promote gender equality, notably its WPS national action plans and an inclusive approach to trade policy. In 2019 Canada appointed its first ambassador for Women, Peace and Security, Jacqueline O'Neill. Another positive point is that Canada applies gender analyses to its policies, using Gender-Based Analysis Plus. This process analyses how differently government policies, programmes and initiatives at home and abroad affect different groups of women, men and gender-diverse people, taking intersectionality into account.

At the G7 summit in Quebec in 2018, Prime Minister Justin

---

* According to Canadian government officials, in 2020–1, 92.6 per cent of Canada's bilateral international assistance integrated gender equality; in 2021–2, nearly all – 99 per cent – of its bilateral international development assistance either targeted or integrated gender equality and the empowerment of women and girls.

Trudeau established the first Gender Equality Advisory Council (GEAC). A GEAC was also convened at the subsequent G7 summits in Biarritz in 2019 and Cornwall in 2021, when it was made a permanent fixture of the G7.* These councils bring together leading international experts on gender equality in different areas of society. Their task is to produce recommendations for the G7 leaders. At the 2019 summit, the actress Emma Watson and the former executive director of UN Women, Phumzile Mlambo-Ngcuka, demanded that all G7 states should have a feminist foreign policy.[23] By establishing the GEAC, Canada dealt a further blow to the patriarchal structures in international politics and provided a forum for feminist issues in a setting where *Realpolitik* is usually far too prominent.

But Canada, like Sweden, doesn't always act consistently. For example, feminist civil society has criticized the decision in 2020 to resume arms exports to Saudi Arabia, which had been suspended after the murder of the journalist Jamal Khashoggi. This contradicts Canada's feminist principles.

As I write this, Canada is developing a public-facing document outlining its feminist foreign policy – taking a comprehensive approach rather than limiting itself to particular areas. In 2020–1 the Canadian government engaged in extensive dialogue with feminist civil society for this paper; I represented CFFP in this process.[24]

France

In March 2019, the French foreign minister, Jean-Yves Le Drian, and the secretary of state for gender equality, Marlène Schiappa, announced in a jointly authored article that France would in future pursue 'feminist diplomacy'.[25] This was the first time France had described its diplomacy as 'feminist', though there had been individual strategies along these lines for some years. Although the article repeatedly uses

---

* The 2020 summit was supposed to take place at Camp David in the USA but was cancelled because of the pandemic.

the term 'feminist diplomacy', its main focus is on new funding for the French development agency, the Agence Française de Développement (AFD). It reports the government's pledge to distribute a budget of €120 million to feminist organizations via the AFD. And it states that the government has tasked the AFD with spending €700 million per year to fund projects to reduce gender inequality.[26]

France has committed to an *International Strategy on Gender Equality (2018 to 2022).** Here the French government recognizes that gender must be taken into account in all government decisions and in all areas of foreign policy. The strategy is the foundation for French feminist diplomacy and has five main objectives: first, to foster a stronger institutional culture of gender equality within the government's work; second, to intensify France's advocacy for gender equality; third, to increase the integration of gender equality into France's official development assistance; fourth, to improve the visibility, transparency and accountability of the actions taken by ministries and government agencies for gender equality; and, fifth, to strengthen ties with civil society actors, the private sector and research stakeholders to fight gender inequality.[27]

In 2021, the French parliament passed a 'law on development, solidarity and the fight against global inequalities', which sets the course for France's development policy and overseas development assistance (ODA) in the years to come. Article 1 of the law expressly states that, in the context of France's feminist diplomacy, this development policy aims to prioritize gender equality and its promotion. There is also a whole section on gender equality, Sustainable Development Goal 5 on gender equality, WPS, sexual and reproductive health and rights, and different initiatives launched by the ministry. The law states that, by 2025, gender-targeted ODA† will need to reach 75 per cent of total

---

* The first of these strategies was published in 2007, and the 2018–22 strategy was being evaluated by the High Council for Equality as this edition of the book was being prepared. The report by the High Council is expected to be published in the first half of 2023 and the new strategy in autumn 2023.

† This includes the gender equality policy markers of the OECD's Development Assistance

ODA, including 20 per cent of funding for programmes and projects where gender equality is the main objective. In addition, France will 'aim for' the EU goal of 85 per cent of gender-targeted ODA.[28]

France was the co-host (with Mexico) of the 2021 Generation Equality Forum, initiated by UN Women, which took place in March in Mexico City and in late June/early July in Paris (mostly online).* By the end of the Paris forum, governments, the private sector and philanthropists had pledged the unprecedented sum of nearly $US40 billion to bring about major advances in global gender equity by 2026.[29]

France's declared commitment to feminist diplomacy is little more than lip service: the content of French diplomacy has barely changed. In a positive step, France asked its own independent advisory body, the High Council for Gender Equality (HCE), to evaluate its international strategy. In its 2020 report, the HCE criticized the limited perspective of French diplomacy and suggested that a feminist analysis should also be applied in the fields of security, defence, the economy and trade.[30] The most problematic issue, however, is that France, as one of the five recognized nuclear states (according to the Treaty on the Non-Proliferation of Nuclear Weapons),† has a nuclear arsenal. The nuclear bomb, with its striving for destruction and dominance, is the most potent expression of toxic masculinity. It is an instrument of the patriarchy – and thus incompatible with a feminist foreign policy. Of course not everything can be turned upside down from one day to the next. But a state that publicly claims the 'feminist' label must be prepared to engage in dialogue with feminist civil society on this

---

Committee, which are used to score aid programmes. Principal (marked 2) means that gender equality is the main objective of the project/programme and is fundamental in its design and expected results. Significant (marked 1) means that gender equality is an important and deliberate objective but not the principal reason for undertaking the project/programme, often explained as gender equality being given prominence in the project/programme.

* The conferences in Mexico City and Paris were actually supposed to take place in 2020 but were postponed because of the pandemic and were largely held online.

† This treaty, commonly known as the Non-Proliferation Treaty (NPT), is not to be confused with the Treaty on the Prohibition of Nuclear Weapons, which has much more extensive goals.

difficult topic – otherwise it can rightly be suspected of mere virtue signalling. So far France has not published any comprehensive document giving a complete picture of its feminist approach. But during the Commission on the Status of Women in March 2021 the country did announce that it would produce a handbook on its own feminist foreign policy.[31]

Mexico

In January 2020, Mexico became the first country in the Global South to adopt a feminist foreign policy, as announced at the 74th UN General Assembly in September 2019. Mexico's agenda for feminist foreign policy for 2020 to 2024, based on an impressive feminist analysis,[32] consists of five core elements:[33] 1) the promotion of a foreign policy with a gender perspective and a feminist agenda; 2) gender parity within the Mexican Foreign Ministry; 3) the fight against gender-specific violence, within the ministry and elsewhere; 4) visible equality; and 5) intersectional feminism.

Mexico has also highlighted the connection between gender-specific discrimination and climate justice. This comprehensive approach was apparent in the work of the Mexican government during the 2019 UN Climate Change Conference (also known as the Conference of the State Parties, COP 25) in Spain. There Mexico demanded gender equality as a non-negotiable component of any agreement on climate and environment, and this has been consistent in all negotiations in international forums ever since. According to Cristopher Ballinas Valdés, general director for human rights and democracy in the Mexican Foreign Ministry, Mexico's feminist foreign policy is a question not just of gender but of human rights in general, including those of the LGBTQ+ community and people with disabilities. He also notes that one of the reasons for this feminist foreign policy is the strong mobilization of feminists and civil society within Mexico and Latin America.[34]

Mexico has set precise timelines for an ambitious number of immediate targets in its five areas of action. By 2024, the government aims to achieve full employment parity, equal pay, and the application of a gender perspective to every foreign policy position, resolution and mandate.[35] Some already see Mexico's feminist foreign policy as a kind of global gold standard.

The problem is that Mexico's feminist foreign policy and its commitment to feminism on the global stage are in sharp contrast to the worsening situation of women inside the country. Representatives of the government say that this is exactly why a feminist foreign policy was announced: to create pressure to align domestic policy with foreign policy and to tackle Mexico's problems. However, local feminist civil society actors have drawn attention to the country's deeply rooted patriarchal structures and the widespread impunity for crimes. These factors interact and produce extreme conditions of domestic and gender-specific violence. In Mexico, around ten women per day are killed because they are women.[36] Some Mexicans would therefore prefer to see a focus on male violence against women in their own country, along with consistent punishment for femicide.[37]

This is not the only contradiction. Although the Mexican government calls itself a 'feminist government',[38] this doesn't apply to its head of state. The Mexican president, Andrés Manuel López Obrador (often abbreviated to 'AMLO'), viewed as a populist 'strongman' by international policy experts,[39] behaves in a way that is anything but feminist and would never claim this label for himself. He shares the views of the religious right and champions 'traditional family values'. This can only be seen as a euphemism, since it means both the oppression of women and the LGBTQ+ community and the denial of their autonomy over their own bodies. In his first year of office, in 2018, AMLO cut funding for women's rights, indigenous rights and civil society, jeopardized overseas funding for civil society work,[40] and imposed political decisions that caused disproportionate harm to women.[41]

While Mexico's national policies can hardly be described as feminist, its foreign policy is based on a genuinely feminist analysis (rather than just a focus on women). I've worked with some of the government representatives dealing with the policy, and they seem to sincerely believe in the concept. The ongoing challenge is to align international and national policies and to keep antifeminist actors – including the president – in check.

Spain

Spain has also had a feminist foreign policy since 2021, announced by the then foreign minister, Arancha González Laya. The country's priorities here are as follows: firstly, to promote the WPS agenda internally and at national, EU and multilateral level; secondly, to fight gender-specific violence; thirdly, to strengthen the human rights of women and girls and to support human rights defenders; fourthly, to foster women's involvement in decision-making processes; and, fifthly, to achieve economic justice with a gender-sensitive trade policy.

One of the tools used by Spain to achieve these goals is gender mainstreaming – in foreign policy, in bilateral, regional and multilateral diplomacy, and in international cooperation. Spain follows internal measures put in place by the Ministry of Equality, pursues sustainable development goals, and seeks greater involvement in the creation of the EU action plan on WPS (2019–24). Its core principles are a transformative approach, committed leadership, ownership, inclusive participation, and support for alliances, intersectionality and diversity. A positive point here is that Spain has considered the need for annual monitoring and evaluation right from the start and plans to appoint an advisory committee for this purpose.[42]

Since October 2021, the implementation of Spain's feminist foreign policy has been in the hands of Maria Jesus Conde Zabala, ambassador-at-large for feminist foreign policy. Although it is too soon to make a conclusive assessment, the Ministry of Foreign Affairs of Spain is, according to Spanish diplomats, undergoing a cultural change. Firstly, the causes of gender inequality and discrimination are being considered in a systemic way in decision-making processes. And, secondly, women now make up 30 per cent of the staff in the diplomatic service, up from only 26 per cent in 2018. Today 25 per cent of Spain's ambassadors and heads of mission are women, compared to 22 per cent in 2018.*

Conde Zabala's predecessor was Clara Cabrera Brasero. I met Clara in June 2019 at the Escuela Diplomatica in Madrid, at a training course for leaders in the diplomatic service. At the time, her area of responsibility was human rights. After a welcome from the Spanish foreign minister, Josep Borrell (now the EU's high representative for foreign affairs), I started the event with a speech on feminist foreign policy. I liked Clara and the other Spanish women diplomats; they were no-nonsense feminists. When a participant said that the Spanish were simply not yet ready to accept a feminist foreign policy, one of the diplomats replied: 'We women were never asked whether we were ready for the patriarchy, but we got it regardless.'

On the evening of the first day of the course, the participants were invited to a reception hosted by Josep Borrell in a palace in the Spanish capital. There's a photo of me talking to Borrell, looking happy and excited. I posted it on Instagram with the following caption: 'Mr Foreign Minister, I think Spain should have a feminist foreign policy.'[43] So I was delighted when Spain announced a feminist foreign policy in spring 2021. Now the government has to show that it means business.

Germany

In November 2021 the newly elected German government, a coalition consisting of the Social Democrats (SPD), the Greens and the Liberals (FDP), presented its eagerly awaited coalition agreement. The afternoon the document was published, I was at the Canadian embassy for an event on women peacebuilders co-hosted by CFFP. Just after I had delivered my speech, I suddenly received a flood of messages congratulating us for shaping government policy. I didn't understand

---

* This information was provided by diplomats of the Spanish foreign service.

initially, but then read the following words in the coalition agreement myself: 'Together with our partners, we aim to strengthen the rights, resources, and representation of women and girls worldwide and promote diversity in the spirit of a Feminist Foreign Policy.'[44] I honestly hadn't seen this coming and was pleasantly surprised, to say the least. Yes, for the last three and a half years we'd been lobbying the German government and political parties, through a variety of channels and formats, to implement a feminist foreign policy. This included advising the Green party in the Bundestag in 2019, when they became the first political party to introduce a motion on feminist foreign policy in plenary. CFFP had also lobbied German politicians in the run-up to the 2021 Bundestag elections, outlining our vision in the 77-page *Manifesto for a Feminist Foreign Policy for Germany*.[45] Even so, I was delighted.

Since the announcement of Germany's feminist foreign policy, Annalena Baerbock has been very outspoken about it, mentioning it in countless interviews and speeches. She has firmly focused on women's and human rights as well as human security in her foreign policy. In early February 2022, for example, during her first visit to Egypt in her new role, she announced that arms exports to Egypt – a top recipient of German arms for years – would henceforth be dependent on the human rights situation there (of course, a genuine feminist foreign policy would not deliver weapons to Egypt at all). When she flew to Madrid to meet her Spanish counterpart, also in February 2022, she first met with Teresa Peramato Martin, Spain's special prosecutor for violence against women. On almost every trip abroad, she tries to meet local women. The difference between Baerbock's foreign policy and that of her male predecessors is further underlined by her decision to bring Jennifer Morgan, the former head of Greenpeace International, into the Foreign Office as special envoy for international climate policy. Another example is her speech on 1 March 2022 at the emergency special session of the UN General Assembly on Ukraine. She began with the words: 'A baby girl was born in a metro station in Kyiv a few days ago. Her name, I have been told, is Mia.'[46]

Throughout the speech, instead of engaging in geopolitical power games, she focused on human security and the effects of the war on the people in Ukraine. She also mentioned the racist discrimination that people of African descent had experienced at EU borders when fleeing the war. Baerbock is consistent in her feminist convictions and her dedication to human security, and she continues to use her political capital to explore new paths. In late November 2022, she travelled to a special session of the UN Human Rights Council in Geneva to push through a resolution (co-sponsored by Iceland) on the deteriorating human rights situation in Iran. The Human Rights Council adopted the resolution to set up an independent international fact-finding mission in Iran to investigate ongoing human rights violations related to the protests that had begun on 16 September 2022.[47] Annalena Baerbock gave further proof of her commitment to feminist foreign policy by hosting the first ever government-organized feminist foreign policy conference, held at the German Foreign Office in mid-September 2022[48] (the first ever summit on feminist foreign policy was held by CFFP in April 2022).

But one fact blatantly contradicts the principles of feminist foreign policy and must be clearly criticized: the current government, the first in Germany to adopt a feminist foreign policy, approves more arms exports than almost any other government before it. In 2022, it approved arms exports worth a total of €8.4 billion. This was the second-highest amount since the Federal Republic of Germany came into existence – exceeded only in 2021, Angela Merkel's last year in office, when the figure was €9.4 billion. And even if we deduct the €2.2 billion worth of arms supplied to Ukraine in 2022, this remains a huge sum. In 2020, in comparison, the CDU–SPD coalition approved arms deliveries worth €5.8 billion.[49] These immense sums for arms exports belie both the commitment to a 'restrictive arms export policy' expressed in the current government's coalition agreement and the pledge to introduce a national arms export control law. And although the coalition agreement also stipulates that no arms will be approved for countries mixed up in the Yemen war, Germany was involved in precisely such arms exports to Saudi Arabia within the framework of a European arms cooperation (Germany approved €17 million worth of arms exports to Saudi Arabia in 2022[50] – the outcry was tremendous).

To ensure that feminist foreign policy will continue to inform German policy-making in the long term, Baerbock initiated the drafting of a strategy on feminist foreign policy covering internal processes at the ministry as well as international foreign policy-making. We, CFFP, have been involved in the process. The strategy was released on 1 March 2023. For this occasion I, among other experts, was invited to share the panel with Foreign Minister Annalena Baerbock to discuss feminist foreign policy in front of a conference hall packed with diplomats, civil society representatives, politicians and journalists. Germany's feminist foreign policy is one of the most comprehensive to date.

Other countries with a feminist foreign policy agenda

Other countries currently working on the development of a feminist foreign policy are Liberia, Chile, Scotland, Colombia, Luxembourg and the Netherlands.

At an event on feminist foreign policy hosted by the German foreign minister Annalena Baerbock during the UN General Assembly High-Level Week in September 2022, Liberia's minister of gender, children and social protection, Williametta Piso Saydee-Tarr, said that her government intended to ensure that, 'at some point, we will be establishing our own feminist foreign policy.'[51]

Chile announced a feminist foreign policy in March 2022 on what was – for me personally – a special and highly apt occasion. The German foreign minister Annalena Baerbock and her ministry had organized 'Unidas Week 2022', a week of events on feminism and foreign policy, including an awards ceremony. The focus was the Unidas network, connecting Germany, Latin America and the Caribbean, which I had built up with my diplomat colleagues during my time as an advisor to the German Foreign Ministry in 2019. The

Chilean foreign minister, Antonia Urrejola, gave a passionate speech announcing the development of a feminist foreign policy.[52] As I revise the text for the English edition of this book, Chile's feminist foreign policy is being developed by the Gender Equality Board of Chile's Ministry of Foreign Affairs, and it is due to be formally launched in spring 2023. 'According to the Minister, there are two aspects, one within the Ministry of Foreign Affairs, which is to incorporate women into the spaces of power. The second is to position the multilateral perspective in foreign policy from the perspective of gender mainstreaming.'[53]

In its 2021–2 programme, the Scottish government committed to developing a feminist approach to foreign policy, and the External Affairs Directorate concluded a wide-ranging stakeholder engagement process with community and third-sector organizations, experts and academics – including actors from the Global South. This incorporated a series of thematic workshops on feminist approaches to foreign policy and peace and security, trade and economic justice, climate justice, and development and aid. These conversations are expected to lead to a policy statement outlining Scotland's feminist approach to foreign policy, to be presented in summer 2023.

Colombia is also currently developing a feminist foreign policy. I was asked to brief the Colombian Foreign Ministry towards the end of 2022 and am hoping to see a strategy published in 2023. Hopes are high, especially since Francia Márquez was named the country's first Afro-Colombian female – and feminist! – vice president after the elections in May and June 2022. Francia is part of the feminist network Unidas, and I met her when I travelled to Latin America with the former German foreign minister Heiko Maas to launch the network. She was also a keynote speaker at the high-level women-only dinner we – CFFP together with the feminist PR agency Hell & Karrer – hosted at the Munich Security Conference in February 2023.

At the end of 2018, the government of Luxembourg announced a feminist foreign policy in its coalition agreement.[54] The foreign minister, Jean Asselborn, subsequently stated that his country wanted to advance gender equality and the rights of women and girls in line with the country's '3D' approach to foreign policy, guided by the pillars of diplomacy, development and defence.[55] In June 2021, during the Generation Equality Forum, the government committed to developing an action plan for feminist foreign policy within a five-year period.[56] As yet, no other official resources have been produced, but the government has announced that it plans to publish a guiding document by mid-2023.

During the summer of 2021, the Dutch government commissioned a study on the added value of a feminist foreign policy for presentation to parliament. In May 2022 the Dutch minister of foreign affairs and the minister of foreign trade and development cooperation informed parliament that the government of the Netherlands would adopt a feminist foreign policy.[57] After months of consultations, the Dutch handbook on feminist foreign policy is due to be published in the summer of 2023. In September 2023 the foreign ministry will hold a conference on feminist foreign policy, taking over from Germany.

There is also a strong civil society campaign in the USA – e.g. by the Coalition for a Feminist Foreign Policy in the United States. CFFP belongs to this coalition, along with representatives of the Rockefeller Foundation, Amnesty International and the Global Fund for Women.[58] In September 2020, female Democrats submitted a proposal for a feminist foreign policy to the US House of Representatives.[59]

Staying power: the Global Partner Network

In November 2019 I set out for Bellagio on Lake Como in Italy. In Germany the weather was already grey and miserable, but in Bellagio the sun shone for the entire four days I was there. I was part of a small group invited to spend a few days at the Rockefeller Foundation's Bellagio Center, an invitation issued by the Foundation itself and the

US-based International Center for Research on Women (ICRW). The gathering brought together various people working with feminist foreign policy. There was one representative of each country that already practised or claimed to practise feminist foreign policy (at the time just Sweden, Canada and France) or that was about to announce a feminist foreign policy (Mexico). There were also about ten representatives of organizations doing significant work on feminism and foreign policy, as well as the most established researchers in this field. I'd been invited to represent CFFP.

The atmosphere during the four days in Bellagio was one of mutual trust. All conversations took place under Chatham House Rules, which stipulate that the things people say may be quoted but the identity of the speaker must not be revealed. We had heated discussions and drank good wine. Our Bellagio Group, as we referred to it informally, was the foundation for the Global Partner Network for Feminist Foreign Policy. Launched online in July 2021 at the Generation Equality Forum in Paris, the network already comprised more than thirty governments and organizations at the time of its founding.[60]

Since the meeting, this group of government and civil society representatives has been in regular dialogue, working to elaborate the concept of feminist foreign policy and gain the support of more and more organizations and states. At a New York press conference led by Lyric Thompson, ICRW's senior director for policy and advocacy at the time, on 11 March 2020 (two days before the pandemic forced me to cut short my US business trip), we presented a concept and framework for a feminist foreign policy. Developed under the leadership of ICRW, after more than a year of research and consultations with over 100 organizations in more than forty countries all over the world, it contains recommended guidelines for governments and supranational organizations. And it is based on the assumption that feminist foreign policy means a radical revision of existing power relations.

Five questions for a feminist foreign policy

The main contribution of the framework is to identify the core components of a feminist foreign policy:

1 What *purpose* does it serve? What we mean here is the specific purpose of a government in adopting a feminist foreign policy. Such a policy must be linked with domestic policies.

2 What *definition* does it follow? What does feminist foreign policy mean for governments or international organizations, based on an intersectional approach?

3 What is the intended *scope* of such a policy? To what extent do measures cover different areas and government entities?

4 What *outcomes* are intended, and what *standards* will be applied? This refers to the specific results that are to be achieved, including a fixed timeline.

5 A *plan* for the implementation of the feminist foreign policy (how and when is it to be implemented?), encompassing resources, representation and inclusion, a timeline for reporting, and capacity building.

As part of the Global Partner Network, CFFP works with others to create frameworks and specific proposals. We know that feminist activism requires staying power – as demonstrated by pioneering campaigners such as those at The Hague. It's a long, slow process, but I know from my experience as an activist that structures and paradigms can change. If I didn't have that certainty, I wouldn't be doing this job.

Small steps

An all-out feminist revolution in foreign policy isn't the only option; it's also possible to start small.[61] This can pave the way for bigger steps towards a truly feminist foreign and security policy. In a study looking at what the USA could do to promote gender equality in foreign policy, Jamille Bigio and Rachel Vogelstein divided the relevant activities of other countries into the three following areas: (1) leadership, (2) policy and (3) resource allocation.

In the area of leadership, a wide range of measures can be introduced. For example, some governments have created high-level positions such as ambassadors or special envoys for gender equality. In 2009, under Barack Obama, the USA became the first country in the world to create the position of ambassador-at-large for global women's issues. In 2019 Canada appointed its first ambassador for WPS. Under the heading 'policy', Bigio and Vogelstein mention strategies for gender equality and national action plans to implement UNSCR 1325. Some countries include commitments to equality in their diplomacy, trade policies and defence policies. In 2012, during Hillary Clinton's tenure as secretary of state, the USA published its first policy guidance on 'Promoting gender equality to achieve our national security and foreign policy objectives', to improve the status of women in the work of the US Department of State. Similar strategies were published in 2016 by Australia and Norway. Under 'resources', Bigio and Vogelstein identified four different financial instruments used by governments to support moves towards gender equality: targets within development aid funding, gender budgeting, pooled funds and collective initiatives. Overall, however, very little money is invested in gender equality. In 2018–19, according to the OECD Development Assistance Committee, only 5 per cent of bilateral development finance from OECD states went to programmes that mention gender equality as their principal objective. Most development funding for gender equality went to programmes that have this as a significant but secondary objective: $US47.4 billion, which makes up 40 per cent of total bilateral aid. 55 per cent of funding for development cooperation was 'gender blind'* – i.e. not focused on gender equality.

---

* If we consider the average share of official development finance focused on gender equality (either as its principal or significant but secondary objective) in 2018 and 2019, Canada

'Gender budgeting' was first introduced in Australia in 1984. The idea is that, when making a budget, countries should consider who (in gender terms) benefits from the provision of public money. The budget should then be adjusted to ensure fair distribution. For example, if stimulus packages during the pandemic give disproportionate financial support to the automotive industry (as in Germany, with the 'innovation bonus' for electric cars), but the care sector gets nothing, then this benefits men, because they are more likely to be employed in the auto industry, while more women work in care.

Some governments, of course, have gone a step further and announced a comprehensive feminist foreign policy. What factors lead to such a decision? The Australia-based International Women's Development Agency has investigated this question with the help of a number of experts, including myself.[62] Its research identified several decisive factors. Generally there is a senior government figure who (often on the basis of a personal preference, as in Sweden and Mexico) is willing to make a bold feminist announcement. This sometimes even surprises civil society in his or her own country – in Germany, CFFP was taken by surprise when the coalition agreement for the new government in November 2021 contained a commitment to a feminist foreign policy. The success of such bold announcements depends on the overall social climate, however: there has to be a largely positive attitude towards feminism. In the case of Germany, CFFP has played a significant role here. The ongoing transformation of this social climate is entirely due to feminist civil society: our work prepares the ground on which the seeds of a feminist foreign policy can thrive. Other contributing factors are political leaders with progressive personal values

takes the top spot, with 92 per cent, followed by Sweden with 84 per cent and France with 32 per cent (Canada has committed to reaching 95 per cent and France 50 per cent by 2022). However, a better indicator of financial support for feminist work in development cooperation is how much money countries invest in programmes focused primarily on gender equality. These figures are considerably lower: in the same years, the figure for Canada is around 24 per cent, Sweden just under 18 per cent, and France around 4 per cent. The average worldwide is 5 per cent.

and suitable opportunities. Such an opportunity may occur when a new government wants to distinguish itself from conservative predecessors or when globally significant phenomena such as #MeToo dominate the public sphere and media. International political occasions such as the G7 or the WPS agenda are also good opportunities for governments to make feminist announcements.[63]

Conclusion: the will for transformation

Feminist foreign policy has its origins in the streets. The eleven countries which officially have a feminist foreign policy or a feminist international assistance policy are indebted to the work done by feminists and feminist civil society since the nineteenth century. Canada, France, Mexico, Luxembourg, Spain, Germany, the Netherlands, Chile, Liberia, Scotland and Colombia must be measured against the visionary work of these women.

I'm fully aware that new and progressive developments always take place within a world that is still essentially patriarchal. My view is that, as a critical civil society, we must keep this in mind when criticizing governments. What we have to do is find the right balance between acknowledging and welcoming feminist political actions on the one hand and continuing to make utopian demands on the other. Without such demands, urgently needed changes cannot be achieved.

It is not a contradiction for us, as members of feminist civil society, occasionally to accept that there are things that cannot be changed overnight, still less by us. One of these things is the normalization of arms trading and militarism in our society; this also applies to weapons of mass destruction and the nuclear bomb. States should be allowed to declare a feminist foreign policy even if their economy is still involved in the international arms trade. But only if – and here I believe there should be no exceptions – they are genuinely willing to examine this problematic status quo. If a government is not prepared to discuss destructive and patriarchal elements of foreign policy such as the possession of nuclear weapons, then feminist foreign policy is nothing but virtue signalling. Our great feminist forebears would be turning in their graves if they knew what passed for 'feminist foreign policy' these days. This is partly because feminism is a polymorphous concept. It stands for transformative social change. If this is what states want to achieve with their foreign policy, then I see no reason why they shouldn't use this term. Finally, I would like to explicitly emphasize what remarkable progress it is that there are now eleven countries that have or are developing a feminist foreign policy. When my book was first published in February 2022, there were seven such states. This is real progress.

Cynthia Enloe:
'Where are the women?'

Cynthia Enloe, born in 1938, has been studying this question for decades. A political scientist, a lecturer, and the author of numerous books, Cynthia turns the world of traditional comparative political science on its head. Her analysis focuses on an area that has previously attracted far too little attention: the stories and visions of women and their activities in politics. Her work on feminism and militarism helped to establish her reputation.

Cynthia argues that foreign policy is much more complex than most political commentators would have us believe. It is shaped not only by power struggles but also by hidden contradictions. For example, a state's outward demonstrations of power may be fuelled by internal insecurity and vulnerability. Often, a state's internal and gender-specific insecurities and weaknesses are overlooked.

In the past, women were always an object of state policy, an object that had to be controlled. Feminist scholars, says Cynthia, expose the dependencies between patriarchy, power, control, oppression and policy-making. She believes it is impossible to talk about states without talking about patriarchy. The two are interdependent. And she warns that, if we are not fully aware of how patriarchy works, it will be impossible to analyse a state's aims and actions reliably.

Cynthia also wants to share the insight that women, in all their diversity and complexity, have always been active in all spheres of power. It's just that we haven't heard their (hi)stories because our textbooks present a purely male-directed history of the world. Men write history about men. That's why most of us haven't heard of the international women's organization to end the transatlantic slave trade or of women's global strategy to secure the right to vote. We know little about the women activists in the Caribbean, the Middle East, Africa and Asia who campaigned both for the end of colonial rule and for greater gender equality. For Cynthia, one thing is certain: the questions we ask are as important as the answers we receive.

Cynthia's best-known book is *Bananas, Beaches and Bases: Making Feminist Sense of International Politics*. Her absolute favourite book is *Three Guineas* by Virginia Woolf.

8 ATTACKS ON WOMEN'S RIGHTS, LGBTQ+ RIGHTS AND HUMAN RIGHTS

*By redefining whose voice is valued,
we redefine our society and its values.*
Rebecca Solnit, *The Mother of All Questions*
(London: Granta, 2017)

Political work, especially activism and networking, involves constant interaction with other people. When you're talking about policies and their effects, you soon get onto highly sensitive and confidential topics which are best discussed face to face. Before the pandemic I'd often groaned at the sheer number of meetings and conferences I had to attend, but in the end such events are crucial for the development of political visions.

Before the pandemic (and the same is true again now), my diary was packed. I gave speeches on small stages in front of twenty people and on large stages in front of hundreds of people, in Prague, Lisbon and Barcelona. I spoke on panels at Harvard University and in New York, Bern, Budapest, Munich, Hamburg and Berlin. In Berlin, my time was divided between the German Foreign Office (where I was working as an advisor), the CFFP office and my desk at home. All the events I attended had one thing in common: however interesting the programme may be, what really counts are the breaks between sessions and the evenings, when you get into conversation with other participants, hear about their views and experiences, and have opportunities for networking.

177

Networking

For three days in January 2020, I took part in an exclusive conference organized by Wilton Park, an agency of the British Foreign, Commonwealth and Development Office. The location was Wiston House, a beautiful old building with large, inviting rooms, an extensive garden and an orangery. Leading thinkers, practitioners and new voices meet there to deliberate on issues of international politics, such as conflict prevention, global health, human rights, defence and security.

I'd been invited to Wilton Park with around fifty other participants – high-ranking UN staff, government representatives and human rights defenders – for an event entitled Human Rights, Peace and Security: Strengthening the Links. The sessions followed various formats and explored how the different policy areas – human rights, development policy, and peace and security – could be brought together. Too often, these are considered and dealt with in isolation from one another. Security is taken to mean not the defence of human rights but 'hard security' – i.e. military strength and armed force. Feminists working in foreign and security policy have always sought to uphold an inclusive concept of security.

I had an amazing time at Wiston House, met some impressive people, and finally got to enjoy something I'd missed since leaving England in 2016 – a breakfast of porridge, hash browns and fried mushrooms. One special result of these three days was my conversations with a very nice woman in a senior role at the Finnish Ministry for Foreign Affairs. We talked mainly about the growing number of attacks on women's and LGBTQ+ rights by antifeminist and right-wing actors. I suggested to her that my team and I could investigate this in order to get a better understanding of how well these actors are interconnected and what exactly their goals are. If we want to tackle these groups, this is what we need to do. She liked my idea, and a few months later we were working together. Synergies like these can only come about if people are able to talk to each other in confidence. The loss of these opportunities during the pandemic was a huge problem.

My remarks in this chapter have arisen from the collaboration between CFFP and the Finnish and German foreign ministries. At our end, the project is headed by Damjan Denkovski, who was the first member of CFFP's staff after me and Nina. Damjan and Nina are the principal authors of our study *Power over Rights – Understanding and Countering the Transnational Anti-Gender Movement*. The findings of this study – and of other publications we have subsequently produced on this topic* – play an important role in this chapter. A feminist foreign policy must do all it can to prevent attacks on human rights by right-wing and antifeminist actors. We cannot confront the greatest challenges of our time and build lasting peace worldwide unless human rights and feminist security are at the centre of all foreign and security policy activities.

Power over Rights

Thanks to funding from the Finnish Ministry for Foreign Affairs and the German Foreign Office, we've been able to build on the work of leading scholars such as Rebecca Sanders, David Paternotte and Roman Kuhar and investigate the anti-gender movement gaining ground in many countries. This is an increasingly transnational, populist, antifeminist movement, hostile to human rights and made up of actors as diverse as the Catholic Church, governments, and right-wing think-tanks. They're often unconnected and don't necessarily see each other as partners, yet they work in similar ways to develop and produce alternative norms that are hostile to the concept of universal and indivisible human rights. This is a well-organized (but not centralized), well-financed transnational movement, working – for various reasons – to undermine women's rights, LGBTQ+ rights, and civil society.

---

* My colleague Annika Kreitlow made a significant contribution to these publications, and I have benefited from her knowledge and expertise while writing this chapter.

One of our methods was to invite experts to round table discussions. At one event we talked about attacks by anti-gender actors in the USA, Mexico and Europe; at another we discussed the attacks in Ireland, Argentina, the EU and the UN system. The participants in these virtual discussions included academics and representatives of NGOs but also real movers and shakers such as the famous Argentine author and feminist Mariana Carbajal, as well as Ailbhe Smyth, a leader of the successful referendum campaign to overturn Ireland's abortion ban in 2018.

Many of the activists we spoke to agreed with us that the current situation has got worse for those affected. This is the worst it's been in a long time. At CFFP, we're doing all we can to defend the human rights advances we've made as a society in recent years. Yet we're fearful of losing this battle, even though we're better informed than ever. What we need is a systematic understanding of the way anti-gender actors influence (inter)national politics.

The origins of anti-gender ideology

Anti-gender actors have been making their opinions heard for many years – for example, at the second International Conference on Population and Development* in Bucharest in 1974 and at the third conference in Mexico City in 1984. Among the topics discussed there were abortion, family planning and diverse family models (some people call them 'new', but in fact they were never new, just forbidden and suppressed). Representatives of the Holy See and the USA took an extremely negative stance on these issues and lobbied for restrictive rules. However, the two events seen as the origin of the international anti-gender movement are the International Conference on Population and Development in Cairo in 1994 and the Fourth World Conference on Women in Beijing in 1995. The objective at the time was to include

---

* These international conferences are a series of UN summits on questions of global population. The first took place in Rome in 1954, the last in Nairobi in 2019.

sexual and reproductive health and rights (SRHR) in the catalogue of human rights. This means complete physical and mental well-being in relation to all areas of human sexuality and reproduction – and it covers access to safe abortions, sexuality education, the prevention of sexualized violence (including genital mutilation), family planning and contraception, and the provision of care during pregnancy and childbirth. The conference in Cairo in 1994 can be described as a historical turning point: for the first time, 179 UN member states agreed to put humans – and not the interests of the state – at the centre of their health policies. The action plan adopted at the conference pledged to protect the sexual and reproductive health and rights of all people.[1] One year later, in Beijing, activists and delegates from 189 countries came together to adopt the most far-reaching and ambitious agenda for women's rights in history. This aimed at nothing less than 'removing all the obstacles to women's active participation in all spheres of public and private life through a full and equal share in economic, social, cultural and political decision-making.'[2]

But more rights for women clearly make some men, especially the anti-gender actors, very afraid that they may have to relinquish some of their own rights and privileges. So the more international discussion there was on women's rights, and the more attention was paid to these issues, the stronger the resistance to these progressive policies grew – particularly from the Holy See. In 1994, resistance from the Vatican prevented the inclusion of abortion as a legitimate form of family planning in the final document of the Cairo conference. And not only that: the document states that abortion is *not* a method of family planning. Despite the best efforts of the anti-gender movement, however, the 1994 and 1995 conferences marked a defeat for the patriarchal understanding of gender and sexuality, since sexual and reproductive health and rights *are* mentioned in the final documents.

After the conferences in Cairo and Beijing, the Vatican and the Catholic Church developed the narrative of 'gender ideology'. The advances made in 1994 and 1995 were labelled as 'ideology' to emphasize their divergent and threatening nature in relation to so-called biological norms (e.g. the differences between men and women). Since its origins in the 1990s, this narrative of 'gender ideology' has been used successfully by anti-gender activists worldwide. This includes Germany. In 2016, Bavaria's conservative party CSU (Christian Social Union) announced in its manifesto: 'We reject a social and educational policy based on gender ideology and early sexualization.'[3] Anyone who uses the term 'gender ideology', whether in Colombia, Bavaria, or anywhere else in the world, is implying that demanding human rights for everyone is ideologically motivated, one-sided and dogmatic. And yet in reality this is a matter not of being one-sided or rigid but of giving everyone the freedom and safety to be themselves. The term 'gender ideology' is an active attempt to delegitimize our work towards freedom and rights for everyone.

The old, the new and the allies

The different antifeminist actors can be divided into three groups: the old, the new and the allies.[4]

The old actors are the Catholic Church and right-wing think-tanks and institutions, many of them from the USA. These established actors have very good connections to the centres of power. They are represented in government agencies, have observer status in international organizations, and have substantial financial resources to advance their agendas. In an investigative report early in 2020, openDemocracy revealed how twenty-eight right-wing US Christian organizations, including the Heritage Foundation and other organizations with links to the Trump administration, had spent at least $280 million globally since 2007 to influence laws, guidelines and public opinion in other countries against women's and LGBTQ+ rights.* The biggest propor-

---

* As Damjan Denkovski and Annika Kreitlow write in CFFP's policy briefing 'Funding (in) equality? A comparative look at the funding landscape for pro- and anti-gender initiatives and campaigns in the European Union (EU)', the sums mentioned here are only part of the truth. The exact figures cannot be ascertained because church organizations in the USA

tion of this gigantic sum (nearly $90 million) was spent in Europe. This reactionary lobbying was mainly orchestrated and conducted via two organizations: the American Center for Law and Justice (ACLJ), founded in 1990, and the Alliance Defending Freedom (ADF). The ACLJ is headed by a conservative lawyer, Jay Sekulow, who defended Donald Trump in his impeachment proceedings. Its European branch, the European Center for Law and Justice (ECLJ), gives it a foothold in Europe. Both the ECLJ and ADF have consultative status at the UN, and in the last ten years they have intervened in dozens of European court cases, among them Poland's landmark anti-abortion ruling. In at least seven cases up to 2020, they have argued against adoption by same-sex couples, supported doctors who refuse to provide services to women and LGBTQ+ individuals, and made written submissions to European courts in favour of Poland's ultraconservative government.[5]

The new actors – encompassing 'concerned citizens' initiatives', political parties and NGOs – have emerged and launched their fight against 'gender ideology' only in the last decade. One example is the Turkish Women and Democracy Association (KADEM), founded in 2013. This women's rights organization, founded by the Turkish government, is an attempt by the right-wing party AKP to undermine the powerful independent feminist movement in Turkey.[6] Another example is the German AfD (Alternative for Germany). Although this party first became known for its anti-immigrant and anti-European focus, it can also be counted among the anti-gender actors, playing off the narrative of 'concerned citizens' against the rights of women and LGBTQ+ individuals.

The third group, the allies, consists of academics, politicians, journalists and media who share and disseminate hostile attitudes towards human rights. In Germany this includes articles in well-known newspapers such as *Die Welt* or the *Frankfurter Allgemeine Zeitung*, since they propagate the narrative that gender is a problem of overprivileged

---

are not necessarily required to give information about their funds, and because there aren't enough regulations on transparency in Europe.

feminists, who are out of touch with reality and have no idea of people's actual problems.[7]

Even if the actors mentioned here don't always share the same worldview and their anti-gender attitudes may have different motivations, they are united by the fact that they construct 'gender ideology' as an assault on at least one of the 'three Ns' (as identified by Roman Kuhar and David Paternotte): nature, nation and normality.[8] They attack gender mainstreaming in institutions, university courses on gender, international human rights conventions such as the Istanbul Convention, LGBTQ+ rights, sexual and reproductive health and rights, and sexuality education in schools. These actors employ various strategies to uphold the patriarchal social order. They are all based on fear and on the idea that securing equality and human rights for everyone is a radical and destabilizing project. The old actors primarily use religious and naturalistic narratives – e.g. that homosexuality is unnatural and contrary to the divine order. Newer actors increasingly use secular and allegedly scientific arguments – e.g. the narrative that there are only two biological sexes – or human-rights-based language, such as Poland's attempt to establish a 'family rights convention' as an alternative to the Istanbul Convention. This is an initiative launched by ultraconservative forces in Poland, who seek to use the language of 'family rights' to sabotage the EU's efforts to promote women's and LGBTQ+ rights.[9]

The language of human rights is increasingly being misused internationally to curtail the human rights of political minorities such as women or the LGBTQ+ community. Another example is the establishment under President Trump in 2019 of the Commission on Unalienable Rights in the US Department of State, which questioned the way international human rights are defined today and emphasized a supposedly traditional, US-specific understanding of rights. Its report refers frequently to the word 'inalienable' in the US Constitution, which means that these rights – especially the right to freedom – must not be restricted by anything or anyone. The Commission's mandate was to provide the secretary of state with advice on human rights 'grounded in our nation's founding principles and the 1948 Universal Declaration of Human Rights'.[10] Although it recognized the 1948 Declaration, the Commission's report categorized later normative and legal developments in the area of human rights, including women's rights and sexual and reproductive rights, as illegitimate. The report clearly prioritizes individual rights such as religious freedom or property rights over collective rights such as the right to health.[11] The Biden administration has abandoned the Commission's recommendations.[12]

Another common argument of anti-gender actors is that gender equality has already been achieved, a claim refuted by the actual data. They also assert that 'gender ideology' is a totalitarian ideology – a harsh accusation, given that this is not about dictatorial subjugation but about liberation.

Defending the international patriarchal social order

On the multilateral level, anti-gender initiatives are launched mainly by the Vatican or by Christian states and then gratefully taken up by other groups. These actors were already active before the 1990s, have been well organized for about a decade, and have gained further strength in the last few years. They are not concerned solely with countering gender awareness or destroying what has been achieved. They want, quite simply, to uphold the patriarchy. These attacks are not merely a backlash or pushback, nor are they isolated events. Their real target is power relations, and their aim is to maintain a destructive power imbalance. Neil Datta, secretary of the European Parliamentary Forum for Sexual and Reproductive Rights, warns: 'They're not against us; we are rather a victim on their path towards a much bolder and more ambitious social, economic and political project.'[13]

In our latest CFFP study, *Disrupting the Multilateral Order?*,[14] supported by the Finnish Ministry for Foreign Affairs, we have taken a closer look at the attacks of anti-gender actors on Europe's multilateral institutions. Our team conducted nearly thirty interviews with staff of different EU institutions, members of the European Parliament and academics in order to identify the precise tactics that anti-gender actors use to influence the different levels of European politics. Annika Kreitlow, who conducted the interviews with Damjan Denkovski and worked on the study, stresses that anti-gender, antifeminist and anti-democratic actors are extremely professional at multilateral level (i.e. in multilateral institutions such as the EU) as well as nationally. They have good networks and are able to adapt well to the different forums and thus maximize their influence on the different levels. Annika also stresses that the language and frameworks of human rights – agreed on internationally by states to protect and guarantee human rights – have been in place for decades. As members of progressive civil society, we must not be taken in by the attempts of antifeminist, anti-gender actors to classify these rights as ideology. Anti-gender actors are working towards the strategic goal of undermining multilateral agreements (such as human rights conventions) and creating new reference works that delegitimize LGBTQ+ and sexual and reproductive rights. They are not just targeting these rights, however; their aim is to call into question the whole multilateral democratic system. For fifteen years, there has been a sustained effort in the Geneva-based United Nations Human Rights Council (UNHRC) to challenge agreed human rights conventions and redefine them along traditionalist and relativist lines. The aims of the actors involved are to prioritize cultural tradition and the family over the fundamental human rights of women and LGBTQ+ people and to delegitimize the idea of universal human rights as imperialist. In the Organization for Security and Co-operation in Europe (OSCE), 'gender' and LGBTQ+ rights have consistently been rejected by Russia and the Holy See, hampering the OSCE in its ability to work progressively. The proportion of MEPs whose politics can be described as antifeminist or anti-gender has doubled in comparison with that of the last legislative period and now stands at 30 per cent. In EU foreign policy, individual member states make declarations in multilateral bodies that clash with the EU's joint declarations. This leads to a growing incoherence between the rhetoric of the EU and that of its member states. Member states of the Council of Europe, for example, have enshrined the protection of the heterosexual family in their constitutions, thus challenging the authority of the Council of Europe in its defence of human rights, democracy and the rule of law. But the focal point for the contestation of equality in the Council of Europe has become the Convention on Preventing and Combating Violence Against Women and Domestic Violence, better known as the Istanbul Convention, after the city where it was signed in 2011. Its opponents have argued that the convention is incompatible with national values, as shown by Turkey's withdrawal from the convention and the successful attempt in Bulgaria to have it declared unconstitutional.[15] The convention was created by the Council of Europe* and sets legally binding standards not only for the punishment of perpetrators but also for the prevention of violence and the protection of victims. It was signed by forty-five of the forty-seven member states of the Council of Europe at the time (the exceptions were Azerbaijan and Russia)[16] and by the EU as an organization. By signing an international treaty, a country declares its intention to transpose the agreement into national law. Only then can the treaty be ratified and take effect within the state. However, several current and former EU members have so far refused to take this step: Bulgaria, Czechia, Hungary, Lithuania, Latvia, Slovakia and the UK. Turkey's withdrawal from the Istanbul Convention in July 2021 (and Poland's plan to do so) is a new development. This is the first time that a country has revoked a previously ratified Council of Europe convention – evidence that conservative governments are showing an increasing disregard for women's rights.

This, however, is just one part of a much bigger plan: to dismantle international protections and violate the rights of women and minorities.[17] This takes the form of physical attacks on the streets or legal attacks via the justice system. Attacks on the street include

---

* The Council of Europe is the leading human rights organization in Europe. It has forty-six member states, of which twenty-seven are members of the European Union – so it is not an EU institution.

demonstrations by church and 'pro-life' groups in front of abortion clinics in the USA (now increasingly common in Germany too)*[18] or violent attacks on LGBTQ+ individuals in public spaces. In 2020 alone, at least 350 trans people were murdered worldwide, the highest number since the beginning of annual reports in 2008. The real number is certain to be much higher in some countries, since many cases are not reported.[19] The attacks carried out via policy-making and the justice system are equally horrifying, if not more so. In Poland, for example, there has been a near total ban on abortion since a momentous ruling by the Polish Constitutional Tribunal in January 2021 – despite large-scale demonstrations. The only exceptions are in cases of rape, incest or danger to the mother's life. Doctors who carry out abortions risk a prison sentence of up to three years. As a result, many Polish women are forced to continue pregnancies against their will, while others go overseas to have abortions.[20] Two women are already known to have died because of this law.[21] Such attacks also occur in national governments and at international level. An example of the latter (which I've already described in chapter 6) was the pressure exerted by the Trump administration in April 2019, which forced the German government to delete a passage on sexual and reproductive health and rights from UN Security Council Resolution 2467.

The activities of the anti-gender movement must be seen in the context of the general decline in freedom and civil liberties worldwide and the shrinking spaces of civil society. Progress in implementing international human rights in past decades (beginning with the adoption of the Universal Declaration of Human Rights by the UN General Assembly in 1948) gave governments and civil society the illusion that things would always go in the same positive direction. 'Up to 2010 there was [in Europe] the understanding of a constant progress towards more rights,'[22] says David Paternotte, one of the lead-

---

* Most recently, for example, there were violent protests by religious fundamentalists at the opening of a new abortion clinic in Dortmund at the end of 2022. See www.ruhr24.de/dortmund/dortmund-abtreibung-klinik-kritik-abtreibung-weltkrieg-schwangerschaftsabbruch-protest-koerne-frauen-91947463.html.

ing scholars researching anti-gender actors, in an interview with my colleague Damjan. But this is a fallacy. Progress isn't an automatic process; it relies on the tireless work of (feminist) civil society. For decades, this work has been the driver of advances in human rights for everyone.

The *Atlas of Civil Society*

As shown by our work and by case studies from the USA, Mexico, Europe, Brazil, Tunisia and other countries, women's rights, LGBTQ+ rights and human rights are under fire worldwide, and civil society has less and less room to manoeuvre – a phenomenon that has been referred to as the 'shrinking spaces of civil society'. A study on the global situation in 2021[23] by the German Christian aid organization Brot für die Welt, for its *Atlas der Zivilgesellschaft* (Atlas of civil society), shows that only 3 per cent (!) of the world's population live in countries with an open civil society, while 9 per cent live in 'narrowed' societies.* 'Worldwide, only around 12 per cent of people can, more or less without hindrance, express their opinion, assemble, and fight injustices.'† This is a clear decline compared to 2019, when the figure was nearly 18 per cent. Eighty-eight per cent of the world's population – that's 6.8 billion people – live in obstructed, repressed or closed societies, under governments that 'curtail their basic rights, harass, persecute, torture or even kill them'.[24] This applies to 58 per cent of the world's states – 114 states in total.

Now, if you're thinking, well, that's dreadful, but it's all happening in far-off places, then I have to disappoint you: even here in the

---

* The five categories in the *Atlas of Civil Society* are open, narrowed, obstructed, repressed and closed.
† A year later, the situation has worsened even further: the *Atlas of Civil Society 2022* shows that 'only 11 per cent of all people worldwide [can], more or less without hindrance, express their opinion, assemble, and fight injustices. They live in open (3 per cent) or narrowed societies (8 per cent).' See www.brot-fuer-die-welt.de/themen/atlas-der-zivilgesell schaft/2022/zusammenfassung-2022/.

European Union, according to the *Atlas*, basic rights are restricted. Only 173 million out of 445 million EU citizens live in open societies; that's just 40 per cent. Nearly 60 per cent live in countries in which their basic rights are 'narrowed'. That's twelve states, with 262 million EU citizens. And the roughly 10 million inhabitants of Hungary live under an authoritarian government, 'which grants its citizens only limited freedom of action.'[25]

The analyses of the *Atlas* also show how the Covid-19 pandemic has been used as a pretext for repression. All too often, reductions in civil society freedoms have been justified with the fight against Covid, when their actual purpose was to bolster repressive governments by further restricting civil liberties and silencing critics. Extensive analyses by reputable human rights organizations such as Human Rights Watch confirm this trend. Many governments, for example, have expanded digital surveillance – in the form of facial recognition or contact-tracing apps – to contain the virus. All these technologies, especially when used by governments in non-open societies, endanger human rights and privacy. Governments have also used the pandemic to crack down on the right to free expression and peaceful assembly. In countries such as Brazil, Kenya or Egypt, military or police forces have physically attacked journalists, bloggers and protesters, including those who were criticizing the government's reaction to Covid-19. Restrictions on the freedom of speech and assembly are still in place in numerous countries.[26] There's an important distinction to be made here, though. In Germany, particularly in 2020, many self-styled lateral thinkers (*Querdenker:innen*), in a loose movement opposed to the government's Covid response, complained vociferously about limitations on their rights and on the freedom of expression. However, the restrictions discussed above have not taken place in Germany. The legal requirement to wear a face mask at demonstrations is not the same as the violent suppression of critical voices by the military. The abuse of power by governments during the pandemic must be reversed as quickly as possible. Feminist foreign policy, with its commitment to feminist security and human rights, prioritizes this demand and advocates for it in international organizations by putting pressure on the states that oppress their citizens.

The myth of gender ideology

There is substantial overlap between the global anti-gender movement and the international right-wing movement. There are points of inter-section: nationalism, racist fears, a susceptibility to conspiracy theories, resistance to the globalization of human rights norms, and criticism of international norms. But although the two movements feed into each other, they are not identical: left-wing actors can be antifeminist and spread anti-gender attitudes or make common cause with anti-gender actors. The current president of Mexico, López Obrador (AMLO), came to power because he was supported both by traditionally left-wing parties such as the Partido del Trabajo and by the evangelical, anti-gender party Encuentro Social. This can be explained by Mexico's increasing poverty – the focus of the left-wing parties – and violence, which right-wing parties ascribe to a moral crisis. So AMLO supports social causes while simultaneously endorsing 'traditional family values' as a strategy to contain this violence. Here 'traditional family values' serves as a euphemism for the suppression of women's and LGBTQ+ rights.

But there is a disturbing crossover between different movements and their goals in Germany too. Again and again, right-wing actors hijack and misuse women's rights and feminist slogans for their racist and nationalist agendas. A typical case is the instrumentalization of the events in Cologne on New Year's Eve 2015–16, when hundreds of sexualized attacks occurred. At the time, right-wing actors chanted racist slogans under the guise of women's rights. This was what prompted us – twenty-two feminists – to launch the campaign 'Against violence and racism. Always. Anywhere. #ausnahmslos' ('noexcuses').

Richard Grenell, the former US ambassador in Berlin and a close associate of Trump, is an excellent example of how right-wing and ultraconservative actors can defend the interests of the LGBTQ+ community while denying the same minority rights to other groups. Grenell, openly gay himself, served as a senior advisor for the Republican National Committee during Trump's re-election campaign. Tasked with political outreach to the LGBTQ+ community, he claimed that Trump was 'the most pro-gay president in American history'. This was while the Trump administration was both attempting to deny the recognition of sexual orientation and the protection of gender identity under Title VII of the Civil Rights Act of 1964 and arguing before the Supreme Court that discrimination against LGBTQ+ employees, parents and customers should be allowed on the basis of religious objections. Whether it be AMLO in Mexico, New Year's Eve in Cologne, or the attitude of the US ambassador to Germany, all these examples show that we have to pay close attention. Just because someone is ostensibly 'left wing', chants feminist slogans or is openly gay, that doesn't mean that he or she supports human rights for everyone. On the contrary, these actors can be openly antifeminist in their actions.

But of course there are also examples where the intersection between right-wing and antifeminist attitudes and policies becomes very clear, as in the case of Hungary, Brazil or the USA under President Trump. Both the former US president and the former Brazilian president, Jair Bolsonaro, maintain very close contacts with right-wing evangelicals in their countries. When Mike Pence – a supporter of the radical Christian right – became vice president under Trump, this was a great victory for right-wing evangelicals.[27] Pence is well known for his reactionary views on LGBTQ+ rights. In 2014, in his time as governor of Indiana, he supported a state bill to constitutionally prohibit same-sex marriage.[28]

The concept of gender ideology that was developed by the Vatican and by Catholic teachers and activists in the 1990s and then pushed into the mainstream helps us to understand how so many very different actors have come together to oppose human rights and the right to self-determination. According to the anti-gender actors, 'radical gender feminists' and gay rights advocates are destroying the 'natural' order of things. What is meant is the patriarchal, heteronormative order, in which women are inferior to men. If this 'natural equilibrium' is abandoned, they argue, this will lead to the destruction of the family and society. They therefore present gender (and even gender-neutral language) as a threat to society. In our policy briefing *How Anti-Feminist and Anti-Gender Ideologies Contribute to Violent Extremism – and What We Can Do about It*, we point out that hostile, sexist attitudes to women (misogyny) and support for violence against women are the factors that are most strongly linked with support for violent extremism. Studies on extremist groups (both religious fundamentalists and right-wing extremists) show that they share a powerful nostalgia for an imaginary 'golden age of male entitlement'. Nonetheless, the connection between antifeminism and violent extremism is still severely under-researched and has been woefully neglected by government policy. With deadly consequences, as shown by the attacks in Isla Vista in 2014, in Toronto in 2018 and in Tallahassee in 2018, to name just a few.[29]

Antifeminist strategies

The new actors use a wide range of strategies to mobilize the public and spare no effort in their propaganda. This includes demonstrations, public speeches, conferences, flyers, billboards, (social) media campaigns, vigils, sit-ins and disinformation campaigns. By harassing and combating progressive activists, antifeminist actors seek to maintain their preferred social order. A 2019 analysis by the Armed Conflict Location & Event Data Project (ACLED) found that peaceful protests by women, all over the world, were disproportionately met with excessive force (including tear gas and arrests) compared to protests by men or mixed-sex groups.[30] In Egypt, the government has been monitoring the online activities of feminist activists for years and has arrested young women for allegedly immoral behaviour because of content posted on TikTok or other platforms.

Another strategy is to interfere in politics on a national and an international* level. On a national level, anti-gender activists in several EU countries (Croatia, Slovenia, Slovakia, Romania and Hungary) have pushed for laws preventing the extension of spousal privileges to same-sex partners. Another equally contemptible strategy of anti-gender actors is to ensure that funding is withdrawn from feminist and LGBTQ+ organizations.

But sometimes joy and sorrow are not far apart. In June 2021 the majority of members of the European Parliament (MEPs) voted for the Matić Report on the extension of sexual and reproductive health and rights – what a success! The report was concerned partly with recognizing the right to abortion as a normal health service for women. It also demanded access to contraception, sexuality education, and an end to genital mutilation and child marriage.[31] These were the most significant recommendations to be adopted in ten years. But, during the vote, MEPs were harassed with an organized spam campaign. 'We were flooded with emails from ultraconservatives,' complained the vice president of the European Parliament, Katarina Barley. The campaign is assumed to have been instigated by a Polish think-tank, Ordo Iuris, whose disinformation was then spread by a coalition of European antifeminist actors, One of Us.[32] Fortunately, they were not successful on this occasion:† 'The vote sends a strong signal that MEPS are fully committed to protect and promote SRHR in the EU at a time when human rights in sexuality and reproduction are increasingly challenged by illiberal leaders,'[33] wrote the EU in its press release.

These international antifeminist actors are essentially mobilizing against four things. Firstly, gender as a concept, presented as a radical

---

* Our previously mentioned study, *Disrupting the Multilateral Order?*, contains many more examples.

† Annika Kreitlow, who was involved in the research and writing of our study *Disrupting the Multilateral Order?*, notes that this success was down to good preparation rather than good fortune. Many progressive forces were prepared for a massive backlash by anti-gender actors during the vote on the Matić Report, because the Estrela Report, which had similar content, had failed in 2013. This time there was much more preparation of the MEPs and better political strategies, so that centrist MEPs could not be so easily intimidated.

idea threatening to destroy all the categories that keep ordered societies together. Secondly, sexual and reproductive health and rights, including the right to abortion. All over Europe, anti-gender actors are pursuing legislative initiatives to remove the grounds for legal abortion and create new obstacles for access. They also want to give greater legal protection to doctors who refuse to offer abortion services for reasons of conscience or religion. Thirdly, they are fighting against sexuality education in schools. Their narrative is that this exposes children to unhealthy ideas which they are unable to process and lures them into abnormal sexual preferences. Fourthly, they attack the rights of the LGBTQ+ community by stirring up hostility towards LGBTQ+ mainstreaming, marriage equality, adoption by same-sex families, and the recognition of diverse gender identities.

When CFFP was investigating these attacks on women's and LGBTQ+ rights, we commissioned academics to write case studies on particular countries and regions such as the USA (under Trump), Mexico, Brazil, the EU, the Middle East and North Africa.[34]

The USA

The USA's attack on international women's rights was spearheaded by conservative NGOs and then transposed into the domestic and foreign policy of the Republican Party under Trump. Activists, politicians and diplomats not only blocked US ratification of CEDAW, the women's rights convention, but also tried to prevent and push back the international recognition of abortion rights and sexual and reproductive health. They criticized sexuality education and the concept of gender in general, particularly the recognition of diverse sexual orientations.

The origins of conservative anti-gender activities go back to the 1970s. Major triggers were the Equal Rights Amendment (1972) and *Roe* v. *Wade*, a landmark ruling by the US Supreme Court in 1973, which legalized abortion (a decision that was overturned on 24 June 2022 by a 6–3 majority in the conservative US Supreme Court). On an international level, anti-gender actors have used the USA's influence to push back similar successes, for example by blocking foreign aid funding for women's health. They have also tried to remove clauses on the protection of women's rights from international conventions, resolutions and outcome documents.

These actors put forward various narratives that are intended to undermine human rights norms: religious narratives, which see women's rights as destabilizing societies; narratives of competing rights, which present women's rights as hostile to other human rights; patriarchal populist narratives, which suggest that feminism is an elitist or foreign threat; and, finally, pseudo-scientific narratives, which aim to delegitimize an established understanding of women's health and to affirm the 'natural existence' of just two biological sexes.

Donald Trump's government had strong links to both national and international anti-gender organizations, and Trump used all these narratives in his speeches. He also introduced what has so far been the most extreme form of the global gag rule:* he cut off funding for all development programmes that did not subscribe to the 'protecting life' narrative. Although this rule was reversed in 2021, activists fear that Trump's policies will cause lasting damage. Fortunately the Biden–Harris administration has set a different course from the start – for example, with the Gender Policy Council established in the White House in March 2021. The council's task is to promote sex and gender equity in both domestic and foreign policy.[35]

A short postscript on *Roe* v. *Wade*: after a draft leaked in May 2022 had revealed that the US Supreme Court was planning to overturn the landmark ruling from 1973, the Supreme Court published its offi-

---

* The global gag rule (also known as the Mexico City policy) has been in place since 1984. It states that funding will go only to those international NGOs that have previously signed a statement that they will not perform or promote abortion. One of the organizations that suffers from this rule is the World Health Organization. The global gag rule is traditionally rescinded by Democratic administrations and reinstated by Republican ones. It was, for example, reinstated after the transition from Barack Obama to Donald Trump and, of course, rescinded in 2020.

cial ruling on 24 June 2022. This abolished the constitutional right to abortion in the USA and transferred decision-making authority to the individual states. Many US states, especially in the South, had already prepared draft legislation which made abortion illegal from the moment of the Supreme Court announcement. There is now a complete ban on abortion in thirteen US states, and in others there are restrictions and time limits. Antifeminist, anti-gender actors have always tried to make it seem as though their demands reflected the views of the majority.[36] But this isn't the case – and nor is it true of *Roe* v. *Wade*: 65 per cent of Americans are opposed to the abolition of the constitutional right to abortion and thus opposed to the Supreme Court's 2022 ruling.[37] By strategically appointing antifeminist judges to the Supreme Court, however, Donald Trump succeeded in creating a majority in the court that does not exist within the population.

What 'protecting unborn life' actually means

But we mustn't allow ourselves to think that attacks on human and women's rights are taking place only elsewhere, in far-flung countries. Attempts to restrict our rights can also come from close quarters – such as the German Bundestag – and wear smart suits. It's not just the right-wing AfD, either. In October 2020, the ruling coalition at the time (made up of the CDU/CSU and the SPD) wanted to table a motion on gender-just foreign policy (something that the Greens had already attempted in February 2019). At first I was pleased. But a few days before the motion was due to be debated in plenary, my co-director Nina and I learned that the CDU/CSU were trying to insert the following words into the motion: 'The German Bundestag urges the federal government, within the limits of the available budgetary resources, to make sexual and reproductive health and rights a focus of development cooperation *while ensuring the protection of unborn life.*' After learning this, we sought contact with members of parliament from both the CDU/CSU and the SPD and made it clear that the term 'protection of unborn life' would give antifeminist actors free rein to further restrict women's rights and the right to abortion. The 'protection of unborn life' is not neutral language, but coded. It's an expression favoured by misogynists such as Trump and Bolsonaro and by various conservative parties. Thanks to well-informed MPs and pressure from feminist civil society, the SPD – fortunately! – axed the motion. In the end it wasn't even tabled in the proposed form, as discussed during the debate on 28 October 2020.[38] SPD MP Daniela De Ridder made it clear that the motion had failed because of this last-minute demand from the Christian Democrats, which crossed a red line for the Social Democrats. I was pleased to hear this. At the same time, I would have liked to see the SPD defending this 'red line' more vigorously during the previous legislative period, when the revision of paragraphs 218 and 219a of the German Criminal Code was on the (political) table. These two paragraphs stipulate that abortion is exempt from punishment only under certain conditions and prohibit doctors from disseminating information. The coalition agreement of the new German government in November 2021 included the pledge to abolish paragraph 219a, a promise that was fulfilled – at long last! – on 24 June 2022. Since then doctors in Germany have finally been allowed to share appropriate information about abortion on their websites, making it slightly easier for women to find out about this medical procedure.*

The right to safe abortion is a human right.[39] And the defence of human rights, be it in our own countries or overseas, must be at the centre of every feminist foreign policy. Instead of the motion planned by the ruling coalition, the Greens (Bündnis 90/Die Grünen) and the Left Party (Die Linke) tabled two motions on feminist foreign policy,

---

* Ironically this was the same day on which the landmark *Roe* v. *Wade* judgement was overturned in the USA. Unfortunately, this is a striking example of how easily setbacks can occur when it comes to sexual and reproductive rights. In its coalition agreement, the new German government also announced that it would establish a commission to assess the possibility of abolishing paragraph 218 and regulating abortion outside the Criminal Code. More than a year after the coalition agreement was signed, however, it is still unclear when exactly this commission is to start its work and who will be part of it.

both of which were rejected. As was to be expected, the AfD once again showed its misogynist and populist face in the ensuing debates. AfD MPs jeered loudly at the word 'feminism' and argued that a feminist or gender-just agenda would destabilize other countries under the guise of peacemaking – a lie serving to advance their misogynist, right-wing agenda. This debate, and the CDU/CSU's last-minute attempt to incorporate the language and thinking of anti-gender actors into a motion on gender-just foreign policy (how ironic!), occurred at almost the same time as the near total ban on abortion confirmed by the Constitutional Tribunal of Poland – despite the hundreds of thousands of women and men who took to the streets in protest. Even when abortion is banned or criminalized, women and girls still terminate unwanted pregnancies. But, tragically, they do so on their own, in secret, and in unsafe conditions. These abortions – often carried out by unqualified personnel – endanger their health and even their lives. Unsafe abortions are the third most common cause of maternal deaths worldwide and, according to the WHO, lead to 5 million largely avoidable hospitalizations for abortion-related complications every year.[40] The decisions made by politicians about access to abortion have a direct impact on human lives. Trump's abortion-related restrictions on the global funding of US health assistance have negative impacts on the healthcare of women in Africa and South Asia. The report by the International Women's Health Coalition, *Crisis in Care*, describes how Trump's global gag rule affected the work of NGOs and the lives of women from early 2017 to early 2019.[41] Once Trump had been voted out, the gag rule was rescinded, but the lasting damage it caused is enormous. In 2017 the rule was tightened so that organizations were not only forbidden to provide abortions with US funds, they were not allowed to provide them at all. The rule was enforced regardless of the local laws on abortion.

All these examples and events are worrying enough. But the full extent of this assault on human rights becomes even more worrying if we look at its funding. A report on the coordination and funding of the antifeminist anti-gender actors, published by the European

Parliamentary Forum for Sexual & Reproductive Rights in June 2021, shows how human rights are being attacked. Between 2009 and 2018, a total of $707.2 million, from the USA, Russia and Europe, was invested in attacks on LGBTQ+ and women's rights in the EU. The annual budget for this movement has nearly quadrupled in this period, from $22.2 million in 2009 to $96 million in 2018.[42]

Conclusion: an unrelenting struggle

To counter the threat from these antifeminist actors, we have to roll up our sleeves, support human rights defenders and create feminist coalitions. For a start, we need to strengthen internal capacity, for example by providing additional training in these areas for police and security forces and government employees. Recognizing the threat also means clearly identifying such campaigns as strategically organized, well-funded and well-connected attacks on basic democratic and human rights. In order to protect sexual and reproductive health and rights and LGBTQ+ rights internationally and to support them in foreign policy, we must also uphold them in domestic policy. This means that countries (including Germany) must ensure unrestricted and unconditional access to abortion within their own borders, not just in the context of development projects.

Because the anti-gender actors have such strong networks, there needs to be a clear response from progressive actors. They must build networks that are just as good or better, and they need state support to do so. Public campaigns, awareness work and strategic communication are also needed in order to break through the narratives of anti-gender actors and take a clear stand for the protection of human rights. This requires both individual politicians and whole governments. Financial and moral support for (feminist) civil society is crucial for the defence of women's and LGBTQ+ rights and the protection of democracies. (Feminist) civil society must be strengthened with long-term, institutional financial support for its work, facilitated by accessible application processes. Progressive governments have a duty to protect these rights internationally. They must commit to this actively and without compromise – leading the way on their own if need be – and invest political capital – e.g. in international negotiations or collaborations for SRHR and LGBTQ+ rights. To understand the anti-gender actors better and react to their attacks, ongoing research funding is absolutely essential. Progressive governments – Germany's political elite likes to see itself in this light – and governments with an official feminist foreign policy must find the staffing, diplomatic and financial resources to confront the anti-gender actors and their attacks on human rights, and they must support feminist civil society in the fight against patriarchal and racist structures.

Anyone who identifies with a politically underrepresented group knows that we can never just sit back and relax. Our rights can be taken away from us faster than we could ever imagine. There never has been and never will be a natural progression towards more human rights. Everything that has been achieved in this area has been fought for by civil society, movements and individual activists, with their influence on governments and their work in international organizations. However tragic this may sound, the rights of women, LGBTQ+ people, people with disabilities, indigenous people and children cannot be taken for granted – and nor can universal human rights. We have always had to fight for these rights in patriarchal societies, since the patriarchy is interested only in concentrating its own power. As members of civil society, we can never rest. However exhausted we often are, we have to keep fighting, because our financial resources are minimal in comparison to those of the antifeminist actors. In patriarchal societies, including Germany, it is mainly men – as wealthy individuals, donors, and the heads of ministerial departments – who control funding. Since power, positions and resources are usually handed down from one man to another, female founders and feminist work receive a disproportionately small share of funding. This gives the antifeminist actors a head start and makes it twice as hard to catch up with them.

Jennifer Cassidy:
'Old White men were teaching
solely about old White men, and that
made me furious.'

Jennifer Cassidy is a lecturer in political science at the University of Oxford and one of the most sought-after political commentators in the UK. One major focus of her research is digital diplomacy; another is diplomacy and gender. During her studies – also at Oxford – she learned that women were categorically excluded from teaching on diplomacy and international relations: old White men taught about old White men, without taking into account the experiences and expertise of women.

Jennifer has served as a diplomatic attaché to Ireland's Permanent Mission to the United Nations, has been posted to the Kingdom of Cambodia with the European External Action Service, and has worked for the Irish Department of Foreign Affairs and Trade. In these roles, she experienced how enduring gender stereotypes are reflected in international relations. The UN General Assembly organizes its work on different subject areas in committees. One day Jennifer was working in the UN's Third Committee (Social, Humanitarian and Cultural) and found she was surrounded by women. At first she thought that the impression she'd got in her studies was wrong, and that there was equality in the world of diplomacy after all. But when she was working in the First Committee (Disarmament and International Security) later that same day, she realized that its members were mainly men. In the realm of international politics, Jennifer concluded, women continued to be associated with 'soft' topics such as development cooperation and peace, while men made decisions about war and security.

And yet women are equally affected (if not more so) by all these things: not just peace, but also war, security, economics – in short, all subject areas. They should therefore be involved in all decision-making, not just in a few isolated areas labelled as 'women's issues'. Jennifer stresses that this is not just about *how many* women are represented, but *where* they are represented.

To bring together her experiences in her studies and in the world of work, and to recognize the influence of women diplomats, Jennifer published the world's first edited volume on *Gender and Diplomacy*. Here she challenged the androcentric teaching she had experienced as a student by investigating the work of female diplomats and exposing the still pervasive role of gender stereotypes in diplomacy.

Her favourite authors include Hannah Arendt and Maya Angelou.

9 FEMINIST GLOBAL HEALTH POLICY

Another world is not only possible, she's on her way. Maybe many of
us won't be here to greet her, but on a quiet day, if I listen very carefully,
I can hear her breathing.

Arundhati Roy, *My Seditious Heart* (Chicago: Haymarket Books, 2019)

The last few years have proved that global health issues are very much a feminist concern. I've noticed this more than ever since the start of the Covid-19 pandemic. Three of my closest friends were pregnant during the pandemic, and it was an anxious time for them. Pregnant women are at particularly high risk of experiencing severe complications if they are infected with Covid-19, but it took a long time for Germany's Standing Committee on Vaccination to issue clear advice to this group.

While most people have now been vaccinated in Germany, this is an exception in global terms. In spring and early summer 2021, Germany and other wealthy countries secured 80 per cent of the available doses of vaccine for themselves. The US government even enlisted the help of dating platforms such as Tinder and Bumble to encourage people to get vaccinated and offered financial rewards to those who did.[1] During this same period – despite the efforts of the vaccine platform Covax – the poorest states received less than 1 per cent of the available doses.[2] Covax had been founded in April 2020, long before the development of the first promising vaccine candidates, by the World Health Organization (WHO), the Global Alliance for Vaccines and Immunization (Gavi) and the Coalition for Epidemic Preparedness (CEPI). Its mandate was to ensure fair distribution of vaccines and equal access worldwide. The plan was that all states would contribute to a joint fund to buy vaccines for everyone. This didn't work, as we know, because the wealthy states pushed in and signed bilateral agreements.[3]

There did seem to be a certain awareness of the problem: the final declaration of the G7 in June 2021 pledged to make 2.3 billion doses of vaccine available globally by the end of 2022.[4] But the significant delays in the fulfilment of this promise suggested that there was little political will to put it into practice. By November 2022, 1.8 billion doses of vaccine had been distributed to 146 countries by Covax. In total, 68 per cent of the global population had received at least one shot by December 2022 – the goal was 70 per cent by the middle of that year. In low-income countries, the vaccination rate was around 25 per cent.[5] Since the majority of financially poor people worldwide are women, the international distribution of vaccines had a particularly severe impact on them. Clearly, global health is a feminist issue. A feminist foreign policy demands concrete health policy concepts and measures that go beyond improved sexual and reproductive health.

Covid is a feminist issue

It is not just the issue of access to vaccines that has shown Covid's relevance for feminism. The pandemic has amplified global injustices. At the beginning, CFFP was one of the first organizations to draw attention to the lack of fairness. In early April 2020 we collaborated with WILPF to produce a paper for the policy planning staff in the German Foreign Office. The paper, entitled *A Feminist Foreign Policy Response to Covid-19*, offered a political analysis of the situation from a feminist perspective. It presented concrete demands for how foreign policy should respond to the pandemic so as to avoid further exacerbation of injustices.[6] We believe it makes sense to adopt a feminist perspective on Covid-19 because women and other politically marginalized groups are worse affected by the pandemic in so many different ways. One of these is the increase in 'domestic violence' – i.e. male attacks on women and children within their own homes. Slogans such as 'Stay home, save lives' make it clear that the authorities responsible for the pandemic response did not acknowledge or take into consideration this form of violence. This is one of many examples revealing the non-diverse viewpoint of the decision-makers. Furthermore, there is an overwhelming preponderance of women in essential occupations such as care work, which meant they were exposed to the virus to a much greater extent. From a global perspective, existing humanitarian crises have worsened because of the virus. In places where people were already going hungry, disruptions to supply chains made it harder to maintain the flow of aid. Access to sexual and reproductive health services was even more limited than usual. Health systems are still struggling because they are massively underfunded on account of a historic shifting of resources towards military security. The pandemic has also increased the concentration of power in the hands of authoritarian rulers – with all the negative consequences this entails, such as restrictions on human rights, especially those of women and LGBTQ+ individuals.

We consulted with the countries that officially had a feminist foreign policy (or parts of one) at the time: Sweden, Canada, France and Mexico. We wanted to understand how these countries were applying their feminist principles to the pandemic response so that we could make foreign policy recommendations to countries of the Global North such as Germany. It is these countries that profit from global injustices, so it is their duty to try to mitigate them – and they certainly have the resources to do so. Our investigations into the countries with feminist foreign policies showed several main areas of activity (with different emphases from country to country). They were investing considerable financial resources to ensure access to sexual and reproductive health and rights and to fight growing male violence against women. They were increasing spending on humanitarian aid, with a particular focus on those most severely affected (feminist humanitarian assistance). They were dedicating substantial sums of money to countering the negative effects of the pandemic on long-term development cooperation. They were also able to draw on many years of capacity building in the form of gender impact assessments (processes to analyse the different effects of political decisions on different genders), gender budgeting (a method of allocating funds so that all genders benefit equally) and gender mainstreaming (the inclusion of gender dimensions) in emergency policy response. This is essential for a gender-just financial and strategic response to the pandemic. Importantly, these states were providing support and additional funding to feminist civil society, recognizing its indispensable role in positive social change. They also repeatedly emphasized feminism and justice in their public relations work – e.g. in op-eds by ministers. In light of these findings, we recommended ways in which the German Foreign Office and governments in the Global North in general could implement similar measures, both immediately and in the long term.

The Covid-19 pandemic actually makes it relatively easy to understand why global health is a feminist issue – and an issue of justice. At the beginning of the pandemic, six feminist thinkers and practitioners – including me as the co-director of CFFP – approached the German Federal Ministry of Health. We asked for an open mindset and tried to raise awareness of the dimension of justice. We gathered our own data and jointly produced a study on the way government agencies were ignoring this dimension in their response to the pandemic. The resulting internal document, 200 pages in length, bears the title *Health Crisis Management in the Covid-19 Pandemic through an Intersectional Lens: Study on Blind Spots and Recommendations to the Federal Ministry of Health for Dealing with Marginalized Groups*. It's true that the Covid-19 virus doesn't choose its host on the basis of sex. Nonetheless, certain population groups are more severely affected by the pandemic than others – for example, people in shared accommodation and those in precarious social situations.

The fact is that our societies discriminate. All over the world, population groups are marginalized because of their sex, skin colour, social status, physical abilities and other characteristics. Whenever an external shock such as a virus or an economic crisis meets discriminatory structures, vulnerable groups become even more vulnerable.

This means that pandemics such as Covid-19 exacerbate injustices and have indirect as well as direct effects on health. I've already mentioned the increase in male violence against women, with all its physical and psychological consequences. This development was so rapid and so obvious that UN Secretary-General António Guterres was already calling for a 'domestic violence ceasefire' in April 2020.[7] In addition to this, people from a 'migration background' and people of colour are particularly affected by the pandemic. In the USA, for example, Black and Hispanic people and Native Americans, calculated by age group, were at two to three times greater risk of dying of Covid.[8] Another reason why injustices are heightened during pandemics is the false assumption that the crisis management policies developed by non-diverse decision-making bodies are somehow 'neutral'. The accumulation of resources, power and privileges in the hands of a small group of people over the centuries has led to a misleading understanding that the political measures decided on by this non-diverse group are universally applicable. This misjudgement leads to poor political decision-making, since the quality of policy-making depends on its ability to incorporate the many lived realities and needs of all groups in our society. In Germany there is considerable room for improvement, as shown by the homogeneous composition of the Covid-19 working group at the Leopoldina:* twenty-four men and two women. Things are no better in the senior management of the big international health organizations: a study of 200 international organizations in the field of health and health policy found that more than 70 per cent of the CEOs were men, and only 5 per cent were women from low- and middle-income countries.[9] The figures come from a report by Global Health 50/50, a new feminist organization working on global health and challenging the status quo – the fact that power in international

---

* The Leopoldina (the German National Academy of Sciences), one of the oldest scientific bodies in Germany, advises policy-makers on evidence-based decision-making. During the Covid-19 pandemic, it formed a working group which published scientific opinions on possible steps towards reopening and other political decisions: www.leopoldina.org/presse -1/nachrichten/ad-hoc-stellungnahme-coronavirus-pandemie/.

health organizations is concentrated in the hands of highly educated White men from the Global North.

A similar picture emerged for Covid-19 task forces and crisis management groups worldwide. Only two of the twenty-seven members of the White House Coronavirus Task Force (under President Trump) were women, only ten of the thirty-one members and advisors of the WHO's Emergency Committee on Covid-19, and only 20 per cent of the twenty-five members of the WHO–China Joint Mission on Coronavirus Disease 2019.[10] As already mentioned, the burden of nursing and care work rests largely on women, who make up 70 per cent of employees in the health sector worldwide.[11] The pandemic put a strain on women in the private sphere, too: when children had to be home schooled, the majority of care work, parenting and education was managed by women. The restrictions in access to sexual and reproductive health and rights were also dramatic. States such as Poland[12] and the USA[13] exploited the pandemic to limit women's bodily autonomy: in the USA, for example, eight states blocked access to abortion by declaring it a 'non-essential' health service. It has also been estimated that 2 million more girls and women will be subjected to genital mutilation over the next decade, mainly because the pandemic hampered the work of international aid programmes and forced some of them to leave the countries where they were operating.[14] In a study in the medical journal *The Lancet* in May 2020, scientists outlined the worst case scenario: that nearly 60,000 more women would die in the next six months because of pregnancy and childbirth complications related to the pandemic.[15] There are as yet no conclusive figures to confirm these prognoses, but a study published in March 2021 suggests a rise in both stillbirths and maternal deaths* in low- and middle-income countries.[16] Furthermore, a study by the Centers for Disease Control and Prevention in the USA has found that in the first year of the pandemic, 2020, maternal mortality rose

---

* The term 'maternal mortality' refers to deaths connected to pregnancy and childbirth but can also include deaths due to unsafe abortions.

by nearly 14 per cent compared to the previous year. This increase was even greater among Black and Hispanic women.[17] Besides gender, another decisive factor is class: socio-economic status is clearly linked with health. In Germany, the risk of Covid-related hospitalization is higher for recipients of unemployment benefit than for those in paid employment: 18 per cent higher for the recently unemployed, who receive a higher benefit (ALG I), and 84 per cent higher for the long-term unemployed, who receive a lower benefit (basic social security or ALG II).[18]

Despite these clear connections between health and forms of discrimination such as classism, sexism and racism, Global Health 50/50 published worrying findings in relation to the pandemic: the vast majority of the health organizations examined in their study do not so much as mention gender dynamics in their programmes and pandemic response policies. Their response to one of the greatest challenges of the twenty-first century is 'gender blind'. These knowledge gaps and this disregard for social gender hierarchies and justice can be found in over 80 per cent of Covid-related health policies, in areas such as vaccine development, prevention, access to treatment, and the protection of health sector workers.

The human right to health

Global health was a feminist concern long before Covid-19. The latest crisis has simply made a bad situation worse, to the point where no one can continue to deny what is going on. Even before the pandemic, marginalized people, particularly those marginalized in multiple ways, were among the most underserved groups in the health system. One example in the USA is the LGBTQ+ community. This remains an underserved and under-researched group,[19] even though its members are at greater risk of depression, anxiety, suicide and substance abuse than heterosexuals.[20] Women and girls face a high risk of violence, especially sexualized violence, throughout their lives. In the USA, nearly 19.3 per cent of women are raped (compared to around 1.7

per cent of men). Nearly half of all women, 43.9 per cent, experience sexual violence in the course of their lives, compared to around a quarter of men (23.4 per cent).[21] Sexualized violence (especially in childhood) often has lifelong effects on the victim's (mental) health. Such experiences lead to a greater risk of health-damaging behaviours, such as smoking and drinking, and many mental illnesses such as depression or anxiety disorders.[22] These groups therefore have special needs, which are often overlooked within our health systems. As already mentioned, there has not been sufficient research on women's health as a whole, since medical textbooks and studies often assume the prototype of the male patient. There is still a strong tendency to ignore the fact that symptoms and the mechanisms of action of drugs are different in women's bodies.[23]

This is why we need a feminist global health policy. This is an approach based on human rights and human needs. It focuses on the needs of marginalized and disadvantaged people, and its core principle is the human right to health. What this means is that no one should experience negative health consequences because of discrimination or poor treatment based on factors such as sex or gender, skin colour, sexual orientation, class, and so on. And yet such negative outcomes do occur because of the male-dominated research, teaching and practice in medicine. As long as studies are carried out only with male test subjects and their health is seen as normative, as long as dermatologists learn only about White skin, and as long as poor people have a significantly shorter life expectancy, there will be no such thing as equitable medical care. A feminist global health policy therefore challenges and dismantles power dynamics and asymmetries in governments, global health organizations and medical facilities. It demands an understanding of gender as a social construct, and it analyses and deconstructs toxic ideals of masculinity and harmful sex and gender stereotypes. A feminist global health policy aims to achieve universal healthcare – one of the UN's Sustainable Development Goals[24] – for everyone in the world, regardless of their gender, origin, sexual orientation and socio-economic status.[25]

Health diplomacy

During the Covid-19 pandemic, there was frequent talk – especially in foreign policy circles – of 'Covid diplomacy'. Experts discussed China's extensive vaccine exports and analysed how these might influence global power dynamics. And they discussed how Europe could improve its global reputation by taking a leading role in vaccine production and making these vaccines available to other countries. The term 'Covid diplomacy' is not clearly defined; it is derived from the equally vague concept of 'health diplomacy'. In most cases, however, this is about using health policy measures and arguments to achieve certain foreign policy objectives.[26] For example, one could hypothesize that countries such as China are exporting their vaccine not out of pure altruism but primarily to increase their foreign policy influence and to improve their diplomatic status in the world. This seems to have been successful in Latin America: at the beginning of the pandemic, China was often blamed for the global situation, and anti-Asian racism was rife, but exports of its vaccine, Sinovac, helped to boost the country's image. At the same time, China refused to export the vaccine to Honduras and Paraguay, because these countries had maintained good diplomatic relations with Taiwan. China regards this democratic island state as a rebel province and demands reunification under Chinese rule.

What does all this have to do with feminism? As stated above, the right to health is a human right. This human right, however, was trampled in the course of the Covid-19 pandemic, when it was used to play global power games. This is the opposite of feminist foreign policy. Health and human lives must be at the centre of a human rights-based policy; they must not become pawns in an international power struggle.

And yet foreign policy and health policy do not have to be in conflict: foreign policy can also be used to improve global health. One of the most high-profile researchers on global health is Professor Ilona Kickbusch, head of the Global Health Programme in Geneva.

212

Kickbusch describes the connection between global health and foreign policy as follows: 'Foreign policy can endanger health when diplomacy breaks down or when trade considerations trump health; health can be used as an instrument of foreign policy in order to achieve other goals; health can be an integral part of foreign policy; and foreign policy can be used to promote health goals.'[27] This statement clearly shows that, although Covid-19 put this topic at the top of the agenda, health was a feminist issue long before the current pandemic.

What is global health?

The World Health Organization defines health as 'a state of complete physical, mental and social wellbeing'[28] – and a human right. So the WHO definition covers much more than the mere absence of disease and includes social and political dimensions. Global health, in contrast, is somewhat harder to define. In simple terms, it encompasses an area of teaching, research and practice which is concerned with the global distribution of health and disease. It focuses particularly on global injustices and the needs of marginalized groups.[29]

(Global) health can never be regarded as an isolated political field but is linked to all other areas of politics. The concept of the 'social determinants of health' refers to the fact that people's health is influenced not just by illnesses but also by non-medical factors such as gender, social status and level of education – or combinations of these factors. These aspects determine 30 to 55 per cent of a person's state of health.[30] This applies to all countries, regardless of their income level. What this means for women, for example, is that because of their sex, and because they are disproportionately poor and less educated, they are also disproportionately likely to have worse health outcomes.

Colonial tendencies in questions of health

Global health as a field of research and policy is inextricably linked with its colonial history. Its origins lie in tropical medicine – a medical speciality that was concerned mainly with the health of colonialists in the African colonies.[31] Global health is the extension of this field of colonial tropical medicine, which was 'designed to control colonized populations and make political and economic exploitation by European and North American powers easier.'[32] Even today, many organizations and institutions working in this area have a reference to 'tropical medicine' in their names – for example, the London School of Hygiene and Tropical Medicine (LSHTM) or the German Society for Tropical Medicine, Travel Medicine and Global Health.[33] And these same organizations still have a major influence on debates and research – a degree from LSHTM, for example, is seen as guaranteeing a successful career in global health.

Because of this historical dimension, a feminist global health policy is closely linked with demands for the decolonization of global health. A recent example of the colonial inheritance of global health policy was the proposal by French scientists that Africa and its inhabitants could be used as test subjects for Covid-19 vaccines (but would have to go to the back of the queue when it came to the actual distribution of the vaccines).[34] As terrible and shocking as this proposal sounds, there's nothing new about it. In 1996, Pfizer conducted clinical studies for a new meningitis drug on children in Kano State, Nigeria – without gaining the parents' consent, and without giving adequate information on the risks and side-effects. Eleven children died in the course of this study.[35] In 2014, a fifteen-year-old girl went blind during a clinical study on HIV drugs in Zimbabwe; the incident was never properly investigated by the pharmaceutical company responsible.[36] There are many similar examples where researchers have acted as though the ethical principles of clinical research didn't apply outside the Global North. This 'tradition' has its roots in colonial history: in 1906, the German physician and bacteriologist Robert Koch set

214

up what he called 'concentration camps' in German East Africa and conducted experiments on humans to establish the optimal dosage of drugs for sleeping sickness (African trypanosomiasis). These were experiments that, in Germany, would have been carried out only on animals. Thousands of people experienced pain, blindness and death as a result, a price that Koch and his team accepted without hesitation.[37] Today, Germany's largest public health institution is named after him: the Robert Koch Institute, now famous for publishing the daily Covid figures in Germany during the pandemic. According to a radio report on the subject by Julia Amberger, 'Medicine played a key role in the colonization of Africa. Without medical progress, Africa could never have been explored and exploited. At the time, the most prestigious experts in tropical medicine came from Germany.'[38] The most prominent of all was the Nobel Prize laureate Robert Koch. 'Colonial medicine was not designed to help people in need. It served to boost the colony's economy and to provide new knowledge for German science and the pharmaceutical industry.'[39]

In recent years there have been increasingly emphatic demands for a decolonization of global health. From January to December 2020, more than fifty scholarly articles were published on this subject.[40] But as the researcher Laura Mkumba notes, the decolonization movement has existed since the 1960s – and every now and then its persistence has been rewarded with success.* One example of the decolonization of institutions of international politics was Oxfam's decision to move its headquarters from the UK to Kenya in 2014. The executive director at the time, Winnie Byanyima, said that this step reflected the need to strengthen the 'voices of the south' in management.[41]

Ignoring the vulnerability of indigenous groups leads to disastrous results. In Arizona, where members of the Navajo Nation live in reser-

---

* In the 1960s the term 'decolonization' still meant the actual end of colonization and the political independence of the former colonies. One of the first people to expand the concept to the cultural realm was Ngũgĩ wa Thiong'o, in his 1986 book *Decolonise the Mind*, in which he evokes ideas from the 1960s. In its beginnings, then, the decolonization movement was not focused primarily on global health.

vations, a disproportionately large number of people died of Covid-19 in 2020. This was because of poor conditions of hygiene and inadequate infrastructure: around 30 per cent of the people in the region have no access to running water or electricity, and supermarkets and hospitals are few and far between.[42] All these things are the result of colonial continuities and the ongoing systematic oppression of non-White people in the USA.

In an article entitled 'Decolonising global health: if not now, when?', the authors demand a paradigm shift, a leadership shift and a knowledge shift. Paradigm change requires a completely new narrative about what health equity is and how it can be achieved. First of all, the world must admit that the greatest threats to health are colonization, racism, sexism, capitalism and other oppressive power dynamics. A change in leadership requires the Global North to take a step back and let previously underrepresented voices, especially women of colour, contribute to decisions on health policy. The call for a 'knowledge shift' takes us back to the question discussed at the beginning of this book – about what kind of knowledge is viewed as legitimate – and dominates or even suppresses other forms of knowledge. If global health is to be decolonized, local medical knowledge must be recognized. Above all, however, other lived realities must be valued. For example, lockdowns and social distancing don't work for those living in crowded conditions, such as refugees in mass accommodation or migrant workers in slums. Nor is regular handwashing an option here.[43]

In times of crisis, the powerful – those who hold interpretive authority within a society – have always created scapegoats to distract people from the real causes of the crisis. In times of plague, Jewish communities were systematically attacked; during the AIDs epidemic in the 1980s, gay men and others in the LGBTQ+ community were ostracized; and during the Covid-19 pandemic, history repeated itself: the names 'Wuhan virus' and 'Chinese virus' led to a rise in hate crimes and violence against Chinese and East Asian population groups.[44] Historically, the search for scapegoats for social and political crises has always served to further oppress already marginalized groups and distract attention from those who are actually responsible.

Global injustices: North versus South

A central pillar of global health is the collection of worldwide health data. The Global Burden of Disease (GBD) study is based on a collaboration between more than 7,000 researchers from 156 countries and has examined the global burden of disease at regular intervals since 1990. Initiated by the School of Public Health at Harvard, the World Health Organization and the World Bank, it is now funded by the Bill and Melinda Gates Foundation and coordinated by the Institute for Health Metrics and Evaluation at the University of Washington. The GBD study assesses the frequency and effects of individual diseases, particular risk factors, and also the average life expectancy in the different countries and regions of the world. A glance at the findings of the last study from 2020 makes it clear that health is nowhere near equally distributed across the world. The average life expectancy in the Global North is around 78 to 82 years; in Lesotho, one of the poorest countries in the world, people live on average for only 52 years.[45]

But it is not just harmful and life-shortening illnesses that are unequally distributed across the globe, it is also access to essential health services and medicine. This remains a huge problem, especially in the Global South. The debate over the patents for Covid-19 vaccines highlights a long-standing problem: findings from publicly funded research are bought by pharmaceutical companies and developed into products, which are then sold for a profit. The priority goes to wealthy countries who can afford the vaccines and can secure access fast enough (as the USA and all the European countries did). True, these countries promised to release leftover doses to other countries via the Covax initiative, but this is still not fair distribution.[46] The European Union has systematically blocked calls to waive the patents on vaccines. Yet this is the only way that companies in other countries could produce their own vaccines and supply them to local populations.[47] The international arena for this debate is the World Trade Organization.

Not only is access to existing drugs unfairly distributed, but research for new drugs is determined by profits. Diseases that occur mainly in tropical climate zones attract so little research that a group of around twenty of them are now referred to by scientists as 'neglected tropical diseases' (NTDs).[48] These diseases occur in around 150 countries and affect about one in five people in the world.[49] One example is intestinal worms, which are common when people have no access to clean drinking water.

These power asymmetries between the Global North and the Global South are also reflected in the composition of decision-making bodies in influential organizations: 70 per cent of the senior figures in global health organizations are men, 84 per cent come from countries in the Global North, and 94 per cent attended a university in the Global North.[50] Feminist foreign policy in the area of global health seeks to smash this '70–80–90' glass wall (with these figures, we're looking at more than just a glass ceiling). We need to close the power gap between North and South, help to distribute power fairly and decolonize the health sector. This would include eradicating all forms of supremacy (such as White supremacy) in all areas of global health: within states, between states and on a global level.

Sexual and reproductive health and rights

The health issue that is perhaps most prominent and most present in the public debate in connection with feminism is sexual and reproductive health and rights (SRHR) – a topic that also occupies an important place in the existing feminist foreign policies of different countries. The term covers the right to sexual self-determination and the right to reproductive and sexual healthcare, which are recognized as central human rights. This includes, for example, the right to decide how many children to have, and when, and the right to freedom from sexual violence.[51] Women's bodies are frequently the subject of public debates, and many parts of the world have laws that restrict pregnant women's bodily autonomy. A particular focus here is abortion. Ultimately it's quite simple: access to abortion is a human right. The United Nations Population Fund clearly defines abortion as part of SRHR.[52] And the Office of the UN High Commissioner for Human Rights defines it as a violation of human rights when access to abortion is denied or obstructed. This also applies when women have to secure third-party authorization before an abortion, as in Germany.[53] Here pregnant women are obliged to attend a counselling session before the procedure – no abortion is carried out without the signature of an official pregnancy advice service such as the family planning association Pro Familia, the Protestant social welfare organization Diakonie, or another provider. The Office of the High Commissioner for Human Rights has clearly shown that the criminalization of abortion is a human rights violation – so Germany alone is violating human rights about 100,000 times a year.[54] The UN makes it clear that it is part of a state's human rights obligations to ensure that women are not denied their human right to health.[55] Germany is therefore violating its own human rights obligations as enshrined in international law. CFFP pointed this out in a policy briefing during the coalition negotiations in November 2021.[56]

In patriarchal societies, it is standard practice to hamper or block women's access to SRHR, since men want to control women's bodies. This includes decisions about pregnancy, since large numbers of offspring increase a patriarch's status and keep his womenfolk busy in their allocated sphere – i.e. the private sphere. The topic of contraception also has a horrifyingly racist history. Medical progress and developments in the area of SRHR are based partly on experiments on indigenous people and people of colour, especially women of colour. In *Medical Apartheid*, Harriet A. Washington details the long history of human experiments, forced treatment and deliberate mistreatment of Black people in the USA. And it's a shocking history. For example, the contraceptive pill was first tested on women in Puerto Rico, at a time when only animal tests had been conducted in the USA.

These women often had a low level of education and were very poor, which explains their interest in contraception and their willingness – probably springing from deprivation and ignorance – to accept the high risk of the untested drug. It is not known exactly why these women were chosen, but is more than likely that they were exposed to far higher risks than would normally be considered acceptable.[57]

Forced sterilization also has a long history and has often been used to prevent marginalized groups from reproducing. There is substantial evidence, for example, that this was a common practice in Canada from the 1930s. In just a few months in 2018, an organization found more than fifty cases of forcibly sterilized indigenous women in the province of Saskatchewan alone.[58] Another example is the Black civil rights activist Fannie Lou Hamer, who went to hospital in Mississippi in 1961 to have a small cyst removed from her stomach and woke up to find that her uterus had been removed without her knowledge or consent.[59] Three years later, Hamer testified in front of a panel in Washington that six out of ten Black women who went to North Sunflower County Hospital for treatment were discharged with their tubes tied – i.e. sterilized.[60] This type of forced sterilization was so common at the time that it was referred to as a 'Mississippi appendectomy'.[61]

But there's no need to look to America for such practices. In Germany, the Nazi state pursued a double standard of sexual politics. For 'Aryan' women, the policy was strictly pronatalist, but abortions for eugenic reasons were supported under the guise of the 'Law for the Prevention of Offspring with Hereditary Diseases'. Abortions for women classed as Jews (or of foetuses classed as Jewish) were also encouraged, for pseudoscientific reasons of 'race hygiene'. And women thought to have disabilities were often forcibly sterilized.[62]

So while (predominantly) White feminists have fought for the right to abortion for centuries, women of colour have sometimes had to fight for the right to become pregnant in the first place – and for the right and the opportunity to raise their own children in healthy conditions. Since many Black feminists did not feel represented in the debate over abortion in the 1990s, they (in particular the organization SisterSong) developed the concept of 'reproductive justice'.

Reproductive justice focuses more on practical access to abortion. What use is a legally guaranteed right if women are actually unable to get an abortion because of the costs, the distance to the nearest provider, or other obstacles? This debate shows, once again, how important it is to take an intersectional approach. The reality of White women from the Global North is not the reality of all women. We need an intersectional feminism which takes into account different circumstances and lived realities.[63] And another thing these examples make clear is that the debate on abortion is not so much about the ethical issue of when life begins as about the control of female bodies by men and patriarchal systems.

Besides the political debate about women's right to bodily autonomy, the quality and status of women's health within a country has an impact on society as a whole. We know, for example, that a country's economic development (measured by its gross domestic product) is directly linked to women's health. If women have better access to contraceptives, if mothers are well cared for, and if women can benefit from health services, this leads, statistically, to a direct increase in GDP, a drop in child mortality, and a higher life expectancy for men.[64]

Forgotten groups in health policy

However, a global feminist health policy requires more than just a focus on sexual and reproductive health and rights. Both domestic health systems and global health suffer from the fact that marginalized groups are discriminated against and their needs are overlooked.

Figures from the USA show how deeply rooted this injustice is. Symptoms (especially pain) of indigenous people and people of colour are taken much less seriously; they are less likely to be prescribed painkillers, and they are often not given the full range of diagnostic procedures.[65] In the UK, maternal mortality is roughly four times higher for Black women than White women, though there may be various reasons for this – probably a mixture of racial discrimination, classism and structural inequalities.[66]

Another group that faces discrimination and neglect in health systems worldwide is LGBTQ+ individuals. For trans people in particular, access to gender-affirming therapies* and mental healthcare is a huge challenge worldwide.[67] The classification of transgender identity as a mental illness (still common in many countries – e.g. Hungary and Russia – despite a statement by the WHO affirming the contrary)[68] and the compulsory medical treatment required to change one's legal sex (e.g. sterilization) further exacerbate the stigmatization and marginalization of trans people.

Recognition of gender as a social construct, and of gender identities beyond the heteronormative norm, is not just lacking in many countries but is also largely absent from the concept and categories of global health. Fewer than 40 per cent of global health organizations work with a definition of gender that goes beyond women and girls. And trans people are only mentioned in about 10 per cent of definitions of gender.[69]

Research on health is not neutral either. Both in medical research and in teaching, male bodies were long considered the norm. For example, symptoms that manifested differently in women were classified as 'atypical' – if they were described at all.† Diseases that affect women and those with uteruses are even more neglected in research. There is, for example, five times as much research on erectile dysfunction (which affects about 19 per cent of all men) as on premenstrual syndrome, from which around 90 per cent of women suffer.[70] Furthermore, non-binary people are hardly ever mentioned in health data and research.

---

* Gender reassignment/gender-affirming therapies are terms used to describe the medical measures undertaken by trans people to adapt their body to their gender identity. These may include hormone therapies and/or operations; the interventions desired vary from patient to patient and cannot be generalized.

† For more on the topic of gender bias in research, see Caroline Criado Perez, *Invisible Women* (London: Chatto & Windus, 2019).

Conclusion: for a feminist global health policy

What might a feminist global health policy look like? What needs to be done to address the numerous injustices in the health sector? First and foremost, gender and feminism must be taken into account in global health. It's not enough to pay lip service to these ideas, and it's not enough for countries such as Germany to campaign for sexual and reproductive health and rights abroad while actively violating human rights at home. The recognition of the human right to health must be reflected equally in both domestic and foreign policy-making.*

Within global health, all organizations and institutions must recognize the fact that gender is a social construct and that this is not just about the health of women and girls. There has to be representation of diverse perspectives in positions of leadership. And there needs to be research that disaggregates data by sex and gender. Women and LGBTQ+ individuals must participate in clinical studies, and more effort and funds must go into research on illnesses that affect mainly women and politically marginalized groups. There needs to be sufficient funding of health facilities, measures and research that focus on these groups and take their needs seriously. It is vital to provide sexual and reproductive health services for all people worldwide, including those caught up in conflicts and humanitarian emergencies.[71]

The current global health system cannot resolve the many structural injustices mentioned above which determine individual health. This means that the existing health system cannot guarantee health. A feminist foreign policy prioritizes the individual health of all people – following the principles of feminist security – and uses all the instruments of diplomacy and foreign policy to ensure that the human right to health is achieved for all.

---

* After a long process, the German government published its new strategy on global health in October 2020. But, while the global goals are very ambitious and fundamentally feminist, the document fails to consider national health policy. This is an element that is essential from a feminist perspective: global health has to start at home.

Beatrice Fihn:
'It's absurd that force and weapons
are seen as guarantors of
(inter)national security.'

Swedish lawyer Beatrice Fihn was the director of the International
Campaign to Abolish Nuclear Weapons (ICAN) until the end of
January 2023. For years, she and her organization have been successfully mobilizing civil society to work towards demilitarization. In
2017 ICAN received the Nobel Peace Prize for its work towards the
Treaty on the Prohibition of Nuclear Weapons, which came into force
in January 2021. The treaty prohibits the ratifying states from possessing or using nuclear weapons.

Again and again, Beatrice has been told that the relevance of the
treaty is questionable, since the nine states that currently possess
nuclear weapons – the USA, France, the UK, Russia, China, Israel,
North Korea, India and Pakistan – will not sign it. She firmly rejects
this argument, stressing the importance of normative change. The
treaty creates a new narrative, which radically questions the traditional
thinking on state security and emphasizes human security. Nor does
she exclude the possibility that the nuclear powers will eventually join
the treaty. After all, many of these countries are democracies, where
the will of the people counts. And societies all over the world are
increasingly vocal in their opposition to nuclear weapons. When civil
society builds up pressure and consistently demands demilitarization,
this can lead to long-term structural change.

As an example, Beatrice mentions the WPS agenda, which often
met with patronizing smiles when it first emerged around the turn
of the millennium. Gradually, however, it began to have an effect on

societal and institutional structures. The awarding of the Nobel Prize to ICAN sends an important signal, she argues: it makes it clear that civil society's often exhausting struggle for demilitarization is worth while – even though long-term successes are seldom directly visible. The successful work of civil society towards international bans on land mines and cluster munitions shows that the understanding of what is right and wrong is changing. The next target, she suggests, should be fully autonomous weapons systems – e.g. autonomous drones.

Beatrice's favourite books include *Read and Riot: A Pussy Riot Guide to Activism* by Nadya Tolokonnikova and *The Rise: Creativity, the Gift of Failure, and the Search for Mastery* by Sarah Lewis.

10 NO CLIMATE JUSTICE WITHOUT FEMINISM

We are unheard, not voiceless.
Fighting for our present, not just our future.
We will not be prisoners of injustice!
Mitzi Jonelle Tan and Fridays For Future MAPA*

20 September 2019. It was early in the morning, but the sun was shining. For weeks, the Fridays for Future movement and its global leaders – Greta Thunberg (Sweden), Luisa Neubauer and Leonie Bremer (Germany), Vanessa Nakate (Uganda), Mitzi Jonelle Tan (Philippines), Maria Reyes (Mexico) and Nicki Becker (Argentina) – had been calling for a third global climate strike. Many other activists from international movements had added their voices. In Germany alone there were around 500 demonstrations, with 1.4 million people taking to the streets. Worldwide, several million people joined the protests, creating a global mass movement.

The 20th of September went down in history as a day of activism. But this same date also marked a historic failure of the German government at the time – a coalition of the centre-left SPD and the conservative CDU/CSU – in its response to the climate crisis. On this Friday in September 2019, the government's 'climate cabinet' presented its key points for more climate protection. When introducing the plans, the finance minister and vice chancellor at the time, Olaf Scholz (SPD), said: 'Fridays for Future has been a wake-up call for all of us, and has reminded us that we need to take steps we haven't taken in past years.' Yet Luisa Neubauer criticized the cabinet's resolutions: 'This isn't a breakthrough, it's a scandal.'[1] The German Constitutional

---

* MAPA stands for 'most affected people and areas'.

Court reached the same conclusion: at the end of April 2021, it ruled that parts of the new law on climate protection were unconstitutional. The law did not contain sufficient provisions for reducing emissions after 2030 – and this, according to the court, violated the fundamental rights of the younger generation.*

Of course we didn't know about any of this when we gathered early on 20 September 2019 near the Brandenburg Gate in Berlin. I was there with my activist friends, Nina, Bianca and Jeannette, and we were holding up the signs we'd made the night before. My one – with the message 'Girls Just Wanna have FunDamental Climate Justice' – would also see action in subsequent climate strikes. Nina's message was 'Destroy Patriarchy Not Our Planet'; Jeannette's was 'There is No Equality on a Dead Planet'; Bianca's was 'Greta & Luisa & Maja & You', a reference to the climate policy pioneers of the Global North, Greta Thunberg, Luisa Neubauer and Maja Göpel. Our placards were unmistakably feminist. But what does the climate have to do with the end of patriarchy? This chapter will explain.

Led by women

It's a striking fact that the international climate movement is led by women. Historically, it has mainly been indigenous women and women of colour who have risked their lives fighting to preserve the basis of our existence. In general this isn't even about the future; it's purely a matter of survival in the present. In many parts of the world, the climate crisis is already having a catastrophic impact, with droughts, storms, wildfires, landslides and floods threatening lives and livelihoods. In Pakistan in summer 2022, more than 1,700 people lost their lives in floods. Already, three times as many people are being displaced by the climate crisis as by conflicts. Worldwide,

---

* Germany once again failed to meet its self-imposed climate targets for 2022. This has been blamed mainly on the coal-fired power plants that are being used as an alternative to gas from Russia.

95 per cent of fish stocks have declined. Deadly heatwaves are on the rise, even in our latitudes, and it has been estimated that around 100,000 heat-related deaths per year globally can be attributed to climate change.[2] Activists, however, lead a particularly dangerous existence. 2020 saw a record number of murders of climate and environmental activists: 227 in total – i.e. more than four per week.[3] In 2021 the figure was over 200 again.[4] More than 1,700 of these activists have been murdered in the last ten years.[5] One of the three most dangerous countries is the Philippines, where 23-year-old Mitzi Jonelle Tan has helped to establish the local Fridays For Future group (Youth Advocates for Climate Action Philippines) and leads the fight for climate justice. The following figures from her country highlight her courage: in 2019, forty-three people fighting for the environment, climate justice and the protection of indigenous lands were murdered, and in the following year twenty-nine people lost their lives fighting for these causes.* This makes the Philippines the most dangerous country in Asia for land and environmental defenders.[6]

This is partly down to the smear campaign by the government of the former president, Rodrigo Duterte, and to the widespread impunity for murderers. At the end of December 2020, police and soldiers gained access to the land of the Tumandok, a community on the Philippine island of Panay, where they killed nine leaders and arrested another seventeen people. The Tumandok and knowledgeable observers have spoken of a deliberate attack aimed at silencing the group. For years they have resisted a proposed dam – the internationally funded Jalaur mega-dam – which would flood the fields and houses of around 17,000 people.[7] The news magazine *Der Spiegel* described the situation as follows: 'Anyone who resists the Duterte regime, anyone who opposes injustices, is branded a communist or terrorist, arrested or killed.'[8]

---

* These and the following figures are all documented murders. It is assumed that the real murder rates are much higher.

Worldwide, more than a third of murdered environmental defenders are indigenous. Although they constitute only 5 per cent of the global population, indigenous peoples own 18 per cent of the global land area,[9] containing around 80 per cent of global biodiversity.[10] In fact, the climate and environmental movement has its origins in indigenous populations, because, historically speaking, they are disproportionately affected by the destruction of the environment. Far too often, their commitment to preserving the environment – the basis of our existence – costs them their lives.[11]

In my interview with Mitzi Jonelle Tan, she confirmed the life-threatening situation of activists in the Philippines and talked about the tangible effects of climate change. When she was growing up, there were about twenty typhoons a year in the Philippines, but these storms have become more and more deadly. The evidence indicates that the Philippines is the country most at risk from the climate crisis.[12] 'That's why we have no choice but to fight,' says Mitzi, who has been involved in climate activism since 2017. But the situation for activists like her has deteriorated, especially since 2020. This has a lot to do with the former president, Rodrigo Duterte. Duterte is known for calling women 'bitches', making public jokes about rape, and ordering soldiers to shoot female guerrillas in the vagina to render them 'useless'.[13] In July 2020 his government adopted an anti-terror law allowing any form of activism or criticism of the government to be labelled as terrorism. This meant that the state could treat activists with the utmost severity.

Greta Thunberg and Amnesty International condemned the law in the strongest terms. It increases the dangers facing climate and environmental activists and hugely restricts fundamental rights.[14] Even before this, human rights activists and rural labourers had been strategically targeted by 'red tagging' – i.e. accused of planning communist uprisings against the Philippine government and constitution. But the anti-terrorism law means that anyone with criticisms of the government's plans or legislation – including the anti-terrorism law itself – can be viewed as a terrorist.[15] When I interviewed Mitzi for this book, her closing words were: 'If you're a climate activist here, you have to expect to be arrested or murdered.'[16]

According to the NGO Global Witness, campaigning for climate and environmental protection is most dangerous in Latin America. More than two-thirds of the murders of climate and environmental activists committed in 2020 took place there, in countries such as Colombia (65 murders), Mexico (30), Brazil (20), Honduras (17), Guatemala (13), Nicaragua (12) and Peru (6).* In 2021, Latin America was still the most dangerous region for land and environmental defenders.[17] One of the best-known cases is that of the environmental activist Berta Cáceres, the leader of the Council of Popular and Indigenous Organizations of Honduras, who was shot dead in 2016. A commission of experts concluded that a conglomerate of actors were responsible for the planning and execution of the murder and the attempted cover-up: officials, state forces such as the police and military, and employees of Agua Zarca, the company that was to operate the planned hydroelectric power station which Cáceres had been protesting against.[18] Seven men, including a manager of this company, were condemned to long prison terms.[19]

Nineteen-year-old Maria Reyes is one of the leaders of Fridays for Future in Mexico. Maria came to climate justice via feminism. As a woman in Mexico, you have to be constantly on your guard: this is one of the most dangerous countries in the world for the female population. Femicides are widespread – every day, ten women and girls are murdered (usually by men) just because of their sex.[20] Maria says that her understanding of her own situation as a woman from a working-class family and a victim of racist discrimination has made her more aware of socio-political contexts and connections. At some point she understood that everything was connected to the climate crisis: the oppression of women, indigenous people and people of colour, the capitalist exploitation of the planet, colonization. When

---

* In 2019 at least five climate and environmental activists were murdered in each of these countries, in descending order.

I interviewed her for this book, she said, 'It's crazy – we're fighting against the whole system. Far too often, people from the Global North treat us as if they were White saviours. I'm working on changing this narrative.'[21]

Climate protection: an intensely feminist issue

The response to the climate crisis is a perfect example of the need for a feminist foreign policy. The climate crisis can never be overcome with national political strategies; it requires global solutions. The necessary foreign policy actions must be agreed on in international forums. Furthermore, the climate crisis requires a response that overturns existing power relations and ensures justice – something that feminism is well equipped to do. In order to achieve climate justice and keep global warming to less than 1.5 degrees Celsius (as stipulated in the Paris Agreement), we need to change our political and economic system. The new system cannot be led by the same people who have helped to construct and lead the current destructive system. These people, with their imperialist, exploitative, capitalist mindset, cannot facilitate a climate-friendly future. This is why positions of power in this new system must go to socially marginalized people. Otherwise old mistakes will be repeated.

So why is the fight against the climate crisis a feminist issue? It's quite simple: the oppressive dynamics of patriarchy, combined with pervasive male violence against women, form part of the reason why our environment is being exploited, oppressed and destroyed. The political scientist Valerie Hudson and her team used their research to prove empirically what feminist intellectuals in the field of ecology had been pointing out for years: 'Societies that subordinate and exploit women also subordinate and exploit Mother Earth.'[22] Patriarchy subjugates not only women and other marginalized groups but also our environment – in the most harmful way possible.

Earth Overshoot Day

Global warming and the resulting climate crisis are threatening our ecosystems, water supply, food security and human health. Every year, this is demonstrated by Earth Overshoot Day, the day when the natural resources for one year have been used up. In 2021 Earth Overshoot Day was at the end of July, but Germany reached its own 'overshoot day' earlier, on 5 May. If we look at the overshoot days of different countries worldwide, it becomes clear that, for countries of the Global North, the date on which the natural resources for a year have been used up tends to be in the first half of the year.[23] For countries of the Global South, it's in the second half. In other words, industrial nations are destroying the Earth, the basis of all human existence, with particular speed and efficiency – at the expense of the countries and people in the Global South.

The time for action was yesterday. Rapid measures in line with scientific demands are indispensable if we are to protect our planet from further disastrous changes and to limit global warming to 1.5 degrees compared to pre-industrial levels. The crucial thing here is that 1.5 degrees is the tipping point: it simply means that the situation will not go from disastrous to catastrophic. So it's not that the climate crisis begins when the temperature rises by 1.5 degrees; rather, this is the point above which it becomes a global catastrophe. For far too many people, communities and countries, even a 1.5 degree rise is a disaster.[24] Even if we as an international community were to succeed in keeping below 1.5 degrees, every half-degree more will lead to regular, devastating natural disasters with countless deaths. In *The Climate Book*, Greta Thunberg writes that the average global temperature has already risen by around 1.2 degrees since pre-industrial times. On the basis of existing policies – if we carry on with business as usual – the Intergovernmental Panel on Climate Change (IPCC) estimates that global warming will reach about 3.2 degrees by the year 2100.[25] The climate crisis can no longer be overcome; all we can do is prevent even worse outcomes. Even if we achieve the 1.5-degree target, the struggle is not over.

The climate crisis doesn't affect everyone equally

In May 2021, I was one of three experts invited to the German Bundestag. My remit was to talk to the subcommittee on civil crisis prevention and conflict resolution about the work of the German government on the WPS agenda. I criticized the fact that climate justice did not yet play a significant role in the government's actions. After my presentation, an MP from the right-wing AfD party commented: 'What do you mean about injustice and global warming? As far as I know, the sun shines on everyone equally.' I expect this snide remark was intended to delegitimize what I had said – but of course it didn't succeed.

Clearly, the whole world is feeling the effects of the steadily worsening climate crisis and the extreme weather conditions it brings. The resulting crises and conflicts also have far-reaching impacts. However, it quickly becomes clear that the climate crisis doesn't affect everyone equally. This is because our societies discriminate: all over the world, people are marginalized because of their sex, skin colour, social status, physical abilities and other characteristics. Whenever external shocks such as the climate crisis meet discriminating structures, groups that are already disadvantaged become even more vulnerable.

In Uganda, for example, women receive no compensation when harvests fail because of weather events such as floods or droughts. This is because compensation goes only to landowners (who are mainly men), even though women work the fields and this is their livelihood.[26] 80 per cent of people displaced by the climate crisis are women, who are exposed to a greater risk of gender-specific violence and human trafficking while on the move.[27] 'While they sleep, wash, bathe or dress in emergency shelters, tents or camps, the risk of sexual violence is a tragic reality of their lives as migrants or refugees,' says Michelle Bachelet, former UN high commissioner for human rights. 'Compounding this is the increased danger of human trafficking, and child, early and forced marriage, which women and girls on the move endure.'[28] At present, however, they are not entitled to any special protection under the Geneva Convention, which defines a refugee as someone forced to flee because of persecution, war or violence.[29]

Oppressive societal or religious gender norms and 'traditions' (such as restrictive dress codes or the burden of unpaid care work) mean that women are less mobile and less able to take action in natural or other disasters.[30] They are also less likely to learn to swim and are not taken into consideration in local emergency planning. During the tsunami in Asia in 2004, in which more than 227,000 people lost their lives, many women were stuck at home with their children when the wave came, while the men were out and about and were better able to flee – 70 per cent of the fatalities were women. Furthermore, women and children are much more exposed to male violence in the aftermath of natural disasters such as floods, droughts, bushfires or other extreme weather events. During displacement, in refugee camps, or after disasters, the rule of law is suspended and normal protections do not exist. Women are also more likely to die in heatwaves. And pregnant women are especially badly affected by extreme weather conditions.[31] In short, the climate crisis exacerbates existing injustices.

A further factor is that women are substantially poorer than men worldwide. For example, the twenty-two richest men in the world have more wealth than all the women in Africa put together.[32] Poor women are much more dependent on natural resources to secure the necessities of life – and it is these resources that are under pressure in the climate crisis. This is doubly unfair given that women, because of gender norms and their precarious financial status, consume less than men and have therefore contributed less to the climate crisis. Women's greater vulnerability has its roots in economic inequality. This is a problem that most governments don't seem to care about:

a 2020 study by the World Bank showed that 100 of the 190 states examined still had no laws to guarantee equal pay for equal work.[33]

But it is not only women who are disproportionately affected by the climate crisis. Racism, classism and ableism also lead to differing degrees of impact. Poor people, Black and indigenous people, people of colour and ethnic minorities, for example, are more often exposed to air pollution – partly because they're more likely to live in polluted areas – and therefore die earlier.[34] At the end of 2020, a nine-year-old Black girl in the UK, Ella Adoo-Kissi-Debrah, became the first person in the world for whom air pollution was officially cited as a cause of death.[35] People with disabilities do not have the same opportunities to flee from climate disasters. In summer 2021, when terrible storms caused catastrophic floods in western Germany, most inhabitants tried to reach safety. But twelve residents in a home for disabled people drowned because they were not rescued in time and were unable to escape the floods on their own.[36]

Climate justice = human justice

For me as a feminist, the implications of this injustice and marginalization are clear: the fight against global warming must be conducted in a way that tackles these injustices. This is the only way to ensure that we can live peacefully, safely and sustainably on a healthy planet. And this is what the concept of 'climate justice' is all about.

Climate justice – mentioned as a priority in the Paris Agreement[37] – requires us to see the climate catastrophe as a complex problem of social injustice and to place the most severely affected people and regions of the world at the centre of political decision-making. This means that a policy of sustainable energy production and emissions reduction is not enough. It's true that the burning of fossil fuels is the main driver of climate change, and that states all over the world subsidize this industry to the tune of $US500 billion every year.[38] Germany alone pays out $70 billion.[39] To save the Earth, however, we need a much broader and more holistic way of thinking. We need to focus on the causes – such as an exploitative economic system with non-sustainable production methods and a racist and patriarchal social system with oppressive structures. In short, we need an intersectional analysis of the climate catastrophe and its consequences.

Climate justice means understanding that we are dealing not simply with a climate catastrophe and global warming but with a climate catastrophe and global warming in an unjust world – a world where human rights do not apply to everyone equally. This means that green technologies alone are not a panacea: even if global society succeeded in staying below 1.5 degrees of warming by the end of the century, marginalized population groups would still be disproportionately affected by the existing climate crisis.

Research by Oxfam and the Stockholm Environment Institute has shown the unjust distribution of CO_2 emissions between 1990 and 2015, a critical period in which emissions rose by 60 per cent year on year. The researchers estimated that, during this period, the richest 10 per cent of the world's population was responsible for 52 per cent of total global CO_2 emissions and the poorest half of the population for just 7 per cent. In 2030, the carbon footprint of the richest 1 per cent of humans will be thirty times higher than the level that would allow us to meet the 1.5-degree target set by the Paris Agreement, while the footprint of the poorest half of the global population will remain well below this level. 'The emissions from a single billionaire space flight would exceed the lifetime emissions of someone in the poorest billion people on Earth. A tiny elite appear to have a free pass to pollute,' says Nafkote Dabi from Oxfam, the organization that published these figures in the run-up to COP26 in Glasgow.[40] A hundred companies worldwide, including leading gas, coal and oil companies such as ExxonMobil, Shell, BP and Chevron, are responsible for 71 per cent of global emissions since 1998,[41] a fact that they do their best to conceal. BP actually invented the concept of the 'carbon footprint' and developed a tool to calculate this. The concept was introduced with a PR campaign costing hundreds of millions, encouraging consumers to go on a 'low-carbon diet'.[42] This is an attempt to shift the blame from the fossil-fuel-based energy economy to the individual consumer.

At the United Nations Climate Change Conference (COP26) in November 2021 in Glasgow, the biggest delegation was from the fossil fuel industry. No state delegation equalled the numbers of these industry lobbyists.[43] At COP27 in Sharm El-Sheikh (Egypt) in November 2022, their numbers rose by 25 per cent, to a total of 636 delegates. That's more than all the delegates of the ten most affected countries put together.[44] This is emblematic of the power the industry has in relation to the climate crisis – and of how it uses this power to sabotage climate protection. COP27 gets a very mixed report card: on the positive side, the community of nations finally agreed to establish a fund for loss and damage. Given that the crisis has been caused by the historical emissions of the Global North (Germany is historically the fourth-biggest CO_2 emitter, with the USA, China and Russia in places one to three), the worst-affected countries have long demanded financial compensation.[45] The small island developing states have been campaigning for such funding since the 1990s.[46] Before 2022, the wealthier countries had refused to set up a dedicated compensation fund, the argument being that they were already supplying humanitarian aid. At COP27, however, the affected countries overcame this powerful resistance. The establishment of a fund to compensate for climate harm is a step towards climate justice. But who exactly pays what to whom – and when – will not be decided until the next COP. The most distressing outcome of COP27 is that the final declaration of the conference contains no pledge to drastically reduce emissions and no mention of ending the use of oil and gas. Even the clear and dramatic words of UN Secretary-General António Guterres – 'Our planet is still in the emergency room' – had no impact here.[47]

When it comes to justice, we also have to consider a broader time frame. Since nothing is being done at present, and no real attempt is being made to tackle the problem, the climate crisis will inevitably have serious consequences for future generations. This is a matter of intergenerational equity – or rather inequity. If we fail to stop or slow down the climate crisis today, the price must be paid later by those who have no power to make the relevant decisions at present – because they are too young to vote, don't yet have politically influential positions, or haven't even been born. This is unfair, because the people who are failing to make the right decisions today can continue to enjoy their current lifestyle with hardly a care in the world. They won't be around any more when things get really uncomfortable. 'Après moi, le déluge' ('After me, the flood') applies quite literally here. This unwillingness to make changes and take action is worsening the state of our environment and will hugely restrict the freedom of future generations.

Surveys show that women and people of colour have more knowledge about climate change – but also more worries about it – than men and White people. They also show clearer pro-environmental attitudes and a greater willingness to do something about the climate crisis.[48] This trend is personified by the fact that the climate movement has historically been led mainly by indigenous groups, plus the mobilizing power of the global Fridays for Future movement led by young women. Men and White people have been proven to have less interest in the issue and less willingness to change their behaviour and politics. This has been linked to their position in society and a less acute sense of personal involvement.[49] White men's relatively low perception of risk with regard to the climate crisis is referred to in scholarly literature as the 'White male effect'.[50] Historically, it has always been the people who were most oppressed and marginalized who have fought most strongly and effectively for justice. The climate crisis is no different.

Applying feminist foreign policy to climate justice therefore requires a multiphase approach to the climate crisis. It must be tackled as a national problem of justice within states, springing from the unfair distribution of power on the basis of sex, origin or socio-economic status. But it must also be dealt with as a problem between states, requiring international and multilateral solutions. In international forums such as the UN or in treaties such as the Paris Agreement, this power imbalance must be addressed in all its details and facets. Only then can the climate crisis be alleviated in the long term. Anything else is just sticking a plaster on a gaping wound.

Control over nature and women

Thanks to organizations such as Fridays for Future, the climate justice movement has attracted a lot of attention in recent years. But it's important to understand that the fight for climate justice has its roots in the activism and the struggle of indigenous people and people of colour. Organizations such as Intersectional Environmentalist[51] draw our attention to this and share their knowledge of the battles that have been fought for environmental protection – e.g. by indigenous people in North America since the colonization of their continent. The protests against the construction of the North Dakota Access Pipeline in the Standing Rock Reservation in 2016 are a well-known example – and were led mainly by women.[52] 'The climate crisis began with colonization, because this was the point when nature was separated from us humans and turned into a resource,' says the Filipino climate activist Mitzi Jonelle Tan.[53]

J. Ann Tickner writes that perceptions of nature began to change in the seventeenth century with the birth of the modern state and the capitalist orientation of the global economy. Nature was no longer seen as a living organism but, rather, viewed as an inert machine. This idea, Tickner argues, was supported by the concepts of the Enlightenment and was linked to exploitative imperialism and European colonization, which led to worldwide ecological changes. Quoting the feminist intellectual Carolyn Merchant, Tickner describes how medieval Europeans viewed nature as a living organism, in which humans and their environment were interdependent. This living system was usually seen as female – as Mother Earth looking after humanity. But once our capitalist system had been established, the destruction of the environment and nature began, and the foundations for global warming were laid.[54]

Ecofeminism combines ecological issues with feminist analyses, emphasizing the structural similarities between the control and subordination of women and nature. Among its best-known proponents are Françoise d'Eaubonne (1920–2005) and Carolyn Merchant (b. 1936). Feminist intellectuals examining the ideas of the Enlightenment argue that the dominance of men over other people, cultures and nature, as part of the process of accumulating wealth and power, can only be understood if gender is used as a central analytical category. Proponents of ecofeminism assume that men's dominance and arrogance towards women mirrors their attitudes towards nature and non-White people. The expansion of the capitalist system and the augmentation of personal wealth required ever more natural resources – and this is why Europeans began to colonize the rest of the world.[55]

The Enlightenment is also the source of the idea that the exploitation of nature and the environment is a sign of human progress. Ultimately this served to justify colonialism and imperialism. In this worldview, indigenous populations with their respectful relationship to nature were considered incapable of carrying out this (supposedly necessary) transformation. In short, since the indigenous population did not exploit and destroy nature, the basis of their survival, but lived in harmony with it, the European colonists saw them as inferior and took this as a justification for oppressing them. Nature was increasingly viewed as wild and uncontrollable, as something to be tamed – like women (or non-White people), according to J. Ann Tickner. It is no coincidence, she argues, that nature and its wildness have always been regarded as female, as for example in that classic text of the realist school of thought, Machiavelli's *The Prince*.

Intellectuals and activists from other schools of thought have now begun to share a core tenet of ecofeminism: that the status quo of the international political order is based on the dominance of White men over other people and nature. Internationally, we can only achieve security for everyone if all these hierarchies are broken down. The exploitation and destruction of nature and the environment is directly linked with the oppression of women, people of colour and other political minorities. Peace and security worldwide depend on the end of this destruction and exploitation of the planet.

Networking between different groups – both mainly White and mainly non-White groups – is on the increase. This is the approach taken by the Climate Justice League, the first group within Fridays for Future to campaign for intersectional climate justice, especially in the most affected countries. These activists bring new perspectives into the heart of the movement. Most of those leading the first long-term campaigns of the Climate Justice League have a MAPA (most affected people and areas) background. Their campaigns thematize the exploitation of resources in the Global South and show that profit flows exclusively to the Global North. So aspects of injustice, human rights violations and the climate crisis are interconnected. The Climate Justice League focuses on the experiences of people who are already affected by the climate crisis on a daily basis. It uses the exchange of knowledge and close friendships between activists of the Global North and the Global South to develop the strongest global campaigns within Fridays for Future. The members of the Climate Justice League include the above-mentioned Mitzi Jonelle Tan (Philippines), Leonie Bremer (Germany), Maria Reyes (Mexico) and Disha Ravi (India).

Disha Ravi, one of the co-founders of Fridays for Future India, was arrested in February 2021 after supporting protests by farmers. 'Sometimes people try to destroy you, precisely because they recognize your power – not because they don't see it, but because they see it and they don't want it to exist,' writes bell hooks.[56] This is an apt description of the imprisonment of then 23-year-old Disha Ravi by the Indian state authorities. Ravi fights for climate justice in a country facing huge environmental problems. According to the World Economic Forum, six of the ten cities with the highest levels of particulate pollution in 2020 were in India. A study published in *The Lancet* found that 1.2 million Indians died from the consequences of air pollution in 2017 alone.[57] Once Ravi had been released on bail in mid-March 2021, after nearly a week in jail, she reported back on social media. Her words were clear: 'Climate Justice is about intersectional equity. It is about being radically inclusive of all groups of people, so that everyone has access to clean air, food and water. As a dear friend always says: "Climate Justice isn't just for the rich and the White."[58] I can only agree with this powerful statement.

The man-made climate crisis

The impact of humans on climate change has been known since the nineteenth century. In the 1950s, major newspapers reported on this topic. In 1972, the Club of Rome – an international association of scientists – published a seminal report, *The Limits to Growth*, for which it received the Peace Prize of the German Book Trade.[59] In 1988, the UN finally established an Intergovernmental Panel on Climate Change (IPCC). This body brings together experts who regularly compile and evaluate the latest knowledge on the climate crisis.[60] In 1992, the United Nations Framework Convention on Climate Change (UNFCCC) was adopted. The convention, currently ratified by 196 states, seeks to reduce human interventions in the climate system so as to avoid harm to ecosystems, limit global warming and mitigate its effects. A core principle is that the industrialized nations have an obligation to significantly reduce their greenhouse gas emissions – acknowledging their responsibility as the biggest emitters. The implementation of the UNFCCC and of the obligations arising from it, including the Kyoto Protocol of 1997 and the Paris Agreement of 2015, is monitored by the UNFCCC secretariat.

In December 2015 in Paris, 197 states reached a new global climate protection agreement to improve the implementation of the UNFCCC. The legally binding Paris Agreement, an example of visionary diplomacy and international politics, came into force in November 2016 and has so far been ratified by nearly 190 states. Based on science, it forms the foundation for demands for a liveable future and is frequently mentioned in connection with international climate movements such as Fridays for Future, Global Citizens, the Sunrise Movement or 350.org. In the Paris Agreement, the international community resolved to limit global warming to well below 2 degrees above pre-industrial levels, preferably 'only' 1.5 degrees – and this is binding under international law. Each state sets out how it can achieve this in its nationally determined contribution (NDC). Although these NDCs are not legally binding, the agreement is a huge step forward: it defines a clear goal for the community of nations to ensure the future of our planet and the generations to come. And it acknowledges that the climate catastrophe threatens human rights and causes disproportionate suffering to vulnerable groups.

Yet there are no grounds for complacency. The IPCC has consistently underlined the urgency of the matter. The clock is ticking; time is running out. Within the next ten years, CO_2 emissions must be drastically reduced to avoid catastrophic consequences for the climate. In August 2021 the IPCC published the first part of its Sixth Assessment Report, with new assessments of the risks of exceeding 1.5 degrees of global warming in the next few decades. The report notes that the target of 1.5 degrees – or even 2 degrees – will become unattainable if greenhouse gas emissions are not reduced immediately and comprehensively. It also makes it clear that some drastic effects of global warming have already occurred and can no longer be halted: there will be more intense rainfall and floods in some areas and droughts in others; sea levels will keep rising steadily; and extreme weather events will continue to increase, especially in cities.[61] At present, less than 1 per cent of the Earth's surface has average temperatures of over 29 degrees Celsius. As the climate crisis progresses, up to 29 per cent of land areas could reach such life-threatening temperatures.[62]

The Paris Agreement and the related structures form the general framework for international efforts to contain the climate crisis. At COP20 in Lima in 2014, the parties to the UNFCCC also agreed on the Lima Work Programme on Gender, which sets out transformative regulations to reinforce the existing gender-specific provisions in climate protection agreements, to identify gaps and to monitor implementation. Up to that time the importance of gender had been evoked now and then, but before 2014 all the measures had focused solely on increasing women's involvement in these conferences. At COP23 in Bonn in 2017, the parties adopted the first Gender Action Plan (within the framework of the Lima Work Programme) to include women on an equal footing and at all levels in policy-making on climate change and the development of gender-specific measures. The second Gender Action Plan (adopted at COP25 in Madrid in 2019) builds on the first, as well as recognizing gender-specific measures as an important element of disaster prevention. The preamble of the Paris Agreement of 2015 also confirms the importance of gender equality and of empowering women in the fight against climate change – but it does not make this a binding requirement.[63]

UN member states are explicitly urged to follow a gender-responsive approach. A handful of the UN's seventeen Sustainable Development Goals for the years 2015 to 2030 also prioritize gender equality. Two of the goals are concerned with reducing the risk of disasters. Also worth mentioning here is the Sendai Framework for Disaster Risk Reduction (2015–30), which was adopted at the third World Conference on Disaster Risk Reduction in Sendai, Japan. It stresses that 'Women and their participation are critical to effectively managing disaster risk and designing, resourcing and implementing gender-sensitive disaster risk reduction policies, plans and programmes.' The framework particularly emphasizes the promotion of 'gender equitable and universally accessible response, recovery, rehabilitation and reconstruction approaches'.[64]

I'm pleased to see the growing attention paid to the connection between gender and the climate crisis. But this approach will not help the global community to move forward unless it is based on an intersectional perspective and a persistent critique of the status quo. These agreements must aim at a new beginning, a systemic change. As Michelle Benzing from CFFP has pointed out, the issue of gender was completely overlooked at COP27, and even Germany had no experts on the gender-specific effects of the climate crisis in its delegation.[65]

Climate and security

It's April 2021. I'm sitting in an online training session on peacebuilding within the EU. A member of the European External Action Service, the EU's diplomatic service, mentions topics that still attract too little attention: 'So far, the connection between climate and conflict hasn't played a major role for the EU,' she says. This is absolutely crazy, since the link between the climate crisis, conflicts and security is so unmistakable and so clearly proven. Yet many international organizations are only gradually realizing its significance. The UN Security Council didn't hold its first debate on the effects of the climate crisis on peace and security until 2007,[66] and, for many years after that, member states such as China and Russia repeatedly questioned whether this was the right place for such debates.[67]

In 2008 and 2009 there was a severe drought in Syria, and the UN asked its member states to help the people affected. The appeal generated only a quarter to a third of the funds needed to provide real assistance.[68] This was before the civil war, which has now been going on for more than ten years. There is no knowing whether a stronger response to the drought could have prevented the civil war. But isn't it possible to envisage the following scenario: that climate-related natural disasters might in future be avoided by a sincere effort on the part of the international community to combat global warming, and that history might therefore take a different course? Natural disasters such as storms and rising sea levels make countries fragile, especially the small island states that are fighting for their very survival. This is why US President Joe Biden, shortly after taking office in January 2021, described the climate crisis as an 'existential threat'. He appointed a former secretary of state, John Kerry, as the special presidential envoy for climate, with a seat in the National Security Council. And the Pentagon classified climate change as a threat to national security.[69]

The climate crisis drives worldwide migration (especially within states and regions) and makes resources scarce. This has led to conflicts in the past and has the potential to cause more in the future. So security doesn't become a problem only when conflicts arise. It's not just brute force and weapons that threaten security but anything that makes people insecure, as the concept of feminist security shows. And this is definitely the case for long-term changes caused by the climate crisis, such as higher sea levels, global rises in temperature, and high levels of air pollution. But even today there are too few studies and publications on this topic and too little effort, in the sphere of (inter-national) politics, to consider feminist security, peace and justice, and thus respond adequately to the climate catastrophe.

In May 2022, the Stockholm International Peace Research Institute (SIPRI) published a ground-breaking report describing in depth the interaction between the climate crisis and the international security situation, and their mutually reinforcing effects. The report, entitled *Environment of Peace: Security in a New Era of Risk*, was produced by a group of researchers under the guidance of a panel of experts chaired by Margot Wallström, the former Swedish foreign minister.[70] It shows in detail how indicators of insecurity are rising worldwide (an increase in conflicts and wars and in the number of people killed and displaced; an increase in worldwide military spending; a height-ened risk of the use of nuclear weapons), while indicators of environ-mental integrity are sinking (an increase in extreme weather events; rising sea levels; increasing water shortages; a decline in mammals and insects; plastic pollution; dying coral reefs; shrinking forests). This is a dangerous mixture with far-reaching effects, and the institutions (and governments) that have the power to find solutions are acting far too slowly, the authors of the study argue.

The report continues: 'The darkening security horizon presents one layer of risks to peace; environmental decline adds a second layer. The interaction of the two trends produces a third, more complex set of risks, whose significance humanity is only beginning to grasp.'[71] The two crises interact: countries that are most ecologically threatened are also, statistically, those where peace is most at risk. Half the current UN peace missions are in countries that are most severely affected by climate change. We therefore need to transform our thinking, including our understanding of peace: since environmental destruction is part of the security problem, the restoration of environmental integrity has to be part of the security solution. Apart from their direct effects, climate change and the environmental crisis contribute more broadly to insecurities: it has been proven, according to the SIPRI report, that they often lead to social and political instability, which, if not resolved, can escalate into violence. Armed conflicts not only harm the environment but also hamper effective environmental policies, and disputes and conflicts obstruct international collaboration on environmental issues.

At the same time, the richest countries are not providing the international financial resources that are needed to fight climate change and biodiversity loss – further exacerbating the risk of conflict. Nor do the funds for adaptation to the climate crisis reach the areas where they are most urgently needed: the most fragile states, which have the greatest need, receive (per capita) only one-eightieth of the climate funding that goes to non-fragile states. Instead, wealthy states pour the money needed to fight the climate crisis into military spending: at the time of COP27, a report was published with the apt title *Climate Collateral: How Military Spending Accelerates Climate Breakdown*. This shows that the richest countries spend thirty times as much on their armed forces as on climate finance for the world's most vulnerable countries – finance which they are legally bound to provide. Seven of the top ten historical greenhouse gas emitters are among the ten countries with the highest military spending in the world: the United States spends by far the most, followed by China, Russia, the United Kingdom, France, Japan and Germany. And, since Russia's war of aggression against Ukraine began in February 2022, global military spending has increased even more, making the arms industry the real winner of the last year.[72] Of course when there is an acute, worsening security situation, as in a war of aggression, it makes sense to help people under threat by supplying weapons. But increasing militarization will never be the solution to the long-term twin crises of the worsening security situation and the deepening climate crisis. No army in the world will help us to tackle the causes of the climate crisis effectively. On the contrary, the armies of this world are contributing to the crisis.

The UN report *Gender, Climate & Security* presents specific examples to show how the climate crisis leads to insecurities and conflicts and why it is a feminist issue. In northern Nigeria, for example, where drought is growing and rain is unpredictable, norms of masculinity intensify conflicts. The desire to feed one's family and protect family wealth is becoming harder and harder to fulfil. Many young men, especially in rural areas, face huge pressure and increasing economic uncertainty, and these pressures often find expression in violence towards other people. This region, severely impacted by the climate crisis, is also prey to armed groups such as the Islamist terrorist militia Boko Haram. These groups stir up further conflicts, leading to more violence against women.[73]

The Nigerian climate activist and feminist Oladosu Adenike explains in an interview why climate, security and women's rights must be considered together. When Boko Haram abducted 276 schoolgirls in 2014, this was linked to the environmental crisis in north-eastern Nigeria, near Lake Chad. The climate-related instability in that region, she argues, has contributed to armed conflict, displacement and extreme poverty. This, in turn, directly affects the education of young girls and their opportunities in life.[74] In Pakistan, women have become victims of male domestic violence because increasing water shortages have made it impossible to run their households as usual. In some cases, water and energy shortages – exacerbated by climate change – have been linked to the mobilization of men in criminal groups. It has been suggested that economic insecurity and the desire to feed their families make young men particularly susceptible to joining armed, often extremist groups. Such connections have been documented worldwide, from Chad, Sudan and Egypt to Colombia, Nepal and Indonesia.[75]

A study by the International Union for Conservation of Nature (IUCN) shows that climate change and environmental destruction

248

lead to more violence against women. For example, when girls are forced into marriage because climate-related changes mean there isn't enough food in the house – marrying off a daughter means having one mouth less to feed. This happens, for example, in Malawi, Ethiopia and South Sudan. Girls and women are also exposed to increasing violence from men when they perform the typically female task of fetching water. When water sources run dry and they have to go further to find water, the likelihood of falling victim to male violence rises. The same goes for collecting firewood. Other forms of exploitation of nature, such as the overfishing of the seas, also exacerbate male violence against women: fish has become such a scarce commodity that women often have to pay for it with sex as well as money. This is so common in western Kenya that there's even a name for it: the Jaboya system.[76]

Despite all this knowledge and all these reports, far too little is being done. This would probably be different if there were more feminist experts worldwide shaping our international politics. When an open debate was held in the UN Security Council in January 2019 on 'Addressing the impacts of climate-related disasters on international peace and security', only five of the seventy-five member states present acknowledged the relevance of gender-specific dynamics in this context.[77] Although feminists in international relations have lobbied for recognition of the link between climate and gender dynamics, the UN Security Council has not included this in any of its sessions. The Paris Agreement was, admittedly, one of the first agreements to recognize and mention the gender perspective. But it failed to consider the effects of the climate crisis on conflicts and feminist security. The WPS agenda would be a good opportunity to thematize the interplay between gender, conflict and security in the context of the climate crisis and to establish requirements for the foreign policy of states worldwide. So far, however, only one resolution in this agenda – Resolution 2242 – has mentioned the climate crisis.[78]

Foreign and security policy must shift its focus away from military security and towards what really makes people safe. No army in the world will be able to fight the insecurities triggered by the climate catastrophe. Feminists in foreign and security policy demand that individual security be considered in combination with national and international security, and that power dynamics be understood and changed to achieve more justice. Without justice, there can be no peaceful, sustainable global coexistence.

Objections and attacks

Achieving climate justice and taking effective steps against the climate catastrophe are the greatest challenges confronting us as humans. However, the policies proposed and (to some extent) implemented by governments worldwide show little sign of the urgent need to act. This is not a lifestyle choice: our very existence is at stake. Paying to have a few trees planted somewhere or other to compensate for the CO_2 emissions from our flights isn't a real option – it just allows us to buy a clear conscience so we can continue the same lifestyle. I'm in my early thirties, and this existential crisis makes me wonder whether I'll ever want to bring children into this world. The status quo of our world and the basis of our survival are so precarious that I'm not sure I want to inflict the pain of this knowledge on another human being. I'm not alone in this: because of the climate crisis, four in ten young people around the world are not sure whether they ever want to have children.[79]

A step in the right direction would be a feminist foreign policy in response to the climate crisis. Vanessa Nakate from Uganda has demanded that ecocide be classified as a crime under international law. This would mean that governments and companies could be held to account for the destruction of the environment. One of her concerns is to give a voice to those who are most affected by the consequences of environmental damage.[80]

The close connections between nationalists, antifeminists and climate change deniers must be recognized. Their aim of upholding existing patriarchal power structures is also apparent in their hatred towards activists in the Global North such as Greta Thunberg, Luisa Neubauer and Alexandria Ocasio-Cortez (the co-initiator of the Green New Deal in the USA). This hatred usually comes from conservative or nationalist quarters, with a strong element of misogyny. In the case of Ocasio-Cortez it is combined with racism and in Thunberg's case with ableist taunts, related to her Asperger's syndrome. The hatred comes mostly from men, who feel threatened in their masculinity by these (young) women. Trump and Putin, with their attempts to mock high-profile figures such as Greta Thunberg, are just the tip of the iceberg. When Greta sailed to the USA in 2020 to take part in the UN climate summit, more than a few men expressed the hope that she would be shipwrecked.

Researchers have found clear connections between nationalists, antifeminists and climate change deniers, all of whom reinforce one another. Men feel threatened in their masculinity and their privileges by (young, female) climate activists and react with hatred and violence. There is also a discrepancy between the sexes in their perceptions of the climate crisis – men tend to perceive climate activism as something fundamentally feminine. For climate sceptics, it is not the environment that is under threat but modern industrial society, which is built on and dominated by a particular form of masculinity.[81] It is therefore not surprising that, at presidential level, the greatest misogynists – such as Trump and Bolsonaro – also show contempt for the environment and environmentalists. Trump withdrew from the Paris Agreement, and Bolsonaro encouraged the deforestation of the Amazon while removing all protection from its indigenous peoples. The clearing of the Amazon reached an all-time high during Bolsonaro's term in office, and threats to indigenous people and environmental defenders rose dramatically. At the same time he slashed funding for the Ministry of the Environment, making it impossible for the agency to act effectively.[82]

Conclusion: climate justice and feminism – now!

The climate crisis is real, it's getting worse every day and, most of all, it's unjust. These facts have already been acknowledged on many national and international levels, in meetings, resolutions and frameworks, and internationally binding commitments have been made to fight this catastrophe. But all these words and declarations have to be translated into action! The injustice of the climate crisis must be acknowledged and fought with all possible means. The clearing of the rainforest and the extraction of coal must be stopped, and the exploitative capitalist system must be replaced by a 'people over profit' approach. We need respect and protection for environmental and human rights defenders; we must value marginalized knowledge and alternative knowledge production; and we must view the climate crisis as a crisis of social justice. And much more is needed: financial support in the form of reparations to countries of the Global South to facilitate their transition to green energies and recognition of ecocide as a violation of international law. The climate crisis must be recognized as a security problem which disproportionately affects women and other marginalized groups. And, of course, the Paris Agreement with its 1.5-degree target must be upheld. Feminist foreign and security policy demands no more and no less than a sincere attempt to bring about justice in the face of the climate crisis.

J. Ann Tickner:
'It doesn't matter what the boys are doing; we're doing much more interesting things anyway.'

The astute American political scientist and author J. Ann Tickner is well known for not just questioning traditional theories in International Relations but reformulating them in feminist terms. Yet Ann became a feminist relatively late. When she studied International Relations in the 1970s, the teaching and research – and the history and politics taught – were entirely in male hands. At the time, however, this seemed so normal that it didn't strike Ann as a problem. It was only when she became a professor herself that she realized her female students had trouble identifying with the teaching material because of the lack of female perspectives – to the extent that some even wanted to drop her course. Ann decided to tackle the problem.

One of her actions was to reformulate a classic model of international relations – Hans Morgenthau's principles of political realism – from a feminist perspective. Ann stresses that Morgenthau wasn't necessarily wrong, and her aim wasn't simply to refute his theory. The problem was that he didn't tell the whole story and didn't show the whole picture of global power relations, since he was only considering men. Ann's achievement, then, was to expand his theory. Yet some male professors still refused to include feminist theories in their courses. They argued that they couldn't understand this feminism and therefore couldn't teach it. Ann is baffled by this argument: 'After all, I'm not a realist, and I still have to teach political realism.'

Ann's harshest criticism of the traditional understanding of international relations is that the theory is too far removed from reality:

a small, elite group of scholars develop abstract theories far from the lived reality of civil society and the relevant actors.

Ann believes that, slowly but surely, people are beginning to change the way they think. She emphasizes the progress that has already been made – for example, the fact that power is now understood in the context of class, skin colour and gender.

The books Ann is currently reading include *Caste: The Origins of Our Discontents* by Isabel Wilkerson and *The Water Defenders: How Ordinary People Saved a Country from Corporate Greed* by Robin Broad and John Cavanagh.

11 MAKING PEACE WITHOUT WEAPONS: DISARMAMENT AS A FUNDAMENTAL DEMAND OF FEMINISM

Men are afraid that women will laugh at them.
Women are afraid that men will kill them.

Margaret Atwood

My personal security flaw

Long before I studied international politics, there was something that was always a complete mystery to me: the fascination with guns. Growing up in Germany, I had plenty of opportunity to witness this. There was the tradition of the *Schützenfest*, a whole festival revolving around a shooting match; there were shooting galleries at every village fair; and there were hunting expeditions in the forests around my village. Even as a teenager, I was often baffled by this social fact. At some point I found I could no longer accept the everyday presence of weapons in many countries, particularly in crisis zones. During this period I was politicized by punk rock, especially German punk. Many of the songs were about international injustices and the violence of powerful states such as the USA – as manifested in military interventions, drone attacks, or the use of nuclear weapons. I couldn't get my head around this discrepancy: the states extolled as the great democracies of the world, the countries delivering grand speeches about world peace, were also the biggest producers and buyers of weapons, the most eager participants in the arms race. None of this made sense to me. But my 'youthful naivety' soon came up against the 'realists' and disciples of the status quo. They told me why things had to be this way, and why arms proliferation couldn't be challenged. To do so would be naive, stupid, typically female and disagreeably left wing.

As if the desire for a world free of violence could be neatly fitted into a political spectrum extending from left to right. As if the rejection of violence, militarism and war was a question requiring political debate. Time and time again, the power of the dominant patriarchal discourse stops us from listening to our gut feeling and our moral compass. I became defiant; I refused to accept that we live in a violent, militarized society.

The arms race spiral

This is a heavily armed age, and it is becoming more so all the time. Most countries were ill-equipped to cope with the greatest threat facing humanity at the beginning of the 2020s, the raging pandemic. It seemed there was not enough money to pay decent wages to nursing staff, provide more intensive-care beds, or buy life-saving ventilators. And yet, according to the peace research institute SIPRI, military spending in 2020 increased markedly compared to the previous year. Worldwide, states invested a total of $US1.98 trillion in defence. Germany was (and still is) seventh on the list of big military spenders, although it is only the nineteenth largest country in terms of population.[1] Germany's defence spending was 28 per cent higher in 2020 than in 2011.[2]

The hypermilitarized state of our world is not a law of nature but the result of political decisions going back decades or even centuries. In 2021 (in the middle of the pandemic, when money was too tight for hospital beds, nursing staff, and the equitable global distribution of vaccines) more than $2 trillion were spent on defence and militarization. This was an all-time record, the first time military spending had surpassed the 2 trillion mark.[3] And it was – of course – accompanied by a rise in wars and conflicts. In the last ten years the number of wars and conflicts has almost doubled, from thirty in 2010 to fifty-six in 2020. One of the consequences has been a doubling of the number of people killed or displaced. In 2010 there were 41 million displaced people worldwide; in 2020 the number had risen to 82.4 million.[4] Since 2015, global military spending has risen year on year.[5] Despite the economic fluctuations caused by the pandemic, the figure in 2021 was 12 per cent higher than in 2012.[6]

The authors of the *SIPRI Yearbook 2022* argue that the $2 trillion spent on arms and armies constitute a wasted opportunity to achieve the Sustainable Development Goals (SDGs) of Agenda 2030 and the aims of the 2015 Paris Agreement on climate change. Diverting just a fraction of this sum could improve security in a broader sense and help to achieve the SDGs. Ultimately, high military expenditure always comes with painful opportunity costs: this is money that cannot be spent on food security, better access to clean water, or the fight against poverty, disease and the worsening climate crisis. According to the *SIPRI Yearbook 2022*, 'States' arms acquisitions, often from foreign suppliers, are largely driven by violent armed conflict and political tensions. There are strong indications that tensions are increasing in most regions and it seems likely that there will be more demand for major arms in the coming years, much of which will be fulfilled by international transfers.'[7]

Global arms proliferation has been exacerbated by the Russian war of aggression. In the months following the Russian invasion, governments worldwide acted as though increased militarization was the only right answer to a state of affairs that is partly a result of militarization. Three days after the start of the war, German Chancellor Olaf Scholz announced a special fund of €100 billion for the German armed forces. According to a report by the Transnational Institute, *Climate Collateral: How Military Spending Accelerates Climate Breakdown*, the European Commission anticipates that member states will boost their military spending by at least €200 billion by combining ad hoc extra funds with longer-term structural increases. For 2023, the USA has approved a record military budget of $840 billion.[8] During the pandemic, the International Campaign to Abolish Nuclear Weapons calculated how much more money would have been available to fight the pandemic if nuclear arms were not part of our global reality. In 2019, the USA spent $35.1 billion on nuclear weapons. This would have covered the cost of 300,000 intensive-care beds, 35,000 ventilators, and the salaries of 150,000 nurses and 75,000 doctors.[9] If the money had gone into the health budget instead of nuclear arms, many of the more than 1 million people who died of Covid in the USA might still be alive.

When the USA dropped two atomic bombs on Hiroshima and Nagasaki at the end of the Second World War, around 300,000 people were killed. The two bombs – given the disturbingly harmless code-names 'Little Boy' (Hiroshima) and 'Fat Man' (Nagasaki) – were puny in comparison to the destructive power of today's nuclear weapons.[10] At present there are around 13,000 nuclear weapons worldwide, most of them stationed in the USA and Russia (but some in Europe, including Germany).[11] The detonation of just one of these weapons over New York would lead to more than half a million deaths.[12] The abundance of the nuclear arsenal is particularly absurd if we consider that more states possess nuclear weapons now than during the Cold War.

But these weapons of mass destruction are not the only threat to human security: worldwide, conventional firearms kill an average of one person every fifteen minutes.[13] Like many other states, Germany claims that one of its core foreign policy objectives is to work towards enduring peace. But how can this be reconciled with Germany's position as the world's fifth biggest arms exporter (after the USA, Russia, France and China)?[14] In 2021, Germany approved €9.4 billion of arms exports, the highest value since the founding of the Federal Republic.[15]

In the chapter on the theoretical foundations of foreign policy, I explained how a completely irrational mode of behaviour – a huge build-up of arms combined with hopes of world peace – came to be seen as rational *Realpolitik*. This springs from a patriarchal understanding of our society, where dominance, oppression and the destruction of others are viewed as legitimate, rational and necessary. In this tradition, the immense capacity of nuclear weapons to oppress, dominate and destroy makes them the most extreme tool of the patriarchy.

Weapons kill women

It doesn't have to be this way, though. The status quo was created by humans – mainly by men – and can therefore be changed. This has already happened on numerous occasions. Many impressive feminists have played their part here, such as Jody Williams and Beatrice Fihn,* both instrumental in the international prohibition of certain types of weapons. Jody Williams received the Nobel Peace Prize in 1997 for her work towards the ban on landmines, and Beatrice Fihn was (until the beginning of 2023) the head of the International Campaign to Abolish Nuclear Weapons (ICAN), which was awarded the same prize for its contribution to the prohibition of nuclear weapons.

Their work is a continuation of the demands made by the feminists who gathered in The Hague in 1915: in one of their twenty resolutions, they demanded that all states nationalize the production of weapons and ammunition and control the international arms trade.[16] How right they were! As long as the production and supply of weapons systems remains a lucrative part of a capitalist system focused on the maximization of profit, there will be no genuine efforts to end their overproduction. And as long as the 'military-industrial complex' exists (i.e. an excessively intimate relationship between the military and the arms industry, between war and profit), real disarmament and stricter controls on the production and export of weapons will remain a distant dream.[17] The world's ten biggest arms manufacturers had a total revenue of nearly $250 billion in 2019;[18] in 2020, states spent nearly $2 trillion on military and defence worldwide.[19] In comparison, only around $6.5 billion were supplied to the UN's peace missions in the same period.[20]

As part of a project entitled 'Why the international arms trade is a feminist issue', CFFP published a short, pop-style video with a serious message.[21] Between 2015 and 2019, the volume of weapons traded internationally reached its highest level since the Cold War ended.

---

* A portrait of Beatrice Fihn can be found at the end of chapter 9.

This is a feminist issue for the following reasons. Firstly, women and girls are more often victims of gender-based violence. If there's a gun in the house (and gun owners are usually men), this substantially increases a woman's chances of being shot dead in an incident of intimate partner violence (also known as domestic violence). In the USA, half of all women who die at the hands of a male partner or ex-partner are killed with a gun; in total, 84 per cent of all murdered women are killed by guns.[22] Guns are involved in more than a third of all femicides worldwide (and in more than half of those in the USA). Furthermore, weapons often facilitate sexualized violence against women and LGBTQ+ individuals during wartime. Secondly, men are overrepresented in political processes relating to weapons. More than 80 per cent of participants in processes of disarmament and arms control are men, who offer only a male perspective.[23] The third factor is gender-specific conceptions of power. Acquiring more and better weapons is generally seen as rational, strong and powerful – qualities associated with masculinity. Disarmament, in contrast, is regarded as weak, naive and unrealistic – characteristics with feminine connotations. According to this logic, weapons are viewed as synonymous with power and armed force is seen as the expression of power. In this patriarchal understanding, 'real' masculinity means using armed force to 'protect' helpless women. This mad, misguided logic hampers the demilitarization of the international system, since governments fear to be seen as weak if they advocate or engage in disarmament.[24]

I personally believe that arms trading and arms proliferation are feminist issues because weapons are an instrument of violence. When it comes to the reality of life on our planet, we can make one very clear generalization: men inflict violence on women. Almost all acts of violence are committed by men. And almost every woman has experienced some form of male violence – be it online hate speech and sexual harassment,[25] intimate partner violence, rape or femicide. The figures for Germany are just as horrifying: a survey by the Ministry of Family Affairs, published in 2004, found that one in three women had experienced physical violence, one in seven in the form of sexual abuse.[26] For millennia, the patriarchy has maintained artificial hierarchies between groups of people in our societies. To uphold this system and keep White men from the Global North at its apex, misogynist or racist violence is deployed. Weapons – especially guns – make this violence more efficient and keep the patriarchy alive.

Arms and arms proliferation increase power imbalances between the sexes, between the Global North and South, and between other powerful and less powerful groups.

When in 2000 the UN Security Council passed Resolution 1325 on Women, Peace and Security, a crucial aspect was missing. This was something feminists had been demanding vigorously for decades: universal disarmament. The same aspect had been omitted in 1918 when US President Woodrow Wilson incorporated many of the resolutions from the women's peace conference in The Hague into his fourteen-point plan.[27] States and international institutions often boast that they are integrating 'women's concerns' and feminist perspectives into international politics. But these are hollow boasts as long as the aspect with the greatest transformative potential – disarmament – is simply swept under the carpet. This is why disarmament, demilitarization and the end of the international arms trade are core concerns of feminist foreign policy.

Militarization

What is militarization, and what does it mean to live in a militarized society? The work of the American political scientist Cynthia Enloe gets to the heart of these questions. She defines militarization as the gradual cultural, symbolic and material preparation for an armed conflict.[28] If a state is militarizing its foreign policy, this means that it is investing in its military strength and capability. For example, it may expand its army, build up its arsenal, and look for military bases and allies. The most obvious aspects are the size of the army and the number of (heavy) weapons systems. But there is more to it: militarization is often accompanied by militarism.

This is when warlike ideas are deeply rooted in society – e.g. in toys, children's games, films, or camouflage-patterned clothing. '[Militarism] is accompanied by and reinforces militarisation – and vice versa,'[29] as stated in our policy briefing on the militarization of German foreign policy. In another publication, our manifesto for a feminist foreign policy for Germany,[30] we argue that the state in a militarized society is constantly working to persuade people that 'military capability is the most meaningful and effective instrument for achieving any or all national goals, and that soldiers, weapons and wars are the most necessary and noble tools for national protection and advancement.'[31]

Core objective: demilitarization

In most societies, the process of militarization has become so much a part of everyday life – military parades, toy pistols and endless heroic war films – that it passes unnoticed. For feminists, this militarization can never be accepted as the norm.[32]

It will have become clear by now that feminist foreign policy prioritizes feminist security over state security. Feminist security requires demilitarization. By definition, not everyone can be safe in a militarized, hierarchic society – on the contrary, most people are unsafe. Especially those who are already marginalized.

Militarization also means that an army encroaches on more and more areas of society. This happens even in a supposedly peaceful country such as Germany: the Bundeswehr regularly visits schools in an attempt to attract new recruits and has a 'showroom' at Friedrichstrasse station, a busy transport hub in Berlin. The recruitment office is full of glossy brochures and models of ships. Videos of military exercises play on big screens, and the slogan 'Wir. Dienen. Deutschland.' (We. Serve. Germany.) appears in large letters above the door. Another example is the support given by the armed forces in disasters and crises, such as the catastrophic Elbe River floods of 2002 and the Ahr Valley floods of 2021. During the Covid-19 pandemic, the military assisted the health authorities with contact tracing, and helpers in army fatigues also appeared in vaccine centres. This encroachment of the military would not be necessary if there were more investment in other structures. As the political scientist Rosa Brooks commented, 'If your only tool is a hammer, everything looks like a nail.'[33]

In our policy briefing *How Militarised is Germany's Foreign Policy?*, published shortly before the elections to the Bundestag in 2021, Nina and her co-authors criticize the country's increasing militarization. In the last twenty years the German defence budget has nearly doubled – from €24.3 billion in 2000 to €45.65 billion in 2020. In the same period, only a fraction of this money – not even a hundredth of the defence budget – has been spent on disarmament, on non-proliferation and arms control, and on crisis prevention, stabilization and peacebuilding.[34] The progressive militarization of Germany is also apparent in Berlin's continued adherence – confirmed in the new government's coalition agreement – to the concept of nuclear deterrence as a guarantee of security. This is used to justify the presence of US nuclear weapons on German soil. Another serious problem is that the German arms industry has excellent access to political decision-makers. A study published by Transparency International Deutschland in 2020 found close links between arms lobbyists and politicians. For example, the civil and military aerospace corporation Airbus sponsored the German Council on Foreign Relations (DGAP) to the tune of over €100,000 per year from 2013 to 2016. The DGAP, a think-tank partly funded by the German Foreign Office, describes itself as an independent, non-partisan and non-profit organization of experts and members, whose work has 'continued to shape the debate on foreign policy issues in Germany' for over sixty years. The current president of the DGAP was previously the CEO of Airbus for many years.[35] The research director has repeatedly expressed public support for arms exports. Independent? Hardly.

This growing militarization has far-reaching consequences in all areas of society: using force and military might becomes the method of choice in all conflict situations. Humanitarian missions (e.g. by organizations such as Médecins Sans Frontières) are increasingly linked with military objectives, and the use of force to defend borders is becoming normalized. This can be seen in the harsh treatment of refugees in the Mediterranean by Frontex, the European Border and Coast Guard Agency. The state's legitimation of violence in conflict situations also legitimizes and normalizes violence within couple relationships, thus increasing the risk of violence for women and the LGBTQ+ community.[36]

The German government's militaristic attitude is out of step with public opinion in Germany, which is generally anti-militaristic. In CFFP's policy briefing on the militarization of Germany, Nina and her co-authors quote the following figures: '66 percent of Germans do not support the concept of nuclear deterrence and are therefore sceptical of Germany's nuclear sharing agreement. 80 percent of Germans do not support arms exports to conflict regions, and 64 percent of citizens do not support arms exports at all.'[37]

Disarmament as a central feminist concern in history

The best thing about my work on feminist foreign policy and my role as co-director of CFFP is that I am privileged to work and interact with some impressive people, among them the academic Dr Louise Arimatsu. One of Louise's many specialties is the history of feminist activism within the disarmament movement. The following description relies mainly on Louise's knowledge, which she shared with me for this book. I have space here for only a very abbreviated account, but sharing this history is an important feminist act, since few people are aware that women and feminists have been challenging the dominant paradigms for over a century by fighting for a truly transformative disarmament agenda.[38]

It was the Russian tsar Nicholas II who, seeing disarmament as a prerequisite for international peace, first suggested that this be discussed in an international forum. When legal experts and politicians from twenty-six states met at the first Hague Peace Conference from May to July 1899, one of the aims was to put this idea into practice. But the plan failed and no progress was achieved in matters of disarmament. The Russian delegate Feodor de Martens said at the time that 'the Utopians, the most dangerous enemies of the progress of international law, expected from this Conference a general disarmament of all the Powers, eternal peace and the abolition of war'[39] – and he was not the only one with this attitude. The greatest utopians were the women activists campaigning for peace at the time. Their campaign was spearheaded by the Women's International League for Peace and Freedom (WILPF), which handed the conference delegates a petition with over half a million signatures in support of disarmament.[40]

For most women and feminists, the outcome of the Hague Peace Conference of 1899 was a great disappointment. From then on, they focused on the links between the social and gender-specific costs of the arms race, on the one hand, and imperialism, militarism and the oppression of women, on the other. Louise Arimatsu makes it clear that the conference of 1899 was a milestone despite its failure, because it spurred women to develop their own feminist agenda for disarmament.[41] Between the first Hague Peace Conference and the second in 1907, military spending increased in nearly all states. The third Hague Conference, scheduled for 1915, was cancelled because of the outbreak of the First World War in July 1914. But this did not deter over a thousand feminists – despite the high personal and financial costs – from meeting in The Hague for the International Congress of Women from April to May 1915. Although many of their demands were incorporated (without acknowledgement) into Woodrow Wilson's fourteen-point plan, their key demand for universal disarmament was omitted; Wilson's document mentions only a reduction in national armaments.[42]

The Treaty of Versailles, marking the end of the First World War, required the disarmament of only one country, Germany. This was one of WILPF's main criticisms of the treaty. Unilateral disarmament, the women argued, could not bring peace and security. They demanded universal, absolute disarmament.

One positive outcome of the Treaty of Versailles was the founding of the League of Nations, whose charter did include the goal of minimizing international armaments. Its creation in 1920 was an important event for feminist activism because it finally gave women access to the forums in which international political decisions were made. During the interwar period, women peace activists focused on two goals: universal disarmament and the regulation of private arms trading. Little was achieved, however. The World Disarmament Conference in Geneva (1932 to 1936) was a turning point for feminist activism. For the first time in history, states sent women as delegates. Other states took steps to include women in the formal processes by granting special status to the Women's Disarmament Committee, a coalition of different women's organizations formed in preparation for the conference. But this conference also failed to reach any agreement on disarmament. Increasing conflicts and militarization, growing nationalism, and the rise of fascism dampened any hopes of peaceful times to come. Louise Arimatsu stresses that these early feminist activists did not merely insist on being allowed to participate in political life: they wanted to change politics completely.[43] And, to achieve this, they combined forces with feminists all over the world. Whenever I'm reminded of what women were thinking, saying and demanding nearly a hundred years ago, a timeless feminist slogan comes to mind: I can't believe I still have to protest this shit.

During the Second World War, international feminist peace activism was largely on hold. But after the war, at the founding of the United Nations, feminists were once again at the forefront: women's rights organizations such as WILPF and the International Council of Women were among the first NGOs accorded observer status at the Economic and Social Council of the UN. This gave them access to UN bodies such as the General Assembly and the Human Rights Council. But during the Cold War, with its rivalry between the Soviet Union and the USA, WILPF was unable to make much progress in its goal of international disarmament. Geopolitics dominated, and there was an ever-widening gulf between the nuclear-armed states and the states calling for a world without nuclear weapons, who formed the Non-Aligned Movement.

Feminists focused more and more on the campaign against nuclear weapons testing.[44] In the early 1950s, for example, WILPF appealed to the recently founded World Health Organization (WHO) to consider the effects of nuclear tests on health. But this demand was refused on the grounds that weapons testing was a political matter. Two decades later, the WHO finally adopted a resolution calling for an immediate end to testing.

Women and feminists have repeatedly been marginalized in different movements and have therefore formed their own organizations and movements. This includes the American women's peace activist group Women Strike for Peace. On 1 November 1961, it mobilized 50,000 women, who demonstrated against nuclear weapons testing in sixty US cities. This is thought to have contributed to some extent to the Kennedy administration's decision to sign a treaty banning nuclear tests in 1963. When the UN decided to make 1975 International Women's Year and to hold its first World Conference on Women in Mexico City, the feminists hoped to put the demand for disarmament on the agenda. But they were thwarted in this because some states objected. Disarmament, it was argued, had nothing to do with women's rights. Feminists promptly organized a parallel event and lobbied so hard that the final declaration of the conference did include a commitment to complete universal disarmament.[45] It was largely thanks to WILPF that disarmament was also on the agendas of the subsequent UN World Conferences on Women in Copenhagen (1980) and Nairobi (1985). The final document of the fourth conference, the Beijing Platform for Action (1995), acknowledges this history of feminist activism, as well as emphasizing the need to prevent armed conflicts in order to achieve women's rights.[46]

Although the Treaty on the Non-Proliferation of Nuclear Weapons, which came into force in 1970, both required states possessing nuclear weapons to work towards complete disarmament and prohibited the acquisition or production of further nuclear weapons, the opposite happened: during the Cold War, more and more nuclear weapons were accumulated, and universal disarmament became increasingly unlikely. Article 26 of the UN Charter was ignored – and is still being ignored today.

With the end of the Cold War, feminists shifted their focus to other forms of armed violence such as small arms and light weapons. At the time, feminists were not the only ones calling for a broader understanding of security centred on the security of the individual and not the state. The *Human Development Report* of 1994 put the concept of 'human security' on the international agenda. The next concept to attract attention was that of 'humanitarian disarmament'. The new emphasis on the effects of armed violence on all people at all times meant that analyses no longer distinguished between armed forces and civilians and between wartime and peacetime. For the first time, the focus was on what weapons do to humans. A holistic approach was adopted, incorporating international humanitarian law and international human rights. This new narrative contributed to the Anti-Personnel Mine Ban Treaty of 1997, also known as the Ottawa Convention. The feminist activist Jody Williams was awarded the Nobel Peace Prize for her role in this. The 2008 Convention on Cluster Munitions can also be linked to this development. At the 2010 review conference for the Treaty on the Non-Proliferation of Nuclear Weapons, the final document acknowledged the 'catastrophic humanitarian consequences that would result from the use of nuclear weapons'.[47] This paved the way for further discussions on the humanitarian effects of nuclear weapons over the next few years. As a result, the Treaty on the Prohibition of Nuclear Weapons (TPNW) was adopted in 2017 and came into force in January 2021.*

---

* As an aside, Germany attended the consultative conferences before the adoption of the TPNW and also participated in the Meeting of the States Parties in June 2022 as an observer, following a pledge in the coalition agreement of the new government. So far, however, it has neither signed the TPNW nor recognized the consequences of nuclear

In short, decades of feminist activism have made a major contribution to international disarmament regimes. Feminists have recognized that 'nuclear weapons are a tool of the patriarchy.'[48] The change in narrative and the focus on humanitarian disarmament,* along with analyses of the interaction between gender, power, militarism and violence, have helped to produce new ways of thinking and new realities.

But there is a danger: this knowledge and the demand for gender analyses can simply lead to demands for more women to be involved in decisions about armaments. These fears are justified, and the decisions are often not easy, as can be seen in the Arms Trade Treaty (ATT). Louise Arimatsu notes that, while feminist legal scholars and activists 'may have played an active role in pressing for the integration of human rights and a novel provision on gender-based violence into the text of the 2013 Arms Trade Treaty',[49] they were aware of the treaty's flaws.[50] The ATT is the first international treaty to thematize the connection between arms trading and gender-based violence. However, its aim is to regulate the international arms trade without fundamentally questioning its existence or encouraging states to restrict it. In fact, the treaty even suggests that international arms trading can contribute to peace and security. Critical voices might say that this kind of feminist activism helps to legitimize the arms trade. The more charitable interpretation is that feminists, by inserting feminist elements into such treaties, are at least getting a foot in the door. Either way, the outcome shows what can happen when feminist demands meet the reality of global power hierarchies.

Feminists know that, as long as the drivers of the arms trade – the public and private machinery of war – are not effectively tackled, there

---

weapons for the security of humanity as a priority (see CFFP, *How Militarised is Germany's Foreign Policy?*).

* As with the concept of human security, that of humanitarian disarmament fails to consider marginalized groups or to acknowledge the different degrees to which individual groups of people are affected. From a feminist perspective, it is essential to acknowledge and eliminate these disproportionate effects. Nonetheless, CFFP welcomes the agreement reached on this concept.

can be no universal disarmament. But women are still largely excluded from the arenas where weapons regulation and arms control are discussed. Louise Arimatsu sees this exclusion as a disastrous failure of state responsibility.[51]

Utopian thought and feminism

People who campaign for social change are often accused of being naive and making utopian demands. Me too: I'm frequently told that my demands, CFFP's demands, are utopian. In April 2021 even the left-wing newspaper *Die Tageszeitung* (commonly known as *taz*) asked me: 'You and your organization advocate the abolition of the patriarchy, demilitarization and global peace. Aren't those completely utopian goals?' I answered: Yes, they are utopias. And, yes, we are campaigning for them. 400 years ago, the abolition of slavery was utopian. At the beginning of the twentieth century, women's suffrage was completely utopian. Only people who have conceived and fought for utopias have ever contributed to social change. Such people have paved the way for how we live today. Yet of course we're still far from obtaining everything we want, such as gender equity.[52] By definition, a utopia is something that hasn't yet been achieved. It's a positive vision of the future which, in the case of feminist politics, can be understood as constructive. This means that anyone can actively contribute to making the utopia a reality.

A 'no' to the arms trade

Despite over 100 years of feminist campaigning to end the international arms trade, arms expenditure continues to grow steadily.[53] However, the 2013 Arms Trade Treaty is the first arms control treaty worldwide to make explicit reference to gender-based violence. In Article 7.4, the weapons-exporting parties pledge to consider the risk that the weapons they export might be used 'to commit or facilitate serious acts of gender-based violence or serious acts of violence against women and children.'[54] The overall aim of the treaty is to regulate the international trade in conventional arms in order to reduce human suffering and make a contribution to peace and international security. If we look at what counts as conventional arms, it becomes clear how much death, suffering and ruin they cause. They include battle tanks, armoured combat vehicles, large-calibre artillery systems, combat air-craft, attack helicopters, warships, missiles and missile launchers, and small arms and light weapons, as well as the ammunition for these weapons and the components to build them. The connection between feminist demands and the international arms trade is not just a the-oretical construct of feminist foreign policy experts and activists but is clearly established in some of the most recognized international norms: not only does the ATT explicitly mention gender-based vio-lence and violence against women and children, but the WPS agenda (in Resolution 2467) also references the ATT.

Nonetheless, the strong commitment of many governments to the WPS agenda – including Germany, especially during its two-year stint as a non-permanent member of the UN Security Council in 2019–20 – does not translate into a restrictive policy on arms (export) control or greater efforts at disarmament. This double standard exposes the hollowness of their commitment to WPS and their calls for 'more women at the negotiating table'. The WPS agenda is not a box of chocolates; you can't just pick and choose the bits you like. A feminist foreign policy must be consistent and coherent. And yet it isn't. Even Sweden, the pioneer of feminist foreign policy, exports large quantities of weapons. In 2018, for example, it exported military equipment to countries that were involved in the war in Yemen.[55]

And what about Germany? Representatives of the government like to claim that Germany doesn't export any small arms and light weapons. But this is deceptive. What the Foreign Office means by this is that Germany doesn't export these weapons to so-called third countries – i.e. states that aren't part of the EU or NATO and aren't classed as 'NATO-equivalent' countries. In actual fact, Germany exported €3.1 million worth of small arms and light weapons to the USA in 2020[56] – that is, to a NATO partner which is the most dangerous high-income country for women when it comes to gun violence. If there's a gun in the house, then the likelihood of a woman being violently killed by her male partner increases by 500 per cent.[57] In accordance with the 'Political Principles of the Federal Government for the Export of Weapons of War and other Military Goods', exports to EU, NATO and NATO-equivalent countries are not scrutinized in terms of their potential effects on human rights.[58]

It's simply not acceptable for a state or a foreign minister to proclaim their commitment to 'women and peace' and then deal so casually with arms exports. So when Greenpeace commissioned CFFP to produce a study on the connection between German arms exports and gender-based violence in 2020, Nina and I formulated very clear demands: the German government must incorporate the risk of gender-based violence as a separate criterion in its 'Political Principles' and must consider this risk when assessing the human rights consequences of arms exports. This includes the risk that exported weapons could facilitate gender-based violence, as mentioned in the ATT. As we discovered in our study, Foreign Office assessments of the risk of human rights violations in importing countries have paid scant attention to this aspect so far.[59] In the long term, we are calling on the German government to develop and implement a strategy, with a clear timetable and clear milestones, to end all exports of German weapons, military equipment, technology and know-how and to stop supporting German subsidiaries of the arms industry abroad.[60] Because conflict prevention can only work if we demilitarize our security structures.

Another reason why the international arms trade is a core feminist issue is that weapons are used as a threat in gender-based violence. This includes rape as a weapon of war, which serves 'almost [as] a weapon of mass destruction'.[61] In Rwanda, for example, between 250,000 and 500,000 rapes were carried out within a three-month period in 1994. Rape practically became the norm, as a UN report observed in 1996.

'Victims [were] as young as two or as old as seventy-five. . . . In some areas, almost all women who survived had been raped.'[62] While men make up 80 per cent of the fatalities in armed violence and conflicts, women, girls and gender non-conforming people are disproportionately affected by gender-based violence, which is almost exclusively perpetrated by men. Various UN institutions have recognized that the export of small arms and light weapons is linked to gender-based violence. The UN report *Securing Our Common Future* states: 'High levels of arms and ammunition in circulation contribute to insecurity, cause harm to civilians, facilitate human rights violations and impede humanitarian access.'[63]

(Gender-based) armed violence will only stop if states cease to produce weapons and sell them at home and abroad. Until we reach that point, a comprehensive implementation of the ATT can make an important contribution to preventing (gender-based) violence.[64] But our core demand still has to be the end of the international arms trade.

A 'no' to nuclear weapons

There are enough weapons in the current nuclear arsenal to end human existence. So it is utterly perplexing that people attempt to justify not only conventional armaments such as small arms and light weapons but also nuclear weapons – with the argument that they make our world a safer place. The irrational patriarchal explanations are unfazed by these dangers. Even the language used shows their deeply patriarchal nature: in 'Sex and Death in the Rational World of Defense Intellectuals', Carol Cohn shows that the discourse on nuclear weapons is dominated by sexualized language ('erector launchers', 'soft lay downs', 'deep penetration', 'orgasmic whumps').[65] This language keeps the reality and the horror of war at a distance. The discourse focuses only on the weapons themselves and glosses over the disastrous human consequences.

It is striking how so-called realists or proponents of *Realpolitik* insist that political and foreign policy decisions must be based on (their) facts and (their) reality and dismiss feminist approaches to foreign and security policy as naive and unrealistic, when in actual fact the justifications for nuclear weapons and concepts such as 'nuclear deterrence' are largely fantasies. As the US peace scholar Ward Wilson contends in his book *Five Myths about Nuclear Weapons*, these justifications are far removed from any kind of reality. He argues, for example, that Japan's capitulation in 1945 was probably not because of Hiroshima and Nagasaki, as nuclear arms advocates always claim. Instead he suggests that the declaration of war by the USSR was the critical factor. This weakens the argument that nuclear weapons have such an extreme effect that they force other states into submission.[66] Wilson is also unconvinced by the widespread argument that 'nuclear deterrence' works effectively in crises and prevents worse outcomes. The event often held up as evidence of this is the Cuban Missile Crisis of October 1962, when the world only just avoided a 'hot' nuclear war. The United States had placed nuclear-armed medium-range ballistic missiles at a NATO base in Turkey in 1961. In response, the Soviet Union stationed similar missiles in Cuba. The US president, John F. Kennedy, then threatened to use nuclear weapons to prevent the further build-up of arms in Cuba. The power of the American nuclear deterrent has repeatedly been cited as the reason why this confrontation between the superpowers did not end in a nuclear war. But Wilson asks why nuclear deterrence did not prevent Kennedy from blockading Cuba if it was assumed at the time that such a blockade could lead to nuclear war. Wilson also points out that in 1948, when the USA had a monopoly on nuclear weapons, this did not stop Stalin from blockading Berlin. In this showdown between the rival superpowers, the Western allies had to organize an airlift to maintain supplies to West Berlin. So nuclear deterrence had no effect there either. 'The history of nuclear deterrence has been distorted; certain episodes that might indicate failures of nuclear deterrence have been allowed to fade quietly into the background, while other episodes have been claimed as successes and given a prominence they may not deserve', writes Wilson.

Since the 1950s, the theory of deterrence and the school of thought it spawned have been enormously important in shaping the thinking of people who make decisions about foreign policy. Robert Jervis called it 'probably the most influential school of thought in the American study of international relations'. But it may be that the very power of that school of thought has had a negative impact on our ability to see the facts.[67]

The argument that nuclear weapons led to decades of peace and prevented a third world war does not convince Wilson, in any case. Firstly, the absence of something (e.g. a third world war) is not taken as convincing proof in any other field, such as medical research or flight safety. Secondly, other factors helped to prevent another world war. On the Soviet side, one factor was the extent of the destruction caused by the Second World War (in which 27 million Soviet citizens were killed), and in the USA there were other key issues such as the Vietnam War and the civil rights movement. Further factors include the beginning of economic integration in Europe, the formation of alliances such as NATO and the Warsaw Pact, and the emergence of international organizations such as the United Nations. It should also be noted that long phases of peace are not unusual in history. The stories and myths we tell ourselves as a society influence our decisions and actions. This is why we urgently need to challenge theories such as that of nuclear deterrence and myths about the supposed security created by nuclear weapons.

According to statements in spring 2021 by the head of the US Strategic Command at the time, Admiral Charles A. Richard, and by the Federation of American Scientists, the danger of a nuclear war is currently higher than ever before.[68] Nuclear bombs are the clearest and most perverse expression of patriarchal violence and of fantasies of dominance and destruction. They reflect the assumption that force and physical strength are essential for security. Anyone who can subordinate and destroy others is powerful – and safe. In 2018, when the North Korean dictator Kim Jong-un boasted online about the nuclear button on his desk, the US president at the time, Donald Trump, responded with this tweet: 'Will someone from his depleted and food starved regime please inform him that I too have a Nuclear Button, but it is a much bigger & more powerful one than his, and my Button works!' It would be hard to imagine a clearer expression of the need to demonstrate strength and power with nuclear weapons. In this logic, such weapons are seen as a guarantee of maximum security.

Major institutions of security policy were established at a time when the primacy of *Realpolitik* went virtually unchallenged and when alternative ways of thinking played no part in international politics. Ever since, fantasies of domination and destruction have been at the core of the existence of these institutions. For NATO, founded in 1949, the theory of nuclear deterrence plays a constitutive role. NATO's own view is that it will remain a nuclear coalition for as long as nuclear weapons exist. Germany, because of its 'nuclear sharing'* role in NATO, is one of five NATO countries (along with Belgium, Italy, the Netherlands and Turkey) that have American nuclear weapons on their territory. Around fifteen to twenty B61 nuclear bombs are stationed at the Bundeswehr air base in the small locality of Büchel in the Eifel region. If the order came from the US president, the nuclear weapons would be delivered by German pilots. Is it any wonder that NATO was less than pleased (to put it diplomatically) when the Treaty on the Prohibition of Nuclear Weapons (TPNW) came into force and thus became international law on 22 January 2021?[69] Hardly. The treaty forbids the development, production, storage and testing of nuclear weapons – as well as their possession and use.[70]

The TPNW is a success story of civil society, specifically of the International Campaign to Abolish Nuclear Weapons (ICAN), a coalition of numerous NGOs. The treaty was adopted on 7 July 2017 by the UN, with two-thirds of all states – 122 countries – voting in

---

* 'Nuclear sharing' consists partly of political involvement – Germany is part of the Nuclear Planning Group and therefore involved in NATO's nuclear strategy – and partly of technical involvement, that is, the stationing of American nuclear weapons on German soil.

favour. It is no coincidence that the best-known faces of this success story, such as Beatrice Fihn, the former executive director of ICAN, or Ray Acheson, author of *Banning the Bomb: Smashing the Patriarchy*, are decidedly feminist. They are fighting to end this extreme expression of patriarchal violence and its potential to cause mass genocidal destruction.

Ray Acheson's book offers a detailed account both of the history of the movement that resulted in the nuclear weapons ban and of the intersectional feminist critique of the nuclear arsenal. Acheson argues that feminist analysis is the prerequisite for understanding nuclear weapons as the culmination of destructive patriarchal thinking. In this worldview, it seems acceptable that the nine states that possess nuclear weapons are able to kill hundreds of thousands of people at the touch of a button while claiming that this makes our world safer – when in actual fact the existence of these weapons keeps the majority of the world's population (who oppose nuclear arms) in a state of insecurity. Nuclear weapons have never made anyone safe; on the contrary, they have always meant death, suffering and destruction.

We mustn't forget that there is nothing random about the current state of our world. It is the product of human actions – the actions of those who hold (military) power. But feminists encourage us to be brave and remind us that it's worth fighting to change violent and destructive systems. ICAN, for example, took inspiration from the international bans on landmines and cluster bombs and from the focus on the humanitarian consequences of such weapons systems. There is still much to be done, however. Although there are now ninety-two signatories to the TPNW, of which sixty-eight are parties (i.e. they have ratified or acceded to the treaty), too many states still refuse to take this important step towards a less violent world[71] – first of all, the nine states that possess nuclear weapons (the USA, the UK, France, Russia and China – the permanent five – plus India, Pakistan, Israel and North Korea), but also the NATO states including Germany. States such as Germany argue that the TPNW contradicts the Non-Proliferation Treaty (NPT) from the late 1960s. This has been refuted:

even the research service of the Bundestag has stated, 'Legally, the TPNW does not contradict the NPT.'[72] Regardless of their pledges in the Non-Proliferation Treaty to reduce the numbers of their nuclear weapons and ultimately eliminate them altogether, the nuclear-armed states continue to spend billions modernizing their nuclear arsenals – in spite of the pandemic and the economic recession.[73] NATO has openly rejected the Treaty on the Prohibition of Nuclear Weapons, justifying this refusal with the obsolete and deeply patriarchal strategy of nuclear deterrence.[74] This is despite an open letter published by fifty-six former heads of state, heads of government and foreign and defence ministers from twenty NATO member states – including the former German foreign minister and vice chancellor Joschka Fischer, the former secretary-general of the UN Ban Ki-moon, and two former secretaries-general of NATO – calling on states to join the nuclear weapons ban treaty. They write that 'nuclear weapons serve no legitimate military or strategic purpose in light of the catastrophic human and environmental consequences of their use.'[75] To coincide with Germany's federal elections in September 2021, CFFP produced a briefing, with the support of ICAN, setting out very clear steps that Germany could take to contribute to nuclear disarmament. A survey from 2020 found that 83 per cent of Germans would like to see US nuclear weapons withdrawn from Germany.[76]

(Nuclear) disarmament is absolutely central to our work as a feminist organization. So of course we want Germany to join the Treaty on the Prohibition of Nuclear Weapons. At the same time, we're aware that there's widespread acceptance of the concept of nuclear deterrence within the political sphere (as opposed to society in general). So we realize that radical change, unfortunately, can't always be achieved straight away and sometimes has to happen gradually. There are steps that the German government could take immediately to advance nuclear disarmament, but others would probably take some time. For example, we urged Germany to participate in the first meeting of the states parties to the TPNW in June 2022 as an observer. In October 2021, the new Norwegian government was the first NATO state to announce its intention to attend this meeting as an observer, and in November 2021 the new German government made the same promise in its coalition agreement. Both states followed through and attended the meeting.[77] Germany should also, like other NATO members such as Norway and the Netherlands, demand an end to the investment of state pension funds in nuclear weapons. It should – at the very least – draw attention to the catastrophic humanitarian, ecological and often racially discriminatory effects of nuclear tests, accidents and attacks. It should request the removal of all American nuclear weapons from German territory. And it should work with other like-minded NATO member states to develop an alternative security concept for NATO as a 'non-nuclear alliance'.[78] In the past, the establishment of an international ban was an essential prerequisite for the elimination of biological and chemical weapons; the TPNW is therefore the right strategy to follow if we want a world without nuclear weapons.

Any foreign policy that wishes to achieve lasting peace must work resolutely towards nuclear disarmament. Nuclear arms are the worst excrescence of patriarchal violence and the diametric opposite of efforts towards peace. They are the product of the 'realist' school of political thought, based on an assumption of international anarchy and a fundamentally negative view of human nature, which can conceive of security only in terms of the threat of total destruction. But nuclear bombs do not give anyone security – far from it. Since the nine nuclear states are among the most influential in the world, however, the fight for nuclear disarmament – which is also a battle against the patriarchy – is no walk in the park. This makes the achievements of the activists and experts associated with ICAN all the more impressive. They have created international law and made history. This fight has always been strongly influenced by feminist thinking, and it serves as a model for other intersectional feminist concerns. There are, after all, other demands that need to be enshrined in international law – such as a ban on fully autonomous weapons systems, or 'killer robots'.

Fully autonomous weapons systems

Reaching Critical Will – the disarmament programme of WILPF – offers the following definition: 'Fully autonomous weapons are weapon systems that can select and fire upon targets on their own, without any human intervention. Fully autonomous weapons can be enabled to assess the situational context on a battlefield and to decide on the required attack according to the processed information.'[79] To do this they use artificial intelligence (AI), which relies on algorithms and data analysis functions. Fully autonomous weapons differ from remotely controlled weapons systems such as the drones that are widely used at present: the latter are controlled by a human, while completely autonomous weapons would no longer have any human guidance once they were programmed.[80] Although no lethal autonomous weapons systems have been used so far, there are precursors which are autonomous and lethal to varying degrees. In total, twelve states are known to be developing or using autonomous weapons systems, including Germany and several nuclear powers.[81] Naturally, these countries resist demands for a ban. They claim that it is too soon for an international treaty, and that their militaries benefit from such weapons systems. The USA, the UK, Israel and South Korea are already using systems of this type.[82]

Autonomous weapons – weapons without proper human control – will not only reinforce the international dynamics of dominance and subordination but will take them to new extremes. Once these weapons are fully operational, governments will be able to use them in or near the battlefield without human involvement. As we have already seen with drones, this remoteness leads to greater use of force and more civilian victims. It is chilling to imagine an arms race with weapons that are neither controlled by humans nor regulated by international humanitarian law.

A 'no' to killer robots

On 21 March 2019 the international Campaign to Stop Killer Robots, founded in 2013, held a press conference and other public events in Berlin. The campaign, which is resolutely feminist and anti-racist in focus and highlights the dangers of AI for political minorities, demands an international ban on autonomous weapons systems. CFFP had joined an alliance of twelve German NGOs, including Greenpeace, Oxfam and Brot für die Welt, to deliver a demand to the German government at the time. We wanted the government to voice clear support for a global prohibition of autonomous weapons systems, as pledged in its coalition agreement. The agreement had stated: 'We reject autonomous weapons systems which are removed from human control. We want to outlaw them worldwide.' The new government has made similar pledges. However, we wanted (and still want) more: we want the German government to express immediate and explicit support for a binding ban on autonomous weapons systems and to call for negotiations on such a ban within the framework of the UN's expert discussions for the Convention on Certain Conventional Weapons (CCW).* 125 states are parties to this convention. The demand to ban autonomous weapons systems is supported globally by more than 180 organizations in over sixty-five countries as part of the international Stop Killer Robots campaign. Many scientists have also affirmed the need for such a ban.[83] In 2018 Heiko Maas, the German minister of foreign affairs at the time, demanded a ban on autonomous weapons, but so far there is no sign that Germany has made any attempt to begin the necessary negotiations. It has, however, taken part in a few international meetings and in April 2020 organized an online conference on this topic.[84] Our press release at the time stated: 'Autonomous weapons, so-called killer robots, must not only distinguish sufficiently between civilians and

---

* This convention, adopted in 1980, regulates the use of conventional weapons that are not nuclear, biological or chemical. Autonomous weapons therefore fall under its provisions.

combatants but must also calculate the effect of any use of weapons in advance and make deliberative decisions as well as choosing their target and weapons.'

Killer robots have been on the agenda of the CCW since 2014, so the parties to the convention have been discussing these weapons systems since then, and a formal process has been under way since 2017. During the pandemic the regular annual meetings in Geneva, bringing together government representatives, diplomats and civil society, were put on hold. One of the reasons why it is so difficult to reach agreement and a potential ban is that CCW resolutions require a consensus.

At the time of writing, there is widespread support for a ban on autonomous or AI-based weapons. According to the Campaign to Stop Killer Robots, the proposal to ban these weapons is backed by thirty states, more than 170 NGOs, 4,500 AI experts and scientists such as Noam Chomsky and Stuart Russell,[85] entrepreneurs such as Elon Musk, UN Secretary-General António Guterres, the European Parliament, twenty-six Nobel Peace Prize laureates, and 61 per cent of the world's population.[86]

Artificial intelligence is based on the data provided by our society. Again and again, AI has been shown to be racist and sexist. It can be assumed that programmed machines would perpetuate the toxic images of masculinity that operate within the military. And it is not just patriarchal gender traditions that are perpetuated in AI but also racial biases and stereotypes, as shown to chilling effect in the documentary *Coded Bias*. Facial recognition technology works best on the faces of White men and is much more likely to misidentify or fail to recognize men and women of colour.[87] In 2018, the AI researcher Joy Buolamwini and Timnit Gebru, a high-profile expert on ethical AI, published a ground-breaking study. They demonstrated that the failure rate of facial recognition software was 0.8 per cent for light-skinned men but 34.7 per cent for dark-skinned women.[88] This racial bias in the design, production, implementation and regulation of such technologies[89] doesn't just have negative consequences for people applying for loans; in the case of erroneous facial recognition by autonomous weapons systems, the consequences could be deadly.

To understand how problematic autonomous weapons systems are, we also need to look closely at the international power imbalance. The imbalance between states of the Global North and the Global South could be exacerbated by killer robots, since it is mainly countries of the Global North that can afford these technologies. The rise in US drone attacks during Obama's term in office, killing at least 3,000 people in Afghanistan, Pakistan, Iran and Syria,[90] shows how lethal the technological advantage of wealthier countries can be and how it can consolidate global power imbalances. WILPF has pointed out that, although the countries of the Global South may not be the ones developing and using these technologies, they will most likely become the battlegrounds for the testing and use of killer robots, just as they have been for armed drones.[91] So it's not surprising that most of the countries supporting the ban on fully autonomous weapons are from the Global South.

For all these reasons, autonomous weapons systems must be eliminated. Feminist foreign policy, which advocates feminist security and opposes the militarization of new technologies, demands an unconditional and legally binding ban. This could take the form of a new protocol of the CCW, where this issue has been debated since 2014. Alternatively, if the proponents of a ban were to join forces politically, killer robots could be prohibited in a separate treaty. Agreements on bans on landmines (1997), cluster munitions (2008) and nuclear weapons (2021) have shown how this can be done.[92]

Such a ban would also be in line with the democratic will of the people: surveys in Germany have found that 72 per cent of the population is opposed to autonomous weapons. And even the Federation of German Industries (BDI) has demanded such a treaty, along with 20,000 computer scientists from the German Informatics Society.[93]

Conclusion: no security in patriarchy

Whatever types of weapon we are talking about – small arms and light weapons, nuclear weapons, fully autonomous weapons or weapon-like methods in cyberspace,* which is becoming increasingly militarized – what all of them have in common is that they are used to oppress other states and ultimately other people and exert power over them. All these forms of violence are tools of the patriarchy and follow a logic of dominance and state security. If we continue to follow this logic, we will never be able to achieve genuine security for everyone. Feminists have known this for a very long time: weapons don't make us safer. They don't bring peace, and they certainly don't bring feminist security. We need a world where everyone can live in safety. Real safety. Countless proponents of *Realpolitik* dismiss this demand as naive. But if the abolition of war, violence and armed conflict and the creation of peace and security are not our ultimate goal, then what is??

---

* In recent years cyberspace has increasingly been described as unsafe and hostile, and 'cyber-security' has become more and more of a priority for national security worldwide. And rightly so. Cyberattacks and threats to critical public infrastructure originating online constitute a very real danger. But feminists have criticized the response to this threat. The militarization of cyberspace can ultimately lead to real physical violence.

Bonnie Jenkins:
'It's our job to question the
status quo – again and again.'

Bonnie Jenkins is one of the most highly qualified security experts in the USA. She has a law degree, two master's degrees, and a PhD in International Relations. She served in the US Air Force and held an ambassador role in the US Department of State in the Bureau of International Security and Nonproliferation. In July 2021 she was confirmed by the Senate as the under secretary of state for arms control and international security affairs. This makes her the first person of colour ever to reach the level of secretary of state.

In 2017 Bonnie founded the organization Women of Color Advancing Peace, Security and Conflict Transformation (WCAPS). Before this there was no organized platform that expressed the perspective and voice of people of colour, specifically Black women. Thanks to Bonnie's tireless commitment, women of colour now have strong political representation.

Even before her work on arms control and diversity, Bonnie gave considerable thought to how she could use her abilities to serve her community and society, bring about changes and make things better. She grew up in the Bronx in New York and attended a school on the affluent Upper East Side. From an early age she got used to being, more often than not, the only Black person and the only woman in the room. She discovered her passion for the topic of arms control more or less by chance during one of her internships in Washington. Gradually she noticed how few diverse voices there were in this field of work. One woman in a room full of men is not enough to have a lasting impact on decisions, she believes. There need to be more voices, more women, more people of colour, more diversity.

According to Bonnie, the discourse on feminist foreign policy has played a crucial role in creating an inclusive space in which the status quo can be critically questioned from various perspectives. But what exactly does it mean to take a feminist approach to security and disarmament? Bonnie's answer is that the emphasis must be on peace, not violence. We need to think intersectionally, focus on the future and on long-term sustainability, and accord higher status to diplomacy.

One of the books Bonnie is currently reading is *Badges without Borders: How Global Counterinsurgency Transformed American Policing*, by Stuart Schrader.

12 THE FUTURE OF FOREIGN POLICY IS FEMINIST

The master's tools will never dismantle the master's house. They may allow us temporarily to beat him at his own game, but they will never enable us to bring about genuine change.

Audre Lorde, 'The master's tools will never dismantle the master's house', in *Sister Outsider* (Feasterville Trevose, PA: Crossing Press, 2007)

We'd made it! In February 2020, after much networking and preparation, Nina and I and our Centre for Feminist Foreign Policy organized the first event on feminist foreign policy at the Munich Security Conference. The conference, which describes itself as 'the world's leading forum for debating . . . the world's most pressing security concerns',[1] takes place annually at the Hotel Bayerischer Hof. It brings together around a thousand participants, including heads of state, government representatives, members of parliament, journalists, business representatives, and the heads of international (civil society) organizations. Alongside the official programme, they discuss the most urgent issues for foreign and security policy. At our event during the 2020 conference, I delivered a speech to around 150 people. I'd been up until well after midnight finishing it off after the previous day's events. I was excited, as there were many high-ranking politicians and decision-makers in the room. Fatou Bensouda, the chief prosecutor of the International Criminal Court at the time, Niels Annen, then minister of state in the German Foreign Office, and the Nobel Peace Prize laureate Beatrice Fihn were all speaking at our event. And there were other people I look up to (mainly women) in the audience, such as the human rights defender Düzen Tekkal, or Claudia Roth, who was vice president of the Bundestag at the time and is currently minister of state for culture and the media.

My wish list for a future-proof foreign policy

Having a vision means calling into question the patriarchal status quo. Let us disarm. Stop the export of weapons. Fund feminist civil society. Let us make gender conflict analyses the norm. Teach International Relations differently. Tackle toxic and violent masculinity. Ban lethal autonomous weapons systems. Distribute power equitably in foreign ministries. Protect human rights defenders. Smash the military-industrial complex. Create ministries of peace. Let us make human security our priority.

This is an extract from my speech during our event at the 2020 Munich Security Conference – a succinct wish list of core elements of a feminist foreign policy. Of course such a policy must always be adapted to the specific context – tailored to a particular state or organization. This is what CFFP did shortly before the elections to the German Bundestag in September 2021: we wrote a manifesto for a feminist foreign policy for Germany. We described our vision for a future German foreign policy – a policy that focuses on human rights, human security, and the destruction of the patriarchy. This is the only form of foreign policy that can truly create lasting peace. There can be no peace in patriarchy. Oppression, destruction and dominance are, and always have been, incompatible with peace and security.

As we were putting the final touches to our manifesto, a foreign policy disaster was playing out before the eyes of the world. It was a disaster that wouldn't have happened (or not in the way it did) if foreign policy had been genuinely focused on feminist security and human rights and if the demands of human rights defenders and feminist civil society had been put at the centre of international political decisions. This disaster was Afghanistan.

Hopeless: Afghanistan 2021

In 2001, after the attacks on the World Trade Center, US President George W. Bush proclaimed a 'War on Terror'. This was a new form of war, targeted not at a particular country but at non-state actors and groups, first and foremost the Taliban. This Islamist terrorist group had governed its home country, Afghanistan, since 1996. The Taliban were suspected of harbouring Osama bin Laden, the mastermind and financier of the 9/11 attacks. Experts say that the USA, in the aftermath of the attacks, was desperate to find a target and a justification for military action.[2] The Taliban's abuse and disenfranchisement of women became a hot topic in the media, and the US Department of State even published a report entitled *The Taliban's War Against Women*. After 'Operation Enduring Freedom', the US-led military attack that overthrew the Taliban in October 2001, First Lady Laura Bush addressed her fellow Americans on the radio. Thanks to the military successes of the USA, she said, Afghan women were no longer confined to their homes. 'The fight against terrorism is also a fight for the rights and dignity of women,' affirmed Bush.[3] Again and again, over the twenty years of the Afghanistan mission, women's rights were cited to justify the military deployment. This supposedly 'feminist' narrative, combined with colonial ideas and racism, has generated the notion of the 'other men' – Muslims – as violators of the rights of women. These women, according to the narrative, need to be rescued by men from the Global North. The narrative, which fuels global Islamophobia and confirms the idea of the White saviour (as mentioned earlier in this book), made it possible to secure broad-based support for the Afghanistan mission among the US population.[4]

Human rights and women's rights should of course be at the centre of foreign policy actions. This is one of our core demands. And sometimes the principle of 'responsibility to protect' (R2P) requires the use of military means to defend people from crimes against humanity. But – and this is also a core demand of feminist foreign policy – a human-rights-based foreign policy must listen to the voices of those affected, particularly the voices of (feminist) civil society, and seek information about their concerns and the threats they face. This is exactly what didn't happen in Afghanistan. Not at the beginning of the operation, and not at the end. This failure was particularly glaring in the months, weeks and dramatic days before the last US soldier left Afghan soil on 30 August 2021. On 18 August, three days after Kabul had fallen to the Taliban, as desperate people tried to cling to departing aeroplanes and fell to their deaths, Sanam Anderlini tweeted: 'For YEARS we called on govts, #UN, journalists to talk to/ensure #Afghan women peace/rights activists heard & heeded. Always patronized/brushed away. Now everyone suddenly concerned/wants to talk to #Afghan women.'[5]

On Sunday 15 August, when Kabul was captured by the Taliban, I was at a museum in Berlin with a friend. Suddenly there was a flurry of news updates and messages, and my phone rang. One of our partner organizations, Medica Mondiale, which has women's rights defenders on the ground in Kabul, urgently needed our support. They asked whether we could help with contacts high up in the German Foreign Office. Things needed to happen fast. The organization had been working in Afghanistan for twenty years, supporting survivors of sexualized violence. They'd already become alarmed in spring 2021, as the international forces prepared for their unconditional withdrawal from Afghanistan and the Taliban advanced into more and more provinces. The women's rights defenders and activists feared for their lives; security measures at their offices in Herat, Mazar-i-Sharif and Kabul were reinforced. Three days before Kabul fell to the Taliban, the activists of Medica Mondiale managed to move the women whose lives were at risk from Herat and Mazar-i-Sharif to the capital, where they thought they would be safe. But, as of 15 August, their lives were in danger there too.

On that same Sunday, we called a senior representative of the German Foreign Office and made sure that the threat facing these women was placed firmly on the agenda. In the days and weeks that followed we received countless desperate emails with names, in the hope that we could somehow help to get these people onto the lists for German evacuation flights. Three days after that Sunday, the human rights defender Düzen Tekkal and I, along with our organizations, Hawar.help and CFFP, launched the initiative Defend Afghan Women's Rights. Our aim was to combine the many offers of money and assistance that we were receiving and put them to use for the organizations affected (in the end €160,000 was collected within two weeks). We also wanted to make political demands with maximum media impact. These included safe passage to the airport for the women's rights defenders and their families, definite confirmation that their names were on the list for evacuation flights, the opening of Kabul airport beyond the end of August, and special evacuation contingents for particularly endangered groups such as women journalists and politicians.[6] Far too many of the women were not rescued and, as I write, are still living in hiding and in mortal danger.

Two weeks later, on 31 August, Düzen and I held a press conference. One of the participants was Zarifa Ghafari, the mayor of the town of Maidan Shahr, who had fled Afghanistan. On the day after the last Western country (the USA) had ended its evacuation flights, she was visibly distraught. This was hardly surprising, given that she had been forced to flee her homeland overnight, leaving her many sisters to face an uncertain future. At the conference Ghafari accused the international community of turning Afghanistan into the war zone that it is today. Speaking into the camera, she said that anyone who remains silent and does not defend the rights of Afghan women now is making a mockery of their talk of women's and human rights.[7]

In the twenty years of the US mission in Afghanistan, Afghan civil society and especially women's organizations had become well established. Throughout this period, they carried out valuable work on the ground – e.g. in politics, the health system and the social sector. They had built up good networks, and sometimes male politicians even asked for their help because of their perceived influence within communities.[8] For years, Afghan women's rights defenders and peace activists had demanded that their work be taken seriously and valued, and they had asked for an equal place at the table – especially the table where a new peace treaty was to be negotiated.

The Taliban and the USA had been holding talks about the future of Afghanistan since 2018, talks where men made decisions at the expense of women and other minorities, and non-Taliban Afghans (including the Afghan government) were excluded. At the end of these negotiations, the US–Taliban deal (the 'Doha Agreement' or 'Agreement for Bringing Peace to Afghanistan') was signed on 29 February 2020. This set out the conditions for the withdrawal of foreign troops from Afghanistan and laid the foundations for the intra-Afghan peace talks which began a few months later, on 12 September 2020 in Doha, Qatar. Although it has been proved that peace talks are more effective and peace lasts longer if women are involved, there were only four women present at the intra-Afghan negotiations in Doha, and at a later round of negotiations in Moscow only one woman was present.[9] Instead, Afghan women peacebuilders who have dedicated their lives to making peace in their country received letters at the beginning of 2020 urging them to remain silent.[10] At the time, the USA, the UN and other international actors were finally preparing to support the peace process. The activists had been calling for peace talks for years, under the condition that all civil society actors – e.g. women, young people, and religious and ethnic minorities – be included and given an equal voice.[11] However, women's rights and women's demands played no part in either the Doha Agreement or the intra-Afghan peace talks.

In April 2021 a coalition of mainly Afghan women's rights and civil society organizations published an open letter to the 'friends of Afghanistan' and to the governments of Turkey, Qatar, the USA, Norway, Canada, the UK, Iran and Pakistan, as well as the UN, the EU, and other European states who were involved in supporting the peace process (Germany among them). The letter urged these states to finally turn their lofty words on the importance of women's rights into actions and fulfil their commitments to women, peace and security. This included real participation by civil society, and particularly women peacebuilders, in peace talks.

The specific demands expressed in the open letter were as follows. The states addressed were asked to advocate the participation of women peacebuilders as a separate, independent delegation, a third party alongside the Taliban and the Afghan government. They were urged to encourage the Afghan government to include more women in its delegation, especially parliamentarians with expertise on women's and human rights. And if Afghan women peacebuilders continued to be excluded, they were advised to include them in their own delegations.[12] These demands were ignored, however. Many of the women had warned, since the beginning of the peace process, that the protection of human rights and the civilian population would be overlooked if women's rights activists and civil society were not involved. They feared that hard-earned progress towards women's rights would be thoughtlessly sacrificed for the prospect of rapid agreement in the negotiations.[13] And they were right. Since the Taliban seized power in August 2021, many countries have evacuated their embassies in Kabul and ended their financial support for the country (except for humanitarian aid, which is delivered via the UN), but in the long term there are bound to be further attempts to hold peace talks in Afghanistan. With the Taliban in power, however, the situation of women in these talks will be even more precarious. Who knows whether they will be allowed to participate at all?[14]

The situation of women and girls in Afghanistan is catastrophic. Targeted discrimination and a series of increasingly strict decrees prevent Afghan women and girls from accessing education and healthcare and take away their freedom of movement and assembly and their right to participate in political and economic life. Women are not permitted to travel or even go to the doctor without a male chaperone. They are not allowed to go to the gym, walk in the park or study at university. The aim of the Taliban is to banish them completely from the public sphere. Afghanistan is the only country in the world that deprives girls of their right to education. In 2022, a document by the UN special rapporteur on the human rights situation in Afghanistan declared that there was no other country where women and girls had disappeared so quickly from all areas of public life and were so disadvantaged in all aspects of life.[15] The Afghan journalist Zahra Nader commented on these developments during the open debate on Women, Peace and Security in the UN Security Council in October 2022:

> *What I can say from what happened in Afghanistan is that the voices of Afghan women, the real voices of Afghan woman [sic], were never heard, were never part of the negotiation, and were never part of any peace deal. What happened was all behind closed doors. A decision was made for Afghan women and they were not part of making that decision. And what we are seeing right now in Afghanistan is the result of a peace deal that didn't include women.[16]*

Since Kabul fell to the Taliban in August 2021, CFFP has been working with leading Afghan women human rights defenders. At the beginning of 2023 we published their demands for the international community. Any collaboration with the Taliban, they urged, must be dependent on the acceptance of women's and human rights; there must be no exceptions to the travel ban on members of the Taliban until the restrictions on girls and women have been lifted; political pressure must be exerted on states that support the Taliban; no more male-only delegations should be sent to negotiations with the Taliban (50 per cent of each delegation should be women); and the demands of women's and human rights defenders must be at the centre of all political discussions on the future of Afghanistan.[17]

I clearly remember an event in Berlin, at the diplomatic mission of a NATO partner, about two years before the withdrawal of troops from Afghanistan. A high-ranking German diplomat talked about the need for compromises. A topic such as the rights of women shouldn't stand in the way of a possible peace process with the Taliban, he said. Sacrifices had to be made. He was totally serious: he believed it was possible to make 'peace' although at least half of society was massively oppressed. This is exactly the one-dimensional patriarchal understanding of international politics that I have been criticizing and that feminist foreign policy seeks to overcome. It is completely contrary to the understanding of peace and security that feminists advocate worldwide.

The CFFP manifesto*

As mentioned above, CFFP produced a document just before the German national elections in 2021 to show what we mean by peace and security and how this translates into specific areas of foreign and security policy. We published the document – our demands for a feminist foreign policy – ten days before the election, presented it at an international online event, and sent it to multiple representatives of the democratic parties, as well as to other contacts in ministries and civil society. This manifesto is a team effort by CFFP, co-authored by Nina Bernarding, Sheena Anderson, Antonia Baskakov, Damjan Denkovski, Annika Kreitlow, Anna Provan, Janika Lohse and myself. We write:

> *A Feminist Foreign Policy acknowledges that the historical practice of foreign and security policy has led to a most insecure, unequal and destructive global status quo that is failing most people. A Feminist Foreign Policy re-envisions a country's national interests by prioritising feminist understandings of security and shifting the focus from the state to the individual as the primary referent of security. A Feminist Foreign Policy questions who has power and why. . . . [It] proactively seeks to eradicate the injustices, oppression and exclusion, which uphold dominant and oppressive power structures. It recognises that existing foreign policy is influenced by patriarchal and racist stereotypes and colonial legacies, and it works to overcome these influences.*[18]

---

* By the time the English translation of this book is published our manifesto will be two years old. I updated large parts of the book for the German paperback edition and the English translation, but I have left the manifesto as it was when it was first published in September 2021 – partly as a document of the time when it was written.

We also identify principles that must underlie any feminist foreign policy. For example, a feminist foreign policy must be based on a comprehensive understanding of gender. This means that structural power differences and hierarchies on the basis of sex and social attributions of characteristics to the different genders must be seen and analysed. Furthermore, a feminist foreign policy must be intersectional, antiracist and anti-militaristic. It must be coherent in its approach – that is, 'grounded in a domestic policy that exercises the same values within the country's own borders as it does outside.' And by recognizing the central role of (feminist) civil society in the historical fight for human rights, especially the rights of minorities, feminist foreign policy builds on these hard-won human rights and takes its lead from (feminist) civil society and broader social movements. Feminist foreign policy relies on cooperation rather than domination, is concerned with climate justice, works transparently and takes responsibility. It pursues precise, measurable goals, so that civil society and all those entrusted with implementing the policy understand exactly *what* the state wishes to achieve with its foreign policy, *when* it plans to achieve these goals, and what resources it intends to use.

Below I give a brief account of the areas covered in detail by our manifesto. Foreign and security policy is an extremely wide-ranging field; we concentrated on selected aspects.

Peace and security

Feminist foreign policy relies on feminist understandings of security instead of militarized ideas of state security. It spends money to overcome structural inequalities and to change violent, militarized power relations – so it is not concerned just with the absence of violent conflicts but with investing in peace. In concrete terms, this means promoting human rights, creating economic and social justice for all, protecting the environment and preserving ecosystems. A feminist foreign policy insists on inclusive and transparent processes in all decisions relating to peace and security – from a local to a global level.

In German foreign policy we're still far removed from many of these principles. The preservation of the state's 'sovereignty' and 'territorial integrity' is still the top priority. This is clearly set out in the German government's policy documents, such as the *White Paper on German Security Policy and the Future of the Bundeswehr*, published in 2016. Although the government has repeatedly emphasized its restrictive export policy for military goods, Germany is still one of the four biggest arms exporters in the world. 'Legitimate security policy and Alliance policy interests' are cited in justification.[19] At the same time, Berlin has steadily increased military spending since 2015. In 2020 the Ministry of Defence had the third-largest budget of all federal ministries, €45.7 billion. By way of comparison, only around €6.6 billion was allocated to the Foreign Office. And although the Foreign Office mentions peace and security as essential components of German policy, in 2020 Germany spent only €40 million on disarmament, non-proliferation of weapons and arms control, and just €400 million on crisis prevention, stabilization and peacebuilding. Furthermore, the Ministry for the Environment, Nature Conservation and Nuclear Safety, the department responsible for responding to the climate crisis (which has already plunged millions of people into terrible insecurity), spent only €776 million of its budget of €3.2 billion on climate-related measures. That's just 2.5 per cent of its total budget.

Another frequent criticism of the German government is that its decision-making on peace and security is anything but transparent and inclusive. This is evident in the huge influence of lobbyists and the privileged access of the defence industry and the automotive industry to decision-making processes. While lobbyists from the auto and arms industries are regular visitors to the Bundestag, representatives of civil society like us struggle to be heard at all. From 2015 to 2017, highranking government representatives had almost nine times as many meetings with auto manufacturers as with environmental organizations.[20] So civil society, which reflects the concerns of the people, still has a far less powerful voice than industry.

To implement a feminist foreign policy, Germany needs to develop a peace strategy containing specific steps to overcome structural inequalities, militarized power relations and the excessive influence of the defence industry. Financial and human resources from the defence budget must be diverted to fight threats to human and feminist security, such as the climate crisis, the pandemic and arms proliferation. We want the official policy documents of the German government to call into question the insane and deeply patriarchal concept of nuclear and conventional deterrence, and we want the defence ministry to be replaced by a ministry of peace. The language we use and the stories we tell shape our reality. A ministry of peace instead of a ministry of defence would help us to tell better stories and, we hope, make better history.

Demilitarization, disarmament and arms (export) control

A feminist foreign policy explicitly calls for the recognition of feminist concepts of security. International demilitarization, disarmament and arms (export) control are therefore one of its central pillars. Advocates of feminist foreign policy do not believe that peace and security can be achieved by subordination, violence and war. On the contrary, a feminist foreign policy examines and questions how militarized structures may help to cause violent conflicts.

It has been estimated that German arms manufacturers have made about €400 million producing weapons for the Afghanistan mission over the last twenty years – and this is just a fraction of Germany's arms exports.[21] Germany also opposes international efforts at disarmament – for example, by refusing to ratify the Treaty on the Prohibition of Nuclear Weapons. Another problem is Germany's own build-up of arms: in 2020, during a pandemic which put a heavy strain on critical resources and overburdened the public health system, the German defence budget was at its highest since 1993.[22] Of the ten countries with the highest military spending in 2020, it was Germany's expenditure that increased the most – a 5.2 per cent rise in comparison to the previous year.[23] Disarmament and arms control are vital elements of feminist foreign policy, as is the goal of ending arms production and arms exports. Germany should be taking serious steps to invest in peace rather than war. In summary, we want the German government to make disarmament and genuinely restrictive arms control a priority, to advocate nuclear disarmament and a ban on fully autonomous weapons ('killer robots'), and to recognize that militarized power structures are a source of conflicts.

Human rights and the rule of law

A feminist foreign policy is based on the recognition of international human rights norms. Its understanding of human rights is inclusive and intersectional. If Germany is to promote human rights credibly and effectively on an international level, it must also fulfil its obligations arising from international human rights norms on a domestic level.

Germany has ratified most international human rights conventions and emphatically advocates the international protection of human rights. But there are major gaps in many areas, especially in domestic policy. In sexual and reproductive justice, for example, there are substantial discrepancies between what Germany says and what it does: women with unwanted pregnancies still have great difficulty accessing safe abortions. At the very least, a German feminist foreign policy would ensure that the obligations enshrined in international human rights norms are fully reflected in German law. If Berlin has ratified these norms, it is obliged to turn them into federal laws. This includes demands from human rights treaties such as the Istanbul Convention, the UN Convention on the Rights of the Child, the Charter of Fundamental Rights of the European Union and the women's rights convention, CEDAW. A feminist foreign policy would also invest substantial resources to prioritize these norms, to reinforce them, and to implement them effectively and sustainably. A feminist foreign policy insists that all states protect and guarantee universal human rights and the rule of law. It demands an international commitment to bringing to justice the perpetrators of human rights violations and ending impunity for international crimes. A feminist foreign policy applies a feminist understanding of international law (as set out in chapter 5).

Climate justice

A feminist foreign policy is fully committed to ending the climate crisis, promoting climate justice, and helping people adapt to changing circumstances. It recognizes that structural, multidimensional inequalities and unfair power dynamics are the greatest obstacles to achieving climate justice. In this respect, Berlin is a long way from our ideals: Germany's climate protection legislation is patchy. Even the Federal Constitutional Court declared that the Climate Protection Law of 2019 was unconstitutional. It remains to be seen whether the new government will make better choices in this area.

As a wealthy industrial nation, Germany bears a huge share of responsibility for the climate crisis. This has been caused largely by the fossil energy economy – the result of the industrial revolution and the associated phenomenon of colonialism. Germany has been producing enormous amounts of CO_2 for more than 200 years, making it one of the biggest environmental polluters in history.[24]

A German feminist foreign policy would recognize the climate crisis as one of the greatest threats to national and international security. It would take an intersectional approach, acknowledging that it is people who are already socially and politically marginalized who are worst affected by the climate crisis. Germany must recognize the power inequalities in the climate crisis and do something about them, and it must admit its own responsibility for this crisis. Our long list of demands for a new government includes a complete phase-out of coal by 2030, a carbon tax for high-income households, a ministry for climate justice and the protection of endangered lives, and investment in public transport. A positive aspect of the coalition agreement signed in November 2021 is the promise to phase out coal by 2030. However, Fridays for Future has criticized many other measures in the agreement as insufficient to reach the 1.5 degree target.[25]

Development cooperation*

Development cooperation also requires a feminist approach. Here intersectional equality and justice are the top priority. From a feminist point of view, economic indicators of poverty reduction such as GDP are of secondary importance.

At present Germany is far behind other countries (ranking only fifteenth among all donor nations) in its official spending on development projects with a gender focus. The German government has still not publicly acknowledged that development cooperation, even today, is influenced by colonial thinking and colonial knowledge production. It therefore ignores the unequal power relations between Germany and its 'partner countries'. The official change of terminology by the Federal Ministry for Economic Cooperation and Development – from 'development aid' to 'development cooperation' – has made very little difference.

A German feminist foreign policy would acknowledge that development cooperation is essentially a structural continuation of colonialism and would actively strive to decolonize this field. This means breaking down the prevailing power asymmetries and investing resources to achieve real justice. Within development cooperation, Germany must spend more money on dismantling existing inequalities. This includes spending to promote equality in education, health, water supply and sanitation, civil society and economic infrastructure.

---

* On 1 March 2023, the German international cooperation and development minister Svenja Schulze presented her ministry's strategy for a feminist international cooperation policy. This is an excellent policy, and we will be observing closely whether the content is translated into action.

And, last but not least, Germany must work closely with feminist civil society, especially in the Global South.

Migration

A feminist foreign policy seeks to eliminate structural inequalities and precarious living conditions, which can lead to (forced) migration. It refuses to treat migration as a militarized security problem and concentrates on its humanitarian dimension. A feminist foreign policy recognizes that border controls, arrests, deportations and racial profiling are a form of violence and that they often exacerbate unequal power relations, reproduce colonial hierarchies, and worsen unsafe conditions, especially for women, children and LGBTQ+ people. Displaced women and LGBTQ+ people face particularly high risks. There are figures showing that up to 90 per cent of all women and girls on the Balkan route are raped, and that women and LGBTQ+ individuals more frequently experience violence and abuses of power by border guards and people smugglers.[26] Until 2019, Germany accepted more asylum seekers than any other EU country. In absolute figures – though not in proportion to the size of the population – it hosts the third-largest refugee population in the world, after Turkey and Colombia.[27] And yet the current government is the first to officially see Germany as a country of immigration. Implementing a feminist foreign policy would mean making radical changes to migration and asylum policy, both inside and outside Germany, and focusing on the people affected rather than perpetuating an outdated understanding that equates state security with impenetrable borders. More specifically, we believe Germany should establish legal and safe refugee routes and decriminalize civilian sea rescue operations.

Global health

Feminist foreign policy is committed to global health that is free of discrimination and power imbalances within and between states.

The core principle here is the human right to health. Feminist foreign policy seeks to achieve health and well-being for everyone – but especially for the most disadvantaged people. It provides all the necessary resources to ensure safe, affordable and high-quality healthcare for all, at home and abroad. Both international and domestic health policy must be informed by feminist values.

On the international stage, Germany has become increasingly vocal about the importance of global health and now tops the list of WHO donors.[28] Inside Germany, however, there are still people who are denied respectful and humane healthcare (e.g. refugees, trans people and pregnant women). A German feminist foreign policy would ensure that both global and national health policies are based on the principle of health as a human right and that every form of discrimination in the German health system is eliminated. It is pleasing to see that the coalition agreement of the current government pledges to improve psychosocial support for refugees, provide free abortion services, and replace the current 'Law on Transsexuals' with a new law allowing self-identification.

Decolonizing foreign policy

Feminist foreign policy takes full responsibility for all colonial crimes and their current effects. This means that the inhabitants of former colonies should have a right to compensation and to the restitution of everything that was taken from them and their communities. It is essential to oppose postcolonial structures and systemic violence, which reinforce racism, White supremacy and unequal power relations. A feminist foreign policy reflects on the colonial histories and traumas that people (and whole countries) are still suffering from today. And it faces these histories and traumas head-on by reappraising past events, providing compensation, and working with the inhabitants of former colonies as equals.

German foreign policy must engage seriously with its colonial past and work on decolonizing its foreign policy discourses. A document published in 2019, 'Eckpunkte zum Umgang mit Sammlungsgut aus kolonialen Kontexten' (Key points for dealing with collections from colonial contexts), is a first step, but it doesn't go nearly far enough. As of 2022, only €1.44 million was available to assess museum collections that are already available for viewing online, to support digitalization in selected museums, to develop a standard for previously unpublished inventories, and to expand the project.[29] It doesn't sound as though this issue will be resolved any time soon.

All German colonial crimes must be acknowledged, all monuments, street names and other tributes to former colonial rulers must be removed, and the many stolen objects and artworks exhibited in German museums must be given back.

Fighting antifeminist attacks on the human rights system

A feminist foreign policy acknowledges that the campaigns of antifeminists and 'anti-gender' actors constitute a global movement which threatens the safety of politically marginalized people and groups worldwide. These campaigns aim at (further) restricting the rights of women, LGBTQ+ people, migrants and racial minorities. A feminist foreign policy opposes the increasingly transnational anti-gender attacks of governments, think-tanks, parties, citizens and religious groups and works actively to promote women's and LGBTQ+ rights at home and abroad.

To implement a feminist foreign policy, the German government must provide more resources to fight these actors. It must support feminist civil society and work internationally to raise awareness of the threat posed by the anti-gender movement.

Participation and leadership

A feminist foreign policy is based on the fair distribution of power – in all institutions and on all levels. Marginalized groups must not be forced to justify their own inclusion or to fight for the long-withheld right to participate. Privileged groups, on the other hand, especially White cis* men, need to justify – and end – their ongoing overrepresentation in positions of power. Only then can the needs, lived experiences and perspectives of all groups be fairly represented.

In the German Foreign Office, 43 per cent of heads and deputy heads of department are now women. This does not constitute full parity, however, and women still tend to face additional challenges in planning and organizing their careers.[30] The same goes for ethnic minorities. Diplomats of Color, an initiative launched by diplomats in the Foreign Office, criticizes the fact that only 12 per cent of civil servants have a 'migration background' (i.e. they are the children or grandchildren of people who were not born in Germany), although around 26 per cent of the population as a whole fall into this category.

A German feminist foreign policy would mean acknowledging the existing structural power hierarchies and actively working to change them. It would mean ensuring equal participation by men and women, offering courses to raise awareness and counter racism, and implementing gender budgeting in all German ministries.

Collaboration and feminist civil society

In a feminist foreign policy, feminist civil society plays a key role and is closely supported by the government. Feminist civil society has always been the strongest driver of social justice, especially when it comes to protecting and promoting marginalized groups.

Implementing a German feminist foreign policy would mean ensuring long-term institutional (rather than project-based) funding for civil society organizations, particularly those working on intersectional feminist topics, and working with them as equals.

---

* 'Cis' is used to refer to people whose gender identity coincides with the biological sex assigned at birth. It is the linguistic counterpart to 'trans' and avoids referring to people living a heteronormative lifestyle as 'normal'.

Conclusion: change and growth

A feminist foreign policy must be transformative. Change and growth occur when there is friction and when we break with traditions and dismantle unjust structures. I'm convinced that our manifesto has the power to bring about change and contribute to a fairer global society – one in which foreign policy disasters like that in Afghanistan can no longer happen.

Samantha Power:
'I want to create diplomatic
progress.'

Samantha Power wants to achieve this 'by shaking things up and punctuating the political bubble with the lived human experiences of those affected'.

Samantha Power, US ambassador to the United Nations from 2013 to 2017, law professor, Pulitzer-awarded author, and head of the US Agency for International Development (USAID) since 2021, is convinced that activism and diplomacy are inextricably linked. In her experience, diplomacy does not consider the needs of the people it affects: too often, diplomats make the same old speeches without listening to the people whose fates are at stake.

As the US ambassador in the UN Security Council, Samantha did her best to ensure that the voices of those most affected by the Security Council's decisions were heard there: for example, the reports of the doctors treating the victims of chemical weapons in Syria. Without the first-hand accounts of those affected and those working on the ground, there would never have been such a sense of urgency.

Samantha Power is an expert on the topic of genocide, which she examined in depth in her book *A Problem from Hell: America in the Age of Genocide*. What motivates people to commit such crimes against humanity? Samantha believes it is a combination of factors: perceived threat, 'values', and systematic dehumanization. Other people are banished from one's own moral universe. The first step is to define who belongs and who is a threat and to create hierarchies and justify them with 'values' such as protection and self-defence. The next step is to exclude whoever is perceived as 'threatening' – those who do not belong, the others – from the morality of those who are 'threatened', thus justifying crimes against them. She emphasizes how important it is continually to interrogate the way nations, groups and individuals define and justify their own interests.

Samantha says that women are bound together by their similar experiences. She herself organized both meetings with other women ambassadors at the UN and weekly get-togethers with female colleagues in a 'Wednesday group' during her time at the White House. What does this achieve? It enables women to encourage and support one another and to remind one another that it is not women who have to adapt but the system that must be changed.

One of the books Samantha Power appreciates is Daniel Kahneman's psychological study *Thinking, Fast and Slow*; another is Lindsey Hilsum's moving account of the life story of war reporter Marie Colvin, *In Extremis*.

13 FEMINIST FOREIGN POLICY IN TIMES OF WAR AND CONFLICT

'Feminist foreign policy, feminist development policy, yes, you can do all that, but not with this budget for the Bundeswehr!' These were the thunderous words of Friedrich Merz, leader of the main opposition party, the conservative CDU, in a general debate in the German Bundestag in March 2022. He was referring to the special fund of €100 billion for the armed forces announced a month earlier by Chancellor Scholz (leader of the centre-left SPD), and the targets of his wrath were the feminist policies of the minister for foreign affairs, Annalena Baerbock, and the minister for economic cooperation and development, Svenja Schulze.

Baerbock responded with a passionate and convincing rebuttal: 'Bringing up the Bundeswehr, and then saying in the same sentence "Yes to the Bundeswehr – and no more of that feminist foreign policy." It breaks my heart.' She continued:

And do you know why? Do you know why? Because I've been to see the mothers of Srebrenica. A week ago. And they told me how the traces of that war are inside them, and those mothers said: Ms Baerbock, back then, no action was taken! In the early nineties, when their daughters, their friends were raped. When rape wasn't recognized as a weapon of war. Wasn't prosecuted by the International Criminal Court. And this is why a twenty-first-century security policy has to include a feminist perspective. This isn't just a lot of fuss over nothing, it's absolutely timely.

Baerbock's words were followed by loud applause from members of parliament.

Merz wanted to deny the importance of feminist foreign policy in times of war and conflict. As if feminist analyses and demands were something you could dabble in now and then if there was nothing else to worry about. A fair-weather project. When this book was first published, on 24 February 2022, the day Putin began his war of aggression against Ukraine, I was asked in interview after interview: 'What's the point of feminist foreign policy in times of war?' The underlying message was that we had to solve the 'real' problems first; that this was a time for 'hard security', not for soft topics such as feminist foreign policy.

Of course this is utter nonsense. Feminists have always tackled the toughest issues, most notably violence – or, to be more precise, male violence. Feminism has always sought to dismantle patriarchal structures and foster non-violent structures. So it's always been about 'hard security'. Anyone who denigrates feminist foreign policy and denies its significance in times of war and conflict is quite simply wrong. Feminist foreign policy (as I showed in my chapter on its origins) was actually forged in a time of war. This new chapter, written for this edition, is dedicated to the relevance of feminist foreign policy in times of war and conflict. Two defining foreign policy topics of 2022 (and beyond) serve as examples: Putin's war of aggression against Ukraine and the feminist revolution in Iran.

Feminist foreign policy aims to make an impact, to radically transform foreign and security policy. So it's particularly convincing when it comes to long-term processes, such as the renunciation of toxic geopolitical power games, underpinned by economic interests and detrimental to human rights. Feminist foreign policy is good at long-term thinking – an ability that isn't especially well developed in society as a whole, where short-term thinking predominates. If that weren't the case, we wouldn't have a climate crisis – this has come about because short-term economic gains have been privileged over the long-term preservation of our planet.

But feminist foreign policy has to do both if it is to be truly effective: short-term feminist interventions, coupled with long-term transformative strategies. In wars and conflicts, we have to act fast to prevent suffering, protect women and all vulnerable groups, and stop or alleviate human rights violations. But we also have to take a long-term approach and try to prevent future violent crises. In feminist foreign policy, short-term feminist interventions go hand in hand with long-term feminist transformations.

Putin's war of aggression against Ukraine

We mustn't forget that the war against Ukraine actually began in February 2014, with the Russian annexation of Crimea. On 24 February 2022, Putin escalated the violence with his war of aggression against the whole territory of Ukraine. By the end of 2022, nearly 8 million Ukrainians, 90 per cent of them women and children, had fled the country. In December 2022, the Ukrainian organization Centre for Civil Liberties was awarded the Nobel Peace Prize for gathering evidence of Russian war crimes. At an event in Berlin in the same month, the head of the organization, the human rights lawyer Oleksandra Matviichuk, said: 'We need more weapons to protect ourselves, our territory and our population. It's strange that I, a human rights defender, am asking for weapons, but this is what we need.' Matviichuk's organization has documented more than 29,000 cases of war crimes between 24 February 2022 and mid-January 2023 and has called for an international war crimes tribunal for Putin and his government.* The international prosecution of war crimes is a vital step towards restoring peace within a society.

'All the acts of violence we are observing in Ukraine are the result of the impunity Russia has enjoyed for decades,' explains Matviichuk. 'Russian troops have committed crimes everywhere: in Chechnya, Moldova, Georgia, Libya and Syria. It had no consequences. And now they think they can do whatever they want.'[1] So the Russian army continues to murder and rape.

This is why we need to help the Ukrainian population to defend itself – and this includes supplying weapons. We must not aban-

---

* Investigative research also shows that Russia remains the second-largest market for arms exports – even from Ukraine. This proves once again that the capitalist drive to maximize profits always seems to trump every other consideration, especially reason and the striving for peace and non-violence.

don the Ukrainian people. This applies especially to Germany, which has supported Russia and Putin with its energy imports. Worse still, Germany is one of ten EU member states that continued to export military goods to Russia at least until 2020, despite the 2014 embargo. The total value of these exports was €346 million, of which Germany (with €122 million worth of exports) had the second-largest share after France.[2] And there are still German arms companies operating in Russia, helping to maintain and produce planes, rockets and tanks. This gives the Russian regime desperately needed access to modern technologies and feeds Putin's destructive war in Ukraine.[3] Nobel Peace Prize laureate Matviichuk is clear in her verdict: 'By collaborating economically with Russia, Germany virtually encouraged it to take the next step towards escalation.'[4] In February 2022 Chancellor Scholz announced a *Zeitenwende* (historic turning point) in German politics, involving not only arms shipments to Ukraine but also a commitment to building up Germany's own military capacity. Even in the foreign policy circles in which I move, this new course has been uncritically embraced. I find this worrying, and I hope that the government will act and communicate with caution. It should be aware – and publicly acknowledge – that militarization will, in the long term, lead to more conflicts, more wars and more violence, even if militarization and arms shipments seem appropriate at present. If we do not balance military spending with heavy investment in multilateralism, international law, human rights and arms control, then sooner or later the next illegal aggression will occur. Another problem is that the glorification of militarization is connected to a rise in nationalism. And nationalism, racism, antifeminism and the exclusion of others do not make the world a safer place to live in.*

---

* Of course there are different forms of nationalism. In this text I am referring to the glorification of militarization and a possible connection with increasing nationalism. In Ukraine we are talking about civic rather than ethnic nationalism, or about existential nationalism. As pointed out by the political scientist Leandra Bias, the strengthening of national identity in Ukraine is not necessarily a bad thing.

In the medium and long term, arms proliferation does not bring stability and security – only more wars and conflicts. More weapons mean more patriarchal violence; more patriarchal violence means more weapons. The goal of feminist foreign policy is a future in which patriarchal regimes such as Putin's, violent systems that breach all international conventions, can no longer exist. It must therefore support those who seek to eliminate or change such systems, everywhere including Russia.

Antifeminist, racist or homophobic heads of state and government tend to be prepared to use force against other states – i.e. to provoke or start conflicts and wars. If the representatives of states act violently within their borders, they will probably also do so outside their borders. Putin's Russia is a prime example. 'What we have here is a masculinist foreign policy. Speaking in general terms, we can draw a direct line between Putin the topless bear-wrangler and the Putin who has invaded Ukraine,'[5] says Leandra Bias.

Detecting such tendencies early on is preventive security policy, and important for the feminist approach. In *The Age of the Strongman: How the Cult of the Leader Threatens Democracy around the World*, Gideon Rachman writes that Putin is the archetype for the current generation of 'strongmen'. The global rise of these men, he says, has fundamentally changed international politics and constitutes the most sustained assault on liberal democratic values since the 1930s. Besides Vladimir Putin, these strongmen are Xi Jinping, Recep Tayyip Erdoğan, Viktor Orbán, Jair Bolsonaro, Donald Trump, Andrés Miguel López Obrador, Rodrigo Duterte and Narendra Modi. Thanks to these men, with their contempt for liberal democratic values, populist and authoritarian leadership is now a defining feature of global politics. Rachman identifies four main characteristics of strongmen: they create a cult of personality, they show contempt for the rule of law, they claim to represent the 'real' people against the elites (also known as populism), and their politics is driven by fear and nationalism. Strongmen are usually also united in their antifeminism and their contempt for women's rights and homosexuality – this is a fifth point that could be added to Rachman's list.

313

The French military expert Pierre Servent comments on Putin's contempt for women and his 'strongman' politics as follows:

> *The concept of the strongman is a leitmotif for Putin, just as it was for the KGB, the former Russian secret service, where he worked for many years. There are KGB songs that Putin quotes at press conferences. One of them goes: 'Like it or not, my beauty, you have to put up with it.' This is the phrase of a rapist. Putin is not quoting these lines secretly.*[6]

So on the one side we have Putin, head of a state that is a permanent member of the UN Security Council, publicly defending rape. And on the other side, as Servent interprets it, we have the Ukrainian president, Volodymyr Zelensky, saying: I won't be your beauty, I won't let myself be raped.

Too many people failed to see the very clear warning signs in Putin's behaviour. Perhaps they didn't want to see them. Such misogynistic and homophobic men seldom confine their violent tendencies to rhetoric but extend them over their sphere of influence. In Putin's case, unfortunately, this sphere of influence is the largest country in the world (in terms of surface area), a huge army, and nearly 6,000 nuclear warheads. A feminist foreign policy would not do business with such men, it would not supply weapons to them, and it would most certainly not allow itself to become dependent on them, as Germany has done with its energy supply. Feminists are very aware of patriarchal power structures; analysing these structures is the basis of our work. Yet, time and time again, we see how little knowledge leading international experts, analysts and political decision-makers have of these categories and how little relevance they ascribe to them. We see this every time one of these patriarchal, violent leaders is underestimated. The same thing happened with Donald Trump. Before his election to the US presidency in 2016, leading political experts took an amused, dismissive attitude towards him. Feminists, however, never dismissed him, because he clearly presented himself as a misogynist with the potential for destructiveness and bursts of violence. If feminists had significant representation in influential positions in this world, we would have made a serious effort to prevent his presidency, instead of letting him get away with his misogyny – even during the election campaign.

These examples show that it is impossible to understand international politics or achieve lasting peace without a feminist analysis and a focus on the rights of women. In her article 'The international of antifeminists', Leandra Bias analyses Putin's antifeminism. She shows how this, coupled with his contempt for Western values, serves to justify the invasion of Ukraine. According to Bias, antifeminism is a tool with multiple functions: 'internally, it justifies authoritarianism and repression, externally, it legitimises aggression, and creates common terrain with right-wing movements.'[7] Putin presents Russian feminists as an internal fifth column who want to destroy Russia with their 'gender ideology'. Feminists within the country are accused of following Western instructions and planning an ambush on Russia – by campaigning for the right to divorce, the right to defend themselves against domestic violence, and the right to safe access to abortion. For Putin, such people and their supporters (e.g. the West, and in particular Ukraine) are traitors and scum, says Bias.

LGBTQ+ rights are another target of the antifeminists. Same-sex marriage is seen as a threat to Russian society, and since 2012 the term 'Gayropa' has often been used instead of 'Evropa' (Europe). According to Leandra Bias, antifeminism and the demonization of 'gender ideology' serve several purposes. Feminism is seen as standing for Western neo-imperialism, which Russia heroically opposes. 'By devaluing feminism, [Putin] sweeps away democracy, the rule of law, and human rights in one stroke,' says Bias. After years of antifeminist policies, it is now hardly possible to pursue feminist activities in Russia any longer. A striking example occurred in 2016, when domestic violence was criminalized for the first time in Russian history, after nearly thirty years of feminist campaigning. But this success was short-lived. The new law was derided as the 'slap bill', supposedly sponsored by the Western feminist lobby. Its opponents argued that it criminalized

Russian mothers and contradicted 'Russian values' – and it was over-turned at the beginning of 2017, after just six months. Since then, the violence experienced by women in their own homes has once again been demoted to the same level as a parking offence.[8]

In Russia's narrative, the Western attack on 'traditional values' justifies not only the persecution of feminism at home but also the attack on a neighbouring country. Putin justified his war of aggression as a preventive measure triggered by the 'morally degraded' West, which is determined to cancel 'millennia-old values'.[9]

Putin's Russia is therefore an important actor within the international antifeminist movement described in chapter 8. The country is now the second-biggest financial supporter of this antifeminist, anti-gender movement.

If our long-term aim is to avoid wars and conflicts and strengthen democracies, we need to develop better strategies and tools to support democratic and feminist civil society worldwide and defuse the power of the antifeminist, autocratic strongmen and the movements they lead.

Alongside this long-term feminist transformation, a feminist foreign policy also requires short-term interventions. When Foreign Minister Baerbock addressed the special session of the UN General Assembly on 1 March 2022, she said she'd heard rumours that people of African descent fleeing Ukraine were experiencing discrimination at the EU's borders. 'Every refugee must receive protection, no matter what their nationality, their origin or the colour of their skin,'[10] affirmed Baerbock. In times of war and conflict, a feminist foreign policy recognizes that people have very different experiences in military conflicts, depending on factors such as sex, skin colour or age. It then takes these differences into account in interventions such as humanitarian aid.

Short-term interventions guided by feminist foreign policy encompass these areas: the protection of particularly vulnerable groups, including the attempt to address gender-based violence; intersectional, gender-based humanitarian aid; and support for the involvement of local initiatives, especially women and feminists, in efforts at peacemaking and reconstruction, as in Ukraine. Most of the following descriptions and demands are already covered by the Women, Peace and Security agenda, which the majority of states have already pledged to support. Yet since 24 February 2022, NATO and its member states have been astonishingly quiet about the gender-specific demands of the WPS agenda – in fact the agenda seems to have been forgotten. The political scientist Katharine Wright comments: '[T]he response to the war in Ukraine by NATO, its members and its partners, many of whom have championed the WPS agenda, draws attention to what many feminists had feared: the disjuncture between the rhetoric and the reality of the global commitment to the WPS agenda.'[11]

There are countless reports that Russian soldiers are committing rape during the war. This is indisputably a war crime. A feminist foreign policy would invest in documenting these crimes so that those responsible can be brought to justice. But it is not enough to document gender-based violence in order to bring prosecutions; there also needs to be transformative justice – for example, long-term funding for feminist civil society to create spaces for healing. Because trials – if they actually happen at all – seldom give a sense of justice.[12]

It is crucial that the victims of these crimes receive all the protection, support and care that they need. This includes sex-segregated refuges, access to medical care, and funding for local women's organizations which document such crimes. There must be deliberate investment in such structures, and everything possible must be done to protect women and children (in particular) from this violence. But it is not just the sexualized violence of Russian soldiers that we must fight. During wars and conflicts, the level of domestic violence also rises, and men who return *after* their military deployment often bring the violence back home with them, to their wives and children. They also bring weapons. Domestic violence can be expected to rise in both Ukraine and Russia after the war. A feminist foreign policy would take preventive measures against this.

A feminist foreign policy would muster the maximum of resources to identify and prevent gender-based and sexualized violence in the Russian war against Ukraine and to bring the perpetrators to justice. This includes putting political pressure on countries like Poland, to ensure that all those affected by sexualized violence can access safe abortions. Since January 2021, Poland has had a near-total ban on abortion, and this also applies to Ukrainian women who have been raped by Russian soldiers and have fled to Poland. Sexual and gender-based violence doesn't happen just during war but also during displacement: according to UNHCR figures, one in five refugee women experience sexualized violence. The first reports about Ukrainian women refugees falling victim to human traffickers began to appear shortly after the outbreak of the war in February 2022 – and more and more cases have subsequently been reported.[13] As well as publicly run facilities, private accommodation for refugees must be monitored to ensure that no attacks or crimes take place there. The LBGTQ+ community is also affected by specific violence. For example, trans people have been prevented from fleeing because the information in their documents did not match their gender identity.[14] Feminist foreign policy would defend trans people, try to prevent such incidents at the border, and support queer organizations that provide immediate assistance.[15]

In the weeks and months after the outbreak of the war, analyses by UN Women and CARE International attempted to draw attention to gender-specific differences in the humanitarian crisis. A report by the two organizations states:

> *The crisis is quickly revealing the different needs of women and men, girls and boys. The data confirm that the impact of the war is particularly disproportionate for marginalized groups, such as female-headed households, IDPs [internally displaced persons], Roma people, LGBTQIA+ and people with disabilities. Women facing multiple forms of discrimination, such as women from minority groups, face particular challenges in accessing humanitarian support and have increased protection needs.*

The report also found that the war was having a huge impact on mental health. Because of traditional gender roles, women are most probably taking on additional emotional care work within the family, while men are less likely to seek support for mental health problems. Feminist interventions in times of war and conflict would therefore try to provide gender-differentiated humanitarian support. This includes safe, sex-segregated and family-segregated shelter; adequate care for specific hygiene needs such as menstrual health; and appropriate, sufficient, and fairly distributed food which meets the dietary needs of pregnant and breastfeeding women and newborn babies. Gender-specific healthcare needs must also be taken into consideration, notably psychological support and a guarantee of sexual and reproductive health, taking in the health of mothers, newborn babies and children.[16]

A feminist foreign policy in times of war and conflicts would support women and feminist organizations to ensure that their voices are considered in any peace process. Even before 2014 – and especially before 24 February 2022 – there was a broad landscape of Ukrainian women's rights organizations working on conflict prevention and incorporating gender analyses into their work. These organizations require ongoing support: women's rights defenders need protection if they are to continue their work in wartime. On a multilateral level, states should be campaigning for the participation of women, other political minorities and other local groups in efforts at peacemaking and reconstruction.[17] The work of mediators must also be supported, and many more women need to be trained for this role. Instead of entrusting such work to large international mediation organizations, it should be given to local and feminist groups with relevant mediation expertise – groups that already have relationships of trust with other actors who may be involved in a potential mediation process. The international community must not repeat its mistakes in the Afghan peace process, where it accepted the exclusion of women. Feminist foreign policy would also ensure that feminist civil society is given a voice – e.g. by inviting its representatives to brief the UN Security Council. And every conference about reconstruction must consider not only the physical infrastructure (roads, buildings, power supply, etc.), but also the social infrastructure. Who is doing the care work? Is there enough childcare? Are all occupations open to women? Are there laws that discriminate against women? A feminist approach would ensure that the process of reconstruction is used to eliminate the historical disadvantage experienced by women and other political minorities.

Short-term feminist action would also take into account the gender-specific global effects of the Russian war of aggression and provide funding to alleviate these. The war has had a devastating impact on women and girls worldwide. According to a report by UN Women, it has widened gender-specific differences and exacerbated food insecurity, malnutrition and energy poverty. The report explains how exactly women and girls in Ukraine and around the globe are affected in situations of conflict, crisis and humanitarian hardship. There are '[a]larming increases in gender-based violence, transactional sex for food and survival, sexual exploitation and trafficking, [and] child marriage with girls forced to leave school, and women's and girls' unpaid care and domestic workloads to provision households and communities are further endangering [their] physical and mental health.'[18]

Feminist foreign policy puts a stop to the simplistic tendency to act as though militarization could solve problems that are largely caused by militarization. If a special fund of €100 billion can be provided for militarization, there should also be generous special funds for humanitarian aid, for the support of civil society in Ukraine, and especially for feminist initiatives working towards the Women, Peace and Security agenda of the UN Security Council – as well as for particularly threatened groups such as the LGBTQ+ community. The current situation must always be considered from an intersectional feminist perspective, which is able to identify who needs special protection and additional support at the present time.

The feminist revolution in Iran

Since the founding of the Islamic Republic of Iran in the 1979 revolution, the mullahs have ruled their theocracy with an iron fist. They smother any stirrings of democracy and ruthlessly oppress women. The supreme ruler is the ayatollah, the country's highest-ranking cleric and its political leader. Before the revolution Iran was a monarchy, led by the shah (Persian for 'ruler'). The last shah, Reza Pahlavi, was ousted during the 1979 revolution. 'Just days after Ayatollah Ruhollah Khomeini alighted from an Air France plane, set foot on Iranian soil and toppled the government of the last monarch, the first target for the sword of his revolution was women,' writes the Tehran-born German TV journalist Golineh Atai in her book *Iran: Die Freiheit ist weiblich* (Iran: Freedom is female).[19] She adds: 'Nearly all the laws that had brought five decades of social gains for women would fall victim to his idea of Islam.'[20] And there were human victims too, such as the physician Farrokhroo Parsa, who had served as minister of education. She had campaigned vigorously for women and their rights, built up organizations and networks for women, and had been the first woman in a senior political office before the regime change. She was executed after the Islamic Revolution.

'Misogyny is one of the political cornerstones of the Islamic Republic,' writes Golineh Atai. She quotes the revolutionary leader Khomeini, who once said: 'If the Islamic revolution is to have no other result than the veiling of women, then that is enough.'[21] Atai points out that Iran is able to hold talks with its arch-enemies but is not capable of negotiating with Iranian women. The political rulers, she suggests, are more afraid of women than of their ideological opponents. It is through women that the regime controls society.

Atai describes how her mother went to a demonstration for women's rights in July 1980, nearly eighteen months after the revolution; the first protest of this kind had taken place in March 1979. A few days before the demonstration in July 1980, the revolutionary leader had issued a decree making the hijab or headscarf compulsory for women.

The protesters chanted: 'The freedom of women is the freedom of society!'[22] More than forty years later, the current uprising against the Iranian regime has been described as a feminist revolution, and the slogan that has reverberated around the world – 'Jin, Jiyan, Azadî' (Woman, life, freedom) – clearly recalls the words of the protesters back in 1980. There has always been feminist resistance to the regime. Another example is the 'Girls of Revolution Street' in 2018, who took off their headscarves and were arrested in droves. Internationally, according to Gilda Sahebi, hardly anyone took any notice.[23] Sahebi, an Iranian journalist and doctor living in Germany, has become one of the most important voices in Germany on the situation in Iran.

Women are second-class citizens in Iran. Numerous prohibitions restrict their everyday lives. They are not permitted to sing or dance in public or to travel without their husband's permission. They must cover their hair, a law enforced by the 'morality police'. Their public life is restricted, as is their private life: men are allowed to have four wives and can divorce whenever they like; women do not have this right. In general, a woman's life is worth only half as much as a man's. In court, a man's statement is worth that of two women; after an accident, a man receives twice as much compensation as a woman. Men can forbid their wives from working and beat and rape them with impunity.

The current protests broke out after the death of 22-year-old Jina Mahsa Amini on 16 September 2022, three days after she was arrested by the morality police. Her alleged crime was to have worn her hijab incorrectly. For more than four decades, women in Iran have lived under social control and male domination.

'Jin, Jiyan, Azadî': this is the Kurdish slogan of the women's protests in Iran. In many parts of the country, women are rising against their oppressors, the Iranian regime. They are taking off their headscarves and setting them alight in front of the security forces. They are cutting off their hair as a sign of protest. 'The slogan clearly shows what kind of system the people in Iran want: democracy and secularism, because it is only in this kind of system that women can have equal rights. It is only in this kind of political system that gender-based discrimination can be stopped,'[24] says Shirin Ebadi, the exiled Iranian Nobel Peace Prize laureate.

Although there have been protests against the regime in past years, this time it is different, says Gilda Sahebi. This is the most widespread protest in Iran since 1979, with people in all parts of the country and across all ethnic groups standing up to the regime together, united by the feminist slogan 'Woman, life, freedom'. They want to overthrow the regime. The brutal response of the Iranian government cannot break their spirit; they carry on regardless. Human rights activists report that women with their hair uncovered are now a common sight in Tehran. In reaction to the persistence of the protesters, the regime began to execute some of them in December 2022. Since the beginning of the protests, the Iranian regime has pronounced seventeen death sentences; by mid-January 2023 four executions had taken place. However, more than 500 protesters had already been killed by security forces by the end of 2022, including around seventy under the age of eighteen. Nearly 18,500 people have been arrested.[25] In the prisons, girls and women are systematically raped.

To understand what a feminist foreign policy can achieve in the case of Iran, I'd like to start by looking at the past. What would a feminist foreign policy have done in the last few decades to try to prevent this kind of escalation? Feminist foreign policy has backbone; it would never congratulate a regime that crushes women as Iran does. And yet this is exactly what Frank-Walter Steinmeier, president of the Federal Republic of Germany, did on the fortieth anniversary of the Islamic Revolution in 2019, warmly congratulating the Iranian regime 'on behalf of my fellow citizens'.[26]* Other German presidents before him had done the same. Shirin Ebadi has this to say:

> *In the past, European governments, including the German government, had a good relationship with the Iranian regime. They ignored*

---

* I find it offensive to read this. It certainly wasn't on my behalf, nor was it on behalf of many of his other fellow citizens.

the systematic violations of human rights and the murders carried out by this state. Now they have to listen to what the Iranians are saying. And the people in Iran are saying: Stop supporting the murderers in Iran. Put yourselves on the right side of history.[27]

Ebadi, who became Iran's first woman judge before the Islamic Revolution, explains why Western governments have focused on economic interests for so long. 'The reality is that human rights have been forgotten at the negotiating table.'[28] The smell of oil, she says, has stopped other countries from looking too closely. A feminist foreign policy would never have put economic interests before human rights.

This criticism refers partly to the nuclear deal with Iran, the Joint Comprehensive Plan of Action (JCPoA). Signed in 2015 by Iran on the one side and the five permanent members of the UN Security Council (China, France, Russia, the UK and the USA) and Germany – the 'P5+1' – on the other, the deal grants an easing of sanctions against Iran in exchange for substantial restrictions on the Iranian nuclear programme. The European Union also took part in the negotiations. In the JCPoA, Iran declared its willingness to dismantle a substantial part of its nuclear programme and to open its nuclear facilities for extensive international inspections in exchange for an easing of sanctions worth billions of dollars. From 2012 to 2014 alone, international sanctions had cost the Iranian economy more than $100 billion in income.[29]

The then US president, Donald Trump, withdrew the USA from the Iran deal in 2018, claiming that it had not succeeded in limiting the Iranian nuclear programme. A year later, Iran began to ignore the restrictions imposed by the deal. In 2021, President Joe Biden declared that the United States would return to the agreement if Iran pledged to comply. At first the resumption of diplomacy seemed promising, but after stop-and-go talks it remains unclear whether the parties will be able to come to an agreement.[30]

Since the protests broke out in September 2022, political discussions have repeatedly centred on the JCPoA and what should be done about it. From a feminist perspective, this is complicated. On the one hand, as I show in my chapter on demilitarization and weapons, disarmament – especially nuclear disarmament – is a core demand of feminist foreign policy. When I interviewed her, Gilda Sahebi argued that it would be an utter disaster – the worst possible scenario – if the regime of the mullahs were to possess nuclear weapons. This is an argument *for* continuing nuclear talks with Iran. On the other hand, since the outbreak of the protests, demonstrators have been demanding that the talks be paused or abandoned, in order to stop giving international legitimacy to the Iranian regime. Gilda also told me that it was 'naive to believe that people who rape women and kill the innocent and hang people from cranes will adhere to agreements.' In her view, *Realpolitik* is only possible if it takes human rights into account; together with democracy, she says, this is the only way to a nuclear-free Iran. However, human rights have never played a part in the nuclear talks. A feminist foreign policy would never disregard women's rights and human rights in negotiations for an international agreement – especially not in a country that is one of the world's worst oppressors of women. A feminist foreign policy would also ensure that sanctions affect the powerful elite and not the civilian population. Yet the sanctions still in place today have caused severe direct and indirect harm to the Iranian population, especially civil society.[31] This is why any attempt to restrict Iran's nuclear capacity must listen to the voices of (feminist) civil society, make women's and human rights a prominent point of negotiation, and establish a sanctions regime that does no harm to civil society.

In view of the violence, human rights activists and protesters fleeing Iran should be granted visas and allowed entry to European countries with a minimum of red tape and delays. The refugees should then be supported to find work in the EU so they can earn their living. Yet Gilda Sahebi keeps hearing that the German embassy in Tehran is rejecting visa applications. Deportations to Iran must be stopped, and Iranians whose residency status is precarious need security. European governments must continue to exert a high level of pressure on the

Iranian regime, and the Islamic Revolutionary Guard Corps must be put on the EU's lists of terrorist organizations. Violations of women's rights must be condemned in the strongest terms, again and again, and an independent investigation into the death of Jina Mahsa Amini – and all Iran's human rights violations – must be called for. Significant financial resources must be provided to women's rights organizations and women's rights defenders on the ground. Political capital must be invested to stop the systematic imprisonment of human rights defenders (documented by feminist civil society organizations such as Femena)[32] and sexualized violence (including rape) against imprisoned female protesters. International attention must be drawn to these abuses.

Iranian human rights defenders have also pointed out how the sanctions against Iran are hampering their work.[33] For years, feminist human rights defenders such as the prize-winning activist Shiva Nazar Ahari have urged international governments to listen to and support feminist civil society in Iran and be guided by their demands. Whenever such steps are taken, whenever money goes to feminist civil society, then feminist policy is more than mere symbolism. Feminist foreign policy is meaningless unless we treat women's and human rights as a red line that must not be crossed. To quote Gilda Sahebi: 'The focus of foreign policy must always be on women's, children's and human rights, not on the economy and armament, because the latter never work in the long term. So far this is not what we are doing, but I hope this will change, and in 100 years it will simply be called "foreign policy", because all foreign policy is inherently feminist.'

Unlike her predecessors, the current German minister for foreign affairs, Annalena Baerbock, has put a new emphasis on the rights of women in Iran. In late November 2022, for example, she travelled to Geneva for a special session of the UN Human Rights Council, where Germany and Iceland successfully proposed a resolution on the deteriorating human rights situation in Iran. The Council voted to deploy an independent international fact-finding mission to investigate the ongoing human rights violations in the Islamic Republic in connection with the protests that began on 16 September 2022. In October 2022, at an online event held by CFFP, 'In Solidarity with the Women on the Streets: Feminist Foreign Policy Demands towards Iran',[34] Baerbock* said: 'The women on the streets don't need our applause, they're much braver than many of us politicians, but we owe it to them to amplify their voices and to remove obstacles.' This hits the nail on the head.

Conclusion: short-term feminist interventions and long-term feminist transformation

For democratic countries, it will always be a challenge to support the civilian population, including human rights defenders and feminist activists, in autocratic regimes. But if feminist foreign policy wants to achieve a successful long-term transformation, it must work to develop the knowledge and expertise needed to provide this support. Beginning in spring 2023, with funding from the German Bundestag, CFFP will be conducting a project to do exactly this. We will be working with civil society from different countries to produce this knowledge. Because this is the main problem with traditional foreign policy, focused on militarization and economic interests: that human rights expertise does not receive sufficient attention or funding. It is unacceptable that we have defence ministries and a well-established arms industry that has excellent contacts with the political elite, but no peace ministries with well-established strategies to support (feminist) civil society in autocracies. Ultimately, what you focus on gets bigger.

'You have thirty seconds and zero budget to solve every problem created by patriarchal structures – and if you don't succeed, that just proves your feminist naivety.' This is how the disarmament expert Ray Acheson, at our conference in April 2022, paraphrased the attitude of those who seek to delegitimize feminist foreign policy. These are

---

* The other participants were Sawsan Chebli, Gilda Sahebi, Natalie Amiri, Sanam Anderlini, Enissa Amani and Dastan Jasim.

exactly the arguments used by people such as Friedrich Merz, along with other critics.

They're wrong. Feminist foreign policy means a clear and rigorous stance, coupled with the tools of de-escalation and diplomacy: short-term feminist interventions combined with long-term feminist transformation. Without feminism, there can be no peace.

Madeleine Rees:
'I took off my velvet gloves a long
time ago.'

Madeleine Rees, a leading human rights lawyer and secretary-general of the Women's International League for Peace and Freedom (WILPF), urges us to think loudly, critically, and in radical utopias. Madeleine began her career as a lawyer in the field of anti-discrimination law, bringing cases before the European Court of Human Rights and the European Court of Justice. She went on to work as a gender expert and head of office in Bosnia and Herzegovina for the Office of the United Nations High Commissioner for Human Rights (OHCHR). Here she became a whistle-blower: in the late 1990s, along with the American police investigator Kathryn Bolkovac, Madeleine revealed that the International Police Task Force and members of the UN mission in Bosnia were committing human rights violations linked to trafficking and sexual exploitation, and that the UN was systematically covering this up. She was horrified and sickened to learn that the UN was not protecting the people with whose protection it was entrusted. Madeleine was not rewarded for her courage, however, but was demoted and later wrongfully dismissed. The film *The Whistleblower* tells this story.

Madeleine also criticizes the United Nations because it puts state and military security rather than human security at the centre of its work. This is reflected in the name of one of its principal organs: not 'Peace Council' or even 'Security and Peace Council', but 'Security Council'. One of the main problems in (inter)national security policy, she argues, is that the wrong questions are asked: 'How can we regulate weapons?' instead of 'How can we eliminate weapons and prioritize human security?'. She points out that the most pressing threats for humanity – such as the pandemic and the climate crisis – are not military in nature.

Again and again, says Madeleine, activists face these questions: How critically can we express ourselves in elite institutions such as the United Nations if we want to fundamentally challenge these institutions, but we also want our voices to be heard there, in the halls of power? Is it better to soften up radically utopian ideas so we can exert influence inside the system, or is it better to remain radical? Madeleine says she has taken off her velvet gloves. We're often too nice, she argues. And yet it's up to us, civil society actors, to criticize power relations and denounce injustices. If we don't do it, who will?

14 EPILOGUE

You don't have to put up with the things you don't like.
If your head's more than just what you put your hat on.
. . . It's not your fault that the world's the way it is.
But it would be your fault if it stayed that way.

Die Ärzte, 'Deine Schuld', *Geräusch* (2004)

'Would it be all right if Angelina Jolie spoke at your event?' – Nina and I were asked this surprising question in January 2020, as we were organizing our event on feminist foreign policy at the Munich Security Conference. Though we tried to play it cool, we were incredibly excited. In the end, ours was by far the most feminist event at the whole conference – even though in the end Angelina Jolie didn't attend the conference at all.

Our event, held in the heart of traditional, *Realpolitik*-based, militarized foreign policy, didn't meet with unmixed approval. There was also criticism, especially from feminist circles. We were letting ourselves be co-opted, they said; our collaboration with the Munich Security Conference was reinforcing problematic structures rather than breaking them down. The criticism was based on different ideas about how change is achieved and what kinds of alliance are permissible to achieve it. I think it also had to do with the leap from theory to practice. In the end, the thing that matters is turning knowledge and ideas into reality. Nonetheless, people are always very quick to criticize. And it's easy to do so when you're standing on the periphery and not in the arena, when you're not exposed to the dynamics, judgements and consequences. People are quick to judge and condemn others but not nearly as quick to try and understand the situations that others are in. I found some of the criticism justified. We always

331

have to ask ourselves: when are we simply contributing to the manifestation of unjust structures, and when can we infiltrate structures and change them from within? I'm convinced that the best way to bring about change is to push simultaneously from the inside and the outside, and to create new, sustainable structures and institutions at the same time. When I started to get involved in feminist causes and to campaign for human rights, I was primarily an activist. Now I'm also an entrepreneur, and I'm trying to create new, progressive structures, partly by employing other critical people. This means that I don't have sole responsibility for producing ideas, and the efficacy of those ideas is not dependent just on my actions. On the contrary, the people in my organization think and develop ideas themselves. I believe this is the most sustainable way for us to bring about change. Yet it wasn't at all obvious that I would take this path.

My personal history: CFFP instead of the UN

When I was living in Myanmar in 2017, I thought about where my career might go from there. For many people with a similar academic history, international organizations such as the United Nations are the dream employer. Since I had a fixed-term consultancy contract with the United Nations Development Programme, the obvious next step was to get a permanent job with the UN. But my unease about the unhealthy structures and power dynamics of development policy wasn't the only thing putting me off this step. I also had an increasingly strong desire to start something of my own. But I didn't have any experience of starting a business, nor did I know any founders personally.

Shortly after my return, my mentor and friend Dr Scilla Elworthy made me a fantastic offer. I'd met Scilla in Oxford in 2015, when she was presenting her latest book at an event at the university. I sat in the audience, hanging on her every word. The political scientist, who was in her early seventies when I met her, is one of the wisest and kindest people I know. Of all the people in my life, she's one of those who have had the biggest influence on me. Scilla was the first person to point out to me the dangers of activist burnout and to teach me that you can only bring about outward change if you're at peace with yourself. That is, if you've acknowledged and dealt with your own pain, and can – in spite of everything – approach others with good will and an open heart. She embodies the mantra described by the author Brené Brown: 'Strong back. Soft front. Wild Heart'. In late 2017 Scilla was in the process of founding her latest peacebuilding organization. She asked if I would like to step in and build it up for her. Her confidence in me was a huge honour. I thought about it but turned it down: it was time to make my dreams a reality.

I had very little in the way of savings, and none of my friends or family were in a position to support me financially. At the end of 2017 I made a joint decision with Marissa Conway (an American living in the UK) to set up CFFP together (she would set up a branch in London, I'd set one up in Berlin). Initially I was working three days a week in a tech start-up and spending the other four getting CFFP established. On 8 March 2018, International Women's Day, I delivered my first speech as the director of my organization. It was a keynote at an event on feminist foreign policy at the Nordic embassies in Berlin. In accordance with one of my mottos – 'Carry yourself with the self-confidence of a mediocre White man' – I was determined to give this speech, so I went ahead and did it. Nothing ventured, nothing gained.

That evening was a godsend: for one thing, I met Nina, who was sitting in the audience and came up and spoke to me after the event. From then on, Nina worked with me as a volunteer at CFFP alongside her day job, and a few months later she became the co-founder and co-director of CFFP in Berlin. For another thing, I was introduced to Jutta, who is now my mentor and our lawyer. I went to see Jutta in her office on the chic Kurfürstendamm boulevard a few days later. She took care of the legal formation of CFFP as a *gemeinnützige GmbH* (non-profit limited liability company) in Berlin. Right from the start, she was – and still is – one of our biggest and most generous supporters. Without Jutta, we wouldn't be where we are today. Because, as women setting up a feminist non-profit social enterprise, we're faced with a triple whammy: firstly, women founders get no money compared to men; secondly, civil society is hugely underfunded; and, thirdly, hardly anyone is ever paid for feminist work.

The triple whammy

The founding of CFFP in Berlin marked the start of a new phase in my life which would turn everything upside down. The birth of a new organization demands undivided attention – one of the reasons many founders talk about it as their 'baby'. My political start-up, CFFP, has demanded more from me than I ever thought I could give, professionally. It is by far the most exhausting and the most fulfilling thing I've ever done.

The start-up scene is an incredibly male world, often a 'bro' culture. Investors – both 'business angels' and venture capitalists – are almost exclusively men. Such investment processes lead to an unequal distribution of start-up funding: women receive less venture capital. Female founders are measured against gendered stereotypes. If they propose risky ventures – in 'typical' start-up fashion – they are less likely to be rewarded for this than men. Women who attempt this are regarded as uninformed and naive, while men are seen as brave risk-takers.[1]

Another problem is that power, positions and capital are passed from man to man via male networks. The approach advocated by the former Facebook chief operating officer Sheryl Sandberg in her book *Lean In* is far too simplistic. It suggests that women can solve the problem themselves with individual competency and courage, and it implies that they might have caused their own underrepresentation in positions of power. Studies have shown that women tend to seek the blame for power inequalities in themselves. This is hardly surprising, when they're told again and again that they could fix the problem by behaving in a certain way – more self-confidence, a deeper voice, etc.[2]

So the more we talk about 'leaning in', the less we talk about systemic change and the accountability of those who benefit from the

unjust situation. If women demand as much as men in salary negotiations, they simply don't get it. A study has shown that men who
negotiate a pay rise are 25 per cent more likely to get one than women
who attempt to do so.[3] Women are punished if they come across as
'bossy' – that is, if they don't comply with traditional roles and behave
modestly and submissively. The more successful a man is, the more
he is liked. The more successful a woman is, the less she is liked. Of
course business angels and venture capitalists can't invest in non-profits
such as CFFP. However, the mechanisms that prevent female founders
from accessing capital are similar in the non-profit sector. Here, too,
it is mainly men – as philanthropists or board members of charitable
foundations – who control the money.

While the mere fact of being led by a woman is enough to make
funding a start-up difficult, things are much worse for enterprises with
a feminist focus. True, governments and international organizations
are increasingly in favour of funding work towards gender equality.
But feminist organizations (especially in the Global South) hardly see
any of this money. From 2016 to 2017, only 1 per cent of all gender-
specific international funding went to women's organizations.[4] At the
same time, right-wing groups are investing millions to influence foreign laws, guidelines and international public opinion against women's
rights and LGBTQ+ people.[5] This imbalance between underfunded
feminist organizations, on the one hand, and financially strong right-
wing organizations, on the other, is not just unfair but extremely dangerous.

This is because systemic change and the protection of human
rights need feminist civil society. But feminist civil society can only
act, and take on right-wing organizations, if it has the necessary
resources at its disposal. CFFP is a social enterprise which survives
purely on its own turnover. We have no investors and are therefore
not answerable to anyone else. The people who work for us have been
educated at elite universities such as London, Oxford and Cambridge
and have many years of experience in international politics and international organizations. The members of our advisory council are

internationally acclaimed individuals, highly respected as academics, political commentators (with large social media followings) or human rights defenders. So we're a political start-up with top employees and impressive supporters. Our 'flaw', in a capitalist society that unfortunately equates value with monetary profit, is that we're working not to maximize profit (we're not allowed to anyway, as a non-profit) but to defend human rights. This immediately reduces our standing and value because of the above-mentioned capitalist logic. We're often asked to provide our services for free, even by ministries. We frequently have to fight for fair pay, while management consultancies demand and receive high daily fees as a matter of course. I've been an advisor to a government department myself, and it was an eye-opener to see how readily lucrative contracts were awarded to law firms, for example, while civil society organizations were treated with the greatest scepticism. The message was: we don't quite trust you.

I wonder why that is, in Germany of all places.

Conclusion: from angst to agency

Many of the numbers, facts and structures in this book are overwhelming; some are horrifying. But we mustn't be discouraged. We must analyse this information and use the analysis to create fairer conditions and structures. After all, CFFP exists in spite of everything. If there's one thing I am, it is stubborn.

In 2006, bell hooks wrote:

Any woman who wishes to be an intellectual, to write nonfiction, to deal with theory, faces a lot of discrimination coming her way and perhaps even self-doubt because there aren't that many who've gone before you. And I think that the most powerful tool we can have is to be clear about our intent. To know what it is we want rather than going into institutions thinking that the institution is going to frame for us.[6]

I feel every syllable of these words with every part of my body.

This is exactly my experience. This is why I began to build a new institution: so that I could work with my team to question existing theories and formulate new ones. But for many years I thought that neither entrepreneurship nor foreign policy would be open to me because I had no background in either of these areas. There were no entrepreneurs in my family, and the mythical figure of the company patriarch is linked with money and masculinity. Books and lectures often try to tell a different story, one of fearlessness, creativity and resilience. But, in reality, most entrepreneurs come from entrepreneurial families and can afford to be founders. Most are men and not women. They have their own seed capital, or can get it from friends and family, and they have enough reserves to allay any initial financial worries. And then there's what the Germans call *Stallgeruch* (literally, the 'smell of the stable'): the mutual sense of familiarity that comes from a shared habitus and lifestyle. If we imagine life as a racecourse, it would look like this: a small number of people start well ahead of the starting line, a few start on the line, and the majority begin far behind the starting line. Some even have extra weights attached to their legs. It's far easier to build a career and lifestyle – and your chances of success are greater – if you inherit an address book full of wealthy and influential people.

I used to think diplomacy and foreign policy weren't for me either, because they're such exclusive, elite fields, open only to the upper echelons of society. The language of many international actors is intimidating, and there's so much knowledge to acquire: about cultures, instruments, treaties, and so on. I thought you had to be much older – and male – to have a say here. That was until I began to understand that habitus and terminology are a deliberate tactic to maintain the exclusivity of this field and to keep the vast majority of people out. Most books on diplomacy and foreign policy are written by men. When this book was first published in German, the colourful cover broke up the monotony of the bookshelves. In the end, the aim is clear and – for me at least – unsurprising. It's easier to get on if we can communicate with empathy and without violence. This is what I want to achieve, and can achieve, with my fellow campaigners. Everything else – information about institutions, the history of states or treaties – is factual knowledge, which anyone can acquire with a bit of reading.

Despite all the resistance we've had to overcome, CFFP has quickly become an internationally respected organization in the field of foreign policy and human rights. We work with, for and against governments and collaborate with other major human rights defenders. I now have access to the world of diplomacy, social capital, and excellent networks. CFFP won't be home and dry for a long time yet, but these days I sleep more peacefully than I did in early 2018. I hope that my work will push open the door for others.

I'm completely serious: if I've been able to do it, then others can do it too. And, where I can, I want to support other human rights defenders in their work. Whatever international challenges we face, be it wars, the climate crisis, attacks on human rights, arms proliferation or pandemics, we can only find long-term solutions if we push for justice and equality at the same time. The future of foreign policy is feminist. This is the way to solve international crises.

PS: only the strong stay soft!

When activists like me face criticism and hate speech, especially of a misogynist nature, we're often advised to grow a thicker skin. It's a strange piece of advice, especially for women who are speaking up in public. And I think it's completely wrong. Sure, you need coping strategies, a clear stance, self-confidence, and a lot of inner work to stay calm and focused. But you don't need a thick skin. It's a toxic fallacy to think that the right attitude involves toughening up and pushing others aside when you're in a leadership role or taking a public stand. Whatever hate, malicious gossip, rumours, accusations and condemnations come your way . . . my personal response is: only the strong stay soft. That's something the German feminist rapper Sookee once said, and I've never forgotten it.

NOTES

Chapter 1 Prologue

1 Rebecca Traister, *Good and Mad: The Revolutionary Power of Women's Anger*. New York: Simon & Schuster, 2018, p. xxiii.

2 Stifterverband, 'Vom Arbeiterkind zum Doktor: Der Hürdenlauf auf dem Bildungsweg der Erststudierenden' [From working-class child to PhD: the obstacle course on the educational path of first-generation students], October 2021, www.stifterverband.org /medien/vom_arbeiterkind_zum_doktor.

3 UN Women UK, *Prevalence and Reporting of Sexual Harassment in UK Public Spaces*, March 2021, www.unwomenuk.org/site/wp-content/uploads/2021/03/APPG-UN-Wo men-Sexual-Harassment-Report_Updated.pdf.

4 Rachel Vogelstein and Meighan Stone, *Awakening: #MeToo and the Global Fight for Women's Rights*. London: Virago, 2021, p. 19.

5 Frauen gegen Gewalt e. V., 'Kampagne "Vergewaltigung verurteilen"' ['Condemning Rape' campaign], 2016, www.frauen-gegen-gewalt.de/de/aktionen-themen/kampagnen /vergewaltigung-verurteilen/zahlen-und-fakten-zum-plakat-vergewaltigung-verurteilen .html.

6 Frank Heer, 'Böse Buben: Warum bei sexualisierter Gewalt im deutschen Rap weggehört wird', *NZZ Magazin*, 10 July 2021, https://magazin.nzz.ch/kultur/metoo-ist-im-deutsc hen-rap-angekommen-ld.1634851?reduced=true.

7 Molly Redden, '"Global gag rule" reinstated by Trump, curbing NGO abortion services abroad', *The Guardian*, 23 January 2017, www.theguardian.com/world/2017/jan/23/tr ump-abortion-gag-rule-international-ngo-funding.

8 Institut für Demokratie und Zivilgesellschaft, *#Hass im Netz: Der schleichende Angriff auf unsere Demokratie* [#Hate online: the insidious attack on our democracy], IDZ, June 2019, www.idz-jena.de/fileadmin/user_upload/_Hass_im_Netz_-_Der_schleiche nde_Angriff.pdf.

9 Plan International, 'Abuse and harassment driving girls off Facebook, Instagram and Twitter', 5 October 2020, https://plan-international.org/news/2020/10/05/abuse-and -harassment-driving-girls-off-facebook-instagram-and-twitter/.

10 Becky Gardiner et al., 'The dark side of Guardian comments', *The Guardian*, 12 April 2016, www.theguardian.com/technology/2016/apr/12/the-dark-side-of-guardian-com ments.

11 Shelley E. Taylor et al., 'Biobehavioral responses to stress in females: tend-and-befriend, not fight-or-flight', *Psychological Review*, 107/3 (2000): 411–29.

12 Gloria Steinem, *My Life on The Road*. London: Oneworld, 2015, p. 115.

13 Ursula Le Guin, *Dancing at the Edge of the World: Thoughts on Words, Women, Places*. New York: Grove Press, 1989, p. 160.

14 '"Bild" verabschiedet sich vom Oben-ohne-"Bild-Girl"' [*Bild* says goodbye to the topless *Bild* girl], *Süddeutsche Zeitung*, 12 March 2018, www.sueddeutsche.de/wirtschaft/medi en-berlin-bild-verabschiedet-sich-vom-oben-ohne-bild-girl-dpa.urn-newsml-dpa-com -20090101-180312-99-443848.

Chapter 2 Why Foreign Policy Must Become Feminist

1 Wolfgang U. Eckart, 'Feminismus trifft Pazifismus' [Feminism meets pacifism], *Süddeutsche Zeitung*, 27 April 2015, www.sueddeutsche.de/kultur/geschichte-feminis mus-trifft-pazifismus-1.2454669.

2 Françoise Girard, 'Philanthropy for the women's movement, not just "empowerment"',

Stanford Social Innovation Review, 4 November 2019, https://ssir.org/articles/entry/phi lanthropy_for_the_womens_movement_not_just_empowerment#.

3   Mala Htun and S. Laurel Weldon, 'The civic origins of progressive policy change: combating violence against women in global perspective, 1975–2005', *American Political Science Review*, 106/3 (2012): 548–69.

4   Alice J. Kang and Aili Mari Tripp, 'Coalitions matter: citizenship, women, and quota adoption in Africa', *Perspectives on Politics*, 16/2 (2018): 73–91.

5   Girard, 'Philanthropy for the women's movement, not just "empowerment"'.

6   Teresa Lloro-Bidart and Michael H. Finewood, 'Intersectional feminism for the environmental studies and sciences: looking inward and outward', *Journal of Environmental Studies and Sciences*, 8 (2018): 142–51.

7   Emilia Roig, *Why We Matter: Das Ende der Unterdrückung* [Why we matter: the end of oppression]. Berlin: Aufbau, 2021, p. 338.

8   Cinzia Arruzza, Tithi Bhattacharya and Nancy Fraser, *Feminism for the 99 Percent: A Manifesto*. London: Verso, 2019, pp. 3–4.

9   Robert Chambers, 'Editorial introduction: vulnerability, coping and policy', *IDS Bulletin*, 20/2 (1989): 1–7.

10 Mitzi Jonelle Tan at a CFFP event, 29 November 2021.

11 'Societies that treat women badly are poorer and less stable', *The Economist*, 11 September 2021, www.economist.com/international/2021/09/11/societies-that-treat-women-badly-are-poorer-and-less-stable.

12 Simone de Beauvoir, *Le deuxième sexe* [The second sex]. Paris: Gallimard, 1949, vol. 1, p. 285.

13 Barbara Finke, 'Feministische Ansätze' [Feminist approaches], in Siegfried Schieder and Manuela Spindler (eds), *Theorien der Internationalen Beziehungen*. 3rd edn, Stuttgart: UTB, 2018, p. 527.

14 Jennifer Newman, 'Assertive women more likely to be sexually harassed at work', LinkedIn, 2 April 2018, www.linkedin.com/pulse/assertive-women-more-likely-sexually-harassed-work-jennifer-newman/.

15 Chuck Collins and Omar Ocampo, 'Global billionaire wealth surges $4 trillion over pandemic', Institute for Policy Studies, 31 March 2021, https://ips-dc.org/global-billionaire-wealth-surges-4-trillion-over-pandemic/.

16 Oxfam International, 'Ten richest men double their fortunes in pandemic while incomes of 99 percent of humanity fall', 17 January 2022, www.oxfam.org/en/press-releases/ten-richest-men-double-their-fortunes-pandemic-while-incomes-99-percent-humanity.

17 Oxfam International, 'Why the majority of the world's poor are women', www.oxfam.org/en/why-majority-worlds-poor-are-women.

18 GrenzEcho, 'Nur in sechs Ländern weltweit haben Frauen gleiche Rechte, und Belgien gehört dazu' [Women have equal rights in only six countries worldwide, and Belgium is one of them], 8 March 2019, www.grenzecho.net/9809/artikel/2019-03-08/nur-sechs-landern-weltweit-haben-frauen-gleiche-rechte-und-belgien-gehort-dazu.

19 Amnesty International, 'Key facts on abortion', www.amnesty.org/en/what-we-do/sexual-and-reproductive-rights/abortion-facts/.

20 'Societies that treat women badly are poorer and less stable'.

21 'Why nations that fail women fail', *The Economist*, 11 September 2021, www.economist.com/leaders/2021/09/11/why-nations-that-fail-women-fail.

22 Rose McDermott and Jonathan Cowden, 'Polygyny and violence against women', *Emory Law Journal*, 64/6 (2015): 1767–814.

23 David P. Barash, *Out of Eden: The Surprising Consequences of Polygamy*. Oxford: Oxford University Press, 2016, pp. 9, 27.

24 UN Resolution adopted by the General Assembly, 10 September 2012, https://humansecuritycourse.info/module-1-the-concept-of-human-security/un-approach/.

25 CFFP Policy Brief, 12 December 2022, https://centreforfeministforeignpolicy.org/how-militarised-is-germanys-foreign-policy.
26 Marlea Clarke, 'Global South: what does it mean and why use the term?', University of Victoria, 8 August 2018, https://onlineacademiccommunity.uvic.ca/globalsouthpolitics/2018/08/08/global-south-what-does-it-mean-and-why-use-the-term/.
27 Cf. Bundeszentrale für politische Bildung, 'Nationalstaat' [Nation state], www.bpb.de/nachschlagen/lexika/politiklexikon/17894/nationalstaat.
28 Email exchange with Sigmar Gabriel, 10 October 2021.
29 Martin E. Hellman and Vinton G. Cerf, 'An existential discussion: what *is* the probability of nuclear war?', *Bulletin of the Atomic Scientists*, 18 March 2021, https://thebulletin.org/2021/03/an-existential-discussion-what-is-the-probability-of-nuclear-war/.

Chapter 3 Diplomacy
1 Jennifer A. Cassidy and Sara Althari, 'Introduction: analyzing the dynamics of modern diplomacy through a gender lens', in Jennifer A. Cassidy (ed.), *Gender and Diplomacy*. Abingdon: Routledge, 2017, pp. 1–12, at p. 3.
2 Ibid.
3 Ibid., p. 1.
4 Helen McCarthy and James Southern, 'Woman, gender and diplomacy: a historical survey', ibid., pp. 15–31, at pp. 15ff.
5 Ibid.
6 German Federal Foreign Office, *Gender Equality in German Foreign Policy and in the Federal Foreign Office*. Berlin, 2020, p. 25, www.globalwps.org/data/DEU/files/Federal%20Foreign%20Office.pdf.
7 Ursula Müller and Christiane Scheidemann (eds), *Gewandt, geschickt und abgesandt – Frauen im diplomatischen Dienst* [Dexterous, skilled and dispatched: women in the diplomatic service]. Munich: Olzog, 2000, p. 99.
8 Ibid., pp. 96ff. Here we also learn that the post-1949 reorganization, for the first time in the history of the Foreign Office, created the conditions for the integration of women into the Senior Foreign Service.
9 Cf. Müller and Scheidemann, *Gewandt, geschickt und abgesandt*, p. 99.
10 Auswärtiges Amt, 'Hinter den Kulissen: Aus Pressebriefingraum wird Ellinor-von-Puttkamer-Saal' [Behind the scenes: the press briefing room becomes the Ellinor von Puttkamer Room], 26 October 2020, www.auswaertiges-amt.de/de/aamt/zugastimaa/tdot-2020/-/2409748.
11 Ibid.
12 Catherine Tsalikis, 'The making of a gender-balanced foreign service: stories from the women driving Canada's diplomatic corps towards equality', *Open Canada*, 3 April 2018, https://opencanada.org/making-gender-balanced-foreign-service/.
13 Ann Towns and Birgitta Niklasson, 'Gender, international status, and ambassador appointments', *Foreign Policy Analysis*, 13/3 (2017): 521–40.
14 *The #Shecurity Index*, https://shecurity.info/wp-content/uploads/2022/10/Report_Shecurity_2022_FiNAL.pdf.
15 Cf. Instagram post by Diversitry, 14 May 2021, at www.instagram.com/p/CO2se22pM0c/.
16 Celia Parbey and Tiaji Sio, '"Die Politik in Deutschland muss für alle Teile unserer Gesellschaft da sein": Im Gespräch mit der Gründerin des Netzwerks Diplomats of Color Tiaji Sio' ['Politics in Germany must be there for all parts of our society': in conversation with the founder of the network Diplomats of Colour Tiaji Sio], *RosaMAG*, 11 December 2020, https://rosa-mag.de/tiaji-sio-die-deutsche-politik-und-die-verwaltung-mussen-fur-alle-teile-unserer-gesellschaft-da-sein/.
17 Colum Lynch, 'The U.N. has a diversity problem: Westerners are overrepresented in

senior positions across the world body', *Foreign Policy*, 16 October 2020, https://foreign policy.com/2020/10/16/un-diversity-problem-workforce-western-ocha/.

18 Marième Soumaré, 'Racism at the UN: internal audit reveals deep-rooted problems', *The Africa Report*, 3 February 2021, www.theafricareport-com.cdn.ampproject.org/c/s/www .theafricareport.com/62757/racism-at-the-un-internal-audit-reveals-deep-rooted-prob lems/amp/.

19 United States Mission to the United Nations, 'Remarks by Ambassador Linda Thomas-Greenfield at a UN General Assembly commemorative meeting for International Day for the Elimination of Racial Discrimination', 19 March 2021, https://usun.usmission .gov/remarks-by-ambassador-linda-thomas-greenfield-at-a-un-general-assembly-commem orative-meeting-for-intl-day-for-the-elimination-of-racial-discrimination/.

20 Nelson Mandela Foundation, 'Annual lecture 2020: Secretary Guterres's full speech', 18 July 2020, www.nelsonmandela.org/news/entry/annual-lecture-2020-secretary-ge neral-guterress-full-speech.

21 Cf. Ha-Joon Chang, *Kicking away the Ladder: Development Strategy in Historical Perspective*. London: Anthem Press, 2002.

22 Maya Salam, 'In her words: where women rule the headlines', 4 January 2019, www.ny times.com/2019/01/04/us/women-quotes-voices.html.

23 Nicola Davis, 'Girls believe brilliance is a male trait, research into gender stereotypes shows', *The Guardian*, 27 January 2017, www.theguardian.com/education/2017/jan/26 /girls-believe-brilliance-is-a-male-trait-research-into-gender-stereotypes-shows.

24 Tomas Chamorro-Premuzic, 'Why do so many incompetent men become leaders?', *Harvard Business Review*, 22 August 2013, https://hbr.org/2013/08/why-do-so-many-in competent-men.

25 Margarete Stokowski, *Untenrum frei*. Reinbek bei Hamburg: Rowohlt, 2016, p. 170.

26 Martha S. Jones, 'For Black women, the 19th Amendment didn't end their fight to vote', *National Geographic*, 7 August 2020, www.nationalgeographic.com/history/article/black -women-continued-fighting-for-vote-after-19th-amendment.

27 Sarah Grimké, *Letters on the Equality of the Sexes, and the Condition of Woman: Addressed to Mary S. Parker, President of the Boston Female Anti-Slavery Society*. Boston: Isaac Knapp, 1838, p. 10.

28 Anna Dünnebier and Ursula Scheu, *Die Rebellion ist eine Frau: Anita G. Augspurg und Lida G. Heymann: Das schillerndste Paar der Frauenbewegung* [Rebellion is a woman: Anita G. Augspurg and Lida G. Heymann: the most dazzling couple in the women's movement]. Basel: Sphinx, 2002, p. 80.

29 Demokratiezentrum Wien, 'Pionierinnen der Frauenbewegung' [Pioneers of the women's movement], www.demokratiezentrum.org/bildung/ressourcen/themenmodule/gen derperspektiven/pionierinnen-der-frauenbewegung-und-frauen-in-der-politik/pionier innen-der-frauenbewegung/.

30 BBC News, 'Suffragettes: the truth about force feeding', 5 February 2018, www.bbc .com/news/av/uk-42943816.

31 Maik Baumgärtner, Roman Höfner, Ann-Katrin Müller and Marcel Rosenbach, 'Feindbild Frau: Eine düstere Welt enthemmter Männer' [Women as the enemy: a dark world of men who have lost their inhibitions], *Spiegel Online*, 12 February 2021, www. spiegel.de/politik/deutschland/frauenfeindlichkeit-im-internet-die-duestere-welt-ent hemmter-maenner-a-00000000-0002-0001-0000-000175304147. Worldwide figures show that women in politics are interrupted by men twice as often as men by women. They are kept in their place with dismissive comments from men; in a survey, far more than half of female politicians (66 per cent) said that they regularly heard misogynist and sexist comments from their male colleagues; 20 per cent of female members of parliament had experienced sexualized violence. Most of these figures are from a global study on sexism, violence and harassment experienced by female politicians in the

Inter-Parliamentary Union, an international association of parliaments worldwide. Cf. Caroline Criado-Perez, *Invisible Women: Exposing Data Bias in a World Designed for Men.* London: Chatto & Windus, 2019, pp. 277ff.
32 Ibid., pp. 265ff.

Chapter 4 Old White Men in Theory

1 Julia Korbik, "'Das Private ist politisch' & was dieser Slogan mit der Fetischisierung persönlicher Erlebnisse zu tun hat' ['The private is political' and what this slogan has to do with the fetishization of personal experience], *This is Jayne Wayne*, 26 August 2020, www.thisisjanewayne.com/news/2020/08/26/das-private-ist-politisch-was-dieser-slo gan-mit-der-fetischisierung-persoenlicher-erlebnisse-zu-tun-hat/.
2 Valerie Hudson et al., *The First Political Order: How Sex Shapes Governance and National Security Worldwide.* New York: Columbia University Press, 2020.
3 Caroline Criado-Perez, *Invisible Women: Exposing Data Bias in a World Designed for Men.* London: Chatto & Windus, 2019. See also Angela Saini, 'Why the preoccupation with sex?', *The Lancet*, 400/10,364 (2022): 1674–1675, and research published by the British Heart Foundation, 'Women more likely to have "typical" heart attack symptoms than men' (2019), https://www.sciencedaily.com/releases/2019/08/190821082244.htm.
4 The lack of data on trans and gender-diverse people continues to pose a significant challenge in reducing inequalities and accounting for everybody's lived experiences and needs.
5 Maya Salam, 'In her words: where women rule the headlines', 4 January 2019, www.nytimes.com/2019/01/04/us/women-quotes-voices.html.
6 Barbara Finke, 'Feministische Ansätze' [Feminist approaches], in Siegfried Schieder and Manuela Spindler (eds), *Theorie der Internationalen Beziehungen.* Leverkusen: UTB, 2003, pp. 477–504, 534.
7 Niccolò Machiavelli, *The Prince*, trans. Rufus Goodwin. Boston: Dante University Press 2003, p. 94.
8 In the German translation of *The Prince*: Machiavelli, *Der Fürst*, trans. A. W. Rehberg. Frankfurt am Main: Fischer Taschenbuch 2010, p. 12.
9 Zillah R. Eisenstein, *The Radical Future of Liberal Feminism.* Boston: Northeastern University Press, 1981, p. 11.
10 Barry Gewen, *The Inevitability of Tragedy: Henry Kissinger and His World.* New York: W. W. Norton, 2020, pp. 201ff.
11 Ibid.
12 Ibid., p. 173.
13 Ibid., back cover.
14 Bernd Greiner, 'Gewalt. Macht. Hegemonie. Zur Aktualität von Henry Kissinger' [Force. Power. Hegemony. On the current relevance of Henry Kissinger], *Blätter für deutsche und internationale Politik*, October 2020, pp. 63–71, at p. 66.
15 Ibid., p. 63.
16 Ibid., p. 66.
17 Ibid., p. 70.
18 Gewen, *The Inevitability of Tragedy*, p. 166.
19 Ibid., p. xvi.
20 Robert S. McNamara, *In Retrospect: The Tragedy and Lessons of Vietnam.* New York: Vintage, 1996, p. 403.
21 Robert D. Dean, *Imperial Brotherhood: Gender and the Making of Cold War Foreign Policy.* Amherst: University of Massachusetts Press, 2001, p. 4.
22 Ibid., p. 243.
23 CBC Arts, 'George Gerbner leaves the mean world syndrome', *Peace, Earth & Justice News*, 8 January 2006, https://web.archive.org/web/20150222055417/https://pejnews

.com/index.php?option=com_content&view=article&id=4053&catid=74:ijustice-news&Itemid=216; quoted in Rutger Bregman, *Humankind: A Hopeful History*, trans. Elizabeth Manton and Erica Moore. New York: Little, Brown, 2020, p. 38.

24 Minna Salami, *Sensuous Knowledge: A Black Feminist Approach for Everyone*. New York: Amistad, 2020, pp. 146–7.

25 Hanna Fenichel Pitkin, *Wittgenstein and Justice: On the Significance of Ludwig Wittgenstein for Social and Political Thought*. Berkeley: University of California Press, 1973, p. 276.

26 Joke J. Hermsen, *A Good and Dignified Life: The Political Advice of Hannah Arendt and Rosa Luxemburg*, trans. Brendan Monaghan. New Haven, CT: Yale University Press, 2022, p. 98.

27 Max Roser, Bastian Herre and Joe Hasell, 'Nuclear weapons', Our World in Data, 2022, https://ourworldindata.org/nuclear-weapons.

28 ICAN, 'The world's nuclear weapons', www.icanw.org/nuclear_arsenals.

29 J. Ann Tickner, *Gendering World Politics: Issues and Approaches in the Post-Cold War Era*. New York: Columbia University Press, 2001, p. 1.

30 Daniel F. Schulz and Jan Tilly, 'Der Liberalismus in den Internationalen Beziehungen' [Liberalism in international relations], in Markus M. Müller (ed.), *Casebook internationale Politik*. Wiesbaden: VS Verlag für Sozialwissenschaften, 2011, p. 27.

31 Kristen R. Ghodsee, 'Die roten Großmütter der Frauenbewegung' [The red grandmothers of the women's movement], *Le Monde Diplomatique*, 8 July 2021, https://monde-diplomatique.de/artikel/!5783386.

32 Ibid.

33 Ibid.

34 Tickner, *Gendering World Politics*, p. 2.

35 Quoted in Heli Ihlefeld, *Mein Bonner Tagebuch* [My Bonn diary]. Munich: Paul List, 1970, p. 106.

36 Laura Sjoberg, 'Introduction', in Sjoberg (ed.), *Gender and International Security: Feminist Perspectives*. London: Routledge, 2010, pp. 3–17; Finke, 'Feministische Ansätze' [Feminist approaches], pp. 477–504.

37 J. Ann Tickner, 'Hans Morgenthau's principles of political realism: a feminist reformulation', *Journal of International Studies*, 17/3 (1988): 429–40, at p. 429.

38 Samantha Power, *Education of an Idealist*. London: HarperCollins, 2019, p. 220.

39 'Bundeshaushalt 2020' [Federal budget 2020], CRP, Politik und Zeitgeschichte, https://crp-infotec.de/deutschland-bundeshaushalt-2020/.

40 ICAN, 'Nuclear spending vs healthcare', 2020, www.icanw.org/healthcare_costs.

41 Email exchange with Elvira Rosert, 3 August 2021.

42 Ramón Grosfoguel, 'The structure of knowledge in Westernized universities: epistemic racism/sexism and the four genocides/epistemicides of the long 16th century', *Human Architecture: Journal of the Sociology of Self-Knowledge*, XI/1 (2013): 73–90.

43 Emilia Roig, *Why We Matter: Das Ende der Unterdrückung* [Why we matter: the end of oppression]. Berlin: Aufbau, 2021, p. 108.

44 Grosfoguel, 'The structure of knowledge in Westernized universities', pp. 73–90.

45 Roig, *Why We Matter*, p. 109.

46 Quoted in Mona Chollet, *In Defence of Witches: The Legacy of the Witch Hunts and Why Women Are Still on Trial*, trans. Sophie R. Lewis. New York: St Martin's Press, 2022, p. 245.

47 Florian Biskamp, 'Kritik der weißen Vernunft: Sollte man Kant als Rassisten bezeichnen?' [Critique of white reason: should one call Kant a racist?], *Der Tagesspiegel*, 21 June 2020, www.tagesspiegel.de/kultur/sollte-man-kant-als-rassisten-bezeichnen-kritik-der-weissen-vernunft/25935036.html.

48 Jürgen Habermas, *Die Moderne – Ein unvollendetes Projekt: Philosophisch-politische Aufsätze* [Modernity – an incomplete project: philosophical-political essays]. Leipzig:

Reclam, 1990; Iris Därmann in conversation with Simone Miller, 'Die dunkle Seite der Philosophie', *Deutschlandfunk*, 2 August 2020, www.deutschlandfunkkultur.de/rechtfer tigung-von-sklaverei-und-gewalt-die-dunkle-seite-100.html.

49 Olivia U. Rutazibwa and Robbie Shilliam, 'Postcolonial politics: an introduction', in Rutazibwa and Shilliam (eds), *Handbook of Postcolonial Politics*. Abingdon: Routledge, 2020, pp. 1–16.

50 Kelebogile Zvobgo and Meredith Loken, 'Why race matters in international relations', *Foreign Policy*, 19 June 2020, https://foreignpolicy.com/2020/06/19/why-race-matters -international-relations-ir/.

51 Ozan Ozavci, 'Bursting the bubbles: on the Peace of Westphalia and the happiness of unlearning', Utrecht University, https://securing-europe.wp.hum.uu.nl/bursting-the-bu bbles-on-the-peace-of-westphalia-and-the-happiness-of-unlearning/.

52 Peace Direct, *Time to Decolonise Aid: Insights and Lessons from a Global Consultation: Full Report*, November 2020, www.peacedirect.org/wp-content/uploads/2021/05/PD-Decol onising-Aid-Report.pdf.

53 In 2017, only 12 per cent of international funds from US foundations went directly to organizations based in the country where the programmes were conducted. See Solomé Lemma and Jennifer Lentfer, 'Racism and philanthropy: how little practices and big resource flows are connected', Thousand Currents, 29 October 2018, https://thousan dcurrents.org/racism-and-philanthropy-how-little-practices-and-big-resource-flows-are -connected-part-2/.

54 Zvobgo and Loken, 'Why race matters in international relations'.

55 Salami, *Sensuous Knowledge*, p. 4.

Chapter 5 The Beginnings of Feminist Foreign Policy

1 Audre Lorde, *Sister Outsider*. Feasterville Trevose, PA: Crossing Press, 2007, p. 110.

2 Freya Baetens, 'The forgotten peace conference: the 1915 International Congress of Women', in Rüdiger Wolfrum (ed.), *Max Planck Encyclopedia of Public International Law*. Oxford: Oxford University Press, 2010.

3 Anna Dünnebier and Ursula Scheu, *Die Rebellion ist eine Frau: Anita G. Augspurg und Lida G. Heymann: Das schillerndste Paar der Frauenbewegung* [Rebellion is a woman: Anita G. Augspurg and Lida G. Heymann: the most dazzling couple in the women's movement]. Basel: Sphinx, 2002, p. 97.

4 IFFF Internationale Frauenliga für Frieden und Freiheit, 'Lida Gustava Heymann (15. März 1868 – 31. Juli 1943)', 22 June 2005, www.wilpf.de/lida-gustava-heymann/.

5 Elke Schüller, 'Anita Augspurg', *Bundeszentrale für politische Bildung*, 13 January 2009, www.bpb.de/gesellschaft/gender/frauenbewegung/35320/anita-augspurg.

6 Dünnebier and Scheu, *Die Rebellion ist eine Frau*, pp. 103ff.

7 Heymann, *Völkerverbindende Frauenarbeit 1914–18*, p. 11, quoted ibid., p. 214.

8 Ibid., p. 215.

9 Ibid.

10 Louise Arimatsu in a phone/Zoom conversation, 15 January 2021.

11 Dünnebier and Scheu, *Die Rebellion ist eine Frau*, p. 224.

12 International Alliance of Women, 'Brief history of the IAW', https://womenalliance.org /old/history.html.

13 Harriet Hyman Alonso, *The Longest Living Women's Peace Organization in World History: The Women's International League for Peace and Freedom, 1915 to the Present*. Alexandria, VA: Alexander Street Press, 2012.

14 Baetens, 'The forgotten peace conference'.

15 Democracy Now!, 'Women's International League for Peace and Freedom marks 100th anniversary as war rages on worldwide', YouTube, 29 April 2015, www.youtube.com/ watch?v=tlbm5Kvwsak.

16 Baetens, 'The forgotten peace conference'.
17 Christian Ritz, 'Emily Greene Balch', Fritz Bauer Bibliothek, www.fritz-bauer-forum.de /datenbank/emily-greene-balch/.
18 Jane Addams, Emily Greene Balch and Alice Hamilton, *Women at the Hague: The International Congress of Women and its Results*. Urbana: University of Illinois Press, 2003.
19 Baetens, 'The forgotten peace conference'.
20 Ibid.
21 Ibid.
22 Dünnebier and Scheu, *Die Rebellion ist eine Frau*, p. 225.
23 Ibid., p. 227.
24 Ritz, 'Emily Green Balch'.
25 Jane Addams, 'The revolt against war', in Jane Addams, Emily Greene Balch and Alice Hamilton, *Women at the Hague*, pp. 55–81, at p. 57.
26 Ritz, 'Emily Green Balch'. See also Dünnebier and Scheu, *Die Rebellion ist eine Frau*, p. 228.
27 Mona L. Siegel, *Peace on Our Terms: The Global Battle for Women's Rights after the First World War*. New York: Columbia University Press, 2020, p. 137.
28 Ibid.
29 Ritz, 'Emily Green Balch'. See also Dünnebier and Scheu, *Die Rebellion ist eine Frau*, p. 228.
30 Erika Kuhlman, 'The "Women's International League for Peace and Freedom" and reconciliation after the Great War', in Alison S. Fell and Ingrid Sharp (eds), *The Women's Movement in Wartime: International Perspectives, 1914–19*. Basingstoke: Palgrave Macmillan, 2007, pp. 227–43.
31 Siegel, *Peace on Our Terms*, p. 137.
32 Ibid., p. 31.
33 Ibid., p. 38.
34 Ibid., p. 137.
35 Ibid., p. 40.
36 Ibid., p. 46.
37 Ibid., p. 251.
38 Ibid., p. 68.
39 Alonso, *The Longest Living Women's Peace Organization in World History*.
40 Siegel, *Peace on Our Terms*, p. 145.
41 Ibid., p. 162.
42 Marcel Fürstenau, 'Versailler Vertrag: Ein fragiler Frieden' [Treaty of Versailles: a fragile peace], *Deutsche Welle*, 27 June 2019, www.dw.com/de/versailler-vertrag-ein-fragiler-fri eden/a-49291640.
43 Siegel, *Peace on Our Terms*, p. 80.
44 Ibid., p. 63.
45 Ibid., p. 83.
46 Ibid., p. 84.
47 IFFF Internationale Frauenliga für Frieden und Freiheit, 'Anita Augspurg (September 1857 – Dezember 1943)', 22 June 2005, www.wilpf.de/anita-augspurg-september-18 57-dezember-1943/.
48 Siegel, *Peace on Our Terms*.
49 Alonso, *The Longest Living Women's Peace Organization in World History*.
50 UN Women, *Preventing Conflict, Transforming Justice, Securing the Peace: A Global Study on the Implementation of United Nations Security Council Resolution 1325*, 2005, wps. unwomen.org/.

51 Council on Foreign Relations, 'Women's participation in peace processes', 2020, www.cfr.org/womens-participation-in-peace-processes/.

52 Inclusive Security, 'The Women Waging Peace Commission', *Inclusive Security*, www.inc lusivesecurity.org/experts/.

53 Nicole Waintraub, 'Regional women mediator networks: the key to feminist approaches to mediation and peacebuilding?', 6 January 2020, www.boell.de/en/2020/01/03 /regional-women-mediator-networks-key-feminist-approaches-mediation-and-peacebu ilding.

54 UN Women, 'The Beijing Platform for Action turns 20', 2015, https://beijing20.un women.org/en/about.

55 Hilary Charlesworth, Christine Chinkin and Shelley Wright, 'Feminist approaches to international law', *American Journal of International Law*, 85/4 (1991): 613–45.

56 Martti Koskenniemi, *The Gentle Civilizer of Nations: The Rise and Fall of International Law 1870–1960*. Cambridge: Cambridge University Press, 2009, www.cambridge.org /core/books/gentle-civilizer-of-nations/DB461DBE95F8A6E05A65438171E6B637

57 Email exchange with Nicola Popovic, 13 November 2021.

58 Sue Harris Rimmer and Kate Ogg, 'Introduction', in Rimmer and Ogg (eds), *Research Handbook on Feminist Engagement with International Law*. Cheltenham: Edward Elgar, 2019, p. 12.

59 United Nations Human Rights Office of the High Commissioner, 'Status of ratification: interactive dashboard', https://indicators.ohchr.org.

60 CFFP, 'No systemic change without legal change: feminist engagements with international law', 19 May 2021, www.youtube.com/watch?v=Gt7DnVeOs_g&t=3s.

61 Ibid.

62 Ibid.

63 Akila Radhakrishnan, Elena Sarver and Grant Shubin, 'Protecting safe abortion in humanitarian settings: overcoming legal and policy barriers', *Reproductive Health Matters: An International Journal on Sexual and Reproductive Health and Rights*, 25(2017): 40–7.

64 Ritz, 'Emily Greene Balch'.

65 For a detailed account, see Robert W. Dimand, 'Emily Greene Balch, political economist', *American Journal of Economics and Sociology*, 70/2 (2011): 464–79, at pp. 472f.

66 IFFF Internationale Frauenliga für Frieden und Freiheit, 'Lida Gustava Heymann'.

67 Schüller, 'Anita Augspurg'.

68 The Nobel Prize, 'Jane Addams', 2021, www.nobelprize.org/prizes/peace/1931/addams /facts/.

69 Ritz, 'Emily Greene Balch'.

70 Ibid.

71 Ibid.

72 Alice Schwarzer, 'Vorwort' [Foreword], in Dünnebier and Scheu, *Die Rebellion ist eine Frau*, p. 9.

73 Vivian M. May, 'Anna Julia Cooper on slavery's afterlife: can international thought "hear" her "muffled" voices and ideas?', in Katharina Rietzler and Patricia Owens (eds), *Women's International Thought: A New History*. Cambridge: Cambridge University Press 2021, pp. 29–51.

Chapter 6 Feminist Activism: UN Resolution 1325

1 Hans-Martin Tillack, 'Bundeswehr-Panzer für den König' [Bundeswehr tanks for the king], *taz*, 3 April 2021, taz.de/Waffenembargo-in-Libyen/!5760303/.

2 'The UN's structures built in 1945 are not fit for 2020, let alone beyond it', *The Economist*, 18 June 2020, www.economist.com/special-report/2020/06/18/the-uns-structures-built-in-1945-are-not-fit-for-2020-let-alone-beyond-it.

3   Reaching Critical Will, 'Article 26 of the UN Charter', www.reachingcriticalwill.org /resources/fact-sheets/critical-issues/4565-article-26-of-the-un-charter.

4   United Nations, *United Nations Charter*, www.un.org/en/about-us/un-charter/full-text.

5   Madeleine Rees, 'Can the Security Council work for women?', WILPF, 20 October 2017, www.peacewomen.org/resource/can-security-council-work-women.

6   Ray Acheson and Madeleine Rees, 'A feminist approach for addressing excessive military spending', in *Rethinking Unconstrained Military Spending*, UNODA Occasional Papers no. 35, United Nations 2020, pp. 39–56, at p. 42.

7   Peace Women, 'Civil society briefers', WILPF, http://peacewomen.org/node/103504.

8   Peace Women, 'Arria-formula meetings', WILPF, www.peacewomen.org/security-coun cil/other-council-work/arria-meetings.

9   Wolfgang Ischinger, *Welt in Gefahr: Deutschland und Europa in unsicheren Zeiten* [World in danger: Germany and Europe in uncertain times]. Berlin: Econ, 2018, p. 177.

10 Ibid., p. 186.

11 Email exchange with Nicola Popovic, 31 July 2021.

12 Council on Foreign Relations, 'Women's participation in peace processes', 2020, www.cfr.org/womens-participation-in-peace-processes/.

13 Laurel Stone, 'Quantitative analysis of women's participation in peace processes', in UN Women, *Preventing Conflict, Transforming Justice, Securing the Peace: A Global Study on the Implementation of United Nations Security Council Resolution 1325*, 2005, wps. unwomen.org/.

14 The personal section is based on an article I wrote for the Deutsche Gesellschaft für die Vereinten Nationen (German Society for the United Nations): Kristina Lunz, 'Steht nach dem "Nein" in Kolumbien nachhaltiger Frieden auf dem Spiel?' [After the 'no' in Colombia, is lasting peace at risk?], Deutsche Gesellschaft für die Vereinten Nationen, 13 October 2016, https://dgvn.de/meldung/steht-nach-dem-nein-in-kolumbien-nachh altiger-frieden-auf-dem-spiel/.

15 Abigail Ruane and Marina Kumskova, *Towards a Feminist Security Council: A Guidance Note for Security Council Members*, WILPF, November 2018, www.wilpf.org/wp-content /uploads/2019/04/WILPF_FeministSecurityCouncilGuide.pdf.

16 I wrote about this at the beginning of 2017 for *Libertine Magazin*: Kristina Lunz, 'Solidarität und Zusammenhalt statt Sabotage' [Solidarity and cohesion, not sabotage], *Libertine Magazin*, 4 January 2017, https://libertine-mag.com/magazin/society-politics /zusammenhalt-statt-sabotage/.

17 Amnesty International, 'Kolumbien 2017/18', December 2017, www.amnesty.de/jahre sbericht/2018/kolumbien.

18 Programa Somos Defensores, *Annual Report 2020: Information System about Aggression against Human Rights Defenders in Colombia*, 2021, https://drive.google.com/file/d/1Q aCwSTrkScbsWA2H4gajBrtGvi_ya94j/view.

19 Johannes Varwick, *NATO in (Un-)Ordnung: Wie transatlantische Sicherheit neu verhan-delt wird* [NATO in (dis)order: How transatlantic security is being renegotiated]. Bonn: Bundeszentrale für politische Bildung, 2017, p. 26.

20 NATO, 'NATO and Women, Peace and Security: strength is in gender diversity and equality', 15 October 2020, www.nato.int/cps/en/natohq/news_178803.htm.

21 Kristina Lunz, 'Interview with Clare Hutchinson', CFFP, 14 June 2018.

22 Katharine Wright, Matthew Hurley and Jesus Ignacio Gil Ruiz, *NATO, Gender and the Military: Women Organising from Within*. London: Routledge, 2019. For a detailed overview of NATO's work on WPS, see chapter 2, 'The long view: situating NATO's engagement with women, peace and security'.

23 Teresa Bücker, 'Sexualisierte Gewalt als Kriegswaffe: Darum stärkt die neue UN-Resolution reproduktive Rechte nicht' [Sexualized violence as a weapon of war: this

is why the new UN resolution does not strengthen reproductive rights], *Edition F*, 25 April 2019, https://editionf.com/un-resolution-sexualisierte-gewalt-feministische-aussenpolitik-interview/.

24 Ibid.

25 Ibid.

26 Anica Heinlein, Jeannette Böhme and Ines Kappert, 'Statement: German government treading on dangerous ground in the UN Security Council', Heinrich-Böll-Stiftung, March 2019, https://static1.squarespace.com/static/57cd7cd9d482e9784e4ccc34/t/5cd 0624ce79c7011d17929ea/1557160531034/statement+1325_EN.pdf.

27 Adelaide Barat, 'Madeleine Rees on UN Security Council Resolution 2467', WILPF, 2019, www.wilpf.org/madeleine-rees-on-un-security-council-resolution-2467/.

28 Women's International League of Peace and Freedom, '1325 national action plans (NAPS)', https://1325naps.peacewomen.org.

29 Françoise Girard, 'Philanthropy for the women's movement, not just "empowerment"', *Stanford Social Innovation Review*, 4 November 2019, https://ssir.org/articles/entry/phi lanthropy_for_the_womens_movement_not_just_empowerment#.

30 M. Szmigiera, 'Largest donors of humanitarian aid worldwide 2020, by country', Statista, 12 March 2021, www.statista.com/statistics/275597/largest-donor-countries-of-aid-worldwide/.

31 Nina Bernarding, Jeannette Böhme, Anica Heinlein and Ines Kappert, *The Women, Peace and Security Agenda Implementation Matters: Policy Briefing on the Third National Action Plan of the German Government*, Heinrich-Böll-Stiftung, 8 June 2020, www.gwi -boell.de/sites/default/files/2020-06/1325 Policy Briefing_EN_2.pdf.

32 Ibid.

33 IFFF Internationale Frauenliga für Frieden und Freiheit, 'Frauen, Frieden und Sicherheit: Zivilgesellschaftliche Stellungnahme zum 3. Nationalen Aktionsplan der Bundesregierung' [Women, peace and security: civil society statement on the 3rd national action plan of the German federal government], 14 April 2021, www.wilpf.de /frauen-frieden-und-sicherheit-zivilgesellschaftliche-stellungnahme-zum-3-nationalen-aktionsplan-der-bundesregierung/.

34 Victoria Scheyer, 'Rechtsradikale Ideologien bedrohen Frauen, Frieden und Sicherheit in Deutschland' [Extreme right-wing ideologies threaten women, peace and security in Germany], PeaceLab, 7 July 2020, https://peacelab.blog/2020/07/rechtsradikale-ideolo gien-bedrohen-frauen-frieden-und-sicherheit-in-deutschland.

35 Dianne Otto, 'Women, peace and security: a critical analysis of the Security Council's vision', LSE, 9 January 2017, https://blogs.lse.ac.uk/wps/2017/01/09/women-peace-and-security-a-critical-analysis-of-the-security-councils-vision/.

36 Sara E. Davies and Jacqui True, *The Oxford Handbook of Women, Peace, and Security*, Oxford: Oxford University Press, 2019.

37 Friedrich Nietzsche, *Beyond Good and Evil*, trans. Helen Zimmern. Hoboken, NJ: Wiley, 2020, p. 86.

38 This is also how we should understand the quotation in the title of this section, which comes from an interview with her: 'Sanam Naraghi Anderlini: Es ist Zeit, wieder in Frieden zu investieren' [Sanam Naraghi Anderline: it's time to invest in peace again], 1 November 2021, www.tu.berlin/ueber-die-tu-berlin/queens-lecture-2021/interview -mit-sanam-naraghi-anderlini.

Chapter 7 The Status Quo of Feminist Foreign Policy

1 Nathalie Rothschild, 'Swedish women vs. Vladimir Putin', *Foreign Policy*, 5 December 2014, https://foreignpolicy.com/2014/12/05/can-vladimir-putin-be-intimidated-by-fem inism-sweden/.

2   Ellen Barry, 'Sweden's proponent of "feminist foreign policy" shaped by abuse', *New York Times*, 17 November 2017, www.nytimes.com/2017/11/17/world/europe/margot-walls trom-sweden.html.

3   Ibid.

4   Merlyn Thomas, 'Sweden ditches "feminist foreign policy"', *BBC News*, 19 October 2022, www.bbc.com/news/world-europe-63311743.

5   International Center for Research on Women, 'Press release: historic legislation calling for a feminist foreign policy reintroduced in U.S. Congress', ICRW, 8 March 2021, www.icrw.org/press-releases/historic-legislation-calling-for-a-feminist-foreign-policy-rei ntroduced-in-u-s-congress/.

6   Mette Mølgaard, 'EU parliament calls for feminist foreign policy', *EUobserver*, 16 November 2020, https://euobserver.com/institutional/150073.

7   Kubernein Initiative, *Understanding the Feminist Foreign Policy: A View from India*, 2021, https://kuberneininitiative.com/wp-content/uploads/2021/08/Understanding -the-FFP_A-View-from-India.pdf.

8   CFFP, *A Feminist Foreign Policy for the European Union*, June 2020, https://centrefor feministforeignpolicy.org/report-feminist-foreign-policy-for-the-eu.

9   Ministry for Foreign Affairs, *Handbook: Sweden's Feminist Foreign Policy*, Stockholm 2019.

10   Valerie Hudson, Donna Lee Bowen and Perpetua Lynne Nielsen, *First Political Order: How Sex Shapes Governance and National Security Worldwide*. New York: Columbia University Press, 2020.

11   Government Offices of Sweden, Ministry of Foreign Affairs, 'The Swedish Foreign Service action plan for feminist foreign policy 2019–2022, including direction and measures for 2021', 2020.

12   Adam Taylor, 'Sweden stood up for human rights in Saudi Arabia: this is how Saudi Arabia is punishing Sweden', *Washington Post*, 20 March 2015, www.washingtonpost .com/news/worldviews/wp/2015/03/20/sweden-stood-up-for-human-rights-in-saudi-a rabia-this-is-how-saudi-arabia-is-punishing-sweden/.

13   David Crouch, 'Clash between Sweden and Saudi Arabia escalates as ambassador is withdrawn', *The Guardian*, 11 March 2015, www.theguardian.com/world/2015/mar /11/clash-sweden-saudi-arabia-escalates-ambassador-withdrawn-human-rights.

14   Government Offices of Sweden, Ministry of Foreign Affairs, '10 points on Sweden's membership of the UN Security Council 2017–2018', 30 December 2018, www.gover nment.se/government-of-sweden/ministry-for-foreign-affairs/sweden-in-the-un-secur ity-council/10-points-on-swedens-membership-of-the-un-security-council-20172018/ ?TSPD_101_R0=082953afa5ab-2000f887e0754bf8619b0e41fd04eb31c098ac49c731 00ab6b30db2c023a1a-ae6741088ef80158143000d9528061ee84c6c3ce9e9718 48d68c4ad23f5f3 cdbee2-6c75c59b4d4e6d2542db4a49a93925ae2fa156575859bb73 34f.

15   Rachel A. George, 'Sweden's feminist foreign policy can't be undone', *Foreign Policy*, 18 November 2022, https://foreignpolicy.com/2022/11/18/sweden-feminist-foreign-policy-billstrom-gender-equality/.

16   Falke Bernadotte Academy, 'Swedish Women's Mediation Network', https://fba.se/en /areas-of-expertise/dialogue-mediation/swedish-womens-mediation-network/.

17   Merlyn Thomas, 'Sweden ditches "feminist foreign policy"', 19 October 2022, www.bbc .com/news/world-europe-63311743.

18   CFFP, 'How feminist is the Swedish feminist foreign policy?', 12 November 2019, https://centreforfeministforeignpolicy.org/?s=How+feminist+is+the+Swedish+feminist+ foreign+policy.

19   Ibid.

20   Bundesministerium für Familie, Senioren, Frauen und Jugend, *Das Gesetz zum Elterngeld*

und zur Elternzeit im internationalen, insbesondere europäischen Vergleich: Länderstudien 2008 [The German law on parental benefit and parental leave compared to other countries, especially in Europe: country studies 2008], October 2008, www.bmfsfj.de/resour ce/blob/76298/46717e8fd28ca4ee89546c5065a38f2e/beeg-laenderstudien-data.pdf.

21 Lyric Thompson, 'Sound the alarm – Sweden drops "feminist" and returns to mere "foreign policy"', *Ms.*, 19 January 2023, https://msmagazine.com/2023/01/19/sweden-femi nist-foreign-policy/.

22 Global Affairs Canada, *Canada's Feminist International Assistance Policy*, 2017, www. international.gc.ca/world-monde/assets/pdfs/iap2-eng.pdf?_ga=21204682321678331 9791625830670–14788464981625830670.

23 Emma Watson, Phumzile Mlambo-Ngcuka, Katja Iversen and Michael Kaufman, 'Every G7 country should have a feminist foreign policy', *The Guardian*, 22 August 2019, www .theguardian.com/global-development/2019/aug/22/every-g7-country-should-have-a-f eminist-foreign-policy-emma-watson.

24 Feminist Foreign Policy Working Group, *Be Brave, Be Bold: Recommendations for Canada's Feminist Foreign Policy*, Amnesty International, 2020, www.amnesty.ca/sites/ default/files/FFP%20Be%20Brave%20Be%20Bold%20EN.pdf.

25 Ministère de L'Europe et des Affaires Étrangères, '"Feminist foreign policy", op-ed by Jean-Yves Le Drian and Marlène Schiappa', 8 March 2019, www.diplomatie.gouv.fr/en /french-foreign-policy/human-rights/news/article/feminist-foreign-policy-op-ed-by- jean-yves-le-drian-and-marlene-schiappa-08-03.

26 CFFP, *A Feminist Foreign Policy Response to Covid-19*, July 2020, https://centreforffp.net /wordpress/wp-content/uploads/2023/01/PolicyBrief_AFeministForeignPolicyRespons etoCOVID-19.pdf.

27 French Ministry for Europe and Foreign Affairs, Directorate-General for Global Affairs, Culture, Education and International Development, *France's International Strategy on Gender Equality (2018–2022)*, www.diplomatie.gouv.fr/IMG/pdf/meae_strategie_-_ _en_cle076525.pdf.

28 Loi n° 2021-1031 du 4 août 2021 de programmation relative au développement solidaire et à la lutte contre les inégalités mondiales [Programming act no. 2021-1031 of 4 August 2021 on inclusive development and the struggle against global inequalities], www.legifrance.gouv.fr/jorf/id/JORFTEXT000043898536/.

29 UN Women, 'Generation Equality Forum concludes in Paris with announcement of revolutionary commitments and Global Acceleration Plan to advance gender equality by 2026', 2 July 2021, https://reliefweb.int/report/world/generation-equality-forum-co ncludes-paris-announcement-revolutionary-commitments-and.

30 Brigitte Grésy, Martine Storti, Cléa Le Cardeur et al., *Feminist Diplomacy: From a Mobilising Slogan to a Real Dynamic of Change?* Paris: Haut Conseil à l'Egalité entre les Femmes et les Hommes, 2020; www.euromedwomen.foundation/pg/en/documents/vi ew/9348/feminist-diplomacy-from-mobilising-slogan-to-real-dynamic-of-change.

31 Lyric Thompson, Spogmay Ahmed and Tanya Khokhar, *Defining Feminist Foreign Policy: A 2021 Update*, www.icrw.org/wp-content/uploads/2021/10/FFP-2021Update_v3.pdf.

32 Centro de Investigación Internacional, *Conceptualizing Feminist Foreign Policy: Notes for Mexico*, April 2020, www.gob.mx/cms/uploads/attachment/file/545654/Note_6-Femin ist_foreign_policy.pdf.

33 Gobierno de México, Secretaría de Relaciones Exteriores, 'Mexico adopts feminist foreign policy', 9 January 2020, www.gob.mx/sre/prensa/mexico-adopts-feminist-foreign -policy?idiom=en.

34 CFFP, *A Feminist Foreign Policy for the European Union*.

35 Lyric Thompson, 'Mexican diplomacy has gone feminist', *Foreign Policy*, 14 January 2020, https://foreignpolicy.com/2020/01/14/mexican-diplomacy-feminist-foreign-pol icy/.

36 Linnea Sandin, 'Femicides in Mexico: impunity and protests', Center for Strategic and International Studies, 19 March 2020, www.csis.org/analysis/femicides-mexico-im punity-and-protests.

37 International Women's Development Agency, 'From seeds to roots: trajectories towards feminist foreign policy', 24 March 2021, https://iwda.org.au/resource/from-seeds-to-ro ots-trajectories-towards-feminist-foreign-policy/.

38 Centro de Investigación Internacional, *Conceptualizing Feminist Foreign Policy*.

39 See Gideon Rachman, *The Age of the Strongman: How the Cult of the Leader Threatens Democracy Around the World*. London: Bodley Head, 2022.

40 Ann Deslandes, 'Why has AMLO accused USAID of a "coup against Mexico"?', *Foreign Policy*, 5 June 2021, https://foreignpolicy.com/2021/06/05/why-has-amlo-accused-usa id-of-a-coup-against-mexico-elections/.

41 Daniela Philipson, 'Mexico: champion of women or detractor?', WILPF, 2021, www.wi lpf.org/mexico-champion-of-women-or-detractor/.

42 Ministerio de Asuntos Exteriores, Unión Europea y Cooperación, *Spain's Feminist Foreign Policy: Promoting Gender Equality in Spain's External Action*, www.exteriores.gob .es/es/ServiciosAlCiudadano/PublicacionesOficiales/2021_02_POLITICA%20EXTE RIOR%20FEMINISTA_ENG.pdf.

43 See kristina_lunz on 27 June 2019 on Instagram, www.instagram.com/p/BzMMBCEo X3a/.

44 SPD, Grüne and FDP, *Mehr Fortschritt wagen: Bündnis für Freiheit, Gerechtigkeit und Nachhaltigkeit* [Dare more progress: alliance for freedom, justice and sustainability], www.spd.de/fileadmin/Dokumente/Koalitionsvertrag/Koalitionsvertrag_2021-2025 .pdf.

45 See our manifesto for a German feminist foreign policy: CFFP, *Make Foreign Policy Feminist: A Feminist Foreign Policy Manifesto for Germany*, 2021, https://static1.squares pace.com/static/57cd7cd9d482e9784e4ccc34/t/61432508e0c62f33f0a54cea/1631790 357163/CFFP-Manifesto-EN-Final4.pdf.

46 Federal Foreign Office, 'Speech by Foreign Minister Annalena Baerbock at the Emergency Special Session of the UN General Assembly on Ukraine', 1 March 2022, www.auswaertiges-amt.de/en/newsroom/news/-/2514706.

47 Oliver Towfigh Nia, 'German foreign minister to push for Iran resolution at Human Rights Council', 23 November 2022, www.aa.com.tr/en/europe/german-foreign-minis ter-to-push-for-iran-resolution-at-human-rights-council/2746435#.

48 Federal Foreign Office, 'Shaping feminist foreign policy: conference at the Federal Foreign Office on 12 September 2022', www.auswaertiges-amt.de/en/aussenpolitik/ themen/feministische-aussenpolitik/2551352.

49 Sven Becker et al., 'Wie die Grünen zur Hoffnung der Rüstungsindustrie werden' [How the Greens are becoming the hope of the arms industry], *Der Spiegel*, 6 January 2023, www.spiegel.de/politik/deutschland/strengeres-gesetz-fuer-ruestungsexporte-das-waffen dilemma-a-89a024a5-e718-4d41-8098-e34969c58fae.

50 Ibid.

51 United Nations, 'Putting feminism into practice in international policymaking and for the achievement of the SDGs: what does feminist multilateralism look like?', *UN Web TV*, 22 September 2022, https://media.un.org/en/asset/k1m/k1mfw9ocjp.

52 Ministry of Foreign Affairs, Chilean Government, 'Foreign Minister Antonia Urrejola: "The development of a feminist foreign policy will be a distinguishing hallmark and a vanguard element of our diplomacy"', 22 March 2022, www.minrel.gob.cl/foreign-minister-antonia-urrejola-the-development-of-a-feminist.

53 Natalia Espinoza, '"Política exterior feminista": Cancillería busca posicionar a Chile con perspectiva de género a nivel mundial' [Feminist foreign policy: Foreign Ministry seeks to position Chile with a gender perspective worldwide], *El Mostrador*, 19 August 2022,

www.elmostrador.cl/braga/2022/08/19/politica-exterior-feminista-cancilleria-busca-posicionar-a-chile-con-perspectiva-de-genero-a-nivel-mundial/ [translation KL].

54 Federal Foreign Office, 'Shaping feminist foreign policy'.

55 JCA, 'Luxembourg presents feminist foreign policy at international meeting', 19 February 2021, https://chronicle.lu/category/abroad/35646-luxembourg-presents-feminist-foreign-policy-at-international-meeting.

56 Thompson, Ahmed and Khokhar: *Defining Feminist Foreign Policy: A 2021 Update*.

57 Government of the Netherlands, 'Letter of 13 May 22 from the minister of foreign affairs and the minister for foreign trade and development cooperation to the senate on the added value for the Netherlands of a feminist foreign policy', www.government.nl/documents/letters/2022/05/17/letter-on-the-added-value-for-the-netherlands-of-a-feminist-foreign-policy.

58 International Center for Research on Women, 'Coalition for feminist foreign policy in the United States', ICRW, 2020, www.icrw.org/wp-content/uploads/2020/12/FFPUSA-AboutUs-Dec.2020-ICRW.pdf.

59 Lois Frankel, 'Press release: Reps Speier, Lee, and Frankel introduce resolution in support of a feminist foreign policy', 23 September 2020, https://frankel.house.gov/news/documentsingle.aspx?DocumentID=3163.

60 ICRW, 'More than 30 governments and organizations now working to advance feminist foreign policy around the world', www.icrw.org/press-releases/more-than-30-governments-and-organizations-now-working-to-advance-feminist-foreign-policy-around-the-world/.

61 Jamille Bigio and Rachel Vogelstein, *Understanding Gender Equality in Foreign Policy: What the United States Can Do*, Council on Foreign Relations, 2020, https://cdn.cfr.org/sites/default/files/pdf/Understanding%20Gender%20Equality%20in%20Foreign%20Policy.pdf.

62 International Women's Development Agency, 'From seeds to roots'.

63 Ibid.

Chapter 8 Attacks on Women's Rights, LGBTQ+ Rights and Human Rights

1 André Madaus, 'UN-Weltbevölkerungskonferenz: Was Bildung mit Bevölkerungswachstum zu tun hat' [UN World Conference on Population and Development: what education has to do with population growth], 12 November 2019, www.andremadaus.de/archiv/www-heute-de-zdf/weltbevölkerungskonferenz/.

2 United Nations, *Report of the Fourth World Conference on Women*, Beijing, 4–15 September 1995, www.un.org/womenwatch/daw/beijing/pdf/Beijing full report E.pdf.

3 CSU, 'Das CSU-Grundsatzprogramm' [The CSU manifesto], 2016, https://csu-grundsatzprogramm.de/grundsatzprogramm-gesamt/.

4 Roman Kuhar and David Paternotte, 'The anti-gender movement in comparative perspective', in Kuhar and Paternotte (eds), *Anti-Gender Campaigns in Europe: Mobilizing Against Equality*. Lanham, MD: Rowman & Littlefield, 2017, pp. 253–72.

5 Claire Provost, Lou Ferreira and Claudia Torrisi, 'Trump's top lawyer in "crusade" against women's and LGBT rights across Europe', openDemocracy, 27 October 2020, www.opendemocracy.net/en/5050/trump-sekulow-war-womens-lgbt-rights-europe/.

6 Damjan Denkovski, Nina Bernarding and Kristina Lunz, *Power over Rights: Understanding and Countering the Transnational Anti-Gender Movement*, Vol. I, CFFP, March 2021, https://static1.squarespace.com/static/57cd7cd9d482e9784e4ccc34/t/60746c48a067197714820c24/1618242637144/Rights+over+Power+-+Volume+I_D_final3.pdf.

7 Ibid., p. 31.

8 Ibid., p. 35.

9 Claudia Ciobanu, 'Poland begins push in region to replace Istanbul Convention with

"Family Rights" treaty', Reporting Democracy, 6 October 2020, https://balkaninsight .com/2020/10/06/family-rights-treaty/.

10 US Department of State, *Report of the Commission on Unalienable Rights*, July 2020, www.state.gov/wp-content/uploads/2020/07/Draft-Report-of-the-Commission-on -Unalienable-Rights.pdf.

11 CFFP (ed.), *Power over Rights: Understanding and Countering the Transnational Anti-Gender Movement*, Vol. II: *Case Studies*, March 2021, p. 12, https://static1. squarespace .com/static/57cd7cd9d482e9784e4ccc34/t/6051e6d0802ecc6d859c42df/1615980243 056/Power+over+Rights+Volume+II-+Case+Studies.pdf.

12 Steve Benen, 'Biden admin gets to work undoing Pompeo's approach to human rights', MSNBC, 31 March 2021, www.msnbc.com/rachel-maddow-show/biden-admin-ge ts-work-undoing-pompeo-s-approach-human-rights-n1262609. See also Associated Press, 'Blinken ends Trump admin's human rights plan to promote conservative agenda abroad', *NBC News*, 30 March 2021, www.nbcnews.com/politics/politics-news/blinken -ends-trump-admin-s-human-rights-plan-promote-conservative-n1262499.

13 Neil Datta in an interview with my colleague Damjan Denkovski, 2020.

14 Damjan Denkovski, *Disrupting the Multilateral Order? The Impact of Anti-Gender Actors on Multilateral Structures in Europe*, CFFP, November 2022, https://centreforfeminis tforeignpolicy.org/?s=Disrupting+the+Multilateral+Order%3F+The+Impact+of+Anti -Gender+Actors+on+Multilateral+Structures+in+Europe.

15 Ibid.

16 Council of Europe, list of Council conventions, www.coe.int/en/web/conventions/full-list?module=signatures-by-treaty&treatynum=210.

17 Freedom House, 'Freedom in the world research methodology', 2021, quoted in Denkovski, Bernarding and Lunz, *Power over Rights*, Vol. I, p. 19.

18 Sina Fontana, *Möglichkeiten gesetzlicher Neuregelungen im Konfliktfeld Gehsteig-belästigungen: Rechtsgutachten im Auftrag des Gunda-Werner-Instituts für Feminismus und Geschlechterdemokratie* [Possibilities for new legislation in the conflict area of 'pavement harassment' (harassment of patients and staff of abortion clinics by anti-abortion campaigners): Legal report commissioned by the Gunda Werner Institute for Feminism and Gender Democracy], Heinrich-Böll-Stiftung, June 2021, www.gwi-boell.de/sites/default/files/2021-06/NEU_E-Paper%20%C2%ABGehsteigbela%CC %88stigungen%C2%BB%20Endf_1.pdf.

19 Trans Respect Versus Transphobia, 'TMM update: Trans Day of Remembrance 2020', 11 November 2020, https://transrespect.org/en/tmm-update-tdor-2020/.

20 Sandrine Amiel, '100 days since Poland banned abortion, Polish women are fighting back', *Euronews*, 12 May 2021, www.euronews.com/2021/05/12/100-days-since-pola nd-banned-abortion-polish-women-are-fighting-back. See also BBC, 'Poland enforces controversial near-total abortion ban', 28 January 2021, www.bbc.co.uk/news/world-europe-55838210.

21 Weronika Strzyżyńska, 'Polish state has "blood on its hands" after death of woman refused an abortion', *The Guardian*, 26 January 2022, www.theguardian.com/global-development/2022/jan/26/poland-death-of-woman-refused-abortion.

22 Interview with David Paternotte, 10 July 2020. See also Kuhar and Paternotte, 'Gender ideology in movement: introduction', in Kuhar and Paternotte (eds), *Anti-Gender Campaigns in Europe: Mobilizing Against Equality*.

23 Brot für die Welt, 'Atlas der Zivilgesellschaft 2021: Zivilgesellschaft weltweit massiv unter Druck' [Atlas of civil society 2021: civil society under massive pressure world-wide], 2021, www.brot-fuer-die-welt.de/themen/atlas-der-zivilgesellschaft/2021/zusam menfassung-2021/.

24 Ibid.

25 Ibid.

26 Human Rights Watch, 'Covid-19 pandemic sparked year of rights crises', 4 March 2021, www.hrw.org/news/2021/03/04/covid-19-pandemic-sparked-year-rights-crises.

27 Andreas Robertz, 'Amerikanische Christen um Mike Pence: Das Evangelium nach Michael' [American Christians around Mike Pence: the gospel according to Michael], *Deutschlandfunk*, 19 January 2017, www.deutschlandfunk.de/amerikanische-christen -um-mike-pence-das-evangelium-nach.886.de.html?dram:article_id=376627.

28 Indiana Democratic Party, 'A timeline of Mike Pence's discrimination against the LGBT community', www.indems.org/a-timeline-of-mike-pences-discrimination-against-the-lgbt-community/.

29 Violence Prevention Network and CFFP, *How Anti-Feminist and Anti-Gender Ideologies Contribute to Violent Extremism – and What We Can Do about It*, December 2021, https://static1.squarespace.com/static/57cd7cd9d482e9784e4ccc34/t/61eec9ad3ad0a2 796c147d07/1643039149698/CFFP2-1.pdf.

30 Mona Lena Krook, 'A global movement to end violence against women in politics and public life', *E-International Relations*, 25 April 2021, www.e-ir.info/2021/04/25/a-glo bal-movement-to-end-violence-against-women-in-politics-and-public-life/. Roudabeh Kishi, Melissa Pavlik and Hilary Matfess, '*Terribly and Terrifyingly Normal': Political Violence Targeting Women*, ACLED, May 2019, https://acleddata.com/acleddatanew/wp -content/uploads/2019/05/ACLED_Report_PoliticalViolenceTargetingWomen_5.20 19.pdf.

31 Johannes Blöcher-Weil, 'Frauenrechte und Abtreibung: EU-Parlament stimmt für Matić-Bericht' [Women's rights and abortion: EU Parliament votes for Matić Report], PRO, 24 June 2021, www.pro-medienmagazin.de/eu-parlament-stimmt-fuer-matic-be richt/.

32 One of Us, 'Statement European Federation One of Us against Matić Report', 16 June 2021, https://oneofus.eu/statement-european-federation-one-of-us-against-matic-report/.

33 European Parliamentary Forum for Sexual & Reproductive Rights, 'European Parliament adopts landmark position on sexual and reproductive rights', 24 June 2021, www.epf web.org/node/838.

34 CFFP, *Power over Rights*, Vol. II.

35 White House, 'Gender Policy Council', March 2021, www.whitehouse.gov/gpc/.

36 Denkovski, *Disrupting the Multilateral Order?*.

37 Alison Durkee, '100 days since Roe v. Wade was overturned: the 11 biggest conse-quences', *Forbes*, 2 October 2022, www.forbes.com/sites/alisondurkee/2022/10/02/100 -days-since-roe-v-wade-was-overturned-the-11-biggest-consequences/?sh=4f2278b8 7464.

38 Deutscher Bundestag, 'Parlamentsfernsehen Livestream' [Parliament TV livestream], www.bundestag.de/mediathek?videoid=7480332#url=bWVkaWF0aGVrb3Zlcmxheht9 2aWRlb2lkPTc0ODAzMzI=&mod=mediathek.

39 Amnesty International, 'Key facts on abortion', www.amnesty.org/en/what-we-do/sexu al-and-reproductive-rights/abortion-facts/.

40 Ibid.

41 International Women's Health Coalition, *Crisis in Care: Year Two Impact of Trump's Global Gag Rule*, 2019, www.ru.ac.za/media/rhodesuniversity/content/criticalstudiesin sexualitiesandreproduction/documents/Crisis_in_Care_-_Year_Two_Impact_of_Trum p's_Global_Gag_Rule__finalWEB.pdf.

42 European Parliamentary Forum for Sexual & Reproductive Rights, 'Tip of the iceberg: religious extremist funders against human rights for sexuality & reproductive health in Europe', 15 June 2021, www.epfweb.org/node/837.

Chapter 9 Feminist Global Health Policy

1 'Anreize in den USA: Aussicht auf Lottogewinne und Dates für Geimpfte' [Incentives in the USA: prospects of lottery wins and dates for the vaccinated], *Frankfurter Allgemeine Zeitung*, 21 May 2021, www.faz.net/aktuell/gesellschaft/gesundheit/coronavirus/anreize -in-den-usa-aussicht-auf-lottogewinne-und-dates-fuer-geimpfte-17353976.html.

2 Sandra Pfister, 'Impfstoff-Initiative Covax verfehlt Ziele: "Reiche Länder haben den Markt quasi leer gekauft"' [Vaccine initiative Covax misses targets: 'Rich countries have cleaned out the market'], *Deutschlandfunk*, 28 April 2021, www.deutschlandfunk.de /impfstoff-initiative-covax-verfehlt-ziele-reiche-laender.769.de.html?dram:article_id=4 96427.

3 'Covax-Initiative: Erfolge und Probleme bei der weltweiten Impfstoffverteilung' [Covax initiative: successes and problems in worldwide vaccine distribution], *Deutschlandfunk*, 14 June 2021, www.deutschlandfunk.de/covax-initiative-erfolge-und-probleme-der-wel tweiten-100.html.

4 'Merkel gibt klare Zusage für 2,3 Milliarden Impfdosen' [Merkel gives clear pledge of 2.3 billion doses of vaccine], *Spiegel online*, 13 June 2021, www.spiegel.de/ausland/g7 -gipfel-merkel-gibt-klare-zusage-fuer-2-3-milliarden-impfdosen-a-4e10c701-f6cd-4f67 -9d75-e175ab2fe9b2.

5 Claire Parker, 'Group leading Covax decides "in principle" to end vaccine-sharing initia- tive', *Washington Post*, 7 December 2022, www.washingtonpost.com/world/2022/12/07 /gavi-covax-phase-out-coronavirus/.

6 CFFP, *A Feminist Foreign Policy Response to Covid-19*, July 2020, https://centreforffp.net /wordpress/wp-content/uploads/2023/01/PolicyBrief_AFeministForeignPolicyRespons etoCOVID-19.pdf.

7 United Nations, 'UN chief calls for domestic violence "ceasefire" amid "horrifying global surge"', *UN News*, 6 April 2020, https://news.un.org/en/story/2020/04/1061052.

8 Carla K. Johnson, Olga R. Rodriguez and Angeliki Kastanis, 'As US COVID-19 death toll nears 600,000, racial gaps persist', *AP News*, 14 June 2021, https://apnews.com/ar ticle/baltimore-california-coronavirus-pandemic-race-and-ethnicity-health-341950a90 2affc651dc268dba6d83264.

9 Global Health 50/50, *Power, Privilege & Priorities: 2020 Global Health 50/50 Report*, https://globalhealth5050.org/2020report/.

10 Malaka Gharib, 'Where the women aren't: on coronavirus task forces', *NPR*, 24 June 2021, www.npr.org/sections/goatsandsoda/2020/06/24/882109538/where-the-women -arent-on-coronavirus-task-forces?mc_cid=8547341c4f&mc_eid=8d4fb9217b. See also Kim Robin van Daalen et al., 'Symptoms of a broken system: the gender gaps in COVID-19 decision-making', in *BMJ Global Health*, 5/10 (2020).

11 Mathieu Boniol et al., *Gender Equity in the Health Workforce: Analysis of 104 Countries*, World Health Organization, March 2019, https://apps.who.int/iris/handle/10665/31 1314.

12 Selen Eşençay, 'When COVID-19 becomes a political ally: Poland's law on abortion', LSE, 24 June 2020, https://blogs.lse.ac.uk/gender/2020/06/24/when-covid-19-becom es-a-political-ally-polands-law-on-abortion/.

13 Jessica Glenza, 'States use coronavirus to ban abortions, leaving women desperate: "You can't pause on pregnancy"', *The Guardian*, 30 April 2020, www.theguardian.com/world /2020/apr/30/us-states-ban-abortions-coronavirus-leave-women-desperate.

14 United Nations, 'Millions more cases of violence, child marriage, female genital mutila- tion, unintended pregnancy expected due to the COVID-19 pandemic', United Nations Population Fund, 28 April 2020, www.unfpa.org/news/millions-more-cases-violence- child-marriage-female-genital-mutilation-unintended-pregnancies.

15 Timothy Roberton et al., 'Early estimates of the indirect effects of the COVID-19 pan-

demic on maternal and child mortality in low-income and middle-income countries: a modelling study', *Lancet Global Health*, 8/7, 1 July 2020.

16 Ibid.

17 Mary Kekatos, 'Maternal mortality rates increased during first year of COVID pandemic: CDC', *ABC News*, 23 February 2022, https://abcnews.go.com/Health/maternal-mortality-rates-increased-1st-year-covid-pandemic/story?id=83061990.

18 AOK Rheinland/Hamburg, 'Corona: Arbeitslose haben höheres Risiko für Krankenhaus-Aufenthalte' [Coronavirus: unemployed have higher risk of hospitalization], 15 June 2020, www.aok.de/pk/rh/inhalt/covid-19-und-soziale-unterschiede-1/.

19 Karen I. Fredriksen-Goldsen, Hyun-Jun Kim, Susan E. Barkan, Anna Muraco and Charles P. Hoy-Ellis, 'Health disparities among lesbian, gay, and bisexual older adults: results from a population-based study', *American Journal of Public Health*, 103/10 (2013): 1802–9.

20 Kerith J. Conron, Matthew J. Mimiaga and Stewart J. Landers, 'A population-based study of sexual orientation identity and gender differences in adult health', *American Journal of Public Health*, 100/10 (2010): 1953–60. See also Nathaniel M. Lewis, 'Mental health in sexual minorities: recent indicators, trends, and their relationships to place in North America and Europe', *Health Place*, 15/4 (2009): 1029–45.

21 Matthew J. Breiding, Sharon G. Smith, Kathleen C. Basile, Mikel L. Walters, Jieru Chen and Melissa T. Merrick, 'Prevalence and characteristics of sexual violence, stalking, and intimate partner violence victimization: national intimate partner and sexual violence survey, United States, 2011', *MMWR Surveillance Summaries*, 63/8 (2014): 1–18.

22 Jeanie Santaularia, Monica Johnson, Laurie Hart, Lori Haskett, Ericka Welsh and Babalola Faseru, 'Relationships between sexual violence and chronic disease: a cross-sectional study', *BMC Public Health*, 14, 16 December 2014, https://bmcpublichealth.bio medcentral.com/articles/10.1186/1471-2458-14-1286.

23 Robert-Koch-Institut, 'Frauengesundheitsbericht' [Report on women's health], 9 December 2020, www.rki.de/DE/Content/Gesundheitsmonitoring/Studien/Geschle cht_Gesundheit/FP_frauengesundheitsbericht.html.

24 World Health Organization, 'Sustainable Development Goals (SDGs)', 2015, www. who.int/health-topics/sustainable-development-goals#tab=tab_1.

25 CFFP, *A Feminist Global Health Policy*, April 2021, https://static1.squarespace.com/sta tic/57cd7cd9d482e9784e4ccc34/t/607d349c4d979c4ac3c1678c/1618818205289/A+ Feminist+Global+Health+Policy-5.pdf.

26 Anna Kobierecka and Michał Marcin Kobierecki, 'Coronavirus diplomacy: Chinese medical assistance and its diplomatic implications', *International Politics*, 58/6 (2021): 937–54.

27 Ilona Kickbusch, 'Global health diplomacy: how foreign policy can influence health', *British Medical Journal*, 16 April 2011, www.bmj.com/content/342/bmj.d3154.

28 World Health Organization, 'Constitution of the World Health Organization', 2006, https://apps.who.int/gb/bd/PDF/bd47/EN/constitution-en.pdf?ua=1.

29 Cf. Jeffrey P. Koplan, T. Christopher Bond, Michael H. Merson, K. Srinath Reddy, Mario Henry Rodriguez, Nelson K. Sewankambo and Judith N. Wasserheit, 'Towards a common definition of global health', *The Lancet*, 6 June 2009, https://pubmed.ncbi.nlm .nih.gov/19493564/.

30 World Health Organization, 'Social determinants of health', www.who.int/health-topics /social-determinants-of-health#tab=tab_1.

31 Wolfgang U. Eckart, *Medizin und Kolonialimperialismus: Deutschland 1884–1945* [Medicine and colonial imperialism: Germany 1884–1945]. Munich: Schöningh, 1997.

32 Lioba A. Hirsch, 'Is it possible to decolonise global health institutions?', *The Lancet*, 16 January 2021, https://pubmed.ncbi.nlm.nih.gov/33453772/.

33 Ngozi A. Erondu, Dorothy Peprah and Mishal S. Khan, 'Can schools of global public health dismantle colonial legacies?', *Nature Medicine*, 26/10 (2020): 1504–5.

34 Rebecca Rosman, 'Racism row as French doctors suggest virus vaccine test in Africa', *Aljazeera*, 4 April 2020, www.aljazeera.com/news/2020/4/4/racism-row-as-french-docto rs-suggest-virus-vaccine-test-in-africa.

35 Karsten Noko, 'Medical colonialism in Africa is not new', *Aljazeera*, 8 April 2020, www. aljazeera.com/opinions/2020/4/8/medical-colonialism-in-africa-is-not-new. See also Thomas Scheen and Roland Lindner, 'Verdacht auf illegale Arzneimitteltests: Nigeria verklagt Pfizer auf Schadenersatz' [Suspicion of illegal drug trials: Nigeria sues Pfizer for damages], *Frankfurter Allgemeine Zeitung*, 6 June 2007, www.faz.net/aktuell/wirtschaft /verdacht-auf-illegale-arzneimitteltests-nigeria-verklagt-pfizer-auf-schadenersatz-14380 78.html.

36 Terence Zimwara, *Clinical Trials Realities in Zimbabwe: Dealing with Possible Unethical Research*, May 2015, www.wemos.nl/wp-content/uploads/2016/06/report-Clinical-Trials-Realities-in-Zimbabwe-Dealing-with-Possible-Unethical-Research.pdf.

37 Julia Amberger, 'Robert Koch und die Verbrechen von Ärzten in Afrika' [Robert Koch and the crimes of doctors in Africa], *Deutschlandfunk*, 26 December 2020, www.deut schlandfunk.de/menschenexperimente-robert-koch-und-die-verbrechen-von.740.de. html?dram:article_id=489445.

38 Ibid.

39 Ibid.

40 Mishal Khan, Seye Abimbola, Tammam Aloudat, Emanuele Capobianco, Sarah Hawkes and Afifah Rahman-Shepherd, 'Decolonising global health in 2021: a roadmap to move from rhetoric to reform', *BMJ Global Health*, 6/3, 7 March 2021.

41 Ibid.

42 Laurel Morales, 'Coronavirus infections continue to rise on Navajo Nation', *NPR*, 11 May 2020, www.npr.org/sections/coronavirus-live-updates/2020/05/11/854157898 /coronavirus-infections-continue-to-rise-on-navajo-nation.

43 Ali Murad Büyüm, Cordelia Kenney, Andrea Koris, Laura Mkumba and Yadurshini Raveendran, 'Decolonising global health: if not now, when?', *BMJ Global Health*, 5/8 (2020), https://gh.bmj.com/content/5/8/e003394.

44 Ibid.

45 GBD 2019 Demographics Collaborators, 'Global age-sex-specific fertility, mortality, healthy life expectancy (HALE), and population estimates in 204 countries and ter-ritories, 1950–2019: a comprehensive demographic analysis for the Global Burden of Disease Study 2019', *The Lancet*, vol. 396, October 2020, pp. 1160–203.

46 Pfister, 'Reiche Länder haben den Markt quasi leer gekauft'.

47 'Patente auf Impfstoffe – Wie die Coronakrise den Patentschutz ins Wanken bringt' [Patents for vaccines – how the Covid crisis is destabilizing patent protection], 8 May 2021, *Deutschlandfunk*, www.deutschlandfunk.de/patente-auf-impfstoffe-wie-die-coron akrise-den-patentschutz-100.html.

48 Deutsches Netzwerk für vernachlässigte Tropenkrankheiten (DNTDs), 'Was sind NTDs?' [What are NTDs?], https://dntds.de/was-sind-ntds.html.

49 Jana Sepehr, 'Blöd, Sie leiden an einer vernachlässigten Krankheit' [Bad luck, you're suffering from a neglected disease], *Fluter*, 30 June 2021, www.fluter.de/wie-vernachlaes sigte-krankheiten-bekaempft-werden.

50 Global Health 50/50, *Gender Equality: Flying Blind in a Time of Crisis: 2021 Global Health 50/50 Report*, https://globalhealth5050.org/wp-content/uploads/Global-Health -5050-2021-Report.pdf?v2.

51 United Nations Human Rights, Office of the High Commissioner, 'Sexual and repro-ductive health and rights', www.ohchr.org/en/issues/women/wrgs/pages/healthrights .aspx.

52   United Nations Population Fund, 'Sexual & reproductive health', 16 November 2016, www.unfpa.org/sexual-reproductive-health.

53   United Nations Human Rights, 'Sexual and reproductive health and rights'.

54   Destatis, 'Pressemitteilung Nr. 144: Zahl der Schwangerschaftsabbrüche im Jahr 2020 leicht zurückgegangen' [Press release no. 144: Number of abortions in 2020 slightly lower], Statistisches Bundesamt, 24 March 2021, www.destatis.de/DE/Presse/Pressemit teilungen/2021/03/PD21_144_233.html.

55   United Nations Human Rights, Office of the High Commissioner, 'Abortion: information series on sexual and reproductive health and rights', 2020, www.ohchr.org/Docu ments/Issues/Women/WRGS/SexualHealth/INFO_Abortion_WEB.pdf.

56   CFFP, 'The right to legal and safe abortions in Germany: Germany violates international human rights obligations', 2021, https://static1.squarespace.com/static/57cd7cd9d482e 9784e4ccc34/t/618abb4872a5c33f7ccd3a67/1636481864909/CFFP+Briefing++%C2 %A7218+-+Englisch+Version-2.pdf.

57   Theresa Varga, 'Guinea pigs or pioneers? How Puerto Rican women were used to test the birth control pill', *Washington Post*, 9 May 2017, www.washingtonpost.com/news/retro polis/wp/2017/05/09/guinea-pigs-or-pioneers-how-puerto-rican-women-were-used-to -test-the-birth-control-pill/.

58   Maurice Law, 'Statement to the Inter-American Commission on Human Rights: forced sterilization of indigenous women in Saskatchewan, Canada', 27 February 2018, www. aptnnews.ca/wp-content/uploads/2018/02/IACHR-STATEMENT-26.02.20181JP .pdf.

59   Women in American History, 'Fannie Lou Hamer', www.pbs.org/wgbh/americanexperi ence/features/freedomsummer-hamer/.

60   Marina Manoukian, 'The tragic real-life story of Fannie Lou Hamer', *Grunge*, 27 October 2020, https://web.archive.org/web/20210410210848/https://www.grunge.com/2680 44/the-tragic-real-life-story-of-fannie-lou-hamer/.

61   Wikipedia, 'Fannie Lou Hamer', https://en.wikipedia.org/wiki/Fannie_Lou_Hamer.

62   For a seminal account, see Gisela Bock, *Zwangssterilisation im Nationalsozialismus: Studien zur Rassenpolitik und zur Geschlechterpolitik* [Forced sterilization during the Nazi period: studies on racial policies and gender politics]. Munster: MV-Wissenschaft, 2010.

63   Loretta J. Ross, 'Reproductive justice as intersectional feminist activism', *Souls: A Critical Journal of Black Politics, Culture and Society*, 19 (2017): 286–314.

64   Kristine Husøy Onarheim, Johanne Helene Iversen and David E. Bloom, 'Economic benefits of investing in women's health: a systematic review', *PLoS One*, 11/3, 30 March 2016, https://journals.plos.org/plosone/article?id=10.1371/journal.pone.0150120; Prathibha Varkey, Sarah Kureshi and Timothy Lesnick, 'Empowerment of women and its association with the health of the community', *Journal of Women's Health*, 19/1 (2010): 71–6; Jeni Klugman, Li Li, Kathryn M. Barker, Jennifer Parsons and Kelly Dale, 'How are the domains of women's inclusion, justice, and security associated with maternal and infant mortality across countries? Insights from the Women, Peace, and Security Index', *SSM – Population Health*, 9, December 2019, www.sciencedirect.com/science/article/pii/S 2352827318302210; U. Stokoe, 'Determinants of maternal mortality in the developing world', *Australian and New Zealand Journal of Obstetrics and Gynaecology*, 31/1 (1991): 8–16.

65   Chloë FitzGerald and Samia Hurst, 'Implicit bias in healthcare professionals: a systematic review', *BMC Medical Ethics*, 18 (2017), https://bmcmedethics.biomedcentral.com /articles/10.1186/s12910-017-0179-8; A. L. Arnold, K. A. Milner and V. Vaccarino, 'Sex and race differences in electrocardiogram use: the national hospital ambulatory medical care survey', *American Journal of Cardiology*, 88/9 (2001): 1037–40.

66   Hannah Summers, 'Black women in the UK four times more likely to die in pregnancy

or childbirth', *The Guardian*, 15 January 2021, www.theguardian.com/global-develop
ment/2021/jan/15/black-women-in-the-uk-four-times-more-likely-to-die-in-pregnan
cy-or-childbirth.

67 Sam Winter, Milton Diamond, Jamison Green, Dan Karasic, Terry Reed, Stephen
    Whittle and Kevan Wylie, 'Transgender people: health at the margins of society', *The
    Lancet*, 388 (2016): 390–400.

68 World Health Organization, 'Gender incongruence and transgender health in the ICD',
    www.who.int/standards/classifications/frequently-asked-questions/gender-incongruen
    ce-and-transgender-health-in-the-icd.

69 Global Health 50/50, *Gender Equality: Flying Blind in a Time of Crisis*.

70 Nicola Slawson, '"Women have been woefully neglected": does medical science have a
    gender problem?', *The Guardian*, 18 December 2019, www.theguardian.com/education
    /2019/dec/18/women-have-been-woefully-neglected-does-medical-science-have-a-gen
    der-problem.

71 CFFP, *A Feminist Global Health Policy*.

Chapter 10 No Climate Justice without Feminism

1   'Klimastreik: Millionen Menschen gehen weltweit für Fridays for Future auf die Straße'
    [Climate strike: millions of people worldwide take to the streets for Fridays for Future],
    Frankfurter Rundschau, 21 September 2019, www.fr.de/politik/klimastreik-demos-frei
    tag-2092019-millionen-fridays-future-zr-13012060.html.

2   Volker Mrasek, 'Der Klimawandel ist schon heute tödlich' [Climate change is already
    deadly today], *Deutschlandfunk*, 1 June 2021, www.deutschlandfunk.de/hitzetote-der-
    klimawandel-ist-schon-heute-toedlich.676.de.html?dram:article_id=498150.

3   Global Witness, 'Last line of defence', 13 September 2021, www.globalwitness.org/en
    /campaigns/environmental-activists/last-line-defence/.

4   Global Witness, *Decade of Defiance*, 29 September 2022, www.globalwitness.org/en
    /campaigns/environmental-activists/decade-defiance/.

5   Global Witness, 'Our verdict on COP27: a polluters' parade', 21 November 2022,
    www.globalwitness.org/en/blog/our-verdict-on-cop27-a-polluters-parade/.

6   Global Witness, *Decade of Defiance*.

7   Nicola Abé, Sonja Peteranderl and Maria Stöhr, 'Gewalt gegen Aktivisten weltweit:
    "Firmen beauftragen Mörder, um Umweltschützer töten zu lassen"' [Violence against
    activists worldwide: 'Firms hire murderers to kill environmentalists'], *Der Spiegel*,
    25 April 2021, www.spiegel.de/ausland/gewalt-gegen-umweltschuetzer-weltweit-firmen
    -beauftragen-moerder-um-umweltschuetzer-toeten-zu-lassen-a-5571dd65-322f-4b57
    -b54f-4c4d710514fd.

8   Ibid.

9   UN Environment Programme, 'Indigenous people: protecting our planet', 8 August
    2017, www.unep.org/news-and-stories/story/indigenous-people-protecting-our-planet.

10 Gleb Raygorodetsky, 'Indigenous peoples defend Earth's biodiversity – but they're in
    danger', *National Geographic*, 16 November 2018, www.nationalgeographic.com/envi
    ronment/article/can-indigenous-land-stewardship-protect-biodiversity-.

11 Ibid.

12 Amnesty International UK, 'Philippines country most at risk from climate crisis',
    29 October 2021, www.amnesty.org.uk/philippines-country-most-risk-climate-crisis.

13 Jason Gutierrez, 'Duterte, "infamous for his sexist jokes", signs law against sexual harass-
    ment', *New York Times*, 16 July 2019, www.nytimes.com/2019/07/16/world/asia/duter
    te-sexual-harassment.html.

14 Sofia Flittner, 'Greta Thunberg supports Filipino campaign against the new anti-
    terror law', *ScandAsia*, 12 July 2020, https://scandasia.com/greta-thunberg-support-
    filipino-campaign-against-the-new-anti-terror-law/. See also Amnesty International,

'Philippines: dangerous anti-terror law yet another setback for human rights', 3 July 2020, www.amnesty.org/en/latest/news/2020/07/philippines-dangerous-antiterror-law -yet-another-setback-for-human-rights/.

15   Karin Louise Hermes, 'Klimagerechtigkeit ist kein Terrorakt, sondern ein Grundrecht' [Climate justice is not a terrorist act, but a basic right], Stiftung Asienhaus, 2021, http:// crossasia-repository.ub.uni-heidelberg.de/4476/1/SAH_Blickwechsel_21-05_Philip pinen-Hermes_Final.pdf.

16   Interview with Mitzi Jonelle Tan, 10 June 2021.

17   Global Witness, *Decade of Defiance*.

18   Erika Harzer, 'Die Oligarchen lässt man laufen' [The oligarchs are allowed to get away], Amnesty International, 5 February 2018, www.amnesty.de/informieren/amnesty-jour nal/honduras-die-oligarchen-laesst-man-laufen.

19   'Berta Cáceres: 50 Jahre Haft für Mord an Umweltaktivistin' [Berta Cáceres: 50 years in prison for murder of environmental activist], *ZEIT Online*, 3 December 2019, www.zeit .de/gesellschaft/zeitgeschehen/2019-12/honduras-berta-caceres-umweltaktivistin-mord -haftstrafe.

20   David Agren, 'Ten women and girls killed every day in Mexico, Amnesty report says', *The Guardian*, 20 September 2021, www.theguardian.com/global-development/2021 /sep/20/mexico-femicide-women-girls-amnesty-international-report.

21   Interview with Maria Reyes, 22 June 2021.

22   Valerie Hudson, Donna Lee Bowen and Perpetua Lynne Nielsen, *First Political Order: How Sex Shapes Governance and National Security Worldwide*. New York: Columbia University Press, 2020, p. 295.

23   Earth Overshoot Day, 'Country overshoot days', 2023, www.overshootday.org/news room/country-overshoot-days/.

24   Nagraj Adve and Samuel Thomas (eds), 'Even 1.5 degrees is too much: rising tempera- tures and wetter futures in South Asian glacier and snow-fed river basins', *HI-AWARE*, 2018, http://hi-aware.org/wp-content/uploads/2018/10/KM1.pdf.

25   Greta Thunberg, *The Climate Book*. London: Allen Lane, 2022.

26   Hilda Flavia Nakabuye and Leonie Bremer, 'Opinion: the climate crisis has a female face', *Thomson Reuters Foundation News*, 8 March 2020, https://news.trust.org/item/20 200308143901-mlk7e/.

27   Amali Tower, 'The gendered impacts of climate displacement', 19 May 2020, www.clima te-refugees.org/perspectives/genderedimpactsofclimatechange.

28   United Nations, 'Put women's rights "front and centre" of climate policies: Bachelet', *UN News*, 27 June 2022, https://news.un.org/en/story/2022/06/1121442.

29   AQOCI, 'A feminist approach to climate justice', 2019, www.ocic.on.ca/wp- content/uploads/2019/06/WD_A-Feminist-Approach-to-Climate-Justice_Final_2019- 05-31.pdf.

30   Sam Wong, 'Can climate finance contribute to gender equity in developing countries?', *Journal of International Development*, 28/3 (2016): 428–44. See also Alyson Brody, Justina Demetriades and Emily Esplen, *Gender and Climate Change: Mapping the Linkages. A Scoping Study on Knowledge and Gaps*, BRIDGE, Institute of Development Studies (IDS), University of Sussex, June 2008, www.adequations.org/IMG/pdf/Gen derAndClimateChange.pdf.

31   Sam Seller, *Gender and Climate Change: A Closer Look at Existing Evidence*, November 2016, http://wedo.org/wp-content/uploads/2016/11/GGCA-RP-FINAL.pdf.

32   Oxfam International, 'World's billionaires have more wealth than 4.6 billion people', 20 January 2020, www.oxfam.org/en/press-releases/worlds-billionaires-have-more- wealth-46-billion-people.

33   World Bank, 'Laws still restrict women's economic opportunities despite progress, study finds', press release, 23 February 2021, www.worldbank.org/en/news/press-release/20

21/02/23/laws-still-restrict-womens-economic-opportunities-despite-progress-study
-finds.

34 American Lung Association, 'Disparities in the impact of air pollution', 20 April 2020,
www.lung.org/clean-air/outdoors/who-is-at-risk/disparities.

35 Francisca Rockey, 'The death of Ella Adoo-Kissi-Debrah: why are black people more
likely to be exposed to toxic air?', *Euronews*, 4 January 2021, www.euronews.com/green
/2021/01/04/the-death-of-ella-adoo-kissi-debrah-why-are-black-people-more-likely-to
-be-exposed-to-toxi.

36 Lena von Seggern, 'Ertrunkene Menschen mit Behinderung: Wie konnte das passieren?'
[Drowned people with disabilities: how could this happen?], *taz*, 27 July 2021, https://
taz.de/Ertrunkene-Menschen-mit-Behinderung/!5785903/.

37 United Nations, *Paris Agreement*, 2015, https://unfccc.int/sites/default/files/english_
paris_agreement.pdf.

38 François Normand, '500 milliards de subventions aux énergies fossiles' [500 billion
in fossil fuel subsidies], *les affaires*, 26 September 2018, www.lesaffaires.com/secteurs-
d-activite/ressources-naturelles/500-milliards-de-subventions-aux-energies-fossiles/605
288.

39 Luisa Neubauer and Dagmar Reemstma, *Gegen die Ohnmacht: Meine Großmutter, die
Politik und ich* [Against powerlessness: my grandmother, politics and me]. Stuttgart:
Tropen, 2022, p. 135.

40 Oxfam, 'Carbon emissions of richest 1% set to be 30 times the 1.5°C limit in 2030',
press release, 5 November 2021, www.oxfam.org/en/press-releases/carbon-emissions-
richest-1-set-be-30-times-15degc-limit-2030.

41 Paul Griffin, *The Carbon Majors Database: CDP Carbon Majors Report 2017*, July 2017,
https://cdn.cdp.net/cdp-production/cms/reports/documents/000/002/327/original
/Carbon-Majors-Report-2017.pdf?1501833772.

42 Mark Kaufman, 'The carbon footprint sham: a "successful, deceptive" PR campaign',
Mashable, 13 July 2020, https://mashable.com/feature/carbon-footprint-pr-campaign
-sham.

43 Global Witness, 'Hundreds of fossil fuel lobbyists flooding COP26 climate talks', press
release, 8 November 2021, www.globalwitness.org/en/press-releases/hundreds-fossil-
fuel-lobbyists-flooding-cop26-climate-talks/.

44 Global Witness, 'Our verdict on COP27'.

45 Thunberg, *The Climate Book*.

46 CFFP, 'COP27 recap – the solutions to the climate crisis are intersectional and feminist',
29 November 2022, https://centreforfeministforeignpolicy.org/2022/11/29/my-first-
featured-blog-post-2-2/.

47 'COP27 einigt sich auf Abschlusserklärung' [COP27 agrees on final declaration],
Tagesschau, 20 November 2022, www.tagesschau.de/ausland/afrika/klimakonferenz-co
p27-eu-abschlusserklarung-klimawandel-101.html.

48 Houria Djoudi, Bruno Locatelli, Chloe Vaast, Kiran Asher, Maria Brockhaus and
Bimbika Basnett Sijapati, 'Beyond dichotomies: gender and intersecting inequalities in
climate change studies', *Ambio*, 45/3 (2016): 248–62. See also Lindsey Jean Roetzel,
'Why women are key to solving the climate crisis', *One Earth*, 25 October 2021,
www.oneearth.org/why-women-are-key-to-solving-the-climate-crisis/.

49 Patricia Perkins, *Climate Justice, Gender and Intersectionality*. Abingdon: Routledge,
2018.

50 Djoudi et al., 'Beyond dichotomies'.

51 Intersectional Environmentalist, 'The intersectional history of environmentalism',
YouTube, 15 March 2021, www.youtube.com/watch?v=cyqYN90PPjE&t=134s.

52 Julian Brave NoiseCat, 'In the fight for climate justice, indigenous people set the path –

and lead the way', *The Guardian*, 19 January 2017, www.theguardian.com/commentis free/2017/jan/19/fight-climate-justice-indigenous-people-lead-the-way.

53 Interview with Mitzi Jonelle Tan, 10 June 2021.

54 J. Ann Tickner, *A Feminist Voyage through International Relations*. Oxford: Oxford University Press, 2014, pp. 51ff.

55 Ibid.

56 bell hooks, *Reel to Real: Race, Class and Sex at the Movies*. New York: Routledge, 1996, p. 149.

57 Patralekha Chatterjee, 'Indian air pollution – loaded dice', *The Lancet*, 3/12 (2019): 500–1.

58 Cf. Instagram post by disharavii, 13 March 2021, www.instagram.com/p/CMW_uDm nArb/.

59 Friedenspreis des Deutschen Buchhandels [Peace prize of the German book trade], 'Friedenspreis [Peace prize] 1973: The Club of Rome', www.friedenspreis-des-deutschen -buchhandels.de/alle-preistraeger-seit-1950/1970-1979/the-club-of-rome.

60 Andrew Revkin, 'Climate change first became news 30 years ago: why haven't we fixed it?', *National Geographic*, July 2018, www.nationalgeographic.com/magazine/article/em bark-essay-climate-change-pollution-revkin.

61 IPCC, 'Climate change widespread, rapid, and intensifying', 9 August 2021, www.ipcc .ch/2021/08/09/ar6-wg1-20210809-pr/.

62 Benjamin von Brackel, 'Was ist dran an den Argumenten der "Letzten Generation"?' [How accurate are the arguments of the 'Last Generation'?], *Süddeutsche Zeitung*, 17 November 2022, www.sueddeutsche.de/wissen/klimaforschung-klimabewegung-die -letzte-generation-erderwaermung-kipppunkte-markus-lanz-1.5697670.

63 Meike Spitzner, Diana Hummel, Immanuel Stieß, Gotelind Alber and Ulrike Röhr, *30/2020: Interdependente Genderaspekte der Klimapolitik* [30/2020: interdepend-ent gender aspects of climate policy]. Dessau-Rosslau: Umweltbundesamt [German Environment Agency], 2020, www.umweltbundesamt.de/publikationen/interdepen dente-genderaspekte-der-klimapolitik. See also Ulrike Röhr and Gotelind Alber, 'Geschlechterverhältnisse und Klima im Wandel: Erste Schritte in Richtung einer transformativen Klimapolitik' [Gender relations and climate in flux: first steps towards a transformative climate policy], *GENDER: Zeitschrift für Geschlecht, Kultur und Gesellschaft*, 10/2 (2018): 112–27.

64 United Nations, Sendai Framework for Disaster Risk Reduction 2015–2030, www.und rr.org/publication/sendai-framework-disaster-risk-reduction-2015-2030.

65 CFFP, 'COP27 recap'.

66 Climate Security Expert Network, 'Climate security at the UNSC: a short history', 2021, https://climate-diplomacy.org/magazine/conflict/climate-security-un-security-co uncil-short-history.

67 Silke Weinlich, 'Climate change before the UN Security Council: head in the sand?', Deutsches Institut für Entwicklungspolitik, 25 July 2011, www.die-gdi.de/en/the-curre nt-column/article/climate-change-before-the-un-security-council-head-in-the-sand/.

68 'Drought pushing millions into poverty', *The New Humanitarian*, 9 September 2010, www.thenewhumanitarian.org/report/90442/syria-drought-pushing-millions-poverty.

69 White House, 'Executive order on tackling the climate crisis at home and abroad', 27 January 2021, www.whitehouse.gov/briefing-room/presidential-actions/2021/01/27 /executive-order-on-tackling-the-climate-crisis-at-home-and-abroad/.

70 R. Black et al., *Environment of Peace: Security in a New Era of Risk*. Stockholm: SIPRI, 2022, www.sipri.org/sites/default/files/2022-05/environment_of_peace_security_in_a_ new_era_of_risk_0.pdf.

71 Ibid., p. 6.

72 Mark Akkerman, Deborah Burton, Nick Buxton, Ho-Chih Lin, Muhammed Al-Kashef and Wendela de Vries, *Climate Collateral: How Military Spending Accelerates Climate Breakdown*. Amsterdam: Transnational Institute, 2022, www.tni.org/en/publication/climate-collateral.

73 United Nations Development Programme, *Gender, Climate & Security: Sustaining Inclusive Peace on the Frontlines of Climate Change*, 9 June 2020, www.undp.org/publications/gender-climate-and-security.

74 Louise Turner, 'Meet Oladusu Adenike, aka the ecofeminist', 26 August 2020, www.wen.org.uk/2020/08/26/whys-climate-justice-a-feminist-issue-oladosu-adenike/.

75 United Nations Environment Programme, 'Gender, climate & security: report summary', June 2020, https://wedocs.unep.org/bitstream/handle/20.500.11822/32672/GCSSum.pdf?sequence=1&isAllowed=y.

76 Jeannette Cwienk, 'Women as victims of climate change', *Deutsche Welle*, 27 February 2020, www.dw.com/en/women-climate-change-sexual-violence-iucn/a-52449269.

77 United Nations Development Programme, *Gender, Climate & Security*.

78 Keina Yoshida et al., *Defending the Future: Gender, Conflict and Environmental Peace*, LSE Centre for Women, Peace and Security, 2021, www.lse.ac.uk/women-peace-security/assets/documents/2021/Defending-the-Future.pdf.

79 Fiona Harvey, 'Four in 10 young people fear having children due to climate crisis', *The Guardian*, 14 September 2021, www.theguardian.com/environment/2021/sep/14/four-in-10-young-people-fear-having-children-due-to-climate-crisis.

80 Vanessa Nakate, 'What foreign policy needs to do to address climate change in the developing world', Wilson Center, 30 September 2020, www.wilsoncenter.org/article/what-foreign-policy-needs-do-address-climate-change-developing-world.

81 Jonas Anshelm and Martin Hultman, 'A green fatwā? Climate change as a threat to the masculinity of industrial modernity', *NORMA: International Journal for Masculinity Studies*, 9 (2014): 84–96. See also Martin Gelin, 'The misogyny of climate deniers', *Apocalypse Soon*, 28 August 2019, https://newrepublic.com/article/154879/misogyny-climate-deniers.

82 Ines Eisele, 'Bolsonaro gibt Waldgebiete zur Adoption frei' [Bolsonaro offers forest areas for adoption], *Deutsche Welle*, 12 February 2021, www.dw.com/de/bolsonaro-gibt-waldgebiete-zur-adoption-frei/a-56540759.

Chapter 11 Making Peace without Weapons

1 Bruno Urmersbach, 'Bevölkerungsreichste Länder 2021' [Most populous countries 2021], *Statista*, 19 October 2021, https://de.statista.com/statistik/daten/studie/1722/umfrage/bevoelkerungsreichste-laender-der-welt/.

2 SIPRI, 'World military spending rises to almost $2 trillion in 2020', 26 April 2021, https://sipri.org/media/press-release/2021/world-military-spending-rises-almost-2-trillion-2020.

3 SIPRI, 'World military expenditure passes $2 trillion for first time', 25 April 2022, www.sipri.org/media/press-release/2022/world-military-expenditure-passes-2-trillion-first-time.

4 R. Black et al., *Environment of Peace: Security in a New Era of Risk*. Stockholm: SIPRI, 2022, www.sipri.org/sites/default/files/2022-05/environment_of_peace_security_in_a_new_era_of_risk_0.pdf.

5 SIPRI, *SIPRI Yearbook 2022: Armament, Disarmament and International Security: Summary*, www.sipri.org/sites/default/files/2022-06/yb22_summary_en_v3.pdf

6 Ibid.

7 Ibid.

8 Mark Akkerman, Deborah Burton, Nick Buxton, Ho-Chih Lin, Muhammed Al-Kashef and Wendela de Vries, *Climate Collateral: How Military Spending Accelerates Climate*

Breakdown. Amsterdam: Transnational Institute, 2022, www.tni.org/en/publication/climate-collateral.

9 ICAN, 'Nuclear spending vs healthcare', 20 March 2020, www.icanw.org/healthcare_costs.

10 Statista, 'Nuclear weapons in 1945 and 2020 in comparison', 3 August 2020, www.statista.com/chart/3714/nuclear-weapons-in-comparison/.

11 SIPRI, *SIPRI Yearbook 2022*.

12 ICAN, 'The world's nuclear weapons', www.icanw.org/nuclear_arsenals.

13 United Nations, Office for Disarmament Affairs, *Securing Our Common Future: An Agenda for Disarmament*, 2018, https://disarmamenthandbook.org/wp-content/uploads/2021/01/disarmament-handbook-2020_v07.pdf.

14 SIPRI, *SIPRI Yearbook 2022*.

15 Sven Becker et al., 'Wie die Grünen zur Hoffnung der Rüstungsindustrie werden' [How the Greens are becoming the hope of the arms industry], *Der Spiegel*, 6 January 2023, www.spiegel.de/politik/deutschland/strengeres-gesetz-fuer-ruestungsexporte-das-waffen dilemma-a-89a024a5-e718-4d41-8098-e34969c58fae.

16 IFFF Internationale Frauenliga für Frieden und Freiheit, 'Deutsche (Ab-)Rüstungspolitik: Eine intersektional-feministische Analyse der WILPF' [German (dis)armament policy: an intersectional feminist analysis by WILPF], 19 February 2021, www.wilpf.de/deutsc he-ab-ruestungspolitik-eine-intersektional-feministische-analyse-der-wilpf/.

17 For the militarization of German foreign policy specifically, see our policy paper: CFFP, *How Militarised is Germany's Foreign Policy?*, 2021, https://centreforffp.net/wordpress/wp-content/uploads/2023/01/CFFP-HeinrichBoll-EN-Final2.pdf.

18 Statista Research Department, 'Umsatz der weltweit größten Rüstungsunternehmen 2019' [Turnover of the world's biggest arms manufacturers, 2019], 14 May 2021, https://de.statista.com/statistik/daten/studie/152177/umfrage/absatz-der-weltweit-gro essten-ruestungsunternehmen/.

19 Statista Research Department, 'Rüstung und Rüstungsindustrie' [Arms and the arms industry], 24 June 2021, https://de.statista.com/themen/666/ruestung/.

20 United Nations, 'Fifth committee approaches $6.51 billion for 13 peacekeeping operations in 2019/20, joint management of active missions' cash balances, as resumed session ends', UN, 3 July 2019, www.un.org/press/en/2019/gaab4328.doc.htm.

21 CFFP, 'The international arms trade – a feminist issue?', YouTube, 15 December 2020, www.youtube.com/watch?v=d62OFvo_HdI.

22 SEESAC, *Gender and SALW: Gender Aspects of SALW and How to Address Them in Practice*, 2018, www.seesac.org/f/docs/Gender-and-Security/Gender-Aspects-of-SALW ---ENG-28-09-2018.pdf. See also Everytown Research & Policy, 'Report: guns and violence against women: America's uniquely lethal intimate partner violence problem', 27 April 2021, https://everytownresearch.org/report/guns-and-violence-against-women -americas-uniquely-lethal-intimate-partner-violence-problem/.

23 Renata Hessmann Dalaqua, Kjølv Egeland and Torbjørn Graff Hugo, *Still behind the Curve: Gender Balance in Arms Control, Non-Proliferation and Disarmament Diplomacy*, UNIDIR, 2019, www.unidir.org/files/publications/pdfs/still-behind-the-curve-en-770 .pdf.

24 CFFP, *Policy Brief: Why the International Arms Trade Is a Feminist Issue – and What Germany Can Do About It*, November 2020, https://centreforffp.net/wordpress/wp-con tent/uploads/2023/01/CFFP_hbs_policybrief_internationalarmstradefeministissue.pdf.

25 Alexandra Topping, 'Four-fifths of young women in the UK have been sexually harassed, survey finds', *The Guardian*, 10 March 2021, www.theguardian.com/world/2021/mar /10/almost-all-young-women-in-the-uk-have-been-sexually-harassed-survey-finds.

26 Bundeszentrale für politische Bildung, 'Gewalt im Geschlechterverhältnis' [Violence in gender relations], 2004, www.bpb.de/apuz/27881/gewalt-im-geschlechterverhaeltnis.

27 National WWI Museum and Memorial, 'The fourteen points: Woodrow Wilson and the U.S. rejection of the Treaty of Versailles', www.theworldwar.org/learn/peace/fourteen-points.

28 Cynthia Enloe, *Maneuvers: The International Politics of Militarizing Women's Lives.* Berkeley: University of California Press, 2000.

29 CFFP, *How Militarised is Germany's Foreign Policy?*, p. 6.

30 CFFP, *Make Foreign Policy Feminist: A Feminist Foreign Policy Manifesto for Germany*, 2021, https://static1.squarespace.com/static/57cd7cd9d482e9784e4ccc34/t/61432508 e0c62f33f0a54cea/1631790357163/CFFP-Manifesto-EN-Final4.pdf.

31 M. V. Naidu, 'Military power, militarism and militarization: an attempt at clarification and classification', *Peace Research*, 17 (1985): 2–10, at pp. 2–3. Quoted in CFFP, *Make Foreign Policy Feminist.*

32 Cf. CFFP, *How Militarised is Germany's Foreign Policy?*.

33 Rosa Brooks, *How Everything Became War and the Military Became Everything: Tales from the Pentagon.* New York: Simon & Schuster, 2016, p. 21.

34 Bundesministerium der Finanzen, *Haushaltsrechnung des Bundes 2020: Bundeshaushalt* [Federal Budget 2020], vol. 1.

35 Hans-Martin Tillack, 'Studie: Der Rüstungslobby wird es in Deutschland zu leicht gemacht' [Study: the arms lobby has it too easy in Germany], *Stern*, 21 October 2020, www.stern.de/politik/deutschland/studie--der-ruestungslobby-wird-es-in-deutschland -zu-leicht-gemacht-9459426.html.

36 CFFP, *How Militarised is Germany's Foreign Policy?*.

37 Munich Security Conference, 'Special edition of the Munich Security Report on German Foreign and Security Policy', 2021, https://securityconference.org/en/pub lications/msr-special-editions/germany-2020/; Stockholm Centre for Freedom, 'Survey shows 83 percent of Germans against selling weapons to Turkey', 2018, https://stockh olmcf.org/survey-shows-83-percent-of-germans-against-selling-weapons-to-turkey/. See also CFFP, *How Militarised is Germany's Foreign Policy?*.

38 Louise Arimatsu, 'Transformative disarmament: crafting a roadmap for peace', *International Law Studies*, 97 (2021): 833–915.

39 Feodor de Martens, 'International arbitration and the peace conference at The Hague', *North American Review*, 604 (1899), quoted ibid.

40 Ibid., pp. 837ff.

41 Ibid., pp. 840ff.

42 National WWI Museum and Memorial, 'The fourteen points'.

43 Arimatsu, 'Transformative disarmament', p. 859.

44 Ibid., pp. 862f.

45 Ibid., pp. 868ff.

46 United Nations, *Report of the Fourth World Conference on Women*, www.un.org/women watch/daw/beijing/pdf/Beijing%20full%20report%20E.pdf.

47 United Nations, *2010 Review Conference of the Parties to the Treaty on the Non-Proliferation of Nuclear Weapons*, Vol. 1, 2010, www.un.org/en/conf/npt/2010/docs.shtml.

48 CFFP, interview with Ray Acheson, 6 December 2018.

49 Aritmatsu, 'Transformative disarmament', p. 897.

50 Peter Maurer (president of the International Committee of the Red Cross), 'Arms Trade Treaty: we must stop irresponsible arms trade or transfers', ICRC, 24 August 2015, www.icrc.org/en/document/first-conference-states-parties-arms-trade-treaty-att, quoted ibid., p. 897.

51 Ibid., pp. 900ff.

52 Patricia Hecht, 'Feminismus in der Außenpolitik: "Mit voller Wucht"' [Feminism in foreign policy: 'With full force'], *taz*, 17 April 2021, https://taz.de/Feminismus-in-der -Aussenpolitik/!5763175/.

53 CFFP, *Policy Brief: Why the International Arms Trade Is a Feminist Issue.*
54 United Nations, *The Arms Trade Treaty*, 2013, https://unoda-web.s3-accelerate.amazon aws.com/wp-content/uploads/2013/06/English7.pdf.
55 Gabriella Irsten, 'How feminist is the Swedish feminist foreign policy?', 28 August 2019, www.boell.de/en/2019/08/28/how-feminist-swedish-feminist-foreign-policy.
56 Bundesregierung [Federal Government of Germany], 'Antwort auf die kleine Anfrage der Abgeordneten Sevim Dağdelen, Heike Hänsel, Matthias Höhn, weiterer Abgeordneter und der Fraktion DIE LINKE. Exporte von Kleinwaffen, Kleinwaffenteilen und Kleinwaffenmunition im Jahr 2020' [Response to the parliamentary question from MPs Sevim Dağdelen, Heike Hänsel, Matthias Höhn, other MPs and the parliamentary party Die Linke: Exports of small arms, small arms components and small arms ammunition in 2020], Deutscher Bundestag, 26 February 2021, www.waffenexporte.org/wp-content/uploads/2021/03/SALW-2020.pdf.
57 Everytown Research & Policy, 'Report: guns and violence against women'.
58 Cf. CFFP, *Exporting Violence and Inequality: The Link between German Arms Exports and Gender-Based Violence*, report commissioned by Greenpeace, October 2020, p. 9, https://centreforffp.net/wordpress/wp-content/uploads/2023/01/Greenpeace_CFFP_GenderBasedViolence_ArmsExport_Final.pdf.
59 Ibid.
60 CFFP, *Policy Brief: Why the International Arms Trade Is a Feminist Issue.*
61 Christina Lamb, *Our Bodies, Their Battlefield: What War Does to Women.* London: William Collins, 2020, p. 7.
62 Ibid., p. 120.
63 United Nations, *Securing Our Common Future*, p. 40.
64 CFFP, *Exporting Violence and Inequality.*
65 Carol Cohn, 'Sex and death in the rational world of defense intellectuals', *Signs*, 12/4 (1987): 687–718, www.qub.ac.uk/Research/GRI/mitchell-institute/FileStore/Filetoupload,896141,en.pdf.
66 Klaus Scherer, 'Japan 1945: Führte die Atombombe auf Nagasaki zur Kapitulation?' [Japan 1945: did the nuclear bomb on Nagasaki lead to capitulation?], *Der Tagesspiegel*, 26 July 2015, www.tagesspiegel.de/gesellschaft/japan-1945-fuehrte-die-atombombe-auf-nagasaki-zur-kapitulation/12101946.html.
67 Ward Wilson, *Five Myths about Nuclear Weapons.* Boston: Mariner Books, 2014, p. 84.
68 Thomas Hajnoczi, *Deutschlands Weg zum Atomwaffenverbotsvertrag* [Germany's path to the Treaty on the Prohibition of Nuclear Weapons], July 2021, www.greenpeace.de/publikationen/gpde_22072021_atomwaffenverbotsvertrag.pdf.
69 NATO, 'North Atlantic Council statement as the Treaty on the Prohibition of Nuclear Weapons enters into force', 15 December 2020, www.nato.int/cps/en/natohq/news_180087.htm.
70 CFFP, 'Wie die nächste Bundesregierung den Atomwaffenverbotsvertrag unterstützen kann' [How the next German government can support the Treaty on the Prohibition of Nuclear Weapons], 2021, https://static1.squarespace.com/static/57cd7cd9d482e978 4e4ccc34/t/614312be80782d2e588dfcc7/1631785714229/ CFFP-PolicyBrief-DE-V3.pdf.
71 ICAN, 'Signature and ratification status', www.icanw.org/signature_and_ratification_status.
72 Deutscher Bundestag, *Ausarbeitung zum rechtlichen Verhältnis zwischen Atomwaffenverbotsvertrag und Nichtverbreitungsvertrag* [Examination of the legal relationship between the Treaty on the Prohibition of Nuclear Weapons and the Non-Proliferation Treaty], 2021, www.bundestag.de/resource/blob/814856/28b27e2d04faabd4a4bc0bfd0579658c/WD-2-111-20-pdf-data.pdf.
73 ICAN, 'Nuclear spending vs healthcare'.

74 ICAN, *Report: Why NATO Members Should Join the UN Nuclear Weapon Ban*, 2021, www.icanw.org/report_why_nato_members_should_join_the_un_nuclear_weapon_ban.

75 ICAN, '56 former leaders and ministers of US allies urge states to join the nuclear weapon ban treaty', 21 September 2020, www.icanw.org/56_former_leaders.

76 Ibid.

77 ICAN, 'Norway first Nato state to commit to participating at the MSP', 2021, www.icanw.org/norway_msp_observer.

78 CFFP, 'Wie die nächste Bundesregierung den Atomwaffenverbotsvertrag unterstützen kann'.

79 Reaching Critical Will, 'Factsheet: fully autonomous weapons', www.reachingcriticalwill.org/resources/fact-sheets/critical-issues/7972-fully-autonomousweapons.

80 Ibid.

81 Ray Acheson, *A WILPF Guide to Killer Robots*, January 2020, www.wilpf.org/wp-content/uploads/2020/04/WILPF_Killer-Robots-Guide_EN-Web.pdf.

82 Human Rights Watch, *Stopping Killer Robots: Country Positions on Banning Fully Autonomous Weapons and Retaining Human Control*, 2020, www.hrw.org/sites/default/files/media_2021/04/arms0820_web_1.pdf.

83 Reaching Critical Will, 'Factsheet: fully autonomous weapons'.

84 Human Rights Watch, *Stopping Killer Robots*.

85 Jonah M. Kessel, 'Killer robots aren't regulated. Yet', *New York Times*, 13 December 2019, www.nytimes.com/2019/12/13/technology/autonomous-weapons-video.html.

86 Campaign to Stop Killer Robots, 'Stop Killer Robots homepage', 2021, www.stopkillerrobots.org.

87 BBC, 'Facial recognition fails on race, government study says', *BBC*, 20 December 2019, www.bbc.com/news/technology-50865437.

88 Larry Hardesty, 'Study finds gender and skin-type bias in commercial artificial-intelligence systems', *MIT News*, 11 December 2018, https://news.mit.edu/2018/study-finds-gender-skin-type-bias-artificial-intelligence-systems-0212.

89 Hayley Ramsay-Jones, 'Intersectionality and racism', 2020, www.stopkillerrobots.org/wp-content/uploads/2020/05/Intersectionality-and-Racism-Hayley-Ramsay-Jones.pdf.

90 Thomas Gutschker, 'Bei jedem fünften Drohnenangriff der Amerikaner stirbt ein Zivilist' [A civilian dies in one in five American drone strikes], *Frankfurter Allgemeine Zeitung*, 3 July 2016, www.faz.net/aktuell/politik/kampf-gegen-den-terror/bilanz-von-obamas-drohneneinsaetzen-14320818.html.

91 Acheson, *A WILPF Guide to Killer Robots*.

92 Human Rights Watch, 'Poll shows strong opposition to "killer robots"', 22 January 2019, www.hrw.org/news/2019/01/22/poll-shows-strong-opposition-killer-robots.

93 Nina Werkhäuser, 'Widerstand gegen Killer-Roboter wächst' [Opposition to killer robots is growing], *Deutsche Welle*, 22 March 2019, www.dw.com/de/widerstand-gegen-killer-roboter-wächst/a-48017815.

Chapter 12 The Future of Foreign Policy is Feminist

1 Munich Security Conference, 'About the Munich Security Conference', https://securityconference.org/en/about-us/about-the-msc/.

2 Janine Rich, '"Saving" Muslim women: feminism, U.S. policy and the War on Terror', *International Affairs Review*, 2014.

3 Laura Bush, 'Radio address by Mrs. Bush', Office of the First Lady, 17 November 2001, https://georgewbush-whitehouse.archives.gov/news/releases/2001/11/20011117.html.

4 Rich, '"Saving" Muslim women'.

5 @sanambna (Sanam Naraghi Anderlini, MBE), 'Apologies for bout of rage', Twitter, 18 August 2021, https://twitter.com/sanambna/status/1428108218060972034.

6 Defend Afghan Women's Rights! – Now, 2021, www.youtube.com/watch?v=JXdXeHl LLl8.

7 Zarifa Ghafari at the 'Defend Afghan Women's Rights' press conference on 31 August 2021. Düzen Tekkal, 'Defend Afghan Women's Rights Pressekonferenz', Facebook, 31 August 2021, www.facebook.com/duezentekkal/videos/811883009502640.

8 Alliance For Peacebuilding, 'U.S. policy in Afghanistan: what withdrawal means for Afghan women & the future', YouTube, 7 May 2021, www.youtube.com/watch?v=m9i oo5P3Hwo.

9 Vrinda Narain, 'Women negotiators in Afghan/Taliban peace talks could spur global change', *The Conversation*, 19 May 2021, https://theconversation.com/women-negoti ators-in-afghan-taliban-peace-talks-could-spur-global-change-159033. See also Lynne O'Donnell, 'Women cut out of the Afghan peace process', *Foreign Policy*, 30 March 2021, https://foreignpolicy.com/2021/03/30/afghanistan-women-taliban-peace-talks-bi den/.

10 Melinda Holmes et al., *Protecting Women Peacebuilders: The Front Lines of Sustainable Peace*, https://icanpeacework.org/wp-content/uploads/2021/07/ICAN_ProtectingWom enPeacebuilders.pdf.

11 Sanam Naraghi Anderlini, 'Why don't Afghan lives matter? Opinion', *Newsweek*, 3 September 2021, www.newsweek.com/why-dont-afghan-lives-matter-opinion-162 5563.

12 ICAN, 'An open letter to friends of Afghanistan and champions of the women, peace and security agenda', 7 April 2021, https://icanpeacework.org/2021/04/07/an-open-let ter-to-friends-of-afghanistan-and-champions-of-the-women-peace-and-security-agen da/.

13 Ibid.

14 Heather Barr, 'When foreign men talk to the Taliban about women's rights', 18 October 2021, www.hrw.org/news/2021/10/18/when-foreign-men-talk-taliban-about-womens -rights.

15 UN Human Rights Council, *Situation of Human Rights in Afghanistan: Report of the United Nations High Commissioner for Human Rights* (A/HRC/51/6), 9 September 2022, www.ohchr.org/en/documents/country-reports/ahrc516-situation-human-rights -afghanistan-report-special-rapporteur.

16 Zahra Nader, 'Creating a platform for Afghan women's voices to be heard', UN Women Asia and the Pacific, 15 November 2022, https://asiapacific.unwomen.org/en/stories/ feature-story/2022/11/afghan-journalist-zahra-nader.

17 CFFP, *At the Centre: Afghan Women Experts' Policy Demands*, 2022, https://centrefor feministforeignpolicy.org/wordpress/wp-content/uploads/2023/02/2023_CFFP_At -the-centre_Afghan-Women-Experts-Policy-Demands.pdf.

18 CFFP, *Make Foreign Policy Feminist: A Feminist Foreign Policy Manifesto for Germany*, 2021, p. 3, https://static1.squarespace.com/static/57cd7cd9d482e9784e4ccc34/t/6143 2508e0c62f33f0a54cea/1631790357163/CFFP-Manifesto-EN-Final4.pdf.

19 BMWK [German Federal Ministry for Economic Affairs and Climate Action], 'A restrictive, responsible policy on the export of military equipment', 2021, www.bmwk .de/Redaktion/EN/Dossier/export-controls-for-military-equipment.html.

20 Christina Deckwirth, 'Lobbykontakte: Bundesregierung bevorzugt die Autoindustrie' [Lobby contacts: German government privileges auto industry], 14 September 2017, www.lobbycontrol.de/lobbyismus-und-klima/lobbykontakte-bundesregierung-bevorzu gt-die-autoindustrie-35968/.

21 'Deutsche Rüstungsgüter gingen für 419 Millionen Euro nach Afghanistan' [419 mil- lion euros' worth of German armaments went to Afghanistan], *Die Zeit*, 22 August 2021, www.zeit.de/politik/ausland/2021-08/afghanistan-ruestungsgueter-deutschland

-ruestungslieferung-nato-einsatz-ruestungsbericht?utm_referrer=https%3A%2F%2F
www.google.com%2F.

22   Francesco Collini, 'Sipri-Bericht: Staaten geben mehr für Militär aus, trotz Pandemie'
[SIPRI report: states spend more on military, despite pandemic], *Der Spiegel*, 26 April
2021, www.spiegel.de/ausland/sipri-bericht-2020-globale-militaerausgaben-stiegen-au
ch-waehrend-der-pandemie-a-c5e2d7ac-a488-41d1-b96c-fb72d5c2b719.

23   SIPRI, *Sipri Yearbook 2020: Armaments, Disarmament and International Security*, www.
sipri.org/sites/default/files/2020-06/yb20_summary_en_v2.pdf.

24   Hannah Ritchie, 'Who has contributed most to global CO_2 emissions?', *Our World in
Data*, 1 October 2019, https://ourworldindata.org/contributed-most-global-co2.

25   Fridays for Future, 'Aufbruch oder Absage: Das solltest du über den neuen Koalitions-
vertrag wissen' [New start or cancellation: this is what you need to know about the
new coalition agreement], November 2021, https://news.fff.link/mailing/170/468700
1/3512441/85081/79b358544f/index.html.

26   UN Women, *Violence against Women Migrant Workers: Report of the Secretary-General*,
26 July 2019, www.unwomen.org/en/digital-library/publications/2019/07/a-74-235-sg
-report-violence-against-women-migrant-workers.

27   UNHCR, 'Refugee data finder', 27 October 2022, www.unhcr.org/refugee-statistics/.

28   'Spahn fordert mehr Beiträge für die WHO' [Spahn demands more contributions for
WHO], *Ärztezeitung*, 25 May 2021, www.aerztezeitung.de/Politik/Spahn-fordert-mehr
-Beitraege-fuer-die-WHO-419854.html.

29   Paul Starzmann, 'Wenig Hoffnung auf schnelle Rückgabe' [Little hope of rapid restitu-
tion], *Der Tagesspiegel*, 23 February 2021, www.tagesspiegel.de/politik/koloniale-raub
kunst-in-deutschen-museen-wenig-hoffnung-auf-schnelle-rueckgabe/26942200.html.

30   Federal Foreign Office, 'Speech by Foreign Minister Heiko Maas at FidAR Forum XII
"Women in Leadership. A good choice. In Germany and internationally". An event in
the run-up to International Women's Day', 10 February 2021, www.auswaertiges-foru
m/2441252?fbclid=IwAR0yfne2O2XXoydgOV8zC3NYybic7lexwutpvjdLLDtRhH0d
w2HSUvTb3Sk.

Chapter 13 Feminist Foreign Policy in Times of War and Conflict

1   Felix Rupprecht, 'Jedes Zögern bringt täglich Tod' [Every hesitation brings death daily],
Bild, 15 January 2023, www.bild.de/politik/ausland/politik-ausland/friedensnobelpreist
raegerin-zu-waffenlieferungen-jedes-zoegern-bringt-taeglich-t-82556764.bild.html.

2   Laure Brillaud et al., 'EU member states exported weapons to Russia after the 2014
embargo', *Investigate Europe*, 17 March 2022, www.investigate-europe.eu/en/2022/eu-
states-exported-weapons-to-russia/.

3   Anton Mykytiuk, 'How Germany's industrial giants helped Russia manufacture weapons of war', *Euromaidan Press*, 12 September 2022, https://euromaidanpress.com/2022
/09/12/how-germanys-industrial-giants-help-russia-manufacture-weapons-of-war/.

4   Rupprecht, 'Jedes Zögern bringt täglich Tod'.

5   Aleksandra Hiltmann, '"Putin stellt die Ukraine als ein Art Frau dar"' [Putin presents
Ukraine as a kind of woman], *Tagesanzeiger*, 7 March 2022, www.tagesanzeiger.ch/putin
-stellt-die-ukraine-als-eine-art-frau-dar-417923004017.

6   Britta Sandberg, '"Wir erleben gerade den Beginn einer anderen Welt"' [We're experiencing the beginning of another world], interview with Pierre Servent, *Der Spiegel*,
9 December 2022, www.spiegel.de/ausland/folgen-des-russland-ukraine-kriegs-wir-erle
ben-gerade-den-beginn-einer-anderen-welt-a-f60f4427-53fb-4ade-9fcb-ef1d28be60e5.

7   Leandra Bias, 'The international of antifeminists', *Engenderings*, 24 February 2023,
https://blogs.lse.ac.uk/gender/2023/02/24/4808/; first pubd as 'Die Internationale der
Antifeministen', *Republik*, 6 June 2022.

8   Ibid.
9   Ibid.
10   Federal Foreign Office, 'Speech by Foreign Minister Annalena Baerbock at the Emergency Special Session of the UN General Assembly on Ukraine', 1 March 2022, www.auswaertiges-amt.de/en/newsroom/news/baerbock-unga-ukraine/2514752.
11   Katharine A. M. Wright, 'Where is Women, Peace and Security? NATO's response to the Russia–Ukraine war', *European Journal of Politics and Gender*, 5/2 (2022): 275–7, https://bristoluniversitypressdigital.com/view/journals/ejpg/5/2/article-p275.xml.
12   Philipp Schulz and Anne-Kathrin Kreft, 'Accountability for conflict-related sexual violence', *International Studies*, 24 February 2022, https://oxfordre.com/internationalstudi es/display/10.1093/acrefore/9780190846626.001.0001/acrefore-9780190846626-e-7 02;jsessionid=3F88ABC22B1F830020E5ACF62E1F5837.
13   Clara Bauer-Babef, trans. Daniel Eck, 'Trafficking and sexual exploitation of Ukrainian refugees on the rise', *EURACTIV France*, 30 November 2022, www.euractiv.com/sec tion/europe-s-east/news/trafficking-and-sexual-exploitation-of-ukrainian-refugees-on -the-rise/.
14   Katherine Berjikian, '"Lawful transphobia" stopping Ukraine's trans community from fleeing', *Euronews*, 23 March 2022, www.euronews.com/2022/03/22/lawful-transpho bia-stopping-ukraine-s-trans-community-from-fleeing.
15   Kvinna till Kvinna, 'A feminist response to Russia's war in Ukraine: recommendations to the international community (Policy Brief II)', 21 December 2022, https://kvinnatillkv inna.org/wp-content/uploads/2023/01/The-Kvinna-till-Kvinna-Foundation-A-feminist-response-to-Russias-war-in-Ukraine-Recommendations-to-the-International-Commu nity.pdf.
16   UN Women, *Rapid Gender Analysis of Ukraine*, 4 May 2022, www.unwomen.org/sites /default/files/2022-05/Rapid-Gender-Analysis-of-Ukraine-en.pdf.
17   Kvinna till Kvinna, 'A feminist response to Russia's war in Ukraine'.
18   UN Women, *Global Gendered Impacts of the Ukraine Crisis on Energy Access and Food Security and Nutrition*, 2022, www.unwomen.org/sites/default/files/2022-09/Policy-paper-Global-gendered-impacts-of-the-Ukraine-crisis-en.pdf.
19   Golineh Atai, *Iran: Die Freiheit ist weiblich* [Iran: Freedom is female]. Berlin: Rowohlt, 2021, p. 10.
20   Ibid.
21   Ibid., p. 21.
22   Ibid., p. 12.
23   Personal interview, 13 January 2023.
24   '"Sie wollen das Regime stürzen"' [They want to overthrow the regime], interview with Shirin Ebadi by Mina Khani and Gilda Sahebi, *taz*, 29 October 2022, https://taz.de/ Shirin-Ebadi-ueber-die-Proteste-in-Iran/!5888438/.
25   'Rights monitor: more than 500 killed since Iran protests began', 19 December 2022, www.voanews.com/a/rights-monitor-more-than-500-killed-since-iran-protests-began /6882138.html.
26   Antje Schippmann, 'Steinmeier wird Iran nicht zur Islamischen Revolution gratulieren' [Steinmeier won't congratulate Iran on Islamic Revolution], *Welt*, 8 February 2020, www.welt.de/politik/deutschland/article205703033/Steinmeier-wird-Iran-nicht-zur-Is lamischen-Revolution-gratulieren.html.
27   '"Sie wollen das Regime stürzen"'.
28   Ibid.
29   Kali Robinson, 'What is the Iran nuclear deal?', Council on Foreign Relations, 20 July 2022, www.cfr.org/backgrounder/what-iran-nuclear-deal.
30   Ibid.

31 Barbara Mittelhammer and Cornelius Adebahr, '"Women, Life, Freedom": a German feminist foreign policy towards Iran', Heinrich Böll Stiftung, 2 January 2023, www.boell .de/en/2023/01/02/women-life-freedom-german-feminist-foreign-policy-towards-iran.
32 Femena, *Iran Protests: Feminists and WHRDs Detained*, 21 November 2022, https:// femena.net/feminists-and-whrds-detained-report-6.
33 Femena, 'Shiva Nazar Ahari', 22 March 2021, https://femena.net/whrd-perspectives /iran-shiva-nazar-ahari.
34 CFFP, 'In Solidarity with the Women on the Streets: Feminist Foreign Policy Demands towards Iran', 21 October 2022, www.youtube.com/watch?v=YgAcy_Sl2Jw.

Chapter 14 Epilogue

1 Dana Kanze, Laura Huang, Mark A. Conley and E. Tory Higgins, 'Male and female entrepreneurs get asked different questions by VCs — and it affects how much funding they get', *Harvard Business Review*, 27 July 2017; Kamal Hassan, Monisha Varadan and Claudia Zeisberger, 'How the VC pitch process is failing female entrepreneurs', *Harvard Business Review*, 13 January 2020; Malin Malström, Jeaneth Johansson and Joakim Wincent, 'Gender stereotypes and venture support decisions: how governmental venture capitalists socially construct entrepreneurs' potential', *Entrepreneurship Theory and Practice*, 41/5 (2017): 833–60.
2 Ephrat Livni, 'All career advice for women is a form of gaslighting', *Quartz*, 21 August 2018, https://qz.com/work/1363399/all-career-advice-for-women-is-a-form-of-gaslight ing/.
3 Ivana Kottasova, 'Women *do* ask for pay raises, they just don't get them', *CNN Money*, 7 September 2016, https://money.cnn.com/2016/09/06/news/women-pay-gap-ask/in dex.html.
4 Kasia Staszewka, Tenzin Dolker and Kellea Miller, 'Only 1% of gender equality fundings is going to women's organisations – why?', *The Guardian*, 2 July 2019, www.the guardian.com/global-development/2019/jul/02/gender-equality-support-1bn-boost-how-to-spend-it.
5 Claire Provost and Nandini Archer, 'Revealed: $280 "dark money" spent by US Christian Right groups globally', openDemocracy, 27 October 2020, www.opendemocracy.net/en /5050/trump-us-christian-spending-global-revealed/.
6 bell hooks, quoted in Minna Salami, *Sensual Knowledge: A Black Feminist Approach for Everyone*. London: Zed Books, 2020, p. 7.

INDEX

Index

Index

Index

Index

Index